richard wright

BLACK BOY
(AMERICAN HUNGER)

A Record of Childhood and Youth

with a foreword by
Edward P. Jones

**THE RESTORED TEXT
ESTABLISHED BY THE LIBRARY OF AMERICA**

HARPER**PERENNIAL** ● MODERN**CLASSICS**

NEW YORK ● LONDON ● TORONTO ● SYDNEY

HARPERPERENNIAL ● MODERN**CLASSICS**

A hardcover edition of *Black Boy* was originally published in 1945 by Harper & Brothers. A paperback edition was published in 1966 by Perennial Library and reissued in 1989. The text as restored by The Library of America was published in 1991 in a volume entitled *Richard Wright: Later Works* that also included *The Outsider*.

P.S.™ is a trademark of HarperCollins Publishers.

HarperCollins books may be published for educational, business, or sales promotional use. For information please write Special Markets Department, HarperCollins Publishers, 10 East 53rd Street, New York, NY 10022.

First HarperPerennial edition published 1993.

First Harper Perennial Modern Classics edition published 2006.

Designed by Nyamekye Waliyaya

The Library of Congress has catalogued the previous edition as follows:

Wright, Richard, 1908–1960.
    Black boy / Richard Wright. — 1st Perennial Classics ed.
        p. cm.
    "Originally published in 1945 by Harper & Brothers . . . The text as restored by the Library of America was published in 1991 . . . First Harper Perennial edition published 1993"—T.p. verso.
    ISBN 0-06-092978-2
    1. Wright, Richard, 1908–1960—Childhood and youth. 2. Afro-Americans—Missippi—Social life and customs. 3. Authors, American—20th century—Biography. 4. Afro-American authors—Biography. I. Title.
PS3545.R815Z96 1998
813'.52—dc21
  [b] *Ing. 6/4/2010 14.99*   98-28840

ISBN: 978-0-06-113024-3 (reissue)
ISBN-10: 0-06-113024-9 (reissue)

   09 10 11 RRD 10 9 8 7

For
ELLEN *and* JULIA
who live always in my heart

ARNOLD RAMPERSAD
WROTE THE NOTES FOR THIS VOLUME

Contents

East Providence Public Library
41 Grove Ave.
East Providence, RI 02914

401-434-2453

Customer ID: **********0171

Title: Black boy : a record of childhood and
youth.
ID: 31499004478563
Due: 09-23-10

Total items: 1
9/2/2010 1:14 PM

Thank you for using the
Weaver Library

Foreword

The Signet paperback copies of BLACK BOY that the teacher, Charlotte Crawford, distributed to her tenth graders in September 1965 had white covers with a large, rather abstract black fist dead in the center of those covers. Fist as in black power, I suppose, though none of her students had ever uttered those words. We were fifteen and sixteen years old, and we were new to high school, as Miss Crawford was new to teaching. The Negro students in that D.C. classroom had none of the consciousness that children of the same color and ages in the civil rights turmoil of Mississippi or Alabama or Georgia or South Carolina might have had. The riots in Washington, D.C., after the murder of Martin Luther King, Jr., were still a long time in the future. We knew worldly things, but it was not yet a very big world. At the top of the book's cover, there were some rather complimentary words from a reviewer, but those words meant nothing to me. The book was only important because my teacher, one of the few arbiters in my life of what was good and what was not good, had given it to me. Below the reviewer's words was Richard Wright's name, which I had discovered two months before, and then the big words BLACK BOY under his name. Wright was nearly six years dead when Miss Crawford—a thin, short woman with eyeglasses and a warm nature—gave us the books, but his death and his life and his work meant nothing to me that afternoon. All of that and more were years and years away. The book was brand-new and it smelled new. Miss Crawford's class had some twenty Negro children, and of the problems we had, poverty was perhaps foremost for most of us. A condition we did not have a name for yet. Some of Miss Crawford's students wanted to know if we could keep the books—for we could count all day and night the things that were tenuous in our lives. The teacher said they were ours to keep, and I have mine to this day. The cover is creased, the pages are dog-eared for I acquired the book before I knew how precious pages were. There are no underlined sentences. There are no notes in the margins. I had not learned that one could and should do those things; but even if I had known to do them, I would have been too amazed, too absorbed to stop. The only record I have of what I experienced as I read is the book itself and what is left of my memory. That edition of BLACK BOY with its red border was to be only the fourth book I ever read in my life.

I had not been a stranger to words—only to words that were unaccompanied by pictures. Before books without pictures of some sort, there were funny books—what the rest of the universe calls comic books—and books of fairy or folk tales, all of them illustrated with at least one picture.

In 1964, my sister and I stayed the entire summer with relatives in South Boston, Virginia. They passed the civil rights bill that summer and my cousins and their friends were excited about being able finally to use the white swimming pool, the only one in the area. It was no big holler for me—I couldn't swim, for one thing, and in D.C., Negroes had a number of places to swim. I had brought some funny books down to South Boston, but by the first of July, I had read them all, as well as an old copy of *Time* that my aunt had lying around. Then, one afternoon, as I sat bored and lost on the porch of the tiny house my cousin and her husband lived in next door to my aunt and my other cousins, I picked up from a small table *Who Killed Stella Pomeroy?* It was a British mystery and it was the first book of any kind that I ever read that came with no pictures. I do not remember any of it, not one character, not who poor Stella was, and not who wanted her dead. There is only the unfailing memory of being thrust into a different world and seeing and knowing that world and its people simply with the words the author gave me. He said in his novel, word after word, that the place and the people were real and I believed him.

The next summer, 1965, my sister and I stayed with another aunt in Brooklyn, New York. From time to time, when my aunt went to clean someone's house, we were left alone and I took to snooping. One day in a cabinet I came upon *Native Son* and *His Eye Is on the Sparrow*, the autobiography of the black actress Ethel Waters. They were the second and third books without pictures that I ever read. And the first books about black people. As I read on, Brooklyn's Franklin Avenue, the world—in a thousand ways I could not have described—got smaller, if only because Wright's Chicago and Waters's midwest told me about territory beyond my own D.C., but territory that was nevertheless populated with people I had known, in one way or another, all my life. Even Bigger Thomas, though I had known him on a much smaller scale and in a far less violent and pathological way.

After *Who Killed Stella Pomeroy?* in 1964 in Virginia, I had returned to Washington and to funny books. But after that summer in Brooklyn in 1965, Miss Crawford gave me BLACK BOY in September, and before very long—certainly, if memory is doing right by me, way before Christmas—funny books were an almost nonexistent part of my life. Not long after I came back from Brooklyn, we had moved once again, for about the fifteenth or sixteenth time since I had come into the world. About once for every year of my life. I no longer had the sturdiness or the heart of a boy of eight or nine or ten who made friends easily in a new neighborhood, so I now had friends beyond those I saw during the school day. And I had been "pubertized," though my first date was nearly four years away.

It is only in rereading BLACK BOY—and in reading for the first time the Chicago section of the book that was not in my Signet edition—that I see much of what held me some thirty years earlier. Wright was living a southern life I knew in the city: one of constant moving from one slum house to another—the heart wears out in having to pick itself up and make a new home so often. A treacherous landscape of crops and bad times and moonlit nights that I knew about from stories told by southern-born adults who had escaped to D.C.; a place where white people with unkind hearts were as plentiful as fertile soil. A father out there somewhere who could have helped but who chose not to. (Wright was perhaps more forgiving. But for what my father did not do, I decided not to buy him a tombstone when he died. His grave may still be unmarked, though I have not seen it since the first time in 1975.) And in BLACK BOY, all the way through, I was again witness to the fear, day after day, that his mother—the one person who stood between him and a world that seemed to enjoy making widows and orphans—would be swept out of his life. Very little of this was in *Native Son,* and it helps explain why reading BLACK BOY again was like reading one's journal that had not been opened for ages. I know this person, you sometimes say aloud; I know what he went through; and I know how far he has come.

At the back of my 1965 copy of BLACK BOY there were a few pages describing other books that Signet published and one by one I began ordering them, and the books I ordered had other back pages describing other books. Those I did not get by mail, I bought in Trover's Bookstore on Eleventh Street. An autobiography of an impoverished black woman and her children living in a Brazilian *favella, Go Tell It on the Mountain; Invisible Man.* I do not know what happened to the funny books I owned in the last months of 1965. I don't believe any of them survived the first months of 1966. I suppose some of them might be worth something today, depending upon their condition. My copy of BLACK BOY has value only to me.

Edward P. Jones
WASHINGTON, D.C.
July 19 and 20, 2005

PART ONE

SOUTHERN NIGHT

His strength shall be hunger-bitten,
And destruction shall be ready at his side.

—JOB

1

One winter morning in the long-ago, four-year-old days of my life I found myself standing before a fireplace, warming my hands over a mound of glowing coals, listening to the wind whistle past the house outside. All morning my mother had been scolding me, telling me to keep still, warning me that I must make no noise. And I was angry, fretful, and impatient. In the next room Granny lay ill and under the day and night care of a doctor and I knew that I would be punished if I did not obey. I crossed restlessly to the window and pushed back the long fluffy white curtains—which I had been forbidden to touch—and looked yearningly out into the empty street. I was dreaming of running and playing and shouting, but the vivid image of Granny's old, white, wrinkled, grim face, framed by a halo of tumbling black hair, lying upon a huge feather pillow, made me afraid.

The house was quiet. Behind me my brother—a year younger than I—was playing placidly upon the floor with a toy. A bird wheeled past the window and I greeted it with a glad shout.

"You better hush," my brother said.

"You shut up," I said.

My mother stepped briskly into the room and closed the door behind her. She came to me and shook her finger in my face.

"You stop that yelling, you hear?" she whispered. "You know Granny's sick and you better keep quiet!"

I hung my head and sulked. She left and I ached with boredom.

"I told you so," my brother gloated.

"You shut up," I told him again.

I wandered listlessly about the room, trying to think of something to do, dreading the return of my mother, resentful of being neglected. The room held nothing of interest except the fire and finally I stood before the shimmering embers, fascinated by the quivering coals. An idea of a new kind of game grew and took root in my mind. Why not throw something into the fire and watch it burn? I looked about. There was only my picture book and my mother would beat me if I burned that. Then what? I hunted around until I saw the broom leaning in a closet. That's it . . . Who would bother about a few straws if I burned them? I pulled out the broom and tore out a batch of straws and tossed them into the fire and watched them smoke, turn black, blaze, and finally become white wisps of ghosts that vanished. Burning straws was a teasing kind of fun and I took more of them from the broom and cast them into the fire. My brother came to my side, his eyes drawn by the blazing straws.

"Don't do that," he said.

"How come?" I asked.

"You'll burn the whole broom," he said.

"You hush," I said.

"I'll tell," he said.

"And I'll hit you," I said.

My idea was growing, blooming. Now I was wondering just how the long fluffy white curtains would look if I lit a bunch of straws and held it under them. Would I try it? Sure. I pulled several straws from the broom and held them to the fire until they blazed; I rushed to the window and brought the flame in touch with the hems of the curtains. My brother shook his head.

"Naw," he said.

He spoke too late. Red circles were eating into the white cloth; then a flare of flames shot out. Startled, I backed away. The fire soared to the ceiling and I trembled with fright. Soon a sheet of yellow lit the room. I was terrified; I wanted to scream but was afraid. I looked around for my brother; he was gone. One half of the room was now ablaze. Smoke was choking me and the fire was licking at my face, making me gasp.

I made for the kitchen; smoke was surging there too. Soon my mother would smell that smoke and see the fire and come and beat me. I had done something wrong, something which I could not hide or deny. Yes, I would run away and never come back. I ran out of the kitchen and into the back yard. Where could I go? Yes, under the house! Nobody would find me there. I crawled under the house and crept into a dark hollow of a brick chimney and balled myself into a tight knot. My mother must not find me and whip me for what I had done. Anyway, it was all an accident; I had not really intended to set the house afire. I had just wanted to see how the curtains would look when they burned. And neither did it occur to me that I was hiding under a burning house.

Presently footsteps pounded on the floor above me. Then I heard screams. Later the gongs of fire wagons and the clopping hoofs of horses came from the direction of the street. Yes, there was really a fire, a fire like the one I had seen one day burn a house down to the ground, leaving only a chimney standing black. I was stiff with terror. The thunder of sound above me shook the chimney to which I clung. The screams came louder. I saw the image of my grandmother lying helplessly upon her bed and there were yellow flames in her black hair. Was my mother afire? Would my brother burn? Perhaps everybody in the house would burn! Why had I not thought of those things before I fired the curtains? I yearned to become invisible, to stop living. The commotion above me increased and I began to cry. It seemed that I had been hiding for ages, and when the stomping and the screaming died down I felt lonely, cast forever out of life. Voices sounded near-by and I shivered.

"Richard!" my mother was calling frantically.

I saw her legs and the hem of her dress moving swiftly about the back yard. Her wails were full of an agony whose intensity told me that my punishment would be measured by its depth. Then I saw her taut face peering under the edge of the house. She had found me! I held my breath and waited to hear her command me to come to her. Her face went away; no, she had not seen me huddled in the dark nook of the chimney. I tucked my head into my arms and my teeth chattered.

"Richard!"

The distress I sensed in her voice was as sharp and painful as the lash of a whip on my flesh.

"Richard! The house is on fire. Oh, find my child!"

Yes, the house was afire, but I was determined not to leave my place of safety. Finally I saw another face peering under the edge of the house; it was my father's. His eyes must have become accustomed to the shadows, for he was now pointing at me.

"There he is!"

"Naw!" I screamed.

"Come here, boy!"

"Naw!"

"The house is on fire!"

"Leave me 'lone!"

He crawled to me and caught hold of one of my legs. I hugged the edge of the brick chimney with all of my strength. My father yanked my leg and I clawed at the chimney harder.

"Come outta there, you little fool!"

"Turn me loose!"

I could not withstand the tugging at my leg and my fingers relaxed. It was over. I would be beaten. I did not care any more. I knew what was coming. He dragged me into the back yard and the instant his hand left me I jumped to my feet and broke into a wild run, trying to elude the people who surrounded me, heading for the street. I was caught before I had gone ten paces.

From that moment on things became tangled for me. Out of the weeping and the shouting and the wild talk, I learned that no one had died in the fire. My brother, it seemed, had finally overcome enough of his panic to warn my mother, but not before more than half the house had been destroyed. Using the mattress as a stretcher, Grandpa and an uncle had lifted Granny from her bed and had rushed her to the safety of a neighbor's house. My long absence and silence had made everyone think, for a while, that I had perished in the blaze.

"You almost scared us to death," my mother muttered as she stripped the leaves from a tree limb to prepare it for my back.

I was lashed so hard and long that I lost consciousness. I was beaten out of my senses and later I found myself in bed, screaming, determined to run away, tussling with my mother and father who were trying to keep me still. I was lost in a fog of fear. A doctor was called—I was afterwards told—and he ordered that I be kept abed, that I be kept quiet, that my very life depended upon it. My body seemed on fire and I could not sleep. Packs of ice were put on my forehead to keep down the fever. Whenever I tried to sleep I would see huge wobbly white bags, like the full udders of cows, suspended from the ceiling above me. Later, as I grew worse, I could see the bags in the daytime with my eyes open and I was gripped by the fear that they were going to fall and drench me with some horrible liquid. Day and night I begged my mother and father to take the bags away, pointing to them, shaking with terror because no one saw them but me. Exhaustion would make me drift toward sleep and then I would scream until I was wide awake again; I was afraid to sleep. Time finally bore me away from the dangerous bags and I got well. But for a long time I was chastened whenever I remembered that my mother had come close to killing me.

Each event spoke with a cryptic tongue. And the moments of living slowly revealed their coded meanings. There was the wonder I felt when I first saw a brace of mountainlike, spotted, black-and-white horses clopping down a dusty road through clouds of powdered clay.

There was the delight I caught in seeing long straight rows of red and green vegetables stretching away in the sun to the bright horizon.

There was the faint, cool kiss of sensuality when dew came on to my cheeks and shins as I ran down the wet green garden paths in the early morning.

There was the vague sense of the infinite as I looked down

upon the yellow, dreaming waters of the Mississippi River from the verdant bluffs of Natchez.

There were the echoes of nostalgia I heard in the crying strings of wild geese winging south against a bleak, autumn sky.

There was the tantalizing melancholy in the tingling scent of burning hickory wood.

There was the teasing and impossible desire to imitate the petty pride of sparrows wallowing and flouncing in the red dust of country roads.

There was the yearning for identification loosed in me by the sight of a solitary ant carrying a burden upon a mysterious journey.

There was the disdain that filled me as I tortured a delicate, blue-pink crawfish that huddled fearfully in the mudsill of a rusty tin can.

There was the aching glory in masses of clouds burning gold and purple from an invisible sun.

There was the liquid alarm I saw in the blood-red glare of the sun's afterglow mirrored in the squared panes of whitewashed frame houses.

There was the languor I felt when I heard green leaves rustling with a rainlike sound.

There was the incomprehensible secret embodied in a whitish toadstool hiding in the dark shade of a rotting log.

There was the experience of feeling death without dying that came from watching a chicken leap about blindly after its neck had been snapped by a quick twist of my father's wrist.

There was the great joke that I felt God had played on cats and dogs by making them lap their milk and water with their tongues.

There was the thirst I had when I watched clear, sweet juice trickle from sugar cane being crushed.

There was the hot panic that welled up in my throat and swept through my blood when I first saw the lazy, limp coils of a blue-skinned snake sleeping in the sun.

There was the speechless astonishment of seeing a hog stabbed through the heart, dipped into boiling water, scraped, split open, gutted, and strung up gaping and bloody.

There was the love I had for the mute regality of tall, moss-clad oaks.

There was the hint of cosmic cruelty that I felt when I saw the curved timbers of a wooden shack that had been warped in the summer sun.

There was the saliva that formed in my mouth whenever I smelt clay dust potted with fresh rain.

There was the cloudy notion of hunger when I breathed the odor of new-cut, bleeding grass.

And there was the quiet terror that suffused my senses when vast hazes of gold washed earthward from star-heavy skies on silent nights . . .

One day my mother told me that we were going to Memphis on a boat, the *Kate Adams,* and my eagerness thereafter made the days seem endless. Each night I went to bed hoping that the next morning would be the day of departure.

"How big is the boat?" I asked my mother.

"As big as a mountain," she said.

"Has it got a whistle?"

"Yes."

"Does the whistle blow?"

"Yes."

"When?"

"When the captain wants it to blow."

"Why do they call it the *Kate Adams?*"

"Because that's the boat's name."

"What color is the boat?"

"White."

"How long will we be on the boat?"

"All day and all night."

"Will we sleep on the boat?"

"Yes, when we get sleepy, we'll sleep. Now, hush."

For days I had dreamed about a huge white boat floating on a vast body of water, but when my mother took me down to the levee on the day of leaving, I saw a tiny, dirty boat that was not at all like the boat I had imagined. I was disappointed and when time came to go on board I cried and my mother thought that I did not want to go with her to Memphis, and I could not tell her what the trouble was. Solace came when I wandered about the boat and gazed at Negroes throwing dice, drinking whisky, playing cards, lolling on boxes, eating, talking, and singing. My father took me down into the engine room and the throbbing machines enthralled me for hours.

In Memphis we lived in a one-story brick tenement. The stone buildings and the concrete pavements looked bleak and hostile to me. The absence of green, growing things made the city seem dead. Living space for the four of us—my mother, my brother, my father, and me—was a kitchen and a bedroom. In the front and rear were paved areas in which my brother and I could play, but for days I was afraid to go into the strange city streets alone.

It was in this tenement that the personality of my father first came fully into the orbit of my concern. He worked as a night porter in a Beale Street drugstore and he became important and forbidding to me only when I learned that I could not make noise when he was asleep in the daytime. He was the lawgiver in our family and I never laughed in his presence. I used to lurk timidly in the kitchen doorway and watch his huge body sitting slumped at the table. I stared at him with awe as he gulped his beer from a tin bucket, as he ate long and heavily, sighed, belched, closed his eyes to nod on a stuffed belly. He was quite fat and his bloated stomach always lapped over his belt. He was always a stranger to me, always somehow alien and remote.

One morning my brother and I, while playing in the rear of our flat, found a stray kitten that set up a loud, persistent meowing. We fed it some scraps of food and gave it water, but it still meowed. My father, clad in his underwear, stumbled sleepily to the back door and demanded that we keep quiet. We told him that it was the kitten that was making the noise and he ordered us to drive it away. We tried to make the kitten leave, but it would not budge. My father took a hand.

"Scat!" he shouted.

The scrawny kitten lingered, brushing itself against our legs, and meowing plaintively.

"Kill that damn thing!" my father exploded. "Do anything, but get it away from here!"

He went inside, grumbling. I resented his shouting and it irked me that I could never make him feel my resentment. How could I hit back at him? Oh, yes . . . He had said to kill the kitten and I would kill it! I knew that he had not really meant for me to kill the kitten, but my deep hate of him urged me toward a literal acceptance of his word.

"He said for us to kill the kitten," I told my brother.

"He didn't mean it," my brother said.

"He did, and I'm going to kill 'im."

"Then he *will* howl," my brother said.

"He can't howl if he's dead," I said.

"He didn't really say kill 'im," my brother protested.

"He did!" I said. "And you heard him!"

My brother ran away in fright. I found a piece of rope, made a noose, slipped it about the kitten's neck, pulled it over a nail, then jerked the animal clear of the ground. It gasped, slobbered, spun, doubled, clawed the air frantically; finally its mouth gaped and its pink-white tongue shot out stiffly. I tied the rope to a nail and went to find my brother. He was crouching behind a corner of the building.

"I killed 'im," I whispered.

"You did bad," my brother said.

"Now Papa can sleep," I said, deeply satisfied.

"He didn't mean for you to kill 'im," my brother said.

"Then why did he *tell* me to do it?" I demanded.

My brother could not answer; he stared fearfully at the dangling kitten.

"That kitten's going to get you," he warned me.

"That kitten can't even breathe now," I said.

"I'm going to tell," my brother said, running into the house.

I waited, resolving to defend myself with my father's rash

words, anticipating my enjoyment in repeating them to him even though I knew that he had spoken them in anger. My mother hurried toward me, drying her hands upon her apron. She stopped and paled when she saw the kitten suspended from the rope.

"What in God's name have you done?" she asked.

"The kitten was making noise and Papa said to kill it," I explained.

"You little fool!" she said. "Your father's going to beat you for this!"

"But he told me to kill it," I said.

"You shut your mouth!"

She grabbed my hand and dragged me to my father's bedside and told him what I had done.

"You know better than that!" my father stormed.

"You told me to kill 'im," I said.

"I told you to drive him away," he said.

"You told me to kill 'im," I countered positively.

"You get out of my eyes before I smack you down!" my father bellowed in disgust, then turned over in bed.

I had had my first triumph over my father. I had made him believe that I had taken his words literally. He could not punish me now without risking his authority. I was happy because I had at last found a way to throw my criticism of him into his face. I had made him feel that, if he whipped me for killing the kitten, I would never give serious weight to his words again. I had made him know that I felt he was cruel and I had done it without his punishing me.

But my mother, being more imaginative, retaliated with an assault upon my sensibilities that crushed me with the moral horror involved in taking a life. All that afternoon she directed toward me calculated words that spawned in my mind a horde of invisible demons bent upon exacting vengeance for what I had done. As evening drew near, anxiety filled me and I was afraid to go into an empty room alone.

"You owe a debt you can never pay," my mother said.

"I'm sorry," I mumbled.

"Being sorry can't make that kitten live again," she said.

Then, just before I was to go to bed, she uttered a paralyzing injunction: she ordered me to go out into the dark, dig a grave, and bury the kitten.

"No!" I screamed, feeling that if I went out of doors some evil spirit would whisk me away.

"Get out there and bury that poor kitten," she ordered.

"I'm scared!"

"And wasn't that kitten scared when you put that rope around its neck?" she asked.

"But it was only a kitten," I explained.

"But it was alive," she said. "Can you make it live again?"

"But Papa said to kill it," I said, trying to shift the moral blame upon my father.

My mother whacked me across my mouth with the flat palm of her hand.

"You stop that lying! You knew what he meant!"

"I didn't!" I bawled.

She shoved a tiny spade into my hands.

"Go out there and dig a hole and bury that kitten!"

I stumbled out into the black night, sobbing, my legs wobbly from fear. Though I knew that I had killed the kitten, my mother's words had made it live again in my mind. What would that kitten do to me when I touched it? Would it claw at my eyes? As I groped toward the dead kitten, my mother lingered behind me, unseen in the dark, her disembodied voice egging me on.

"Mama, come and stand by me," I begged.

"You didn't stand by that kitten, so why should I stand by you?" she asked tauntingly from the menacing darkness.

"I can't touch it," I whimpered, feeling that the kitten was staring at me with reproachful eyes.

"Untie it!" she ordered.

Shuddering, I fumbled at the rope and the kitten dropped to the pavement with a thud that echoed in my mind for many days and nights. Then, obeying my mother's floating voice, I hunted for a spot of earth, dug a shallow hole, and buried the stiff kitten; as I handled its cold body my skin prickled. When I had completed the burial, I sighed and started back to the flat, but my mother caught hold of my hand and led me again to the kitten's grave.

"Shut your eyes and repeat after me," she said.

I closed my eyes tightly, my hand clinging to hers.

"Dear God, our Father, forgive me, for I knew not what I was doing . . ."

"Dear God, our Father, forgive me, for I knew not what I was doing," I repeated.

"And spare my poor life, even though I did not spare the life of the kitten . . ."

"And spare my poor life, even though I did not spare the life of the kitten," I repeated.

"And while I sleep tonight, do not snatch the breath of life from me . . ."

I opened my mouth but no words came. My mind was frozen with horror. I pictured myself gasping for breath and dying in my sleep. I broke away from my mother and ran into the night, crying, shaking with dread.

"No," I sobbed.

My mother called to me many times, but I would not go to her.

"Well, I suppose you've learned your lesson," she said at last.

Contrite, I went to bed, hoping that I would never see another kitten.

Hunger stole upon me so slowly that at first I was not aware of what hunger really meant. Hunger had always been more or less at my elbow when I played, but now I began to wake up at night to find hunger standing at my bedside, staring at me gauntly. The hunger I had known before this had been no grim, hostile stranger; it had been a normal hunger that had made me beg constantly for bread, and when I ate a crust or two I was satisfied. But this new hunger baffled me, scared me, made me angry and insistent. Whenever I begged for food now my mother would pour me a cup of tea which would still the clamor in my stomach for a moment or two; but a little later I would feel hunger nudging my ribs, twisting my empty guts until they ached. I would grow dizzy and my vision would dim. I became less active in my play, and for the first time in my life I had to pause and think of what was happening to me.

"Mama, I'm hungry," I complained one afternoon.

"Jump up and catch a kungry," she said, trying to make me laugh and forget.

"What's a *kungry?*"

"It's what little boys eat when they get hungry," she said.

"What does it taste like?"

"I don't know."

"Then why do you tell me to catch one?"

"Because you said that you were hungry," she said, smiling.

I sensed that she was teasing me and it made me angry.

"But I'm hungry. I want to eat."

"You'll have to wait."

"But I want to eat now."

"But there's nothing to eat," she told me.

"Why?"

"Just because there's none," she explained.

"But I want to eat," I said, beginning to cry.

"You'll just have to wait," she said again.

"But why?"

"For God to send some food."

"When is He going to send it?"

"I don't know."

"But I'm hungry!"

She was ironing and she paused and looked at me with tears in her eyes.

"Where's your father?" she asked me.

I stared in bewilderment. Yes, it was true that my father had not come home to sleep for many days now and I could make as much noise as I wanted. Though I had not known why he was absent, I had been glad that he was not there to shout his restrictions at me. But it had never occurred to me that his absence would mean that there would be no food.

"I don't know," I said.

"Who brings food into the house?" my mother asked me.

"Papa," I said. "He always brought food."

"Well, your father isn't here now," she said.

"Where is he?"

"I don't know," she said.

"But I'm hungry," I whimpered, stomping my feet.

"You'll have to wait until I get a job and buy food," she said.

As the days slid past the image of my father became associated with my pangs of hunger, and whenever I felt hunger I thought of him with a deep biological bitterness.

My mother finally went to work as a cook and left me and my brother alone in the flat each day with a loaf of bread and a pot of tea. When she returned at evening she would be tired and dispirited and would cry a lot. Sometimes, when she was in despair, she would call us to her and talk to us for hours, telling us that we now had no father, that our lives would be different from those of other children, that we must learn as soon as possible to take care of ourselves, to dress ourselves, to prepare our own food; that we must take upon ourselves the responsibility of the flat while she worked. Half frightened, we would promise solemnly. We did not understand what had happened between our father and our mother and the most that these long talks did to us was to make us feel a vague dread. Whenever we asked why father had left, she would tell us that we were too young to know.

One evening my mother told me that thereafter I would have to do the shopping for food. She took me to the corner store to show me the way. I was proud; I felt like a grownup. The next afternoon I looped the basket over my arm and went down the pavement toward the store. When I reached the corner, a gang of boys grabbed me, knocked me down, snatched the basket, took the money, and sent me running home in panic. That evening I told my mother what had happened, but she made no comment; she sat down at once, wrote another note, gave me more money, and sent me out to the grocery again. I crept down the steps and saw the same gang of boys playing down the street. I ran back into the house.

"What's the matter?" my mother asked.

"It's those same boys," I said. "They'll beat me."

"You've got to get over that," she said. "Now, go on."

"I'm scared," I said.

"Go on and don't pay any attention to them," she said.

I went out of the door and walked briskly down the sidewalk, praying that the gang would not molest me. But when I came abreast of them someone shouted.

"There he is!"

They came toward me and I broke into a wild run toward home. They overtook me and flung me to the pavement. I yelled, pleaded, kicked, but they wrenched the money out of my hand. They yanked me to my feet, gave me a few slaps, and sent me home sobbing. My mother met me at the door.

"They b-beat m-me," I gasped. "They t-t-took the m-money."

I started up the steps, seeking the shelter of the house.

"Don't you come in here," my mother warned me.

I froze in my tracks and stared at her.

"But they're coming after me," I said.

"You just stay right where you are," she said in a deadly tone. "I'm going to teach you this night to stand up and fight for your-self."

She went into the house and I waited, terrified, wondering what she was about. Presently she returned with more money and another note; she also had a long heavy stick.

"Take this money, this note, and this stick," she said. "Go to the store and buy those groceries. If those boys bother you, then fight."

I was baffled. My mother was telling me to fight, a thing that she had never done before.

"But I'm scared," I said.

"Don't you come into this house until you've gotten those groceries," she said.

"They'll beat me; they'll beat me," I said.

"Then stay in the streets; don't come back here!"

I ran up the steps and tried to force my way past her into the house. A stinging slap came on my jaw. I stood on the sidewalk, crying.

"Please, let me wait until tomorrow," I begged.

"No," she said. "Go now! If you come back into this house without those groceries, I'll whip you!"

She slammed the door and I heard the key turn in the lock. I shook with fright. I was alone upon the dark, hostile streets and gangs were after me. I had the choice of being beaten at home or away from home. I clutched the stick, crying, trying to reason. If I were beaten at home, there was absolutely nothing that I could do about it; but if I were beaten in the streets, I had a chance to fight and defend myself. I walked slowly down the sidewalk, coming closer to the gang of boys, holding the stick tightly. I was so full of fear that I could scarcely breathe. I was almost upon them now.

"There he is again!" the cry went up.

They surrounded me quickly and began to grab for my hand.

"I'll kill you!" I threatened.

They closed in. In blind fear I let the stick fly, feeling it crack against a boy's skull. I swung again, lamming another skull, then another. Realizing that they would retaliate if I let up for but a second, I fought to lay them low, to knock them cold, to kill them so that they could not strike back at me. I flayed with tears in my eyes, teeth clenched, stark fear making me throw every ounce of my strength behind each blow. I hit again and again, dropping the money and the grocery list. The boys scattered, yelling, nursing their heads, staring at me in utter disbelief. They had never seen such frenzy. I stood panting, egging them on, taunting them to come on and fight. When they refused, I ran after them and they tore out for their homes, screaming. The parents of the boys rushed into the streets and threatened me, and for the first time in my life I shouted at grownups, telling them that I would give them the same if they bothered me. I finally found my grocery list and the money and went to the store. On my way back I kept my stick poised for instant use, but there was not a single boy in sight. That night I won the right to the streets of Memphis.

Of a summer morning, when my mother had gone to work, I

would follow a crowd of black children—abandoned for the day by their working parents—to the bottom of a sloping hill whose top held a long row of ramshackle, wooden outdoor privies whose opened rear ends provided a raw and startling view. We would crouch at the foot of the slope and look up—a distance of twenty-five feet or more—at the secret and fantastic anatomies of black, brown, yellow, and ivory men and women. For hours we would laugh, point, whisper, joke, and identify our neighbors by the signs of their physiological oddities, commenting upon the difficulty or projectile force of their excretions. Finally some grownup would see us and drive us away with disgusted shouts. Occasionally children of two and three years of age would emerge from behind the hill with their faces smeared and their breath reeking. At last a white policeman was stationed behind the privies to keep the children away and our course in human anatomy was postponed.

To keep us out of mischief, my mother often took my brother and me with her to her cooking job. Standing hungrily and silently in a corner of the kitchen, we would watch her go from the stove to the sink, from the cabinet to the table. I always loved to stand in the white folks' kitchen when my mother cooked, for it meant that I got occasional scraps of bread and meat; but many times I regretted having come, for my nostrils would be assailed with the scent of food that did not belong to me and which I was forbidden to eat. Toward evening my mother would take the hot dishes into the dining room where the white people were seated, and I would stand as near the dining-room door as possible to get a quick glimpse of the white faces gathered around the loaded table, eating, laughing, talking. If the white people left anything, my brother and I would eat well; but if they did not, we would have our usual bread and tea.

Watching the white people eat would make my empty stomach churn and I would grow vaguely angry. Why could I not eat when I was hungry? Why did I always have to wait until others were through? I could not understand why some people had enough food and others did not.

I now found it irresistible to roam during the day while my mother was cooking in the kitchens of the white folks. A block away from our flat was a saloon in front of which I used to loiter all day long. Its interior was an enchanting place that both lured and frightened me. I would beg for pennies, then peer under the swinging doors to watch the men and women drink. When some neighbor would chase me away from the door, I would follow the drunks about the streets, trying to understand their mysterious mumblings, pointing at them, teasing them, laughing at them, imitating them, jeering, mocking, and taunting them about their lurching antics. For me the most amusing spectacle was a drunken woman stumbling and urinating, the dampness seeping down her stockinged legs. Or I would stare in horror at a man retching. Somebody informed my mother about my fondness for the saloon and she beat me, but it did not keep me from peering under the swinging doors and listening to the wild talk of drunks when she was at work.

One summer afternoon—in my sixth year—while peering under the swinging doors of the neighborhood saloon, a black man caught hold of my arm and dragged me into its smoky and noisy depths. The odor of alcohol stung my nostrils. I yelled and struggled, trying to break free of him, afraid of the staring crowd of men and women, but he would not let me go. He lifted me and sat me upon the counter, put his hat upon my head and ordered a drink for me. The tipsy men and women yelled with delight. Somebody tried to jam a cigar into my mouth, but I twisted out of the way.

"How do you feel, setting there like a man, boy?" a man asked.

"Make 'im drunk and he'll stop peeping in here," somebody said.

"Let's buy 'im drinks," somebody said.

Some of my fright left as I stared about. Whisky was set before me.

"Drink it, boy," somebody said.

I shook my head. The man who had dragged me in urged me to drink it, telling me that it would not hurt me. I refused.

"Drink it; it'll make you feel good," he said.

I took a sip and coughed. The men and women laughed. The entire crowd in the saloon gathered about me now, urging me to drink. I took another sip. Then another. My head spun and I laughed. I was put on the floor and I ran giggling and shouting among the yelling crowd. As I would pass each man, I would take a sip from an offered glass. Soon I was drunk.

A man called me to him and whispered some words into my ear and told me that he would give me a nickel if I went to a woman and repeated them to her. I told him that I would say them; he gave me the nickel and I ran to the woman and shouted the words. A gale of laughter went up in the saloon.

"Don't teach that boy that," someone said.

"He doesn't know what it is," another said.

From then on, for a penny or a nickel, I would repeat to anyone whatever was whispered to me. In my foggy, tipsy state the reaction of the men and women to my mysterious words enthralled me. I ran from person to person, laughing, hiccoughing, spewing out filth that made them bend double with glee.

"Let that boy alone now," someone said.

"It ain't going to hurt 'im," another said.

"It's a shame," a woman said, giggling.

"Go home, boy," somebody yelled at me.

Toward early evening they let me go. I staggered along the pavements, drunk, repeating obscenities to the horror of the women I passed and to the amusement of the men en route to their homes from work.

To beg drinks in the saloon became an obsession. Many evenings my mother would find me wandering in a daze and take me home and beat me; but the next morning, no sooner had she gone to her job than I would run to the saloon and wait for someone to take me in and buy me a drink. My mother protested tearfully to the proprietor of the saloon, who ordered me to keep out of his place. But the men—reluctant to surrender their sport— would buy me drinks anyway, letting me drink out of their flasks on the streets, urging me to repeat obscenities.

I was a drunkard in my sixth year, before I had begun school. With a gang of children, I roamed the streets, begging pennies from passers-by, haunting the doors of saloons, wandering farther and farther away from home each day. I saw more than I could

understand and heard more than I could remember. The point of
life became for me the times when I could beg drinks. My mother
was in despair. She beat me; then she prayed and wept over me,
imploring me to be good, telling me that she had to work, all of
which carried no weight to my wayward mind. Finally she placed
me and my brother in the keeping of an old black woman who
watched me every moment to keep me from running to the doors
of the saloons to beg for whisky. The craving for alcohol finally left
me and I forgot the taste of it.

In the immediate neighborhood there were many school children
who, in the afternoons, would stop and play en route to their
homes; they would leave their books upon the sidewalk and I
would thumb through the pages and question them about the baffling black print. When I had learned to recognize certain words, I
told my mother that I wanted to learn to read and she encouraged
me. Soon I was able to pick my way through most of the children's
books I ran across. There grew in me a consuming curiosity about
what was happening around me and, when my mother came home
from a hard day's work, I would question her so relentlessly about
what I had heard in the streets that she refused to talk to me.

One cold morning my mother awakened me and told me that,
because there was no coal in the house, she was taking my brother
to the job with her and that I must remain in bed until the coal she
had ordered was delivered. For the payment of the coal, she left a
note together with some money under the dresser scarf. I went
back to sleep and was awakened by the ringing of the doorbell. I
opened the door, let in the coal man, and gave him the money and
the note. He brought in a few bushels of coal, then lingered, asking
me if I were cold.

"Yes," I said, shivering.

He made a fire, then sat and smoked.

"How much change do I owe you?" he asked me.

"I don't know," I said.

"Shame on you," he said. "Don't you know how to count?"

"No, sir," I said.

"Listen and repeat after me," he said.

He counted to ten and I listened carefully; then he asked me to count alone and I did. He then made me memorize the words twenty, thirty, forty, etc., then told me to add one, two, three, and so on. In about an hour's time I had learned to count to a hundred and I was overjoyed. Long after the coal man had gone I danced up and down on the bed in my nightclothes, counting again and again to a hundred, afraid that if I did not keep repeating the numbers I would forget them. When my mother returned from her job that night I insisted that she stand still and listen while I counted to one hundred. She was dumfounded. After that she taught me to read, told me stories. On Sundays I would read the newspapers with my mother guiding me and spelling out the words.

I soon made myself a nuisance by asking far too many questions of everybody. Every happening in the neighborhood, no matter how trivial, became my business. It was in this manner that I first stumbled upon the relations between whites and blacks, and what I learned frightened me. Though I had long known that there were people called "white" people, it had never meant anything to me emotionally. I had seen white men and women upon the streets a thousand times, but they had never looked particularly "white." To me they were merely people like other people, yet somehow strangely different because I had never come in close touch with any of them. For the most part I never thought of them; they simply existed somewhere in the background of the city as a whole. It might have been that my tardiness in learning to sense white people as "white" people came from the fact that many of my relatives were "white"-looking people. My grandmother, who was white as any "white" person, had never looked "white" to me. And when word circulated among the black people of the neighborhood that a "black" boy had been severely beaten by a "white" man, I felt that the "white" man had had a right to beat the "black" boy, for I naïvely assumed that the "white" man must have been the "black" boy's father. And did not all fathers, like my father, have the right to beat their children? A paternal right was the only right, to my understanding, that a man had to beat a child. But when my mother told me that the "white" man was not the father of the "black" boy, was no kin to him at all, I was puzzled.

"Then why did the 'white' man whip the 'black' boy?" I asked my mother.

"The 'white' man did not *whip* the 'black' boy," my mother told me. "He *beat* the 'black' boy."

"But why?"

"You're too young to understand."

"I'm not going to let anybody beat me," I said stoutly.

"Then stop running wild in the streets," my mother said.

I brooded for a long time about the seemingly causeless beating of the "black" boy by the "white" man and the more questions I asked the more bewildering it all became. Whenever I saw "white" people now I stared at them, wondering what they were really like.

I began school at Howard Institute at a later age than was usual; my mother had not been able to buy me the necessary clothes to make me presentable. The boys of the neighborhood took me to school the first day and when I reached the edge of the school grounds I became terrified, wanted to return home, wanted to put it off. But the boys simply took my hand and pulled me inside the building. I was frightened speechless and the other children had to identify me, tell the teacher my name and address. I sat listening to pupils recite, knowing and understanding what was being said and done, but utterly incapable of opening my mouth when called upon. The students around me seemed so sure of themselves that I despaired of ever being able to conduct myself as they did.

On the playground at noon I attached myself to a group of older boys and followed them about, listening to their talk, asking countless questions. During that noon hour I learned all the four-letter words describing physiological and sex functions, and discovered that I had known them before—had spoken them in the saloon—although I had not known what they meant. A tall black boy recited a long, funny piece of doggerel, replete with filth, describing the physiological relations between men and women, and I memorized it word for word after having heard it but once.

Yet, despite my retentive memory, I found it impossible to recite when I went back into the classroom. The teacher called upon me and I rose, holding my book before my eyes, but I could make no words come from me. I could feel the presence of the strange boys and girls behind me, waiting to hear me read, and fear paralyzed me.

Yet when school let out that first day I ran joyously home with a brain burdened with racy and daring knowledge, but not a single idea from books. I gobbled my cold food that had been left covered on the table, seized a piece of soap and rushed into the streets, eager to display all I had learned in school since morning. I went from window to window and printed in huge soap-letters all my newly acquired four-letter words. I had written on nearly all the windows in the neighborhood when a woman stopped me and drove me home. That night the woman visited my mother and informed her of what I had done, taking her from window to window and pointing out my inspirational scribblings. My mother was horrified. She demanded that I tell her where I had learned the words and she refused to believe me when I told her that I had learned them at school. My mother got a pail of water and a towel and took me by the hand and led me to a smeared window.

"Now, scrub until that word's gone," she ordered.

Neighbors gathered, giggling, muttering words of pity and astonishment, asking my mother how on earth I could have learned so much so quickly. I scrubbed at the four-letter soap-words and grew blind with anger. I sobbed, begging my mother to let me go, telling her that I would never write such words again; but she did not relent until the last soap-word had been cleaned away. Never again did I write words like that; I kept them to myself.

After my father's desertion, my mother's ardently religious disposition dominated the household and I was often taken to Sunday school where I met God's representative in the guise of a tall, black preacher. One Sunday my mother invited the tall, black preacher to a dinner of fried chicken. I was happy, not because the preacher was coming but because of the chicken. One or two neighbors also were invited. But no sooner had the preacher arrived than I began to resent him, for I learned at once that he, like my father, was used to having his own way. The hour for dinner came and I was wedged at the table between talking and laughing adults. In the center of the table was a huge platter of golden-brown fried chicken. I compared the bowl of soup that sat before me with the crispy chicken and decided in favor of the chicken. The others began to eat their soup, but I could not touch mine.

"Eat your soup," my mother said.

"I don't want any," I said.

"You won't get anything else until you've eaten your soup," she said.

The preacher had finished his soup and had asked that the platter of chicken be passed to him. It galled me. He smiled, cocked his head this way and that, picking out choice pieces. I forced a spoonful of soup down my throat and looked to see if my speed matched that of the preacher. It did not. There were already bare chicken bones on his plate, and he was reaching for more. I tried eating my soup faster, but it was no use; the other people were now serving themselves chicken and the platter was more than half empty. I gave up and sat staring in despair at the vanishing pieces of fried chicken.

"Eat your soup or you won't get anything," my mother warned.

I looked at her appealingly and could not answer. As piece after piece of chicken was eaten, I was unable to eat my soup at all. I grew hot with anger. The preacher was laughing and joking and the grownups were hanging on his words. My growing hate of the preacher finally became more important than God or religion and I could no longer contain myself. I leaped up from the table, knowing that I should be ashamed of what I was doing, but unable to stop, and screamed, running blindly from the room.

"That preacher's going to eat *all* the chicken!" I bawled.

The preacher tossed back his head and roared with laughter, but my mother was angry and told me that I was to have no dinner because of my bad manners.

When I awakened one morning my mother told me that we were going to see a judge who would make my father support me and my brother. An hour later all three of us were sitting in a huge crowded room. I was overwhelmed by the many faces and the voices which I could not understand. High above me was a white face which my mother told me was the face of the judge. Across the huge room sat my father, smiling confidently, looking at us. My mother warned me not to be fooled by my father's friendly manner; she told me that the judge might ask me questions, and if he did I must tell him the truth. I agreed, yet I hoped that the judge would not ask me anything.

For some reason the entire thing struck me as being useless; I felt that if my father were going to feed me, then he would have done so regardless of what a judge said to him. And I did not want my father to feed me; I was hungry, but my thoughts of food did not now center about him. I waited, growing restless, hungry. My mother gave me a dry sandwich and I munched and stared, longing to go home. Finally I heard my mother's name called; she rose and began weeping so copiously that she could not talk for a few moments; at last she managed to say that her husband had deserted her and her two children, that her children were hungry, that they stayed hungry, that she worked, that she was trying to raise them alone. Then my father was called; he came forward jauntily, smiling. He tried to kiss my mother, but she turned away from him. I only heard one sentence of what he said.

"I'm doing all I can, Your Honor," he mumbled, grinning.

It had been painful to sit and watch my mother crying and my father laughing and I was glad when we were outside in the sunny streets. Back at home my mother wept again and talked complainingly about the unfairness of the judge who had accepted my father's word. After the court scene, I tried to forget my father; I did not hate him; I simply did not want to think of him. Often when we were hungry my mother would beg me to go to my father's job and ask him for a dollar, a dime, a nickel . . . But I would never consent to go. I did not want to see him.

My mother fell ill and the problem of food became an acute,

daily agony. Hunger was with us always. Sometimes the neighbors would feed us or a dollar bill would come in the mail from my grandmother. It was winter and I would buy a dime's worth of coal each morning from the corner coalyard and lug it home in paper bags. For a time I remained out of school to wait upon my mother, then Granny came to visit us and I returned to school.

At night there were long, halting discussions about our going to live with Granny, but nothing came of it. Perhaps there was not enough money for railroad fare. Angered by having been hauled into court, my father now spurned us completely. I heard long, angrily whispered conversations between my mother and grandmother to the effect that "that woman ought to be killed for breaking up a home." What irked me was the ceaseless talk and no action. If someone had suggested that my father be killed, I would perhaps have become interested; if someone had suggested that his name never be mentioned, I would no doubt have agreed; if someone had suggested that we move to another city, I would have been glad. But there was only endless talk that led nowhere and I began to keep away from home as much as possible, preferring the simplicity of the streets to the worried, futile talk at home.

Finally we could no longer pay the rent for our dingy flat; the few dollars that Granny had left us before she went home were gone. Half sick and in despair, my mother made the rounds of the charitable institutions, seeking help. She found an orphan home that agreed to assume the guidance of me and my brother provided my mother worked and made small payments. My mother hated to be separated from us, but she had no choice.

The orphan home was a two-story frame building set amid trees in a wide, green field. My mother ushered me and my brother one morning into the building and into the presence of a tall, gaunt, mulatto woman who called herself Miss Simon. At once she took a fancy to me and I was frightened speechless; I was afraid of her the moment I saw her and my fear lasted during my entire stay in the home.

The house was crowded with children and there was always a storm of noise. The daily routine was blurred to me and I never quite grasped it. The most abiding feeling I had each day was hunger and fear. The meals were skimpy and there were only two of them. Just before we went to bed each night we were given a slice of bread smeared with molasses. The children were silent, hostile, vindictive, continuously complaining of hunger. There was an over-all atmosphere of nervousness and intrigue, of children telling tales upon others, of children being deprived of food to punish them.

The home did not have the money to check the growth of the wide stretches of grass by having it mown, so it had to be pulled by hand. Each morning after we had eaten a breakfast that seemed like no breakfast at all, an older child would lead a herd of us to the vast lawn and we would get to our knees and wrench the grass loose from the dirt with our fingers. At intervals Miss Simon would make a tour of inspection, examining the pile of pulled grass beside each child, scolding or praising according to the size of the pile. Many mornings I was too weak from hunger to pull the grass; I would grow dizzy and my mind would become blank and I would find myself, after an interval of unconsciousness, upon my hands and knees, my head whirling, my eyes staring in bleak astonishment at the green grass, wondering where I was, feeling that I was emerging from a dream . . .

During the first days my mother came each night to visit me and my brother, then her visits stopped. I began to wonder if she, too, like my father, had disappeared into the unknown. I was rapidly learning to distrust everything and everybody. When my mother did come, I asked her why had she remained away so long and she told me that Miss Simon had forbidden her to visit us, that Miss Simon had said that she was spoiling us with too much attention. I begged my mother to take me away; she wept and told me to wait, that soon she would take us to Arkansas. She left and my heart sank.

Miss Simon tried to win my confidence; she asked me if I would like to be adopted by her if my mother consented and I said no. She would take me into her apartment and talk to me, but her words had no effect. Dread and distrust had already become a daily part of my being and my memory grew sharp, my senses more impressionable; I began to be aware of myself as a distinct personality striving against others. I held myself in, afraid to act or speak until I was sure of my surroundings, feeling most of the time that I was suspended over a void. My imagination soared; I dreamed of running away. Each morning I vowed that I would leave the next morning, but the next morning always found me afraid.

One day Miss Simon told me that thereafter I was to help her in the office. I ate lunch with her and, strangely, when I sat facing her at the table, my hunger vanished. The woman killed something in me. Next she called me to her desk where she sat addressing envelopes.

"Step up close to the desk," she said. "Don't be afraid."

I went and stood at her elbow. There was a wart on her chin and I stared at it.

"Now, take a blotter from over there and blot each envelope after I'm through writing on it," she instructed me, pointing to a blotter that stood about a foot from my hand.

I stared and did not move or answer.

"Take the blotter," she said.

I wanted to reach for the blotter and succeeded only in twitching my arm.

"Here," she said sharply, reaching for the blotter and shoving it into my fingers.

She wrote in ink on an envelope and pushed it toward me. Holding the blotter in my hand, I stared at the envelope and could not move.

"Blot it," she said.

I could not lift my hand. I knew what she had said; I knew what she wanted me to do; and I had heard her correctly. I wanted to look at her and say something, tell her why I could not move; but my eyes were fixed upon the floor. I could not summon enough courage while she sat there looking at me to reach over the yawning space of twelve inches and blot the wet ink on the envelope.

"Blot it!" she spoke sharply.

Still I could not move or answer.

"Look at me!"

I could not lift my eyes. She reached her hand to my face and I twisted away.

"What's wrong with you?" she demanded.

I began to cry and she drove me from the room. I decided that as soon as night came I would run away. The dinner bell rang and I did not go to the table, but hid in a corner of the hallway. When I heard the dishes rattling at the table, I opened the door and ran down the walk to the street. Dusk was falling. Doubt made me stop. Ought I go back? No; hunger was back there, and fear. I went on, coming to concrete sidewalks. People passed me. Where was I going? I did not know. The farther I walked the more frantic I became. In a confused and vague way I knew that I was doing more running *away* from than running *toward* something. I stopped. The streets seemed dangerous. The buildings were massive and dark. The moon shone and the trees loomed frighteningly. No, I could not go on. I would go back. But I had walked so far and had turned too many corners and had not kept track of the direction. Which way led back to the orphan home? I did not know. I was lost.

I stood in the middle of the sidewalk and cried. A "white" policeman came to me and I wondered if he was going to beat me. He asked me what was the matter and I told him that I was trying to find my mother. His "white" face created a new fear in me. I was remembering the tale of the "white" man who had beaten the "black" boy. A crowd gathered and I was urged to tell where I lived. Curiously, I was too full of fear to cry now. I wanted to tell the "white" face that I had run off from an orphan home and that Miss Simon ran it, but I was afraid. Finally I was taken to the police station where I was fed. I felt better. I sat in a big chair where I was surrounded by "white" policemen, but they seemed to ignore me. Through the window I could see that night had completely fallen and that lights now gleamed in the streets. I grew sleepy and dozed. My shoulder was shaken gently and I opened my eyes and looked into a "white" face of another policeman who was sitting beside me. He asked me questions in a quiet, confidential tone, and quite before I knew it he was not "white" any more. I told him that I had run away from an orphan home and that Miss Simon ran it.

It was but a matter of minutes before I was walking alongside a policeman, heading toward the home. The policeman led me to the front gate and I saw Miss Simon waiting for me on the steps. She identified me and I was left in her charge. I begged her not to beat me, but she yanked me upstairs into an empty room and lashed me thoroughly. Sobbing, I slunk off to bed, resolved to run away again. But I was watched closely after that.

My mother was informed upon her next visit that I had tried to run away and she was terribly upset.

"Why did you do it?" she asked.

"I don't want to stay here," I told her.

"But you must," she said. "How can I work if I'm to worry about you? You must remember that you have no father. I'm doing all I can."

"I don't want to stay here," I repeated.

"Then, if I take you to your father . . ."

"I don't want to stay with him either," I said.

"But I want you to ask him for enough money for us to go to my sister's in Arkansas," she said.

Again I was faced with choices I did not like, but I finally agreed. After all, my hate for my father was not so great and urgent as my hate for the orphan home. My mother held to her idea and one night a week or so later I found myself standing in a room in a frame house. My father and a strange woman were sitting before a bright fire that blazed in a grate. My mother and I were standing about six feet away, as though we were afraid to approach them any closer.

"It's not for me," my mother was saying. "It's for your children that I'm asking you for money."

"I ain't got nothing," my father said, laughing.

"Come here, boy," the strange woman called to me.

I looked at her and did not move.

"Give him a nickel," the woman said. "He's cute."

"Come here, Richard," my father said, stretching out his hand.

I backed away, shaking my head, keeping my eyes on the fire.

"He is a cute child," the strange woman said.

"You ought to be ashamed," my mother said to the strange woman. "You're starving my children."

"Now, don't you-all fight," my father said, laughing.

"I'll take that poker and hit you!" I blurted at my father.

He looked at my mother and laughed louder.

"You told him to say that," he said.

"Don't say such things, Richard," my mother said.

"You ought to be dead," I said to the strange woman.

The woman laughed and threw her arms about my father's neck. I grew ashamed and wanted to leave.

"How can you starve your children?" my mother asked.

"Let Richard stay with me," my father said.

"Do you want to stay with your father, Richard?" my mother asked.

"No," I said.

"You'll get plenty to eat," he said.

"I'm hungry now," I told him. "But I won't stay with you."

"Aw, give the boy a nickel," the woman said.

My father ran his hand into his pocket and pulled out a nickel.

"Here, Richard," he said.

"Don't take it," my mother said.

"Don't teach him to be a fool," my father said. "Here, Richard, take it."

I looked at my mother, at the strange woman, at my father, then into the fire. I wanted to take the nickel, but I did not want to take it from my father.

"You ought to be ashamed," my mother said, weeping. "Giving your son a nickel when he's hungry. If there's a God, He'll pay you back."

"That's all I got," my father said, laughing again and returning the nickel to his pocket.

We left. I had the feeling that I had had to do with something unclean. Many times in the years after that the image of my father and the strange woman, their faces lit by the dancing flames, would surge up in my imagination so vivid and strong that I felt I could reach out and touch it; I would stare at it, feeling that it possessed some vital meaning which always eluded me.

A quarter of a century was to elapse between the time when I saw my father sitting with the strange woman and the time when I was to see him again, standing alone upon the red clay of a Mississippi plantation, a sharecropper, clad in ragged overalls, holding a muddy hoe in his gnarled, veined hands—a quarter of a century during which my mind and consciousness had become so greatly and violently altered that when I tried to talk to him I realized that, though ties of blood made us kin, though I could see a shadow of my face in his face, though there was an echo of my voice in his voice, we were forever strangers, speaking a different language, living on vastly distant planes of reality. That day a quarter of a century later when I visited him on the plantation—he was standing against the sky, smiling toothlessly, his hair whitened, his body bent, his eyes glazed with dim recollection, his fearsome aspect of twenty-five years ago gone forever from him—I was overwhelmed to realize that he could never understand me or the scalding experiences that had swept me beyond his life and into an area of living that he could never know. I stood before him, poised, my mind aching as it embraced the simple nakedness of his life, feeling how completely his soul was imprisoned by the slow flow of the seasons, by wind and rain and sun, how fastened were his memories to a crude and raw past, how chained were his actions and emotions to the direct, animalistic impulses of his withering body . . .

From the white landowners above him there had not been handed to him a chance to learn the meaning of loyalty, of sentiment, of tradition. Joy was as unknown to him as was despair. As a creature of the earth, he endured, hearty, whole, seemingly indestructible, with no regrets and no hope. He asked easy, drawling questions about me, his other son, his wife, and he laughed, amused, when I informed him of their destinies. I forgave him and pitied him as my eyes looked past him to the unpainted wooden shack. From far beyond the horizons that bound this bleak plantation there had come to me through my living the knowledge that my father was a black peasant who had gone to the city seeking life, but who had failed in the city; a black peasant whose life had been hopelessly snarled in the city, and who had at last fled the city—that same city which had lifted me in its burning arms and borne me toward alien and undreamed-of shores of knowing.

2

The glad days that dawned gave me liberty for the free play of impulse and, from anxiety and restraint, I leaped to license and thoughtless action. My mother arrived one afternoon with the news that we were going to live with her sister in Elaine, Arkansas, and that en route we would visit Granny, who had moved from Natchez to Jackson, Mississippi. As the words fell from my mother's lips, a long and heavy anxiety lifted from me. Excited, I rushed about and gathered my ragged clothes. I was leaving the hated home, hunger, fear, leaving days that had been as dark and lonely as death.

While I was packing, a playmate came to tell me that one of my shirts was hanging damp upon the clothesline. Filled more with the sense of coming freedom than with generosity, I told him that he could have it. What was a shirt to me now? The children stood about and watched me with envious eyes as I crammed my things into a suitcase, but I did not notice them. The moment I had learned that I was to leave, my feelings had recoiled so sharply and quickly from the home that the children simply did not exist for me any more. Their faces possessed the power of evoking in me a million memories that I longed to forget, and instead of my leaving drawing me to them in communion, it had flung me forever beyond them.

I was so eager to be gone that when I stood in the front hallway, packed and ready, I did not even think of saying good-bye to

the boys and girls with whom I had eaten and slept and lived for so
many weeks. My mother scolded me for my thoughtlessness and
bade me say good-bye to them. Reluctantly I obeyed her, wishing
that I did not have to do so. As I shook the dingy palms extended
to me I kept my eyes averted, not wanting to look again into faces
that hurt me because they had become so thoroughly associated in
my feelings with hunger and fear. In shaking hands I was doing
something that I was to do countless times in the years to come:
acting in conformity with what others expected of me even though,
by the very nature and form of my life, I did not and could not
share their spirit.

(After I had outlived the shocks of childhood, after the habit of
reflection had been born in me, I used to mull over the strange
absence of real kindness in Negroes, how unstable was our tenderness, how lacking in genuine passion we were, how void of great
hope, how timid our joy, how bare our traditions, how hollow our
memories, how lacking we were in those intangible sentiments that
bind man to man, and how shallow was even our despair. After I
had learned other ways of life I used to brood upon the unconscious irony of those who felt that Negroes led so passional an existence! I saw that what had been taken for our emotional strength
was our negative confusions, our flights, our fears, our frenzy under
pressure.

(Whenever I thought of the essential bleakness of black life in
America, I knew that Negroes had never been allowed to catch the
full spirit of Western civilization, that they lived somehow in it but
not of it. And when I brooded upon the cultural barrenness of
black life, I wondered if clean, positive tenderness, love, honor, loyalty, and the capacity to remember were native with man. I asked
myself if these human qualities were not fostered, won, struggled
and suffered for, preserved in ritual from one generation to
another.)

Granny's home in Jackson was an enchanting place to explore.
It was a two-story frame structure of seven rooms. My brother and
I used to play hide and seek in the long, narrow hallways, and on
and under the stairs. Granny's son, Uncle Clark, had bought her

this home, and its white plastered walls, its front and back porches, its round columns and banisters, made me feel that surely there was no finer house in all the round world.

There were wide green fields in which my brother and I roamed and played and shouted. And there were the timid children of the neighbors, boys and girls to whom my brother and I felt superior in worldly knowledge. We took pride in telling them what it was like to ride on a train, what the yellow, sleepy Mississippi River looked like, how it felt to sail on the *Kate Adams,* what Memphis looked like, and how I had run off from the orphan home. And we would hint that we were pausing for but a few days and then would be off to even more fabulous places and marvelous experiences.

To help support the household my grandmother boarded a colored schoolteacher, Ella, a young woman with so remote and dreamy and silent a manner that I was as much afraid of her as I was attracted to her. I had long wanted to ask her to tell me about the books that she was always reading, but I could never quite summon enough courage to do so. One afternoon I found her sitting alone upon the front porch, reading.

"Ella," I begged, "please tell me what you are reading."

"It's just a book," she said evasively, looking about with apprehension.

"But what's it about?" I asked.

"Your grandmother wouldn't like it if I talked to you about novels," she told me.

I detected a note of sympathy in her voice.

"I don't care," I said loudly and bravely.

"Shhh— You mustn't say things like that," she said.

"But I want to know."

"When you grow up, you'll read books and know what's in them," she explained.

"But I want to know now."

She thought a while, then closed the book.

"Come here," she said.

I sat at her feet and lifted my face to hers.

"Once upon a time there was an old, old man named Bluebeard," she began in a low voice.

She whispered to me the story of *Bluebeard and His Seven Wives* and I ceased to see the porch, the sunshine, her face, everything. As her words fell upon my new ears, I endowed them with a reality that welled up from somewhere within me. She told how Bluebeard had duped and married his seven wives, how he had loved and slain them, how he had hanged them up by their hair in a dark closet. The tale made the world around me be, throb, live. As she spoke, reality changed, the look of things altered, and the world became peopled with magical presences. My sense of life deepened and the feel of things was different, somehow. Enchanted and enthralled, I stopped her constantly to ask for details. My imagination blazed. The sensations the story aroused in me were never to leave me. When she was about to finish, when my interest was keenest, when I was lost to the world around me, Granny stepped briskly onto the porch.

"You stop that, you evil gal!" she shouted. "I want none of that Devil stuff in my house!"

Her voice jarred me so that I gasped. For a moment I did not know what was happening.

"I'm sorry, Mrs. Wilson," Ella stammered, rising. "But he asked me—"

"He's just a foolish child and you know it!" Granny blazed.

Ella bowed her head and went into the house.

"But, granny, she didn't finish," I protested, knowing that I should have kept quiet.

She bared her teeth and slapped me across my mouth with the back of her hand.

"You shut your mouth," she hissed. "You don't know what you're talking about!"

"But I want to hear what happened!" I wailed, dodging another blow that I thought was coming.

"That's the Devil's work!" she shouted.

My grandmother was as nearly white as a Negro can get without being white, which means that she was white. The sagging flesh of her face quivered; her eyes, large, dark, deep-set, wide apart, glared at me. Her lips narrowed to a line. Her high forehead wrinkled. When she was angry her eyelids drooped halfway down over her pupils, giving her a baleful aspect.

"But I liked the story," I told her.

"You're going to burn in hell," she said with such furious conviction that for a moment I believed her.

Not to know the end of the tale filled me with a sense of emptiness, loss. I hungered for the sharp, frightening, breathtaking, almost painful excitement that the story had given me, and I vowed that as soon as I was old enough I would buy all the novels there were and read them to feed that thirst for violence that was in me, for intrigue, for plotting, for secrecy, for bloody murders. So profoundly responsive a chord had the tale struck in me that the threats of my mother and grandmother had no effect whatsoever. They read my insistence as mere obstinacy, as foolishness, something that would quickly pass; and they had no notion how desperately serious the tale had made me. They could not have known that Ella's whispered story of deception and murder had been the first experience in my life that had elicited from me a total emotional response. No words or punishment could have possibly made me doubt. I had tasted what to me was life, and I would have more of it, somehow, someway. I realized that they could not understand what I was feeling and I kept quiet. But when no one was looking I would slip into Ella's room and steal a book and take it back of the barn and try to read it. Usually I could not decipher enough words to make the story have meaning. I burned to learn to read novels and I tortured my mother into telling me the meaning of every strange word I saw, not because the word itself had any value, but because it was the gateway to a forbidden and enchanting land.

One afternoon my mother became so ill that she had to go to bed. When night fell Granny assumed the task of seeing that my brother and I bathed. She set two tubs of water in our room and ordered us to pull off our clothes, which we did. She sat at one end of the room, knitting, lifting her eyes now and then from the wool to watch us and direct us. My brother and I splashed in the water, playing, laughing, trying our utmost to fling suds into each other's eyes. The floor was getting so sloppy that Granny scolded us.

"Stop that foolishness and wash yourselves!"

"Yes, ma'am," we answered automatically and proceeded with our playing.

I scooped up a double handful of suds and called to my brother. He looked and I flung the suds, but he ducked and the white foam spattered on to the floor.

"Richard, stop that playing and bathe!"

"Yes, ma'am," I said, watching my brother to catch him unawares so that I could fling more suds at him.

"Come here, you Richard!" Granny said, putting her knitting aside.

I went to her, walking sheepishly and nakedly across the floor. She snatched the towel from my hand and began to scrub my ears, my face, my neck.

"Bend over," she ordered.

I stooped and she scrubbed my anus. My mind was in a sort of daze, midway between daydreaming and thinking. Then, before I knew it, words—words whose meaning I did not fully know—had slipped out of my mouth.

"When you get through, kiss back there," I said, the words rolling softly but unpremeditatedly.

My first indication that something was wrong was that Granny became terribly still, then she pushed me violently from her. I turned around and saw that her white face was frozen, that her black, deep-set eyes were blazing at me unblinkingly. Taking my cue from her queer expression, I knew that I had said something awful, but I had no notion at that moment just how awful it was. Granny rose slowly and lifted the wet towel high above her head and brought it down across my naked back with all the outraged fury of her sixty-odd-year-old body, leaving an aching streak of fire burning and quivering on my skin. I gasped and held my breath, fighting against the pain; then I howled and cringed. I had not realized the meaning of what I had said; its moral horror was unfelt by me, and her attack seemed without cause. She lifted the wet towel and struck me again with such force that I dropped to my knees. I knew that if I did not get out of her reach she would kill me. Naked, I rose and ran out of the room, screaming. My mother hurried from her bed.

"What's the matter, mama?" she asked Granny.

I lingered in the hallway, trembling, looking at Granny, trying to speak but only moving my lips. Granny seemed to have gone out of her mind, for she stood like stone, her eyes dead upon me, not saying a word.

"Richard, what have you done?" my mother asked.

Poised to run again, I shook my head.

"What's the matter, for God's sake?" my mother asked of me, of Granny, of my brother, turning her face from one to another.

Granny wilted, half turned, flung the towel to the floor, then burst into tears.

"He . . . I was trying to wash him," Granny whimpered, "here," she continued, pointing, "and . . . that black little Devil . . ." Her body was shaking with insult and rage. "He told me to kiss him there when I was through."

Now my mother stared without speaking.

"No!" my mother exclaimed.

"He did," Granny whimpered.

"He didn't say *that*," my mother protested.

"He did," Granny sighed.

I listened, vaguely knowing now that I had committed some awful wrong that I could not undo, that I had uttered words I could not recall even though I ached to nullify them, kill them, turn back time to the moment before I had talked so that I could have another chance to save myself. My mother picked up the wet towel and came toward me. I ran into the kitchen, naked, yelling. She came hard upon my heels and I scuttled into the back yard, running blindly in the dark, butting my head against the fence, the tree, bruising my toes on sticks of wood, still screaming. I had no way of measuring the gravity of my wrong and I assumed that I had done something for which I would never be forgiven. Had I known just how my words had struck them, I would have remained still and taken my punishment, but it was the feeling that anything could or would happen to me that made me wild with fear.

"Come here, you little filthy fool!" my mother called.

I dodged her and ran back into the house, then again into the hallway, my naked body flashing frantically through the air. I crouched in a dark corner. My mother rushed upon me, breathing hard. I ducked, crawled, stood, and ran again.

"You may as well stand still," my mother said. "I'm going to beat you tonight if it is the last thing I do on this earth!"

Again she charged me and I dodged, just missing the stinging swish of the wet towel, and scooted into the room where my brother stood.

"What's the matter?" he asked, for he had not heard what I had said.

A blow fell on my mouth. I whirled. Granny was upon me. She struck me another blow on my head with the back of her hand. Then my mother came into the room, I fell to the floor and crawled under the bed.

"You come out of there," my mother called.

"Naw," I cried.

"Come out or I'll beat you to within an inch of your life," she said.

"Naw," I said.

"Call Papa," Granny said.

I trembled. Granny was sending my brother to fetch Grandpa, of whom I was mortally afraid. He was a tall, skinny, silent, grim, black man who had fought in the Civil War with the Union Army. When he was angry he gritted his teeth with a terrifying, grating sound. He kept his army gun in his room, standing in a corner, loaded. He was under the delusion that the war between the states would be resumed. I heard my brother rush out of the room and I knew it was but a matter of minutes before Grandpa would come. I balled myself into a knot and moaned:

"Naw, naw, naw . . ."

Grandpa came and ordered me from under the bed. I refused to move.

"Come out of there, little man," he said.

"Naw."

"Do you want me to get my gun?"

"Naw, sir. Please don't shoot me!" I cried.

"Then come out!"

I remained still. Grandpa took hold of the bed and pulled it. I clung to a bedpost and was dragged over the floor. Grandpa ran at me and tried to grab my leg, but I crawled out of reach. I rested on all fours and kept in the center of the bed and each time the bed moved, I moved, following it.

"Come out and get your whipping!" my mother called.

I remained still. The bed moved and I moved. I did not think; I did not plan; I did not plot. Instinct told me what to do. There was painful danger and I had to avoid it. Grandpa finally gave up and went back to his room.

"When you come out, you'll get your whipping," my mother said. "No matter how long you stay under there, you're going to get it. And no food for you tonight."

"What did he do?" my brother asked.

"Something he ought to be killed for," Granny said.

"But what?" my brother asked.

"Shut you up and get to bed," my mother said.

I stayed under the bed far into the night. The household went to sleep. Finally hunger and thirst drove me out; when I stood up I found my mother lurking in the doorway, waiting for me.

"Come into the kitchen," she said.

I followed her and she beat me, but she did not use the wet towel; Grandpa had forbade that. Between strokes of the switch she would ask me where had I learned the dirty words and I could not tell her; and my inability to tell her made her furious.

"I'm going to beat you until you tell me," she declared.

And I could not tell her because I did not know. None of the obscene words I had learned at school in Memphis had dealt with perversions of any sort, although I might have learned the words while loitering drunkenly in saloons. The next day Granny said emphatically that she knew who had ruined me, that she knew I had learned about "foul practices" from reading Ella's books, and when I asked what "foul practices" were, my mother beat me afresh. No matter how hard I tried to convince them that I had not read the words in a book or that I could not remember having heard anyone say them, they would not believe me. Granny finally charged Ella with telling me things that I should not know and Ella, weeping and distraught, packed her things and moved. The tremendous upheaval that my words had caused made me know that there lay back of them much more than I could figure out, and I resolved that in the future I would learn the meaning of why they had beat and denounced me.

The days and hours began to speak now with a clearer tongue. Each experience had a sharp meaning of its own.

There was the breathlessly anxious fun of chasing and catching flitting fireflies on drowsy summer nights.

There was the drenching hospitality in the pervading smell of sweet magnolias.

There was the aura of limitless freedom distilled from the rolling sweep of tall green grass swaying and glinting in the wind and sun.

There was the feeling of impersonal plenty when I saw a boll of cotton whose cup had spilt over and straggled its white fleece toward the earth.

There was the pitying chuckle that bubbled in my throat when I watched a fat duck waddle across the back yard.

There was the suspense I felt when I heard the taut, sharp song of a yellow-black bee hovering nervously but patiently above a white rose.

There was the drugged, sleepy feeling that came from sipping glasses of milk, drinking them slowly so that they would last a long time, and drinking enough for the first time in my life.

There was the bitter amusement of going into town with Granny and watching the baffled stares of white folks who saw an old white woman leading two undeniably Negro boys in and out of stores on Capitol Street.

There was the slow, fresh, saliva-stimulating smell of cooking cotton seeds.

There was the excitement of fishing in muddy country creeks with my grandpa on cloudy days.

There was the fear and awe I felt when Grandpa took me to a sawmill to watch the giant whirring steel blades whine and scream as they bit into wet green logs.

There was the puckery taste that almost made me cry when I ate my first half-ripe persimmon.

There was the greedy joy in the tangy taste of wild hickory nuts.

There was the dry hot summer morning when I scratched my bare arms on briers while picking blackberries and came home with my fingers and lips stained black with sweet berry juice.

There was the relish of eating my first fried fish sandwich, nibbling at it slowly and hoping that I would never eat it up.

There was the all-night ache in my stomach after I had climbed a neighbor's tree and eaten stolen, unripe peaches.

There was the morning when I thought I would fall dead from fear after I had stepped with my bare feet upon a bright little green garden snake.

And there were the long, slow, drowsy days and nights of drizzling rain . . .

At last we were at the railroad station with our bags, waiting for the train that would take us to Arkansas; and for the first time I noticed that there were two lines of people at the ticket window, a "white" line and a "black" line. During my visit at Granny's a sense of the two races had been born in me with a sharp concreteness that would never die until I died. When I boarded the train I was aware that we Negroes were in one part of the train and that the whites were in another. Naïvely I wanted to go and see how the whites looked while sitting in their part of the train.

"Can I go and peep at the white folks?" I asked my mother.

"You keep quiet," she said.

"But that wouldn't be wrong, would it?"

"Will you keep still?"

"But why can't I?"

"Quit talking foolishness!"

I had begun to notice that my mother became irritated when I questioned her about whites and blacks, and I could not quite understand it. I wanted to understand these two sets of people who lived side by side and never touched, it seemed, except in violence. Now, there was my grandmother . . . Was she white? Just how white was she? What did the whites think of her whiteness?

"Mama, is Granny white?" I asked as the train rolled through the darkness.

"If you've got eyes, you can see what color she is," my mother said.

"I mean, do the white folks think she's white?"

"Why don't you ask the white folks that?" she countered.

"But you know," I insisted.

"Why should I know?" she asked. "I'm not white."

"Granny looks white," I said, hoping to establish one fact, at least. "Then why is she living with us colored folks?"

"Don't you want Granny to live with us?" she asked, blunting my question.

"Yes."

"Then why are you asking?"

"I want to *know*."

"Doesn't Granny live with us?"

"Yes."

"Isn't that enough?"

"But does she *want* to live with us?"

"Why didn't you ask Granny that?" my mother evaded me again in a taunting voice.

"Did Granny become colored when she married Grandpa?"

"Will you stop asking silly questions!"

"But did she?"

"Granny didn't *become* colored," my mother said angrily. "She was *born* the color she is now."

Again I was being shut out of the secret, the thing, the reality I felt somewhere beneath all the words and silences.

"Why didn't Granny marry a white man?" I asked.

"Because she didn't want to," my mother said peevishly.

"Why don't you want to talk to me?" I asked.

She slapped me and I cried. Later, grudgingly, she told me that Granny came of Irish, Scotch, and French stock in which Negro blood had somewhere and somehow been infused. She explained it all in a matter-of-fact, offhand, neutral way; her emotions were not involved at all.

"What was Granny's name before she married Grandpa?"

"Bolden."

"Who gave her that name?"

"The white man who owned her."

"She was a slave?"

"Yes."

"And Bolden was the name of Granny's father?"

"Granny doesn't know who her father was."

"So they just gave her any name?"

"They gave her a name; that's all I know."

"Couldn't Granny find out who her father was?"

"For what, silly?"

"So she could know."

"Know for what?"

"Just to know."

"But for *what*?"

I could not say. I could not get anywhere.

"Mama, where did Father get his name?"

"From his father."

"And where did the father of my father get his name?"

"Like Granny got hers. From a white man."

"Do they know who he is?"

"I don't know."

"Why don't they find out?"

"For what?" my mother demanded harshly.

And I could think of no rational or practical reason why my father should try to find out who his father's father was.

"What has Papa got in him?" I asked.

"Some white and some red and some black," she said.

"Indian, white, and Negro?"

"Yes."

"Then what am I?"

"They'll call you a colored man when you grow up," she said. Then she turned to me and smiled mockingly and asked: "Do you mind, Mr. Wright?"

I was angry and I did not answer. I did not object to being called colored, but I knew that there was something my mother was holding back. She was not concealing facts, but feelings, attitudes, convictions which she did not want me to know; and she became angry when I prodded her. All right, I would find out someday. Just wait. All right, I was colored. It was fine. I did not know enough to be afraid or to anticipate in a concrete manner. True, I had heard that colored people were killed and beaten, but so far it all had seemed remote. There was, of course, a vague uneasiness about it all, but I would be able to handle that when I came to it. It would be simple. If anybody tried to kill me, then I would kill them first.

When we arrived in Elaine I saw that Aunt Maggie lived in a bungalow that had a fence around it. It looked like home and I was glad. I had no suspicion that I was to live here for but a short time and that the manner of my leaving would be my first baptism of racial emotion.

A wide dusty road ran past the house and on each side of the road wild flowers grew. It was summer and the smell of clay dust was everywhere, day and night. I would get up early every morning to wade with my bare feet through the dust of the road, reveling in the strange mixture of the cold dew-wet crust on top of the road and the warm, sun-baked dust beneath.

After sunrise the bees would come out and I discovered that by slapping my two palms together smartly I could kill a bee. My mother warned me to stop, telling me that bees made honey, that it was not good to kill things that made food, that I would eventually be stung. But I felt confident of outwitting any bee. One morning I slapped an enormous bee between my hands just as it had lit upon a flower and it stung me in the tender center of my left palm. I ran home screaming.

"Good enough for you," my mother commented dryly.

I never crushed any more bees.

Aunt Maggie's husband, Uncle Hoskins, owned a saloon that catered to the hundreds of Negroes who worked in the surrounding sawmills. Remembering the saloon of my Memphis days, I begged Uncle Hoskins to take me to see it and he promised; but my mother said no; she was afraid that I would grow up to be a drunkard if I went inside of a saloon again while still a child. Well, if I could not see the saloon, at least I could eat. And at mealtime Aunt Maggie's table was so loaded with food that I could scarcely believe it was real. It took me some time to get used to the idea of there being enough to eat; I felt that if I ate enough there would not be anything left for another time. When I first sat down at Aunt Maggie's table, I could not eat until I had asked:

"Can I eat all I want?"

"Eat as much as you like," Uncle Hoskins said.

I did not believe him. I ate until my stomach hurt, but even then I did not want to get up from the table.

"Your eyes are bigger than your stomach," my mother said.

"Let him eat all he wants to and get used to food," Uncle Hoskins said.

When supper was over I saw that there were many biscuits piled high upon the bread platter, an astonishing and unbelievable sight to me. Though the biscuits were right before my eyes, and though there was more flour in the kitchen, I was apprehensive lest there be no bread for breakfast in the morning. I was afraid that somehow the biscuits might disappear during the night, while I was sleeping. I did not want to wake up in the morning, as I had so often in the past, feeling hungry and knowing that there was no food in the house. So, surreptitiously, I took some of the biscuits from the platter and slipped them into my pocket, not to eat, but to keep as a bulwark against any possible attack of hunger. Even after I had got used to seeing the table loaded with food at each meal, I still stole bread and put it into my pockets. In washing my clothes my mother found the gummy wads and scolded me to break me of the habit; I stopped hiding the bread in my pockets and hid it about the house, in corners, behind dressers. I did not break the habit of stealing and hoarding bread until my faith that food would be forthcoming at each meal had been somewhat established.

Uncle Hoskins had a horse and buggy and sometimes he used to take me with him to Helena, where he traded. One day when I was riding with him he said:

"Richard, would you like to see this horse drink water out of the middle of the river?"

"Yes," I said, laughing. "But this horse can't do that."

"Yes, he can," Uncle Hoskins said. "Just wait and see."

He lashed the horse and headed the buggy straight for the Mississippi River.

"Where're you going?" I asked, alarm mounting in me.

"We're going to the middle of the river so the horse can drink," he said.

He drove over the levee and down the long slope of cobblestones to the river's edge and the horse plunged wildly in. I looked at the mile stretch of water that lay ahead and leaped up in terror.

"Naw!" I screamed.

"This horse has to drink," Uncle Hoskins said grimly.

"The river's deep!" I shouted.

"The horse can't drink here," Uncle Hoskins said, lashing the back of the struggling animal.

The buggy went farther. The horse slowed a little and tossed his head above the current. I grabbed the sides of the buggy, ready to jump, even though I could not swim.

"Sit down or you'll fall out!" Uncle Hoskins shouted.

"Let me out!" I screamed.

The water now came up to the hubs of the wheels of the buggy. I tried to leap into the river and he caught hold of my leg. We were now surrounded by water.

"Let me out!" I continued to scream.

The buggy rolled on and the water rose higher. The horse wagged his head, arched his neck, flung his tail about, walled his eyes, and snorted. I gripped the sides of the buggy with all the strength I had, ready to wrench free and leap if the buggy slipped deeper into the river. Uncle Hoskins and I tussled.

"Whoa!" he yelled at last to the horse.

The horse stopped and neighed. The swirling yellow water was so close that I could have touched the surface of the river. Uncle Hoskins looked at me and laughed.

"Did you really think that I was going to drive this buggy into the middle of the river?" he asked.

I was too scared to answer; my muscles were so taut that they ached.

"It's all right," he said soothingly.

He turned the buggy around and started back toward the levee. I was still clutching the sides of the buggy so tightly that I could not turn them loose.

"We're safe now," he said.

The buggy rolled onto dry land and, as my fear ebbed, I felt that I was dropping from a great height. It seemed that I could smell a sharp, fresh odor. My forehead was damp and my heart thumped heavily.

"I want to get out," I said.

"What's the matter?" he asked.

"I want to get out!"

"We're back on land now, boy."

"Naw! Stop! I want to get out!"

He did not stop the buggy; he did not even turn his head to look at me; he did not understand. I wrenched my leg free with a lunge and leaped headlong out of the buggy, landing in the dust of the road, unhurt. He stopped the buggy.

"Are you really that scared?" he asked softly.

I did not answer; I could not speak. My fear was gone now and he loomed before me like a stranger, like a man I had never seen before, a man with whom I could never share a moment of intimate living.

"Come on, Richard, and get back into the buggy," he said. "I'll take you home now."

I shook my head and began to cry.

"Listen, son, don't you trust me?" he asked. "I was born on that old river. I know that river. There's stone and brick way down under that water. You could wade out for half a mile and it would not come over your head."

His words meant nothing and I would not re-enter the buggy.

"I'd better take you home," he said soberly.

I started down the dusty road. He got out of the buggy and walked beside me. He did not do his shopping that day and when he tried to explain to me what he had been trying to do in frightening me I would not listen or speak to him. I never trusted him after that. Whenever I saw his face the memory of my terror upon the river would come back, vivid and strong, and it stood as a barrier between us.

Each day Uncle Hoskins went to his saloon in the evening and did not return home until the early hours of the morning. Like my father, he slept in the daytime, but noise never seemed to bother Uncle Hoskins. My brother and I shouted and banged as much as we liked. Often I would creep into his room while he slept and stare at the big shining revolver that lay near his head, within quick reach of his hand. I asked Aunt Maggie why he kept the gun so close to him and she told me that men had threatened to kill him, white men . . .

One morning I awakened to learn that Uncle Hoskins had not come home from the saloon. Aunt Maggie fretted and worried. She wanted to visit the saloon and find out what had happened, but Uncle Hoskins had forbidden her to come to the place. The day wore on and dinnertime came.

"I'm going to find out if anything's happened," Aunt Maggie said.

"Maybe you oughtn't," my mother said. "Maybe it's dangerous."

The food was kept hot on the stove and Aunt Maggie stood on the front porch staring into the deepening dusk. Again she declared that she was going to the saloon, but my mother dissuaded her once more. It grew dark and still he had not come. Aunt Maggie was silent and restless.

"I hope to God the white people didn't bother him," she said.

Later she went into the bedroom and when she came out she whimpered:

"He didn't take his gun. I wonder what could have happened?"

We ate in silence. An hour later there was the sound of heavy footsteps on the front porch and a loud knock came. Aunt Maggie ran to the door and flung it open. A tall black boy stood sweating, panting, and shaking his head. He pulled off his cap.

"Mr. Hoskins . . . he done been shot. Done been shot by a white man," the boy gasped. "Mrs. Hoskins, he dead."

Aunt Maggie screamed and rushed off the porch and down the dusty road into the night.

"Maggie!" my mother screamed.

"Don't you-all go to that saloon," the boy called.

"Maggie!" my mother called, running after Aunt Maggie.

"They'll kill you if you go there!" the boy yelled. "White folks say they'll kill all his kinfolks!"

My mother pulled Aunt Maggie back to the house. Fear drowned out grief and that night we packed clothes and dishes and loaded them into a farmer's wagon. Before dawn we were rolling away, fleeing for our lives. I learned afterwards that Uncle Hoskins had been killed by whites who had long coveted his flourishing liquor business. He had been threatened with death and warned many times to leave, but he had wanted to hold on a while longer to amass more money. We got rooms in West Helena, and Aunt Maggie and my mother kept huddled in the house all day and night, afraid to be seen on the streets. Finally Aunt Maggie defied her fear and made frequent trips back to Elaine, but she went in secret and at night and would tell no one save my mother when she was going.

There was no funeral. There was no music. There was no period of mourning. There were no flowers. There were only silence, quiet weeping, whispers, and fear. I did not know when or where Uncle Hoskins was buried. Aunt Maggie was not even allowed to see his body nor was she able to claim any of his assets. Uncle Hoskins had simply been plucked from our midst and we, figuratively, had fallen on our faces to avoid looking into that white-hot face of terror that we knew loomed somewhere above us. This was as close as white terror had ever come to me and my mind reeled. Why had we not fought back, I asked my mother, and the fear that was in her made her slap me into silence.

Shocked, frightened, alone without their husbands or friends, my mother and Aunt Maggie lost faith in themselves and, after much debate and hesitation, they decided to return home to Granny and rest, think, map out new plans for living. I had grown used to moving suddenly and the prospects of another trip did not excite me. I had learned to leave old places without regret and to accept new ones for what they looked like. Though I was nearly nine years of age, I had not had a single, unbroken year of school, and I was not conscious of it. I could read and count and that was about as much as most of the people I met could do, grownups or children. Again our household was torn apart; belongings were sold, given away, or simply left behind, and we were off for another long train ride.

A few days later—after we had arrived at Granny's—I was play-ing alone in a wild field, digging in the ground with an old knife. Suddenly a strange rhythmic sound made me turn my head. Flowing threateningly toward me over the crest of a hill was a wave of black men draped in weird mustard-colored clothing. Unconsciously I jumped to my feet, my heart pounding. What was this? Were these men coming after me? Line by line, row by row, the fantastic men in their wild colors were descending straight at me, trotting, their feet pounding the earth like someone beating a vast drum. I wanted to fly home but, as in a dream, I could not move. I cast about wildly for a clue to tell me what this was, but I could find nothing. The wall of men was drawing closer. My heart was beating so strongly that it shook my body. Again I tried to run, but I could not budge. My mother's name was on the tip of my tongue and I opened my mouth to scream, but no words came, for now the surging men, each looking exactly like the other, parted and poured around me, jarring the earth, their feet stomping in unison. As they flooded past I saw that their black faces were looking at me and that some of them were smiling. Then I noticed that each man was holding a long, dark, heavy, sticklike object upon his shoulder. One of the men yelled something at me which I did not understand. They were past me now, disappearing in a great cloud of brown dust that looked like a part of their clothing, that made them seem akin to the elemental earth itself. As soon as they were far enough away for me to conquer my fear, I dashed home and babbled to my mother what I had seen, asking her who the strange men were.

"Those were soldiers," she said.

"What are soldiers?" I asked.

"Men who fight in wars."

"Why do they fight?"

"Because their country tells them to."

"And what are those long black sticks they have on their shoulders?"

"Rifles."

"What's a rifle?"

"It's a gun that shoots a bullet."

"Like a pistol?"

"Yes."

"Would the bullet kill you?"

"Yes, if it hits you in the right place."

"Who are they going to shoot?"

"Germans."

"Who are Germans?"

"They are the enemy."

"What's an enemy?"

"The people who want to kill you and take your country away from you."

"Where do they live?"

"'Way across the sea," my mother explained. "Don't you remember that I told you that war has been declared?"

I remembered; but when she had told me, it had not seemed at all important. I asked my mother what the war was about and she spoke of England, France, Russia, Germany, of men dying, but the reality of it was too vast and alien for me to be moved or further interested.

Upon another day I was playing out of doors in front of the house and I accidentally looked down the road and saw what seemed to me to be a herd of elephants coming slowly toward me. There was in me this time none of that naked terror I had felt when I had seen the soldiers, for these strange creatures were moving slowly, silently, with no suggestion of threat. Yet I edged cautiously toward the steps of the house, holding myself ready to run if they should prove to be more violent than they appeared. The strange elephants were a few feet from me now and I saw that their faces were like the faces of men! I stared, my mind trying to adjust memory to reality. What kind of men were these? I saw that there were two lines of creatures that looked like men on either side of the road; that there were a few white faces and a great many black faces. I saw that the white faces were the faces of white men and they were dressed in ordinary clothing; but the black faces were men wearing what seemed to me to be elephant's clothing. As the strange animals came abreast of me I saw that the legs of the black animals were held together by irons and that their arms were linked with heavy chains that clanked softly and musically as they moved. The black creatures were digging a shallow ditch on each side of the road, working silently, grunting as they lifted spades of earth and flung them into the middle of the roadway. One of the strange, striped animals turned a black face upon me.

"What are you doing?" I asked in a whisper, not knowing if one actually spoke to elephants.

He shook his head and cast his eyes guardedly back at a white man, then dug on again. Suddenly I noticed that the white men were holding the long, heavy black sticks—rifles!—on their shoulders. After they had passed I ran breathlessly into the house.

"Mama!" I yelled.

"What?" she answered from the kitchen.

"There are elephants in the street!"

She came to the kitchen door and stared at me.

"Elephants?" she asked.

"Yes. Come and see them. They're digging in the street."

My mother dried her hands on her apron and rushed to the front door. I followed, wanting her to interpret the baffling spectacle I had seen. She looked out of the door and shook her head.

"Those are not elephants," she said.

"What are they?"

"That's a chain gang."

"What's a chain gang?"

"It's just what you see," she said. "A gang of men chained together and made to work."

"Why?"

"Because they've done something wrong and they're being punished."

"What did they do?"

"I don't know."

"But why do they look like that?"

"That's to keep them from running away," she said. "You see, everybody'll know that they're convicts because of their stripes."

"Why don't the white men wear stripes?"

"They're the guards."

"Do white men ever wear stripes?"

"Sometimes."

"Did you ever see any?"

"No."

"Why are there so many black men wearing stripes?"

"It's because . . . Well, they're harder on black people."

"The white people?"

"Yes."

"Then why don't all the black men fight all the white men out there? There are more black men than white men . . ."

"But the white men have guns and the black men don't," my mother said. She looked at me and asked: "What made you call them elephants?"

I could not answer her at the moment. But later, brooding over the black-and-white striped clothing of the black men, I remembered that in Elaine I had had a book that carried the gaudy pictures and names of jungle beasts. What had struck me most vividly were the striped zebras that looked as if someone had painted them. The other animals that had gripped my imagination were the elephants, and by association the zebras and the elephants had become linked and identified in my mind to such an extent that when I had seen the convicts dressed in the white and black stripes of zebras, I had thought they were elephants, beasts of the jungle.

Again, after an undetermined stretch of time, my mother announced that we were going to move, that we were going back to West Helena. She had grown tired of the strict religious routine of Granny's home; of the half dozen or more daily family prayers that Granny insisted upon; her fiat that the day began at sunrise and that night commenced at sundown; the long, rambling Bible readings; the individual invocations muttered at each meal; and her declaration that Saturday was the Lord's Sabbath and that no one who lived in her house could work upon that day. In West Helena we could have a home of our own, a condition that now loomed desirable after a few months of Granny's anxiety about the state of our souls. Naturally a trip was agreeable to me. Again we packed. Again we said good-bye. Again we rode the train. Again we were in West Helena.

We rented one half of a double corner house in front of which ran a stagnant ditch carrying sewage. The neighborhood swarmed with rats, cats, dogs, fortune-tellers, cripples, blind men, whores, salesmen, rent collectors, and children. In front of our flat was a huge roundhouse where locomotives were cleaned and repaired. There was an eternal hissing of steam, the deep grunting of steel engines, and the tolling of bells. Smoke obscured the vision and cinders drifted into the house, into our beds, into our kitchen, into our food; and a tarlike smell was always in the air.

Bareheaded and barefooted, my brother and I, along with nameless and countless other black children, used to stand and watch the men crawl in, out, over, and under the huge black metal engines. When the men were not looking, we would climb into the engineer's cab and pull our small bodies to the window and look out, imagining that we were grown and had got a job as an engineer running a train and that it was night and there was a storm and we had a long string of passenger cars behind us, trying to get them safely home.

"Whooooooooeeeeeeeee!" we would say.

"Dong! Dong! Dong!"

"Huff-huff! Huff-huff-huff! Huff-huff-huff-huff!" we would say.

But our greatest fun came from wading in the sewage ditch where we found old bottles, tin cans that held tiny crawfish, rusty spoons, bits of metal, old toothbrushes, dead cats and dogs, and occasional pennies. We made wooden boats out of cigar boxes, devised wooden paddles to which we twisted pieces of rubber and sent the cigar-box boats sailing down the ditch under their own power. Many evenings the fathers of the children would come out, take off their shoes, and make and sail the boats themselves.

My mother and Aunt Maggie cooked in the kitchens of white folks and my brother and I were free to wander where we pleased during their working hours. Each day we were left a dime apiece to spend for lunch and all morning we would dream and discuss what we would buy. At ten or eleven o'clock we would go to the corner grocery—owned by a Jew—and buy a nickel's worth of ginger snaps and a bottle of Coca-Cola; that was lunch as we understood it.

I had never seen a Jew before and the proprietor of the corner grocery was a strange thing in my life. Until that time I had never heard a foreign language spoken and I used to linger at the door of the corner grocery to hear the odd sounds that Jews made when they talked. All of us black people who lived in the neighborhood hated Jews, not because they exploited us, but because we had been taught at home and in Sunday school that Jews were "Christ killers." With the Jews thus singled out for us, we made them fair game for ridicule.

We black children—seven, eight, and nine years of age—used to run to the Jew's store and shout:

> *Jew, Jew, Jew*
> *What do you chew?*

Or we would form a long line and weave back and forth in front of the door, singing:

> *Jew, Jew,*
> *Two for five*
> *That's what keeps*
> *Jew alive.*

Or we would chant:

> *Bloody Christ killers*
> *Never trust a Jew*
> *Bloody Christ killers*
> *What won't a Jew do?*

To one of the redheaded Jewish boys we sang:

> *Red head*
> *Jewish bread*
> *Five cents*
> *A Jewish head.*

To the fat Jewish woman we sneered:

> *Red, white, and blue*
> *Your pa was a Jew*
> *Your ma a dirty Dago*
> *What the hell is you?*

And when the baldheaded proprietor would pass by, we black children, poor, half-starved, ignorant, victims of racial prejudice, would sing with a proud lilt:

> *A rotten egg*
> *Never fries*
> *A cheating dog*
> *Never thrives.*

There were many more folk ditties, some mean, others filthy, all of them cruel. No one ever thought of questioning our right to do this; our mothers and parents generally approved, either actively or passively. To hold an attitude of antagonism or distrust toward Jews was bred in us from childhood; it was not merely racial prejudice, it was a part of our cultural heritage.

One afternoon a group of black boys and girls were standing about outside playing, laughing, talking. A black man dressed in overalls went up the steps and into the flat adjoining the one in which I lived.

"This is Saturday," a black girl said to me.

"Yeah. But why you say it?" I asked.

"They gonna make a lotta money in there today," she said, pointing to the door through which the man had disappeared.

"How?"

Another black man went up the steps and into the flat.

"Don't you know?" the girl asked, incredulous.

"Know what?"

"What they selling . . . ?"

"Where?"

"In there where them men went," she said.

"Nobody sells things in there," I said.

"You kidding?" the girl said in honest disbelief.

"I ain't. What they selling? Tell me."

"You know what they selling," she said, looking at me with a teasing smile.

"They don't sell nothing in there," I said.

"Aw, you just a baby," she said, slapping her dingy palm through the air at me in a contemptuous gesture.

I was puzzled. Was there something happening next door to where I lived that I did not know? I thought I had poked my nose into every bit of conceivable business in the neighborhood; if something was being sold next door, then I certainly wanted to know about it. The building in which I lived was a double frame house of one story; the building originally had been a one-dwelling unit and had been converted into two flats, for there were doors in our flat that led into the flat adjoining. These doors had been locked, bolted, and nailed securely. The family next door seemed quiet; men came and went, but that did not seem odd to me. But now the girl's hints made me want to know what was happening over there. I entered our house and locked the door, then put my ear to the thin wall that divided the two flats and listened. I heard faint sounds, but could make nothing of them. I listened at a bolted door and the sounds came a little louder, but I still could understand nothing.

Quietly I pulled up a chair, placed a box upon it, and climbed up and peered through a crack at the top of the door. I saw, in the dim shadows of the room beyond, a naked man and a naked woman upon a bed, the man on top of the woman. I lost my balance and toppled backwards to the floor. I lay still, wondering if the man and woman next door had heard me. But all seemed quiet and my curiosity returned. Just as I had climbed up again to look, a sharp rapping came on the windowpane behind me; I turned my head and saw the landlady from next door looking at me. My heart thumped and I scrambled down. The landlady's black face was pressed hard against the windowpane; her mouth was moving violently and her eyes were glaring. I was afraid to stay in the house or go out. Why had I not thought of lowering the shade? Evidently I had done something terrible, if the wild anger written on the woman's face was any indication. Her face went from the window and a moment later a loud pounding came at the front door.

"Open this door, you boy!"

I trembled and did not answer.

"Open this door or I'll have to break it!"

"My mama ain't here," I said vaguely.

"This is my house and you open this door!" she shouted.

Her voice overpowered me and I opened the door. She rushed

in, then stopped and stared at the clumsy scaffolding I had rigged up to look into her flat. Why hadn't I taken it down before I opened the door?

"Boy, what do you mean?" she asked.

I could not answer.

"You scared my customers," she said.

"Customers?" I repeated vaguely.

"You little snot!" she blazed. "I got a good mind to beat you!"

"Naw, you won't!" I said.

"I'm gonna make your folks move outta here," she railed. "I got to make a living and you go and spoil my Saturday for me!"

"I . . . I was just looking . . ."

"Looking . . . ?" She smiled suddenly, relenting a little. "Why don't you come on over like the rest and spend a quarter?"

"I don't want to go to your old house," I told her with my nine-year-old indignation.

"You're a plague," she said, deciding that I would not be a customer. "I'm gonna get you outta here!"

When my mother and Aunt Maggie came home that night, there was a scalding argument. The women shouted at each other over the wooden railings on the front porch and their voices could be heard for half a mile. Neighbors listened. Children gathered and gaped. The argument boiled down to one issue: the landlady demanded that my mother beat me and, for once, my mother refused.

"You oughtn't have *that* in your house," my mother told her.

"It's my house and I'll have in it what I damn please," the landlady said.

"I wouldn't've moved in here if I had thought you were running *that* kind of business," my mother said.

"Don't talk to me like that, you high-toned bitch!" the landlady shouted.

"What do you expect children to do when you do *that*?" my mother asked.

"Them bastard brats of yours ain't no angels!" the landlady said.

"You're just a common prostitute!" Aunt Maggie pitched in.

"And what kind of whore is you?" the landlady shouted.

"Don't you talk to my sister like that!" my mother warned.

"Pack up your rags, you black bastards, and get!" the landlady ordered.

It ended with our packing and moving that night into another frame house on the same street, a few doors away. I still had only a hazy notion of what the landlady was selling. The boys later told me the name of it, but I had no exact conception of it in my mind. Though I knew that others felt it was something terribly bad, I was still curious. In time I would find out what it was.

Something secret was happening in our house and it had reached a serious stage before I knew it. Each night, just as I was dozing off to sleep, I would hear a light tapping on Aunt Maggie's windowpane, a door creaking open, whispers, then long silences. Once I got out of bed and crept to the door of the front room and stole a look. There was a well-dressed black man sitting on the sofa talking in a soft voice to Aunt Maggie. Why was it that I could not meet the man? I crept back to bed, but was awakened later by low voices saying good-bye. The next morning I asked my mother who had been in the house, and she told me that no one had been there.

"But I heard a man talking," I said.

"You didn't," she said. "You were sleeping."

"But I saw a man. He was in the front room."

"You were dreaming," my mother said.

I learned a part of the secret of the night visits one Sunday morning when Aunt Maggie called me and my brother to her room and introduced us to the man who was going to be our new "uncle," a Professor Matthews. He wore a high, snow-white collar and rimless eyeglasses. His lips were thin and his eyelids seemed never to blink. I felt something cold and remote in him and when he called me I would not go to him. He sensed my distrust and softened me up with the gift of a dime, then knelt and prayed for us two "poor fatherless young men," as he called us. After prayer Aunt Maggie told us that she and Professor Matthews were leaving soon for the North. I was saddened, for I had grown to feel that Aunt Maggie was another mother to me.

I did not meet the new "uncle" again, though each morning I saw evidences of his having been in the house. My brother and I were puzzled and we speculated as to what our new "uncle" could be doing. Why did he always come at night? Why did he always speak in so subdued a voice, hardly above a whisper? And how did he get the money to buy such white collars and such nice blue suits? To add to our bewilderment, our mother called us to her one day and cautioned us against telling anyone that "uncle" ever visited us, that people were looking for "uncle."

"What people?" I asked.

"White people," my mother said.

Anxiety entered my body. Somewhere in the unknown the white threat was hovering near again.

"What do they want with him?" I asked.

"You never mind," my mother said.

"What did he do?"

"You keep your mouth shut or the white folks'll get you too," she warned me.

Knowing that we were frightened and baffled about our new "uncle," my mother—I guess—urged Aunt Maggie to tell "uncle" to bribe us into silence and trust. Every morning now was like Christmas; we would climb out of bed and race to the kitchen and look on the table to see what "uncle" had left for us. One morning I found that he had brought me a little female poodle, upon which I bestowed the name of Betsy and she became my pet and companion.

Strangely, "uncle" began visiting us in the daytime now, but when he came all the shades in the house were drawn and we were forbidden to go out of doors until he left. I asked my mother a thousand whispered questions about the silent, black, educated "uncle" and she always replied:

"It's something you can't know. Now keep quiet and go play."

One night the sound of sobbing awakened me. I got up and went softly to the front room and peeped around the jamb of the door; there was "uncle" sitting on the floor by the window, peering into the night from under the lifted curtain. My mother was bent over a small trunk, packing hurriedly. Fear gripped me. Was my mother leaving? Why was Aunt Maggie crying? Were the white people coming after us?

"Hurry up," "uncle" said. "We must get out of here."

"Oh, Maggie," my mother said. "I don't know if you ought to go."

"You keep out of this," "uncle" said, still peering into the dark street.

"But what did you do?" Aunt Maggie asked.

"I'll tell you later," "uncle" said. "We got to get out of here before they come!"

"But you've done something terrible," Aunt Maggie said. "Or you wouldn't be running like this."

"The house is on fire," "uncle" said. "And when they see it, they'll know who did it."

"Did you set the house afire?" my mother asked.

"There was nothing else to do," "uncle" said impatiently. "I took the money. I had hit her. She was unconscious. If they found her, she'd tell. I'd be lost. So I set the fire."

"But she'll burn up," Aunt Maggie said, crying into her hands.

"What could I do?" "uncle" asked. "I had to do it. I couldn't just leave her there and let somebody find her. They'd know somebody hit her. But if she burns, nobody'll ever know."

Fear filled me. What was happening? Were white people coming after all of us? Was my mother going to leave me?

"Mama!" I wailed, running into the room.

"Uncle" leaped to his feet; a gun was in his hand and he was pointing it at me. I stared at the gun, feeling that I was going to die at any moment.

"Richard!" my mother whispered fiercely.

"You're going away!" I yelled.

My mother rushed to me and clapped her hand over my mouth.

"Do you want us all to be killed?" she asked, shaking me.

I quieted.

"Now you go back to sleep," she said.

"You're leaving," I said.

"I'm not."

"You are leaving. I see the trunk!" I wailed.

"You stop that noise," my mother said; and she caught my arms in so tight a grip of fury that my crying ceased because of the pain. "Now you get back in bed."

She led me back to bed and I lay awake, listening to whispers, footsteps, doors creaking in the dark, and the sobs of Aunt Maggie. Finally I heard the sound of a horse and buggy rolling up to the house; I heard the scraping of a trunk being dragged across the floor. Aunt Maggie came into my room, crying softly; she kissed me and whispered good-bye. She kissed my brother, who did not even waken. Then she was gone.

The next morning my mother called me into the kitchen and talked to me for a long time, cautioning me that I must never mention what I had seen and heard, that white people would kill me if they even thought I knew.

"Know what?" I could not help but ask.

"Never you mind, now," she said. "Forget what you saw last night."

"But what did 'uncle' do?"

"I can't tell you."

"He killed somebody," I ventured timidly.

"If anybody heard you say that, you'll die," my mother said.

That settled it for me; I would never mention it. A few days later a tall white man with a gleaming star on his chest and a gun on his hip came to the house. He talked with my mother a long time and all I could hear was my mother's voice:

"I don't know what you're talking about. Search the house if you like."

The tall white man looked at me and my brother, but he said nothing to us. For weeks I wondered what it was that "uncle" had done, but I was destined never to know, not even in all the years that followed.

With Aunt Maggie gone, my mother could not earn enough to feed us and my stomach kept so consistently empty that my head ached most of the day. One afternoon hunger haunted me so acutely that I decided to try to sell my dog Betsy and buy some food. Betsy was a tiny, white, fluffy poodle and when I had washed, dried, and combed her, she looked like a toy. I tucked her under my arm and went for the first time alone into a white neighborhood where there were wide clean streets and big white houses. I went from door to door, ringing the bells. Some white people slammed the door in my face. Others told me to come to the rear of the house, but pride would never let me do that. Finally a young white woman came to the door and smiled.

"What do you want?" she asked.

"Do you want to buy a pretty dog?" I asked.

"Let me see it."

She took the dog into her arms and fondled and kissed it.

"What's its name?"

"Betsy."

"She is cute," she said. "What do you want for her?"

"A dollar," I said.

"Wait a moment," she said. "Let me see if I have a dollar."

She took Betsy into the house with her and I waited on the porch, marveling at the cleanliness, the quietness of the white world. How orderly everything was! Yet I felt out of place. I had no desire to live here. Then I remembered that these houses were the homes in which lived those white people who made Negroes leave their homes and flee into the night. I grew tense. Would someone say that I was a bad nigger and try to kill me here? What was keeping the woman so long? Would she tell other people that a nigger boy had said something wrong to her? Perhaps she was getting a mob? Maybe I ought to leave now and forget about Betsy? My mounting anxieties drowned out my hunger. I wanted to rush back to the safety of the black faces I knew.

The door opened and the woman came out, smiling, still hugging Betsy in her arms. But I could not see her smile now; my eyes were full of the fears I had conjured up.

"I just love this dog," she said, "and I'm going to buy her. I haven't got a dollar. All I have is ninety-seven cents."

Though she did not know it, she was now giving me my opportunity to ask for my dog without saying that I did not want to sell her to white people.

"No, ma'am," I said softly. "I want a dollar."

"But I haven't got a dollar in the house," she said.

"Then I can't sell the dog," I said.

"I'll give you the other three cents when my mother comes home tonight," she said.

"No, ma'am," I said, looking stonily at the floor.

"But, listen, you said you wanted a dollar . . ."

"Yes, ma'am. A dollar."

"Then here is ninety-seven cents," she said, extending a handful of change to me, still holding on to Betsy.

"No, ma'am," I said, shaking my head. "I want a dollar."

"But I'll give you the other three cents!"

"My mama told me to sell her for a dollar," I said, feeling that I was being too aggressive and trying to switch the moral blame for my aggressiveness to my absent mother.

"You'll get a dollar. You'll get the three cents tonight."

"No, ma'am."

"Then leave the dog and come back tonight."

"No, ma'am."

"But what could you want with a dollar *now?*" she asked.

"I want to buy something to eat," I said.

"Then ninety-seven cents will buy you a lot of food," she said.

"No, ma'am. I want my dog."

She stared at me for a moment and her face grew red.

"Here's your dog," she snapped, thrusting Betsy into my arms. "Now, get away from here! You're just about the craziest nigger boy I ever did see!"

I took Betsy and ran all the way home, glad that I had not sold her. But my hunger returned. Maybe I ought to have taken the ninety-seven cents? But it was too late now. I hugged Betsy in my arms and waited. When my mother came home that night, I told her what had happened.

"And you didn't take the money?" she asked.

"No, ma'am."

"Why?"

"I don't know," I said uneasily.

"Don't you know that ninety-seven cents is *almost* a dollar?" she asked.

"Yes, ma'am," I said, counting on my fingers. "Ninety-eight, ninety-nine, one hundred. But I didn't want to sell Betsy to white people."

"Why?"

"Because they're white," I said.

"You're foolish," my mother said.

A week later Betsy was crushed to death beneath the wheels of a coal wagon. I cried and buried her in the back yard and drove a barrel staving into the ground at the head of her grave. My mother's sole comment was:

"You could have had a dollar. But you can't eat a dead dog, can you?"

I did not answer.

Up or down the wet or dusty streets, indoors or out, the days and nights began to spell out magic possibilities.

If I pulled a hair from a horse's tail and sealed it in a jar of my own urine, the hair would turn overnight into a snake.

If I passed a Catholic sister or mother dressed in black and smiled and allowed her to see my teeth, I would surely die.

If I walked under a leaning ladder, I would certainly have bad luck.

If I kissed my elbow, I would turn into a girl.

If my right ear itched, then something good was being said about me by somebody.

If I touched a hunchback's hump, then I would never be sick.

If I placed a safety pin on a steel railroad track and let a train run over it, the safety pin would turn into a pair of bright brand-new scissors.

If I heard a voice and no human being was near, then either God or the Devil was trying to talk to me.

Whenever I made urine, I should spit into it for good luck.

If my nose itched, somebody was going to visit me.

If I mocked a crippled man, then God would make me crippled.

If I used the name of God in vain, then God would strike me dead.

If it rained while the sun was shining, then the Devil was beating his wife.

If the stars twinkled more than usual on any given night, it meant that the angels in heaven were happy and were flitting across the doors of heaven; and since stars were merely holes ventilating heaven, the twinkling came from the angels flitting past the holes that admitted air into the holy home of God.

If I broke a mirror, I would have seven years of bad luck.

If I was good to my mother, I would grow old and rich.

If I had a cold and tied a worn, dirty sock about my throat before I went to bed, the cold would be gone the next morning.

If I wore a bit of asafetida in a little bag tied about my neck, I would never catch a disease.

If I looked at the sun through a piece of smoked glass on Easter Sunday morning, I would see the sun shouting in praise of a Risen Lord.

If a man confessed anything on his deathbed, it was the truth; for no man could stare death in the face and lie.

If you spat on each grain of corn that was planted, the corn would grow tall and bear well.

If I spilt salt, I should toss a pinch over my left shoulder to ward off misfortune.

If I covered a mirror when a storm was raging, the lightning would not strike me.

If I stepped over a broom that was lying on the floor, I would have bad luck.

If I walked in my sleep, then God was trying to lead me somewhere to do a good deed for Him.

Anything seemed possible, likely, feasible, because I wanted everything to be possible . . . Because I had no power to make things happen outside of me in the objective world, I made things happen within. Because my environment was bare and bleak, I endowed it with unlimited potentialities, redeemed it for the sake of my own hungry and cloudy yearning.

A dread of white people now came to live permanently in my feelings and imagination. As the war drew to a close, racial conflict flared over the entire South, and though I did not witness any of it, I could not have been more thoroughly affected by it if I had participated directly in every clash. The war itself had been unreal to me, but I had grown able to respond emotionally to every hint, whisper, word, inflection, news, gossip, and rumor regarding conflicts between the races. Nothing challenged the totality of my personality so much as this pressure of hate and threat that stemmed from the invisible whites. I would stand for hours on the doorsteps of neighbors' houses listening to their talk, learning how a white woman had slapped a black woman, how a white man had killed a black man. It filled me with awe, wonder, and fear, and I asked ceaseless questions.

One evening I heard a tale that rendered me sleepless for nights. It was of a Negro woman whose husband had been seized and killed by a mob. It was claimed that the woman vowed she would avenge her husband's death and she took a shotgun, wrapped it in a sheet, and went humbly to the whites, pleading that she be allowed to take her husband's body for burial. It seemed that she was granted permission to come to the side of her dead husband while the whites, silent and armed, looked on. The woman, so went the story, knelt and prayed, then proceeded to unwrap the sheet; and, before the white men realized what was happening, she had taken the gun from the sheet and had slain four of them, shooting at them from her knees.

I did not know if the story was factually true or not, but it was emotionally true because I had already grown to feel that there existed men against whom I was powerless, men who could violate my life at will. I resolved that I would emulate the black woman if I were ever faced with a white mob; I would conceal a weapon, pretend that I had been crushed by the wrong done to one of my loved ones; then, just when they thought I had accepted their cruelty as the law of my life, I would let go with my gun and kill as many of them as possible before they killed me. The story of the woman's deception gave form and meaning to confused defensive feelings that had long been sleeping in me.

My imaginings, of course, had no objective value whatever. My spontaneous fantasies lived in my mind because I felt completely helpless in the face of this threat that might come upon me at any time, and because there did not exist to my knowledge any possible course of action which could have saved me if I had ever been confronted with a white mob. My fantasies were a moral bulwark that enabled me to feel I was keeping my emotional integrity whole, a support that enabled my personality to limp through days lived under the threat of violence.

These fantasies were no longer a reflection of my reaction to the white people, they were a part of my living, of my emotional life; they were a culture, a creed, a religion. The hostility of the whites had become so deeply implanted in my mind and feelings that it had lost direct connection with the daily environment in which I lived; and my reactions to this hostility fed upon itself, grew or diminished according to the news that reached me about the whites, according to what I aspired or hoped for. Tension would set in at the mere mention of whites and a vast complex of emotions, involving the whole of my personality, would be aroused. It was as though I was continuously reacting to the threat of some natural force whose hostile behavior could not be predicted. I had never in my life been abused by whites, but I had already become as conditioned to their existence as though I had been the victim of a thousand lynchings.

I lived in West Helena an undeterminedly long time before I returned to school and took up regular study. My mother luckily secured a job in a white doctor's office at the unheard-of-wages of five dollars per week and at once she announced that her "sons were going to school again." I was happy. But I was still shy and half paralyzed when in the presence of a crowd, and my first day at the new school made me the laughingstock of the classroom. I was sent to the blackboard to write my name and address; I knew my name and address, knew how to write it, knew how to spell it; but standing at the blackboard with the eyes of the many girls and boys looking at my back made me freeze inside and I was unable to write a single letter.

"Write your name," the teacher called to me.

I lifted the white chalk to the blackboard and, as I was about to write, my mind went blank, empty; I could not remember my name, not even the first letter. Somebody giggled and I stiffened.

"Just forget us and write your name and address," the teacher coaxed.

An impulse to write would flash through me, but my hand would refuse to move. The children began to twitter and I flushed hotly.

"Don't you know your name?" the teacher asked.

I looked at her and could not answer. The teacher rose and walked to my side, smiling at me to give me confidence. She placed her hand tenderly upon my shoulder.

"What's your name?" she asked.

"Richard," I whispered.

"Richard what?"

"Richard Wright."

"Spell it."

I spelled my name in a wild rush of letters, trying desperately to redeem my paralyzing shyness.

"Spell it slowly so I can hear it," she directed me.

I did.

"Now, can you write?"

"Yes, ma'am."

"Then write it."

Again I turned to the blackboard and lifted my hand to write, then I was blank and void within. I tried frantically to collect my senses, but I could remember nothing. A sense of the girls and boys behind me filled me to the exclusion of everything. I realized how utterly I was failing and I grew weak and leaned my hot forehead against the cold blackboard. The room burst into a loud and prolonged laugh and my muscles froze.

"You may go to your seat," the teacher said.

I sat and cursed myself. Why did I always appear so dumb when I was called upon to perform something in a crowd? I knew how to write as well as any pupil in the classroom, and no doubt I could read better than any of them, and I could talk fluently and expressively when I was sure of myself. Then why did strange faces make me freeze? I sat with my ears and neck burning, hearing the pupils whisper about me, hating myself, hating them; I sat still as stone and a storm of emotion surged through me.

While sitting in class one day I was startled to hear whistles blowing and bells ringing. Soon the bedlam was deafening. The teacher lost control of her class and the girls and boys ran to the windows. The teacher left the room and when she returned she announced:

"Everybody, pack your things and go home!"

"Why?"

"What's happened?"

"The war is over," the teacher said.

I followed the rest of the children into the streets and saw that white and black people were laughing and singing and shouting. I felt afraid as I pushed through crowds of white people, but my fright left when I entered my neighborhood and saw smiling black faces. I wandered among them, trying to realize what war was, what it meant, and I could not. I noticed that many girls and boys were pointing at something in the sky; I looked up too and saw what seemed to be a tiny bird wheeling and sailing.

"Look!"

"A plane!"

I had never seen a plane.

"It's a bird," I said.

The crowd laughed.

"That's a plane, boy," a man said.

"It's a bird," I said. "I see it."

A man lifted me upon his shoulder.

"Boy, remember this," he said. "You're seeing man fly."

I still did not believe it. It still looked like a bird to me. That night at home my mother convinced me that men could fly.

Christmas came and I had but one orange. I was hurt and would not go out to play with the neighborhood children who were blowing horns and shooting firecrackers. I nursed my orange all of Christmas Day; at night, just before going to bed, I ate it, first taking a bite out of the top and sucking the juice from it as I squeezed it; finally I tore the peeling into bits and munched them slowly.

3

Having grown taller and older, I now associated with older boys and I had to pay for my admittance into their company by subscribing to certain racial sentiments. The touchstone of fraternity was my feeling toward white people, how much hostility I held toward them, what degrees of value and honor I assigned to race. None of this was premeditated, but sprang spontaneously out of the talk of black boys who met at the crossroads.

It was degrading to play with girls and in our talk we relegated them to a remote island of life. We had somehow caught the spirit of the role of our sex and we flocked together for common moral schooling. We spoke boastfully in bass voices; we used the word "nigger" to prove the tough fiber of our feelings; we spouted excessive profanity as a sign of our coming manhood; we pretended callousness toward the injunctions of our parents; and we strove to convince one another that our decisions stemmed from ourselves and ourselves alone. Yet we frantically concealed how dependent we were upon one another.

Of an afternoon when school had let out I would saunter down the street, idly kicking an empty tin can, or knocking a stick against the palings of a wooden fence, or whistling, until I would stumble upon one or more of the gang loitering at a corner, standing in a field, or sitting upon the steps of somebody's house.

"Hey." Timidly.

"You eat yet?" Uneasily trying to make conversation.

"Yeah, man. I done really fed my face." Casually.

"I had cabbage and potatoes." Confidently.

"I had buttermilk and black-eyed peas." Meekly informational.

"Hell, I ain't gonna stand near you, nigger!" Pronouncement.

"How come?" Feigned innocence.

"'Cause you gonna smell up this air in a minute!" A shouted accusation.

Laughter runs through the crowd.

"Nigger, your mind's in a ditch." Amusingly moralistic.

"Ditch, nothing! Nigger, you going to break wind any minute now!" Triumphant pronouncement creating suspense.

"Yeah, when them black-eyed peas tell that buttermilk to move over, that buttermilk ain't gonna wanna move and there's gonna be war in your guts and your stomach's gonna swell up and bust!" Climax.

The crowd laughs loud and long.

"Man, them white folks oughta catch you and send you to the zoo and keep you for the next war!" Throwing the subject into a wider field.

"Then when that fighting starts, they oughta feed you on buttermilk and black-eyed peas and let you break wind!" The subject is accepted and extended.

"You'd win the war with a new kind of poison gas!" A shouted climax.

There is high laughter that simmers down slowly.

"Maybe poison gas is something good to have." The subject of white folks is associationally swept into the orbit of talk.

"Yeah, if they hava race riot round here, I'm gonna kill all the white folks with my poison." Bitter pride.

Gleeful laughter. Then silence, each waiting for the other to contribute something.

"Them white folks sure scared of us, though." Sober statement of an old problem.

"Yeah, they send you to war, make you lick them Germans,

teach you how to fight and when you come back they scared of you, want to kill you." Half boastful and half complaining.

"My mama says that old white woman where she works talked 'bout slapping her and Ma said: 'Miz Green, if you slaps me, I'll kill you and go to hell and pay for it!' " Extension, development, sacrificial boasting.

"Hell, I woulda just killed her if she hada said that to me." An angry grunt of supreme racial assertion.

Silence.

"Man, them white folks sure is mean." Complaining.

"That's how come so many colored folks leaving the South." Informational.

"And, man, they sure hate for you to leave." Pride of personal and racial worth implied.

"Yeah. They wanna keep you here and work you to death."

"The first white sonofabitch that bothers me is gonna get a hole knocked in his head!" Naïve rebellion.

"That ain't gonna do you no good. Hell, they'll catch you." Rejection of naïve rebellion.

"Ha-ha-ha . . . Yeah, goddammit, they really catch you, now." Appreciation of the thoroughness of white militancy.

"Yeah, white folks set on their white asses day and night, but leta nigger do something, and they get every bloodhound that was ever born and put 'em on his trail." Bitter pride in realizing what it costs to defeat them.

"Man, you reckon these white folks is ever gonna change?" Timid, questioning hope.

"Hell, no! They just born that way." Rejecting hope for fear that it could never come true.

"Shucks, man. I'm going north when I get grown." Rebelling against futile hope and embracing flight.

"A colored man's all right up north." Justifying flight.

"They say a white man hit a colored man up north and that colored man hit that white man, knocked him cold, and nobody did a damn thing!" Urgent wish to believe in flight.

"Man for man up there." Begging to believe in justice.

Silence.

"Listen, you reckon them buildings up north is as tall as they say they is?" Leaping by association to something concrete and trying to make belief real.

"They say they gotta building in New York forty stories high!" A thing too incredible for belief.

"Man, I'd be scareda them buildings!" Ready to abandon the now suppressed idea of flight.

"You know, they say that them buildings sway and rock in the wind." Stating a miracle.

"Naw, nigger!" Utter astonishment and rejection.

"Yeah, they say they do." Insisting upon the miracle.

"You reckon that could be?" Questioning hope.

"Hell, naw! If a building swayed and rocked in the wind, hell, it'd fall! Any fool knows that! Don't let people maka fool outta you, telling you them things!" Moving body agitatedly, stomping feet impatiently, and scurrying back to safe reality.

Silence. Somebody would pick up a stone and toss it across a field.

"Man, what makes white folks so mean?" Returning to grapple with the old problem.

"Whenever I see one I spit." Emotional rejection of whites.

"Man, ain't they ugly?" Increased emotional rejection.

"Man, you ever get right close to a white man, close enough to smell 'im?" Anticipation of statement.

"They say we stink. But my ma says white folks smell like dead folks." Wishing the enemy was dead.

"Niggers smell from sweat. But white folks smell *all* the time." The enemy is an animal to be killed on sight.

And the talk would weave, roll, surge, spurt, veer, swell, having no specific aim or direction, touching vast areas of life, expressing the tentative impulses of childhood. Money, God, race, sex, color, war, planes, machines, trains, swimming, boxing, anything . . . The culture of one black household was thus transmitted to another black household, and folk tradition was handed from group to group. Our attitudes were made, defined, set, or corrected; our ideas were discovered, discarded, enlarged, torn apart, and accepted. Night would fall. Bats would zip through the air. Crickets would cry from the grass. Frogs would croak. The stars would come out. Dew would dampen the earth. Yellow squares of light would glow in the distance as kerosene lamps were lit in our homes. Finally, from across the fields or down the road a long slow yell would come:

"Youuuuuuuu, Daaaaaaaavee!"

Easy laughter among the boys, but no reply.

"Calling the hogs."

"Go home, pig."

Laughter again. A boy would slowly detach himself from the gang.

"Youuuuuuu, Daaaaaaaavee!"

He would not answer his mother's call, for that would have been a sign of dependence.

"I'll do you-all like the farmer did the potato," the boy would say.

"How's that?"

"Plant you now and dig you later!"

The boy would trot home slowly and there would be more easy laughter. More talk. One by one we would be called home to fetch water from the hydrant in the back yard, to go to the store and buy greens and meal for tomorrow, to split wood for kindling.

On Sundays, if our clothes were presentable, my mother would take me and my brother to Sunday school. We did not object, for church was not where we learned of God or His ways, but where we met our school friends and continued our long, rambling talks. Some of the Bible stories were interesting in themselves, but we always twisted them, secularized them to the level of our street life, rejecting all meanings that did not fit into our environment. And we did the same to the beautiful hymns. When the preacher intoned:

Amazing grace, how sweet it sounds

we would wink at one another and hum under our breath:

A bulldog ran my grandma down

We were now large enough for the white boys to fear us and both of us, the white boys and the black boys, began to play our traditional racial roles as though we had been born to them, as though it was in our blood, as though we were being guided by instinct. All the frightful descriptions we had heard about each other, all the violent expressions of hate and hostility that had seeped into us from our surroundings, came now to the surface to guide our actions. The roundhouse was the racial boundary of the neighborhood, and it had been tacitly agreed between the white boys and the black boys that the whites were to keep to the far side of the roundhouse and we blacks were to keep to our side. Whenever we caught a white boy on our side we stoned him; if we strayed to their side, they stoned us.

Our battles were real and bloody; we threw rocks, cinders, coal, sticks, pieces of iron, and broken bottles, and while we threw them we longed for even deadlier weapons. If we were hurt, we took it quietly; there was no crying or whimpering. If our wounds were not truly serious, we hid them from our parents. We did not want to be beaten for fighting. Once, in a battle with a gang of white boys, I was struck behind the ear with a piece of broken bottle; the cut was deep and bled profusely. I tried to stem the flow of blood by dabbing at the cut with a rag and when my mother came from work I was forced to tell her that I was hurt, for I needed medical attention. She rushed me to a doctor who stitched my scalp; but when she took me home she beat me, telling me that I must never fight white boys again, that I might be killed by them, that she had to work and had no time to worry about my fights. Her words did not sink in, for they conflicted with the code of the streets. I promised my mother that I would not fight, but I knew that if I kept my word I would lose my standing in the gang, and the gang's life was my life.

My mother became too ill to work and I began to do chores in the neighborhood. My first job was carrying lunches to the men who worked in the roundhouse, for which I received twenty-five cents a week. When the men did not finish their lunches, I would salvage what few crumbs remained. Later I obtained a job in a small café carting wood in my arms to keep the big stove going and taking trays of food to passengers when trains stopped for a half hour or so in a near-by station. I received a dollar a week for this work, but I was too young and too small to perform the duties; one morning while trying to take a heavily loaded tray up the steps of a train, I fell and dashed the tray of food to the ground.

Inability to pay rent forced us to move into a house perched atop high logs in a section of the town where flood waters came. My brother and I had great fun running up and down the tall, shaky steps.

Again paying rent became a problem and we moved nearer the center of town, where I found a job in a pressing shop, delivering clothes to hotels, sweeping floors, and listening to Negro men boast of their sex lives.

Yet again we moved, this time to the outskirts of town, near a wide stretch of railroad tracks to which, each morning before school, I would take a sack and gather coal to heat our frame house, dodging in and out between the huge, black, puffing engines.

My mother, her health failing rapidly, spoke constantly now of Granny's home, of how ardently she wanted to see us grow up before she died. Already there had crept into her speech a halting, lisping quality that, though I did not know it, was the shadow of her future. I was more conscious of my mother now than I had ever been and I was already able to feel what being completely without her would mean. A slowly rising dread stole into me and I would look at my mother for long moments, but when she would look at me I would look away. Then real fear came as her illness recurred at shorter intervals. Time stood still. My brother and I waited, hungry and afraid.

One morning a shouting voice awakened me.

"Richard! Richard!"

I rolled out of bed. My brother came running into the room.

"Richard, you better come and see Mama. She's very sick," he said.

I ran into my mother's room and saw her lying upon her bed, dressed, her eyes open, her mouth gaped. She was very still.

"Mama!" I called.

She did not answer or turn her head. I reached forward to shake her, but drew back, afraid that she was dead.

"Mama!" I called again, my mind unable to grasp that she could not answer.

Finally I went to her and shook her. She moved slightly and groaned. My brother and I called her repeatedly, but she did not speak. Was she dying? It seemed unthinkable. My brother and I looked at each other; we did not know what to do.

"We better get somebody," I said.

I ran into the hallway and called a neighbor. A tall, black woman bustled out of a door.

"Please, won't you come and see my mama? She won't talk. We can't wake her up. She's terribly sick," I told her.

She followed me into our flat.

"Mrs. Wright!" she called to my mother.

My mother lay still, unseeing, silent. The woman felt my mother's hands.

"She ain't dead," she said. "But she's sick, all right. I better get some more of the neighbors."

Five or six of the women came and my brother and I waited in the hallway while they undressed my mother and put her to bed. When we were allowed back in the room, a woman said:

"Looks like a stroke to me."

"Just like paralysis," said another.

"And she's so young," someone else said.

My brother and I stood against a wall while the bustling women worked frantically over my mother. A stroke? Paralysis? What were those things? Would she die? One of the women asked me if there was any money in the house; I did not know. They searched through the dresser and found a dollar or two and sent for a doctor. The doctor arrived. Yes, he told us, my mother had suffered a stroke of paralysis. She was in a serious condition. She needed someone with her day and night; she needed medicine.

Where was her husband? I told him the story and he shook his head.

"She'll need all the help that she can get," the doctor said. "Her entire left side is paralyzed. She cannot talk and she will have to be fed."

Later that day I rummaged through drawers and found Granny's address; I wrote to her, pleading with her to come and help us. The neighbors nursed my mother day and night, fed us and washed our clothes. I went through the days with a stunned consciousness, unable to believe what had happened. Suppose Granny did not come? I tried not to think of it. She *had* to come. The utter loneliness was now terrifying. I had been suddenly thrown emotionally upon my own. Within an hour the half-friendly world that I had known had turned cold and hostile. I was too frightened to weep. I was glad that my mother was not dead, but there was the fact that she would be sick for a long, long time, perhaps for the balance of her life. I became morose. Though I was a child, I could no longer feel as a child, could no longer react as a child. The desire for play was gone and I brooded, wondering if Granny would come and help us. I tried not to think of a tomorrow that was neither real nor wanted, for all tomorrows held questions that I could not answer.

When the neighbors offered me food, I refused, already ashamed that so often in my life I had to be fed by strangers. And after I had been prevailed upon to eat I would eat as little as possible, feeling that some of the shame of charity would be taken away. It pained me to think that other children were wondering if I were hungry, and whenever they asked me if I wanted food, I would say no, even though I was starving. I was tense during the days I waited for Granny, and when she came I gave up, letting her handle things, answering questions automatically, obeying, knowing that somehow I had to face things alone. I withdrew into myself.

I wrote letters that Granny dictated to her eight children— there were nine of them, including my mother—in all parts of the country, asking for money with which "to take Ella and her two little children to our home." Money came and again there were days of packing household effects. My mother was taken to the train in an ambulance and put on board upon a stretcher. We rode to Jackson in silence and my mother was put abed upstairs. Aunt Maggie came from Detroit to help nurse and clean. The big house was quiet. We spoke in lowered voices. We walked with soft tread. The odor of medicine hung in the air. Doctors came and went. Night and day I could hear my mother groaning. We thought that she would die at any moment.

Aunt Cleo came from Chicago. Uncle Clark came from Green-wood, Mississippi. Uncle Edward came from Carters, Mississippi. Uncle Charles from Mobile, Alabama. Aunt Addie from a religious school in Huntsville, Alabama. Uncle Thomas from Hazelhurst, Mississippi. The house had an expectant air and I caught whispered talk of "what is to become of her children?" I felt dread, knowing that others—strangers even though they were relatives—were debating my destiny. I had never seen my mother's brothers and sisters before and their presence made live again in me my old shyness. One day Uncle Edward called me to him and he felt my skinny arms and legs.

"He needs more flesh on him," he commented impersonally, addressing himself to his brothers and sisters.

I was horribly embarrassed, feeling that my life had somehow been full of nameless wrong, an unatonable guilt.

"Food will make him pick up in weight," Granny said.

Out of the family conferences it was decided that my brother and I would be separated, that it was too much of a burden for any one aunt or uncle to assume the support of both of us. Where was I to go? Who would take me? I became more anxious than ever. When an aunt or an uncle would come into my presence, I could not look at them. I was always reminding myself that I must not do anything that would make any of them feel they would not want me in their homes.

At night my sleep was filled with wild dreams. Sometimes I would wake up screaming in terror. The grownups would come running and I would stare at them, as though they were figures out of my nightmare, then go back to sleep. One night I found myself standing in the back yard. The moon was shining bright as day. Silence surrounded me. Suddenly I felt that someone was holding my hand. I looked and saw an uncle. He was speaking to me in a low, gentle voice.

"What's the matter, son?"

I stared at him, trying to understand what he was saying. I seemed to be wrapped in a kind of mist.

"Richard, what are you doing?"

I could not answer. It seemed that I could not wake up. He shook me. I came to myself and stared about at the moon-drenched yard.

"Where are we going?" I asked him.

"You were walking in your sleep," he said.

Granny gave me fuller meals and made me take naps in the afternoon and gradually my sleepwalking passed. The uneasy days and nights made me resolve to leave Granny's home as soon as I was old enough to support myself. It was not that they were unkind, but I knew that they did not have money enough to feed me and my brother. I avoided going into my mother's room now; merely to look at her was painful. She had grown very thin; she was still speechless, staring, quiet as stone.

One evening my brother and I were called into the front room where a conference of aunts and uncles was being held.

"Richard," said an uncle, "you know how sick your mother is?"

"Yes, sir."

"Well, Granny's not strong enough to take care of you two boys," he continued.

"Yes, sir," I said, waiting for his decision.

"Well, Aunt Maggie's going to take your brother to Detroit and send him to school."

I waited. Who was going to take me? I had wanted to be with Aunt Maggie, but I did not dare contest the decision.

"Now, where would you like to go?" I was asked.

The question caught me by surprise; I had been waiting for a fiat, and now a choice lay before me. But I did not have the courage to presume that anyone wanted me.

"Anywhere," I said.

"Any of us are willing to take you," he said.

Quickly I calculated which of them lived nearest to Jackson. Uncle Clark lived in Greenwood, which was but a few miles distant.

"I'd like to live with Uncle Clark, since he's close to the home here," I said.

"Is that what you really want?"

"Yes, sir."

Uncle Clark came to me and placed his hand upon my head.

"All right. I'll take you back with me and send you to school. Tomorrow we'll go and buy clothes."

My tension eased somewhat, but stayed with me. My brother was happy. He was going north. I wanted to go, but I said nothing.

A train ride and I was in yet another little southern town. Home in Greenwood was a four-room bungalow, comprising half of a double house that sat on a quiet shady road. Aunt Jody, a medium-sized, neat, silent, mulatto girl, had a hot supper waiting on the table. She baffled me with her serious, reserved manner; she seemed to be acting in conformity with a code unknown to me, and I assumed that she regarded me as a "wrong one," a boy who for some reason did not have a home; I felt that in her mind she would push me to the outskirts of life and I was awkward and self-conscious in her presence. Both Uncle Clark and Aunt Jody talked to me as though I were a grownup and I wondered if I could do what was expected of me. I had always felt a certain warmth with my mother, even when we had lived in squalor; but I felt none here. Perhaps I was too apprehensive to feel any.

During supper it was decided that I was to be placed in school the next day. Uncle Clark and Aunt Jody both had jobs and I was told that at noon I would find lunch on the stove.

"Now, Richard, this is your new home," Uncle Clark said.

"Yes, sir."

"After school, bring in wood and coal for the fireplaces."

"Yes, sir."

"Split kindling and lay a fire in the kitchen stove."

"Yes, sir."

"Bring in a bucket of water from the yard so that Jody can cook in the mornings."

"Yes, sir."

"After your chores are done, you may spend the afternoon studying."

"Yes, sir."

I had never been assigned definite tasks before and I went to bed a little frightened. I lay sleepless, wondering if I should have come, feeling the dark night holding strange people, strange houses, strange streets. What would happen to me here? How would I get along? What kind of woman was Aunt Jody? How ought I act around her? Would Uncle Clark let me make friends with other boys? I awakened the next morning to see the sun shining into my room; I felt more at ease.

"Richard!" my uncle was calling me.

I washed, dressed, and went into the kitchen and sat wordlessly at the table.

"Good morning, Richard," Aunt Jody said.

"Oh, good morning," I mumbled, wishing that I had thought to say it first.

"Don't people say good morning where you come from?" she asked.

"Yes, ma'am."

"I thought they did," she said pointedly.

Aunt Jody and Uncle Clark began to question me about my life and I grew so self-conscious that my hunger left me. After breakfast, Uncle Clark took me to school, introduced me to the principal. The first half of the school day passed without incident. I sat looking at the strange reading book, following the lessons. The subjects seemed simple and I felt that I could keep up. My anxiety was still in me; I was wondering how I would get on with the boys. Each new school meant a new area of life to be conquered. Were the boys tough? How hard did they fight? I took it for granted that they fought.

At noon recess I went into the school grounds and a group of boys sauntered up to me, looked at me from my head to my feet, whispering among themselves. I leaned against a wall, trying to conceal my uneasiness.

"Where you from?" a boy asked abruptly.

"Jackson," I answered.

"How come they make you people so ugly in Jackson?" he demanded.

There was loud laughter.

"You're not any too good-looking yourself," I countered instantly.

"Oh!"

"Aw!"

"You hear what he told 'im?"

"You think you're smart, don't you?" the boy asked, sneering.

"Listen, I ain't picking a fight," I said. "But if you want to fight, I'll fight."

"Hunh, hard guy, ain't you?"

"As hard as you."

"Do you know who you can tell that to?" he asked me.

"And you know who you can tell it back to?" I asked.

"Are you talking about my mama?" he asked, edging forward.

"If you want it that way," I said.

This was my test. If I failed now, I would have failed at school, for the first trial came not in books, but in how one's fellows took one, what value they placed upon one's willingness to fight.

"Take back what you said," the boy challenged me.

"Make me," I said.

The crowd howled, sensing a fight. The boy hesitated, weighing his chances of beating me.

"You ain't gonna take what that new boy said, is you?" someone taunted the boy.

The boy came close. I stood my ground. Our faces were four inches apart.

"You think I'm scared of you, don't you?" he asked.

"I told you what I think," I said.

Somebody, eager and afraid that we would not fight, pushed the boy and he bumped into me. I shoved him away violently.

"Don't push me!" the boy said.

"Then keep off me!" I said.

He was pushed again and I struck out with my right and caught him in the mouth. The crowd yelled, milled, surging so close that I could barely lift my arm to land a blow. When either of us tried to strike the other, we would be thrown off balance by the screaming boys. Every blow landed elicited shouts of delight. Knowing that if I did not win or make a good showing I would have to fight a new boy each day, I fought tigerishly, trying to leave a scar, seeking to draw blood as proof that I was not a coward, that I could take care of myself. The bell rang and the crowd pulled us apart. The fight seemed a draw.

"I ain't through with you!" the boy shouted.

"Go to hell!" I answered.

In the classroom the boys asked me questions about myself; I was someone worth knowing. When the bell rang for school to be dismissed, I was set to fight again; but the boy was not in sight.

On my way home I found a cheap ring in the streets and at once I knew what I was going to do with it. The ring had a red stone held by tiny prongs which I loosened, took the stone out, leaving the sharp tiny prongs jutting up. I slid the ring on to my finger and shadow boxed. Now, by God, let a goddamn bully come and I would show him how to fight; I would leave a crimson streak on his face with every blow.

But I never had to use the ring. After I had exhibited my new weapon at school, a description of it spread among the boys. I challenged my enemy to another fight, but he would not respond. Fighting was not now necessary. I had been accepted.

No sooner had I won my right to the school grounds than a new dread arose. One evening, before bedtime, I was sitting in the front room, reading, studying. Uncle Clark, who was a contracting carpenter, was at his drawing table, drafting models of houses. Aunt Jody was darning. Suddenly the doorbell rang and Aunt Jody admitted the next-door neighbor, the owner of the house in which we lived and its former occupant. His name was Burden; he was a tall, brown, stooped man and when I was introduced to him I rose and shook his hand.

"Well, son," Mr. Burden told me, "it's certainly a comfort to see another boy in this house."

"Is there another boy here?" I asked eagerly.

"My son was here," Mr. Burden said, shaking his head. "But he's gone now."

"How old is he?" I asked.

"He was about your age," Mr. Burden mumbled sadly.

"Where did he go?" I asked stupidly.

"He's dead," Mr. Burden said.

"Oh," I said.

I had not understood him. There was a long silence. Mr. Burden looked at me wistfully.

"Do you sleep in there?" he asked, pointing to my room.

"Yes, sir."

"That's where my boy slept," he said.

"In *there?*" I asked, just to make sure.

"Yes, right in there."

"On *that* bed?" I asked.

"Yes, that was his bed. When I heard that you were coming, I gave your uncle that bed for you," he explained.

I saw Uncle Clark shaking his head vigorously at Mr. Burden, but he was too late. At once my imagination began to weave ghosts. I did not actually believe in ghosts, but I had been taught that there was a God and I had given a kind of uneasy assent to His existence, and if there was a God, then surely there must be ghosts. In a moment I built up an intense loathing for sleeping in the room where the boy had died. Rationally I knew that the dead boy could not bother me, but he had become alive for me in a way that I could not dismiss. After Mr. Burden had gone, I went timidly to Uncle Clark.

"I'm scared to sleep in there," I told him.

"Why? Because a boy died in there?"

"Yes, sir."

"But, son, that's nothing to be afraid of."

"I know. But I am scared."

"We all must die someday. So why be afraid?"

I had no answer for that.

"When you die, do you want people to be afraid of *you?*"

I could not answer that either.

"This is nonsense," Uncle Clark went on.

"But I'm scared," I told him.

"You'll get over it."

"Can't I sleep somewhere else?"

"There's nowhere else for you to sleep."

"Can I sleep here on the sofa?" I asked.

"*May* I sleep here on the sofa?" Aunt Jody corrected me in a mocking tone.

"May I sleep here on the sofa?" I repeated after her.

"No," Aunt Jody said.

I groped into the dark room and fumbled for the bed; I had the illusion that if I touched it I would encounter the dead boy. I trembled. Finally I jumped roughly into the bed and jerked the covers over my face. I did not sleep that night and my eyes were red and puffy the next morning.

"Didn't you sleep well?" Uncle Clark asked me.

"I can't sleep in that room," I said.

"You slept in it before you heard of that boy who died in there, didn't you?" Aunt Jody asked me.

"Yes, ma'am."

"Then why can't you sleep in it now?"

"I'm just scared."

"You stop being a baby," she told me.

The next night was the same; fear kept me from sleeping. After Uncle Clark and Aunt Jody had gone to bed, I rose and crept into the front room and slept in a tight ball on the sofa, without any cover. I awakened the next morning to find Uncle Clark shaking me.

"Why are you doing this?" he asked.

"I'm scared to sleep in there," I said.

"You go back into that room and sleep tonight," he told me. "You've got to get over this thing."

I spent another sleepless, shivering night in the dead boy's room—it was not my room any longer—and I was so frightened that I sweated. Each creak of the house made my heart stand still. In school the next day I was dull. I came home and spent another long night of wakefulness and the following day I went to sleep in the classroom. When questioned by the teacher, I could give no answer. Unable to free myself from my terror, I began to long for home. A week of sleeplessness brought me near the edge of nervous collapse.

Sunday came and I refused to go to church and Uncle Clark and Aunt Jody were astonished. They did not understand that my refusal to go to church was my way of silently begging them to let me sleep somewhere else. They left me alone in the house and I spent the entire day sitting on the front steps; I did not have enough courage to go into the kitchen to eat. When I became thirsty, I went around the house and drank water from the hydrant in the back yard rather than venture into the house. Desperation made me raise the issue of the room again at bedtime.

"Please, let me sleep on the sofa in the front room," I pleaded.

"You've got to get out of that fear," my uncle said.

I made up my mind to ask to be sent home. I went to Uncle Clark, knowing that he had incurred expense in bringing me here, that he had thought he was helping me, that he had bought my clothes and books.

"Uncle Clark, send me back to Jackson," I said.

He was bent over a little table and he straightened and stared at me.

"You're not happy here?" he asked.

"No, sir," I answered truthfully, fearing that the ceiling would crash down upon my head.

"And you really want to go back?"

"Yes, sir."

"Things will not be as easy for you at home as here," he said. "There's not much money for food and things."

"I want to be where my mother is," I said, trying to strengthen my plea.

"It's really about the room?"

"Yes, sir."

"Well, we tried to make you happy here," my uncle said, sighing. "Maybe we didn't know how. But if you want to go back, then you may go."

"When?" I asked eagerly.

"As soon as school term has ended."

"But I want to go now!" I cried.

"But you'll break up your year's schooling," he said.

"I don't mind."

"You will, in the future. You've never had a single year of steady schooling," he said.

"I want to go home," I said.

"Have you felt this way a long time?" he asked.

"Yes, sir."

"I'll write Granny tonight," he said, his eyes lit with surprise.

Daily I asked him if he had heard from Granny only to learn that there had been no word. My sleeplessness made me feel that my days were a hot, wild dream and my studies suffered at school. I had been making high marks and now I made low ones and finally began to fail altogether. I was fretful, living from moment to moment.

One evening, in doing my chores, I took the water pail to the hydrant in the back yard to fill it. I was half asleep, tired, tense, all but swaying on my feet. I balanced the handle of the pail on the jutting tip of the metal faucet and waited for it to fill; the pail slipped and water drenched my pants and shoes and stockings.

"That goddamn lousy bastard sonofabitching bucket!" I spoke in a whisper of hate and despair.

"Richard!" Aunt Jody's amazed voice sounded in the darkness behind me.

I turned. Aunt Jody was standing on the back steps. She came into the yard.

"What did you say, boy?" she asked.

"Nothing," I mumbled, looking contritely at the ground.

"Repeat what you said!" she demanded.

I did not answer. I stooped and picked up the pail. She snatched it from me.

"What did you say?" she asked again.

I still kept my head down, vaguely wondering if she were intimidating me or if she really wanted me to repeat my curses.

"I'm going to tell your uncle on you," she said at last.

I hated her then. I thought that hanging my head and looking mutely at the ground was a kind of confession and a petition for forgiveness, but she had not accepted it as such.

"I don't care," I said.

She gave me the pail, which I filled with water and carried to the house. She followed me.

"Richard, you are a very bad, bad boy," she said.

"I don't care," I repeated.

I avoided her and went to the front porch and sat. I had had no intention of letting her hear me curse, but since she had heard me and since there was no way to appease her, I decided to let things develop as they would. I would go home. But where was home? Yes, I would run away.

Uncle Clark came and called me into the front room.

"Jody says that you've been using bad language," he said.

"Yes, sir."

"You admit it?"

"Yes, sir."

"Why did you do it?"

"I don't know."

"I'm going to whip you. Pull off your shirt."

Wordlessly I bared my back and he lashed me with a strap. I gritted my teeth and did not cry.

"Are you going to use that language again?" he asked me.

"I want to go home," I said.

"Put on your shirt."

I obeyed.

"I want to go home," I said again.

"But this is your home."

"I want to go to Jackson."

"You have no home in Jackson."

"I want to go to my mother."

"All right," he relented. "I'll send you home Saturday." He looked at me with baffled eyes. "Tell me, where did you learn those words Jody heard you say?"

I looked at him and did not answer; there flashed through my mind a quick, running picture of all the squalid hovels in which I had lived and it made me feel more than ever a stranger as I stood before him. How could I have told him that I had learned to curse before I had learned to read? How could I have told him that I had been a drunkard at the age of six?

When he took me to the train that Saturday morning, I felt guilty and did not want to look at him. He gave me my ticket and I climbed hastily aboard the train. I waved a stiff good-bye to him through the window as the train pulled out. When I could see his face no longer, I wilted, relaxing. Tears blurred my vision. I leaned back and closed my eyes and slept all the way.

I was glad to see my mother. She was much better, though still abed. Another operation had been advised by the doctor and there was hope for recovery. But I was anxious. Why another operation? A victim myself of too many hopes that had never led anywhere, I was for letting my mother remain as she was. My feelings were governed by fear and I spoke to no one about them. I had already begun to sense that my feelings varied too far from those of the people around me for me to blab about what I felt.

I did not re-enter school. Instead, I played alone in the back yard, bouncing a rubber ball off the fence, drawing figures in the soft clay with an old knife, or reading what books I found about the house. I ached to be of an age to take care of myself.

Uncle Edward arrived from Carters to take my mother to Clarksdale for the operation; at the last moment I insisted upon being taken with them. I dressed hurriedly and we went to the station. Throughout the journey I sat brooding, afraid to look at my mother, wanting to return home and yet wanting to go on. We reached Clarksdale and hired a taxi to the doctor's office. My mother was jolly, brave, smiling, but I knew that she was as doubtful as I was. When we reached the doctor's waiting room the conviction settled in me that my mother would never be well again. Finally the doctor came out in his white coat and shook hands with me, then took my mother inside. Uncle Edward left to make arrangements for a room and a nurse. I felt crushed. I waited. Hours later the doctor came to the door.

"How's my mother?"

"Fine!" he said.

"Will she be all right?"

"Everything'll clear up in a few days."

"Can I see her now?"

"No, not now."

Later Uncle Edward returned with an ambulance and two men who carried a stretcher. They entered the doctor's office and brought out my mother; she lay with closed eyes, her body swathed in white. I wanted to run to the stretcher and touch her, but I could not move.

"Why are they taking mama that way?" I asked Uncle Edward.

"There are no hospital facilities for colored, and this is the way we have to do it," he said.

I watched the men take the stretcher down the steps; then I stood on the sidewalk and watched them lift my mother into the ambulance and drive away. I knew that my mother had gone out of my life; I could feel it.

Uncle Edward and I stayed at a boardinghouse; each morning he went to the rooming house to inquire about my mother and each time he returned gloomy and silent. Finally he told me that he was taking my mother back home.

"What chance has mama, really?" I asked him.

"She's very sick," he said.

We left Clarksdale; my mother rode on a stretcher in the baggage car with Uncle Edward attending her. Back home, she lay for days, groaning, her eyes vacant. Doctors visited her and left without making any comment. Granny grew frantic. Uncle Edward, who had gone home, returned and still more doctors were called in. They told us that a blod clot had formed on my mother's brain and that another paralytic stroke had set in.

Once, in the night, my mother called me to her bed and told me that she could not endure the pain, that she wanted to die. I held her hand and begged her to be quiet. That night I ceased to react to my mother; my feelings were frozen. I merely waited upon her, knowing that she was suffering. She remained abed ten years, gradually growing better, but never completely recovering, relapsing periodically into her paralytic state. The family had stripped itself of money to fight my mother's illness and there was no more forthcoming. Her illness gradually became an accepted thing in the house, something that could not be stopped or helped.

My mother's suffering grew into a symbol in my mind, gathering to itself all the poverty, the ignorance, the helplessness; the painful, baffling, hunger-ridden days and hours; the restless moving, the futile seeking, the uncertainty, the fear, the dread; the meaningless pain and the endless suffering. Her life set the emotional tone of my life, colored the men and women I was to meet in the future, conditioned my relation to events that had not yet happened, determined my attitude to situations and circumstances I had yet to face. A somberness of spirit that I was never to lose settled over me during the slow years of my mother's unrelieved suffering, a somberness that was to make me stand apart and look upon excessive joy with suspicion, that was to make me self-conscious, that was to make me keep forever on the move, as though to escape a nameless fate seeking to overtake me.

At the age of twelve, before I had had one full year of formal schooling, I had a conception of life that no experience would ever erase, a predilection for what was real that no argument could ever gainsay, a sense of the world that was mine and mine alone, a notion as to what life meant that no education could ever alter, a conviction that the meaning of living came only when one was struggling to wring a meaning out of meaningless suffering.

At the age of twelve I had an attitude toward life that was to endure, that was to make me seek those areas of living that would keep it alive, that was to make me skeptical of everything while seeking everything, tolerant of all and yet critical. The spirit I had caught gave me insight into the sufferings of others, made me grav-

itate toward those whose feelings were like my own, made me sit
for hours while others told me of their lives, made me strangely tender and cruel, violent and peaceful.

It made me want to drive coldly to the heart of every question
and lay it open to the core of suffering I knew I would find there. It
made me love burrowing into psychology, into realistic and natural-
istic fiction and art, into those whirlpools of politics that had the
power to claim the whole of men's souls. It directed my loyalties to
the side of men in rebellion; it made me love talk that sought
answers to questions that could help nobody, that could only keep
alive in me that enthralling sense of wonder and awe in the face of
the drama of human feeling which is hidden by the external drama
of life.

4

Granny was an ardent member of the Seventh-Day Adventist Church
and I was compelled to make a pretense of worshiping her God,
which was her exaction for my keep. The elders of her church
expounded a gospel clogged with images of vast lakes of eternal
fire, of seas vanishing, of valleys of dry bones, of the sun burning to
ashes, of the moon turning to blood, of stars falling to the earth, of
a wooden staff being transformed into a serpent, of voices speaking
out of clouds, of men walking upon water, of God riding whirl-
winds, of water changing into wine, of the dead rising and living, of
the blind seeing, of the lame walking; a salvation that teemed with
fantastic beasts having multiple heads and horns and eyes and feet;
sermons of statues possessing heads of gold, shoulders of silver, legs
of brass, and feet of clay; a cosmic tale that began before time and
ended with the clouds of the sky rolling away at the Second
Coming of Christ; chronicles that concluded with the Arma-
geddon; dramas thronged with all the billions of human beings who
had ever lived or died as God judged the quick and the dead . . .

While listening to the vivid language of the sermons I was
pulled toward emotional belief, but as soon as I went out of the
church and saw the bright sunshine and felt the throbbing life of
the people in the streets I knew that none of it was true and that
nothing would happen.

Once again I knew hunger, biting hunger, hunger that made

my body aimlessly restless, hunger that kept me on edge, that made my temper flare, hunger that made hate leap out of my heart like the dart of a serpent's tongue, hunger that created in me odd cravings. No food that I could dream of seemed half so utterly delicious as vanilla wafers. Every time I had a nickel I would run to the corner grocery store and buy a box of vanilla wafers and walk back home, slowly, so that I could eat them all up without having to share them with anyone. Then I would sit on the front steps and dream of eating another box; the craving would finally become so acute that I would force myself to be active in order to forget. I learned a method of drinking water that made me feel full temporarily whether I had a desire for water or not; I would put my mouth under a faucet and turn the water on full force and let the stream cascade into my stomach until it was tight. Sometimes my stomach ached, but I felt full for a moment.

No pork or veal was ever eaten at Granny's, and rarely was there meat of any kind. We seldom ate fish and then only those that had scales and spines. Baking powder was never used; it was alleged to contain a chemical harmful to the body. For breakfast I ate mush and gravy made from flour and lard and for hours afterwards I would belch it up into my mouth. We were constantly taking bicarbonate of soda for indigestion. At four o'clock in the afternoon I ate a plate of greens cooked with lard. Sometimes on Sundays we bought a dime's worth of beef which usually turned out to be uneatable. Granny's favorite dish was a peanut roast which she made to resemble meat, but which tasted like something else.

My position in the household was a delicate one; I was a minor, an uninvited dependent, a blood relative who professed no salvation and whose soul stood in mortal peril. Granny intimated boldly, basing her logic on God's justice, that one sinful person in a household could bring down the wrath of God upon the entire establishment, damning both the innocent and the guilty, and on more than one occasion she interpreted my mother's long illness as the result of my faithlessness. I became skilled in ignoring these cosmic threats and developed a callousness toward all metaphysical preachments.

But Granny won an ally in her efforts to persuade me to confess her God; Aunt Addie, her youngest child, had just finished the Seventh-Day Adventist religious school in Huntsville, Alabama, and came home to argue that if the family was compassionate enough to feed me, then the least I could do in return was to follow its guidance. She proposed that, when the fall school term started, I should be enrolled in the religious school rather than a secular one. If I refused, I was placing myself not only in the position of a horrible infidel but of a hardhearted ingrate. I raised arguments and objections, but my mother sided with Granny and Aunt Addie and I had to accept.

The religious school opened and I put in a sullen attendance. Twenty pupils, ranging in age from five to nineteen and in grades from primary to high school, were crowded into one room. Aunt Addie was the only teacher and from the first day an acute, bitter antagonism sprang up between us. This was the first time she had ever taught school and she was nervous, self-conscious because a blood relative of hers—a relative who would not confess her faith and who was not a member of her church—was in her classroom. She was determined that every student should know that I was a sinner of whom she did not approve, and that I was not to be granted consideration of any kind.

The pupils were a docile lot, lacking in that keen sense of rivalry which made the boys and girls who went to public school a crowd in which a boy was tested and weighed, in which he caught a glimpse of what the world was. These boys and girls were will-less, their speech flat, their gestures vague, their personalities devoid of anger, hope, laughter, enthusiasm, passion, or despair. I was able to see them with an objectivity that was inconceivable to them. They were claimed wholly by their environment and could imagine no other, whereas I had come from another plane of living, from the swinging doors of saloons, the railroad yard, the roundhouses, the street gangs, the river levees, an orphan home; had shifted from town to town and home to home; had mingled with grownups more than perhaps was good for me. I had to curb my habit of cursing, but not before I had shocked more than half of them and had embarrassed Aunt Addie to helplessness.

As the first week of school drew to a close, the conflict that smoldered between Aunt Addie and me flared openly. One afternoon she rose from her desk and walked down the aisle and stopped beside me.

"You know better than that," she said, tapping a ruler across my knuckles.

"Better than what?" I asked, amazed, nursing my hand.

"Just look at that floor," she said.

I looked and saw that there were many tiny bits of walnut meat scattered about; some of them had been smeared into grease spots on the clean, white pine boards. At once I knew that the boy in front of me had been eating them; my walnuts were in my pocket, uncracked.

"I don't know anything about that," I said.

"You know better than to eat in the classroom," she said.

"I haven't been eating," I said.

"Don't lie! This is not only a school, but God's holy ground," she said with angry indignation.

"Aunt Addie, my walnuts are here in my pocket . . ."

"I'm Miss Wilson!" she shouted.

I stared at her, speechless, at last comprehending what was really bothering her. She had warned me to call her Miss Wilson in the classroom, and for the most part I had done so. She was afraid that if I called her Aunt Addie I would undermine the morale of the students. Each pupil knew that she was my aunt and many of them had known her longer than I had.

"I'm sorry," I said, and turned from her and opened a book.

"Richard, get up!"

I did not move. The room was tense. My fingers gripped the book and I knew that every pupil in the room was watching. I had not eaten the nuts; I was sorry that I had called her Aunt Addie; but I did not want to be singled out for gratuitous punishment. And, too, I was expecting the boy who sat in front of me to devise some lie to save me, since it was really he who was guilty.

"I asked you to get up!" she shouted.

I still sat, not taking my eyes off my book. Suddenly she caught me by the back of my collar and yanked me from the seat. I stumbled across the room.

"I spoke to you!" she shouted hysterically.

I straightened and looked at her; there was hate in my eyes.

"Don't you look at me that way, boy!"

"I didn't put those walnuts on the floor!"

"Then who did?"

My street gang code was making it hard for me. I had never informed upon a boy in the public school, and I was waiting for the boy in front of me to come to my aid, lying, making up excuses, anything. In the past I had taken punishment that was not mine to protect the solidarity of the gang, and I had seen other boys do the same. But the religious boy, God helping him, did not speak.

"I don't know who did it," I said finally.

"Go to the front of the room," Aunt Addie said.

I walked slowly to her desk, expecting to be lectured; but my heart quickened when I saw her go to the corner and select a long, green, limber switch and come toward me. I lost control of my temper.

"I haven't done anything!" I yelled.

She struck me and I dodged.

"Stand still, boy!" she blazed, her face livid with fury, her body trembling.

I stood still, feeling more defeated by the righteous boy behind me than by Aunt Addie.

"Hold out your hand!"

I held out my hand, vowing that never again would this happen to me, no matter what the price. She stung my palm until it was red, then lashed me across my bare legs until welts rose. I clamped my teeth to keep from uttering a single whimper. When she finished I continued to hold out my hand, indicating to her that her blows could never really reach me, my eyes fixed and unblinking upon her face.

"Put down your hand and go to your seat," she said.

I dropped my hand and turned on my heels, my palm and legs on fire, my body taut. I walked in a fog of anger toward my desk.

"And I'm not through with you!" she called after me.

She had said one word too much; before I knew it, I had whirled and was staring at her with an open mouth and blazing eyes.

"Through with me?" I repeated. "But what have I done to you?"

"Sit down and shut up!" Aunt Addie bellowed.

I sat. I was sure of one thing: I would not be beaten by her again. I had often been painfully beaten, but almost always I had felt that the beatings were somehow right and sensible, that I was in the wrong. Now, for the first time, I felt the equal of an adult; I knew that I had been beaten for a reason that was not right. I sensed some emotional problem in Aunt Addie other than her concern about my eating in school. Did my presence make her feel so insecure that she felt she had to punish me in front of the pupils to impress them? All afternoon I brooded, wondering how I could quit the school.

The moment Aunt Addie came into the house—I reached home before she did—she called me into the kitchen. When I entered, I saw that she was holding another switch. My muscles tightened.

"You're not going to beat me again!" I told her.

"I'm going to teach you some manners!" she said.

I stood fighting, fighting as I had never fought in my life, fighting with myself. Perhaps my uneasy childhood, perhaps my shifting from town to town, perhaps the violence I had already seen and felt took hold of me, and I was trying to stifle the impulse to go to the drawer of the kitchen table and get a knife and defend myself. But this woman who stood before me was my aunt, my mother's sister, Granny's daughter; in her veins my own blood flowed; in many of her actions I could see some elusive part of my own self; and in her speech I could catch echoes of my own speech. I did not want to be violent with her, and yet I did not want to be beaten for a wrong I had not committed.

"You're just mad at me for something!" I said.

"Don't tell me I'm mad!"

"You're too mad to believe anything I say."

"Don't speak to me like that!"

"Then how can I talk to you? You beat me for throwing walnuts on the floor! But I didn't do it!"

"Then who did?"

Since I was alone now with her, and desperate, I cast my loyalties aside and told her the name of the guilty boy, feeling that he merited no consideration.

"Why didn't you tell me before?" she asked.

"I don't want to tell tales on other people."

"So you lied, hunh?"

I could not talk; I could not explain how much I valued my code of solidarity.

"Hold out your hand!"

"You're not going to beat me! I didn't do it!"

"I'm going to beat you for lying!"

"Don't, don't hit me! If you hit me I'll fight you!"

For a moment she hesitated, then she struck at me with the switch and I dodged and stumbled into a corner. She was upon me, lashing me across the face. I leaped, screaming, and ran past her and jerked open the kitchen drawer; it spilled to the floor with a thunderous sound. I grabbed up a knife and held it ready for her.

"Now, I told you to stop!" I screamed.

"You put down that knife!"

"Leave me alone or I'll cut you!"

She stood debating. Then she made up her mind and came at me. I lunged at her with the knife and she grasped my hand and tried to twist the knife loose. I threw my right leg about her legs and gave her a shove, tripping her; we crashed to the floor. She was stronger than I and I felt my strength ebbing; she was still fighting for my knife and I saw a look on her face that made me feel she was going to use it on me if she got possession of it. I bit her hand and we rolled, kicking, scratching, hitting, fighting as though we were strangers, deadly enemies, fighting for our lives.

"Leave me alone!" I screamed at the top of my voice.

"Give me that knife, you boy!"

"I'll kill you! I'll kill you if you don't leave me alone!"

Granny came running; she stood thunderstruck.

"Addie, what are you doing?"

"He's got a knife!" she gasped. "Make 'im put it down!"

"Richard, put down that knife!" Granny shouted.

My mother came limping to the door.

"Richard, stop it!" she shouted.

"I won't! I'm not going to let her beat me!"

"Addie, leave the boy alone," my mother said.

Aunt Addie rose slowly, her eyes on the knife, then she turned and walked out of the kitchen, kicking the door wide open before her as she went.

"Richard, give me that knife," my mother said.

"But, mama, she'll beat me, beat me for nothing," I said. "I'm not going to let her beat me; I don't care what happens!"

"Richard, you are bad, bad," Granny said, weeping.

I tried to explain what had happened, but neither of them would listen. Granny came toward me to take the knife, but I dodged her and ran into the back yard. I sat alone on the back steps, trembling, emotionally spent, crying to myself. Grandpa came down; Aunt Addie had told him what had happened.

"Gimme that knife, mister," he said.

"I've already put it back," I lied, hugging my arm to my side to conceal the knife.

"What's come over you?" he asked.

"I don't want her to beat me," I said.

"You're a child, a boy!" he thundered.

"But I don't want to be beaten!"

"What did you do?"

"Nothing."

"You can lie as fast as a dog can trot," Grandpa said. "And if it wasn't for my rheumatism, I'd take down your pants and tan your backside good and proper. The very idea of a little snot like you threatening somebody with a knife!"

"I'm not going to let her beat me," I said again.

"You're bad," he said. "You better watch your step, young man, or you'll end up on the gallows."

I had long ceased to fear Grandpa; he was a sick old man and he knew nothing of what was happening in the house. Now and then the womenfolk called on him to throw fear into someone, but I knew that he was feeble and was not frightened of him. Wrapped in the misty memories of his young manhood, he sat his days out in his room where his Civil War rifle stood loaded in a corner, where his blue uniform of the Union Army lay neatly folded.

Aunt Addie took her defeat hard, holding me in a cold and silent disdain. I was conscious that she had descended to my own emotional level in her effort to rule me, and my respect for her sank. Until she married, years later, we rarely spoke to each other, though we ate at the same table and slept under the same roof, though I was but a skinny, half-frightened boy and she was the secretary of the church and the church's day-school teacher. God blessed our home with the love that binds . . .

I continued at the church school, despite Aunt Addie's never calling upon me to recite or go to the blackboard. Consequently I stopped studying. I spent my time playing with the boys and found that the only games they knew were brutal ones. Baseball, marbles, boxing, running were tabooed recreations, the Devil's work; instead they played a wildcat game called popping-the-whip, a seemingly innocent diversion whose excitement came only in spurts, but spurts that could hurl one to the edge of death itself. Whenever we were discovered standing idle on the school grounds, Aunt Addie would suggest that we pop-the-whip. It would have been safer for our bodies and saner for our souls had she urged us to shoot craps.

One day at noon Aunt Addie ordered us to pop-the-whip. I had never played the game before and I fell in with good faith. We formed a long line, each boy taking hold of another boy's hand until we were stretched out like a long string of human beads. Although I did not know it, I was on the tip end of the human whip. The leading boy, the handle of the whip, started off at a trot, weaving to the left and to the right, increasing speed until the whip of flesh was curving at breakneck gallop. I clutched the hand of the boy next to me with all the strength I had, sensing that if I did not hold on I would be tossed off. The whip grew taut as human flesh and bone could bear and I felt that my arm was being torn from its socket. Suddenly my breath left me. I was swung in a small, sharp arc. The whip was now being popped and I could hold on no more; the momentum of the whip flung me off my feet into the air, like a bit of leather being flicked off a horsewhip, and I hurtled headlong through space and landed in a ditch. I rolled over, stunned, head bruised and bleeding. Aunt Addie was laughing, the first and only time I ever saw her laugh on God's holy ground.

In the home Granny maintained a hard religious regime. There were prayers at sunup and sundown, at the breakfast table and dinner table, followed by a Bible verse from each member of the family. And it was presumed that I prayed before I got into bed at night. I shirked as many of the weekday church services as possible, giving as my excuse that I had to study; of course, nobody believed me, but my lies were accepted because nobody wanted to risk a row. The daily prayers were a torment and my knees became sore from kneeling so long and often. Finally I devised a method of kneeling that was not really kneeling; I learned, through arduous repetition, how to balance myself on the toes of my shoes and rest my head against a wall in some convenient corner. Nobody, except God, was any the wiser, and I did not think that He cared.

Granny made it imperative, however, that I attend certain all-night ritualistic prayer meetings. She was the oldest member of her church and it would have been unseemly if the only grandchild in her home could not be brought to these important services; she felt that if I were completely remiss in religious conformity it would cast doubt upon the stanchness of her faith, her capacity to convince and persuade, or merely upon her ability to apply the rod to my backside.

Granny would prepare a lunch for the all-night praying session, and the three of us—Granny, Aunt Addie, and I—would be off, leaving my mother and Grandpa at home. During the passionate prayers and the chanted hymns I would sit squirming on a bench, longing to grow up so I could run away, listening indifferently to the theme of cosmic annihilation, loving the hymns for their sensual caress, but at last casting furtive glances at Granny and wondering when it would be safe for me to stretch out on the bench and go to sleep. At ten or eleven I would munch a sandwich and Granny would nod her permission for me to take a nap. I would awaken at intervals to hear snatches of hymns or prayers that would lull me to sleep again. Finally Granny would shake me and I would open my eyes and see the sun streaming through stained-glass windows.

Many of the religious symbols appealed to my sensibilities and I responded to the dramatic vision of life held by the church, feeling that to live day by day with death as one's sole thought was to be so compassionately sensitive toward all life as to view all men as slowly dying, and the trembling sense of fate that welled up, sweet and melancholy, from the hymns blended with the sense of fate that I had already caught from life. But full emotional and intellectual belief never came. Perhaps if I had caught my first sense of life from the church I would have been moved to complete acceptance, but the hymns and sermons of God came into my heart only long after my personality had been shaped and formed by uncharted conditions of life. I felt that I had in me a sense of living as deep as that which the church was trying to give me, and in the end I remained basically unaffected.

My body grew, even on mush and lard gravy, a miracle which the church certainly should have claimed credit for. I survived my twelfth year on a diet that would have stunted an average-sized dog, and my glands began to diffuse through my blood, like sap rising upward in trees in spring, those strange chemicals that made me look curiously at girls and women. The elder's wife sang in the choir and I fell in love with her as only a twelve-year-old can worship a distant and unattainable woman. During the services I would stare at her, wondering what it was like to be married to her, pondering over how passionate she was. I felt no qualms about my first lust for the flesh being born on holy ground; the contrast between budding carnal desires and the aching loneliness of the hymns never evoked any sense of guilt in me.

It was possible that the sweetly sonorous hymns stimulated me sexually, and it might have been that my fleshy fantasies, in turn, having as their foundation my already inflated sensibility, made me love the masochistic prayers. It was highly likely that the serpent of sin that nosed about the chambers of my heart was lashed to hunger by hymns as well as dreams, each reciprocally feeding the other. The church's spiritual life must have been polluted by my base yearnings, by the leaping hunger of my blood for the flesh, because I would gaze at the elder's wife for hours, attempting to draw her eyes to mine, trying to hypnotize her, seeking to communicate with her with my thoughts. If my desires had been converted into a concrete religious symbol, the symbol would have looked something like this: a black imp with two horns; a long, curving, forked tail; cloven hoofs, a scaly, naked body; wet, sticky fingers; moist, sensual lips; and lascivious eyes feasting upon the face of the elder's wife . . .

A religious revival was announced and Granny felt that it was her last chance to bring me to God before I entered the precincts of sin at the public school, for I had already given loud and final notice that I would no longer attend the church school. There was a discernible lessening in Aunt Addie's hostility; perhaps she had come to the conclusion that my lost soul was more valuable than petty pride. Even my mother's attitude was: "Richard, you ought to know God through *some* church."

The entire family became kind and forgiving, but I knew the motives that prompted their change and it drove me an even greater emotional distance from them. Some of my classmates— who had, on the advice of their parents, avoided me—now came to visit and I could tell in a split second that they had been instructed in what to say. One boy, who lived across the street, called on me one afternoon and his self-consciousness betrayed him; he spoke so naïvely and clumsily that I could see the bare bones of his holy plot and hear the creaking of the machinery of Granny's maneuvering.

"Richard, do you know we are all worried about you?" he asked.

"Worried about me? Who's worried about me?" I asked in feigned surprise.

"All of us," he said, his eyes avoiding mine.

"Why?" I asked.

"You're not saved," he said sadly.

"I'm all right," I said, laughing.

"Don't laugh, Richard. It's serious," he said.

"But I tell you that I'm all right."

"Say, Richard, I'd like to be a good friend of yours."

"I thought we were friends already," I said.

"I mean true brothers in Christ," he said.

"We know each other," I said in a soft voice tinged with irony.

"But not in Christ," he said.

"Friendship is friendship with me."

"But don't you want to save your soul?"

"I simply can't feel religion," I told him in lieu of telling him that I did not think I had the kind of soul he thought I had.

"Have you really tried to feel God?" he asked.

"No. But I know I can't feel anything like that."

"You simply can't let the question rest there, Richard."

"Why should I let it rest?"

"Don't mock God," he said.

"I'll never feel God, I tell you. It's no use."

"Would you let the fate of your soul hang upon pride and vanity?"

"I don't think I have any pride in matters like this."

"Richard, think of Christ's dying for you, shedding His blood, His precious blood on the cross."

"Other people have shed blood," I ventured.

"But it's not the same. You don't understand."

"I don't think I ever will."

"Oh, Richard, brother, you are lost in the darkness of the world. You must let the church help you."

"I tell you, I'm all right."

"Come into the house and let me pray for you."

"I don't want to hurt your feelings . . ."

"You can't. I'm talking for God."

"I don't want to hurt God's feelings either," I said, the words slipping irreverently from my lips before I was aware of their full meaning.

He was shocked. He wiped tears from his eyes. I was sorry.

"Don't say that. God may never forgive you," he whispered.

It would have been impossible for me to have told him how I felt about religion. I had not settled in my mind whether I believed in God or not; His existence or nonexistence never worried me. I reasoned that if there did exist an all-wise, all-powerful God who knew the beginning and the end, who meted out justice to all, who controlled the destiny of man, this God would surely know that I doubted His existence and He would laugh at my foolish denial of Him. And if there was no God at all, then why all the commotion? I could not imagine God pausing in His guidance of unimaginably vast worlds to bother with me.

Embedded in me was a notion of the suffering in life, but none of it seemed like the consequences of original sin to me; I simply could not feel weak and lost in a cosmic manner. Before I had been made to go to church, I had given God's existence a sort of tacit assent, but after having seen His creatures serve Him at first hand, I had had my doubts. My faith, such as it was, was welded to the common realities of life, anchored in the sensations of my body and in what my mind could grasp, and nothing could ever shake this faith, and surely not my fear of an invisible power.

"I'm not afraid of things like that," I told the boy.

"Aren't you afraid of God?" he asked.

"No. Why should I be? I've done nothing to Him."

"He's a jealous God," he warned me.

"I hope that He's a kind God," I told him.

"If *you* are kind to Him, He is a kind God," the boy said. "But God will not look at you if you don't look at Him."

During our talk I made a hypothetical statement that summed up my attitude toward God and the suffering in the world, a statement that stemmed from my knowledge of life as I had lived, seen, felt, and suffered it in terms of dread, fear, hunger, terror, and loneliness.

"If laying down my life could stop the suffering in the world, I'd do it. But I don't believe anything can stop it," I told him.

He heard me but he did not speak. I wanted to say more to him, but I knew that it would have been useless. Though older than I, he had neither known nor felt anything of life for himself; he had been carefully reared by his mother and father and he had always been told what to feel.

"Don't be angry," I told him.

Frightened and baffled, he left me. I felt sorry for him.

Immediately following the boy's visit, Granny began her phase of the campaign. The boy had no doubt conveyed to her my words of blasphemy, for she talked with me for hours, warning me that I would burn forever in the lake of fire. As the day of the revival grew near, the pressure upon me intensified. I would go into the dining room upon some petty errand and find Granny kneeling, her head resting on a chair, uttering my name in a tensely whispered prayer. God was suddenly everywhere in the home, even in Aunt Addie's scowling and brooding face. It began to weigh upon me. I longed for the time when I could leave. They begged me so continuously to come to God that it was impossible for me to ignore them without wounding them. Desperately I tried to think of some way to say no without making them hate me. I was determined to leave home before I would surrender.

Then I blundered and wounded Granny's soul. It was not my intention to hurt or humiliate her; the irony of it was that the plan I conceived had as its purpose the salving of Granny's frustrated feelings toward me. Instead, it brought her the greatest shame and humiliation of her entire religious life.

One evening during a sermon I heard the elder—I took my eyes off his wife long enough to listen, even though she slumbered in my senses all the while—describe how Jacob had seen an angel. Immediately I felt that I had found a way to tell Granny that I needed proof before I could believe, that I could not commit myself to something I could not feel or see. I would tell her that if I were to see an angel I would accept that as infallible evidence that there was a God and would serve Him unhesitatingly; she would surely understand an attitude of that sort. What gave me courage to voice this argument was the conviction that I would never see an angel; if I had ever seen one, I had enough common sense to have gone to a doctor at once. With my bright idea bubbling in my mind, wishing to allay Granny's fears for my soul, wanting to make her know that my heart was not all black and wrong, that I was actually giving serious thought to her passionate pleadings, I leaned to her and whispered:

"You see, granny, if I ever saw an angel like Jacob did, then I'd believe."

Granny stiffened and stared at me in amazement; then a glad smile lit up her old wrinkled white face and she nodded and gently patted my hand. That ought to hold her for a while, I thought. During the sermon Granny looked at me several times and smiled. Yes, she knows now that I'm not dismissing her pleas from my mind . . . Feeling that my plan was working, I resumed my worship of the elder's wife with a cleansed conscience, wondering what it would be like to kiss her, longing to feel some of the sensuous emotions of which my reading had made me conscious. The service ended and Granny rushed to the front of the church and began talking excitedly to the elder; I saw the elder looking at me in surprise. Oh, goddamn, she's telling him! I thought with anger. But I had not guessed one-thousandth of it.

The elder hurried toward me. Automatically I rose. He extended his hand and I shook it.

"Your grandmother told me," he said in awed tones.

I was speechless with anger.

"I didn't want her to tell you that," I said.

"She says that you have seen an angel." The words literally poured out of his mouth.

I was so overwhelmed that I gritted my teeth. Finally I could speak and I grabbed his arm.

"No . . . N-nooo, sir! No, sir!" I stammered. "I didn't say that. She misunderstood me."

The last thing on earth I wanted was a mess like this. The elder blinked his eyes in bewilderment.

"What did you tell her?" he asked.

"I told her that if I ever saw an angel, then I would believe," I said, feeling foolish, ashamed, hating and pitying my believing granny. The elder's face became bleak and stricken. He was stunned with disappointment.

"You . . . you didn't see an angel?" he asked.

"No, *sir!*" I said emphatically, shaking my head vigorously so that there could be no possible further misunderstanding.

"I see," he breathed in a sigh.

His eyes looked longingly into a corner of the church.

"With God, you know, anything is possible," he hinted hopefully.

"But I didn't see *anything*," I said. "I'm sorry about this."

"If you pray, then God will come to you," he said.

The church grew suddenly hot. I wanted to bolt out of it and never see it again. But the elder took hold of my arm and would not let me move.

"Elder, this is all a mistake. I didn't want anything like this to happen," I said.

"Listen, I'm older than you are, Richard," he said. "I think that you have in your heart the gift of God." I must have looked dubious, for he said: "Really, I do."

"Elder, please don't say anything to anybody about this," I begged.

Again his face lit with vague hope.

"Perhaps you don't want to tell me because you are bashful?" he suggested. "Look, this is serious. If you saw an angel, then tell me."

I could not deny it verbally any more; I could only shake my head at him. In the face of his hope, words seemed useless.

"Promise me you'll pray. If you pray, then God will answer," he said.

I turned my head away, ashamed for him, feeling that I had unwittingly committed an obscene act in rousing his hopes so wildly high, feeling sorry for his having such hopes. I wanted to get out of his presence. He finally let me go, whispering:

"I want to talk to you sometime."

The church members were staring at me. My fists doubled. Granny's wide and innocent smile was shining on me and I was filled with dismay. That she could make such a mistake meant that she lived in a daily atmosphere that urged her to expect something like this to happen. She had told the other members and everybody knew it, including the elder's wife! There they stood, the church members, with joyous astonishment written on their faces, whispering among themselves. Perhaps at that moment I could have mounted the pulpit and led them all; perhaps that was to be my greatest moment of triumph!

Granny rushed to me and hugged me violently, weeping tears of joy. Then I babbled, speaking with emotional reproof, censuring her for having misunderstood me; I must have spoken more loudly and harshly than was called for—the others had now gathered about me and Granny—for Granny drew away from me abruptly and went to a far corner of the church and stared at me with a cold, set face. I was crushed. I went to her and tried to tell her how it had happened.

"You shouldn't've spoken to me," she said in a breaking voice that revealed the depths of her disillusionment.

On our way home she would not utter a single word. I walked anxiously beside her, looking at her tired old white face, the wrinkles that lined her neck, the deep, waiting black eyes, and the frail body, and I knew more than she thought I knew about the meaning of religion, the hunger of the human heart for that which is not and can never be, the thirst of the human spirit to conquer and transcend the implacable limitations of human life.

Later, I convinced her that I had not wanted to hurt her and she immediately seized upon my concern for her feelings as an opportunity to have one more try at bringing me to God. She wept and pleaded with me to pray, really to pray, to pray hard, to pray until tears came . . .

"Granny, don't make me promise," I begged.

"But you must, for the sake of your soul," she said.

I promised; after all, I felt that I owed her something for inadvertently making her ridiculous before the members of her church.

Daily I went into my room upstairs, locked the door, knelt, and tried to pray, but everything I could think of saying seemed silly. Once it all seemed so absurd that I laughed out loud while on my knees. It was no use. I could not pray. I could never pray. But I kept my failure a secret. I was convinced that if I ever succeeded in praying, my words would bound noiselessly against the ceiling and rain back down upon me like feathers.

My attempts at praying became a nuisance, spoiling my days; and I regretted the promise I had given Granny. But I stumbled on a way to pass the time in my room, a way that made the hours fly with the speed of the wind. I took the Bible, pencil, paper, and a rhyming dictionary and tried to write verses for hymns. I justified this by telling myself that, if I wrote a really good hymn, Granny might forgive me. But I failed even in that; the Holy Ghost was simply nowhere near me . . .

One day while killing my hour of prayer, I remembered a series of volumes of Indian history I had read the year before. Yes, I knew what I would do; I would write a story about the Indians . . . But what about them? Well, an Indian girl . . . I wrote of an Indian maiden, beautiful and reserved, who sat alone upon the bank of a still stream, surrounded by eternal twilight and ancient trees, waiting . . . The girl was keeping some vow which I could not describe and, not knowing how to develop the story, I resolved that the girl had to die. She rose slowly and walked toward the dark stream, her face stately and cold; she entered the water and walked on until the water reached her shoulders, her chin; then it covered her. Not a murmur or a gasp came from her, even in dying.

"And at last the darkness of the night descended and softly kissed the surface of the watery grave and the only sound was the lonely rustle of the ancient trees," I wrote as I penned the final line.

I was excited; I read it over and saw that there was a yawning void in it. There was no plot, no action, nothing save atmosphere and longing and death. But I had never in my life done anything like it; I had made something, no matter how bad it was; and it was mine . . . Now, to whom could I show it? Not my relatives; they would think I had gone crazy. I decided to read it to a young woman who lived next door. I interrupted her as she was washing dishes and, swearing her to secrecy, I read the composition aloud. When I finished she smiled at me oddly, her eyes baffled and astonished.

"What's that for?" she asked.

"Nothing," I said.

"But why did you write it?"

"I just wanted to."

"Where did you get the idea?"

I wagged my head, pulled down the corners of my mouth, stuffed my manuscript into my pocket and looked at her in a cocky manner that said: Oh, it's nothing at all. I write stuff like this all the time. It's easy, if you know how. But I merely said in an humble, quiet voice:

"Oh, I don't know. I just thought it up."

"What're you going to do with it?"

"Nothing."

God only knows what she thought. My environment contained nothing more alien than writing or the desire to express one's self in writing. But I never forgot the look of astonishment and bewilderment on the young woman's face when I had finished reading and glanced at her. Her inability to grasp what I had done or was trying to do somehow gratified me. Afterwards whenever I thought of her reaction I smiled happily for some unaccountable reason.

5

No longer set apart for being sinful, I felt that I could breathe again,
live again, that I had been released from a prison. The cosmic
images of dread were now gone and the external world became a
reality, quivering daily before me. Instead of brooding and trying
foolishly to pray, I could run and roam, mingle with boys and girls,
feel at home with people, share a little of life in common with others, satisfy my hunger to be and live.

Granny and Aunt Addie changed toward me, giving me up for
lost; they told me that they were dead to the world, and those of
their blood who lived in that world were therefore dead to them.
From urgent solicitude they dropped to coldness and hostility.
Only my mother, who had in the meantime recovered somewhat,
maintained her interest in me, urging me to study hard and make
up for squandered time.

Freedom brought problems; I needed textbooks and had to
wait for months to obtain them. Granny said that she would not
buy worldly books for me. My clothes were a despair. So hostile did
Granny and Aunt Addie become that they ordered me to wash and
iron my own clothes. Eating was still skimpy, but I had now
adjusted myself to the starch, lard, and greens diet. I went to
school, feeling that my life depended not so much upon learning as
upon getting into another world of people.

Until I entered Jim Hill public school, I had had but one year of unbroken study; with the exception of one year at the church school, each time I had begun a school term something happened to disrupt it. Already my personality was lopsided; my knowledge of feeling was far greater than my knowledge of fact. Though I was not aware of it, the next four years were to be the only opportunity for formal study in my life.

The first school day presented the usual problem and I was emotionally prepared to meet it. Upon what terms would I be allowed to remain upon the school grounds? With pencil and tablet, I walked nonchalantly into the schoolyard, wearing a cheap, brand-new straw hat. I mingled with the boys, hoping to pass unnoticed, but knowing that sooner or later I would be spotted for a newcomer. And trouble came quickly. A black boy bounded past me, thumping my straw hat to the ground, and yelling:

"Straw katy!"

I picked up my hat and another boy ran past, slapping my hat even harder.

"Straw katy!"

Again I picked up my hat and waited. The cry spread. Boys gathered around, pointing, chanting:

"Straw katy! Straw katy!"

I did not feel that I had been really challenged so far; no particular boy had stood his ground and taunted me. I was hoping that the teasing would cease, and tomorrow I would leave my straw hat at home. But the boy who had begun the game came close.

"Mama bought me a straw hat," he sneered.

"Watch what you're saying," I warned him.

"Oh, look! He talks!" the boy said.

The crowd howled with laughter, waiting, hoping.

"Where you from?" the boy asked me.

"None of your business," I said.

"Now, look, don't you go and get sassy, or I'll cut you down," he said.

"I'll say what I please," I said.

The boy picked up a tiny rock and put it on his shoulder and walked close again.

"Knock it off," he invited me.

I hesitated for a moment, then acted; I brushed the rock from his shoulder and ducked and grabbed him about the legs and dumped him to the ground. A volcano of screams erupted from the crowd. I jumped upon the fallen boy and started pounding him. Then I was jerked up. Another boy had begun to fight me. My straw hat had been crushed and forgotten.

"Don't you hit my brother!" the new boy yelled.

"Two fighting one ain't fair!" I yelled.

Both of them now closed in on me. A blow landed on the back of my head. I turned and saw a brick rolling away and I felt blood oozing down my back. I looked around and saw several brickbats scattered about. I scooped up a handful. The two boys backed away. I took aim as they circled me; I made a motion as if to throw and one of the boys turned and ran. I let go with the brick and caught him in the middle of his back. He screamed. I chased the other halfway around the schoolyard. The boys howled their delight; they crowded around me, telling me that I had fought with two bullies. Then suddenly the crowd quieted and parted. I saw a woman teacher bearing down upon me. I dabbed at the blood on my neck.

"Was it you who threw that brick?" she asked.

"Two boys were fighting me," I told her.

"Come," she said, taking my hand.

I entered school escorted by the teacher, under arrest. I was taken to a room and confronted with the two brothers.

"Are these the boys?" she asked.

"Both of 'em fought me," I said. "I had to fight back."

"He hit me first!" one brother yelled.

"You're lying!" I yelled back.

"Don't you use that language in here," the teacher said.

"But they're not telling the truth," I said. "I'm new here and they tore up my hat."

"He hit me first," the boy said again.

I reached around the teacher, who stood between us, and smacked the boy. He screamed and started at me. The teacher grabbed us.

"The very idea of you!" the teacher shouted at me. "You are trying to fight right in school! What's the matter with you?"

"He's not telling the truth," I maintained.

She ordered me to sit down; I did, but kept my eyes on the two brothers. The teacher dragged them out of the room and I sat until she returned.

"I'm in a good mind not to let you off this time," she said.

"It wasn't my fault," I said.

"I know. But you hit one of those boys right in here," she said.

"I'm sorry."

She asked me my name and sent me to a room. For a reason I could not understand, I was assigned to the fifth grade. Would they detect that I did not belong there? I sat and waited. When I was asked my age I called it out and was accepted.

I studied night and day and within two weeks I was promoted to the sixth grade. Overjoyed, I ran home and babbled the news. The family had not thought it possible. How could a bad, bad boy do that? I told the family emphatically that I was going to study medicine, engage in research, make discoveries. Flushed with success, I had not given a second's thought to how I would pay my way through a medical school. But since I had leaped a grade in two weeks, anything seemed possible, simple, easy.

I was now with boys and girls who were studying, fighting, talking; it revitalized my being, whipped my senses to a high, keen pitch of receptivity. I knew that my life was revolving about a world that I had to encounter and fight when I grew up. Suddenly the future loomed tangibly for me, as tangible as a future can loom for a black boy in Mississippi.

Most of my schoolmates worked mornings, evenings, and Saturdays; they earned enough to buy their clothes and books, and they had money in their pockets at school. To see a boy go into a grocery store at noon recess and let his eyes roam over filled shelves and pick out what he wanted—even a dime's worth—was a hairbreadth short of a miracle to me. But when I broached the idea of my working to Granny, she would have none of it; she laid down the injunction that I could not work on Saturdays while I slept under her roof. I argued that Saturdays were the only days on which I could earn any worth-while sum, and Granny looked me straight in the eyes and quoted Scripture:

But the seventh day is the sabbath of the Lord thy God: in it thou shalt not do any work, thou, nor thy son, nor thy daughter, nor thy manservant, nor thy maidservant, nor thine ax, nor thine ass, nor any of thy cattle, nor thy stranger that is within thy gates; that thy manservant and thy maidservant may rest as well as thou . . .

And that was the final word. Though we lived just on the borders of actual starvation, I could not bribe Granny with a promise of half or two-thirds of my salary; her answer was no and never. Her refusal wrought me up to a high pitch of nervousness and I cursed myself for being made to live a different and crazy life. I told Granny that she was not responsible for my soul, and she replied that I was a minor, that my soul's fate rested in her hands, that I had no word to say in the matter.

To protect myself against pointed questions about my home and my life, to avoid being invited out when I knew that I could not accept, I was reserved with the boys and girls at school, seeking their company but never letting them guess how much I was being kept out of the world in which they lived, valuing their casual friendships but hiding it, acutely self-conscious but covering it with a quick smile and a ready phrase. Each day at noon I would follow the boys and girls into the corner store and stand against a wall and watch them buy sandwiches, and when they would ask me: "Why don't you eat a lunch?" I would answer with a shrug of my shoulders: "Aw, I'm not hungry at noon, ever." And I would swallow my saliva as I saw them split open loaves of bread and line them with juicy sardines. Again and again I vowed that someday I would end this hunger of mine, this apartness, this eternal difference; and I did not suspect that I would never get intimately into their lives, that I was doomed to live with them but not of them, that I had my own strange and separate road, a road which in later years would make them wonder how I had come to tread it.

I now saw a world leap to life before my eyes because I could explore it, and that meant not going home when school was out, but wandering, watching, asking, talking. Had I gone home to eat my plate of greens, Granny would not have allowed me out again, so the penalty I paid for roaming was to forfeit my food for twelve hours. I would eat mush at eight in the morning and greens at seven or later at night. To starve in order to learn about my environment was irrational, but so were my hungers. With my books slung over my shoulder, I would tramp with a gang into the woods, to rivers, to creeks, into the business district, to the doors of poolrooms, into the movies when we could slip in without paying, to neighborhood ball games, to brick kilns, to lumberyards, to cottonseed mills to watch men work. There were hours when hunger would make me weak, would make me sway while walking, would make my heart give a sudden wild spurt of beating that would shake my body and make me breathless; but the happiness of being free would lift me beyond hunger, would enable me to discipline the sensations of my body to the extent that I could temporarily forget.

In my class was a tall, black, rebellious boy who was bright in his studies and yet utterly fearless in his assertion of himself; he could break the morale of the class at any moment with his clowning and the teacher never found an adequate way of handling him. It was he who detected my plaguing hunger and suggested to me a way to earn some money.

"You can't sit in school all day and not eat," he said.

"What am I going to eat?" I asked.

"Why don't you do like me?"

"What do you do?"

"I sell papers."

"I tried to get a paper route, but they're all full," I said. "I'd like to sell papers because I could read them. I can't find things to read."

"You too?" he asked, laughing.

"What do you mean?" I asked.

"That's why I sell papers. I like to read 'em and that's the only way I can get hold of 'em," he explained.

"Do your parents object to your reading?" I asked.

"Yeah. My old man's a damn crackpot," he said.

"What papers are you selling?"

"It's a paper published in Chicago. It comes out each week and it has a magazine supplement," he informed me.

"What kind of a paper is it?"

"Well, I never read the newspaper. It isn't much. But boy, the magazine supplement! What stories . . . I'm reading the serial of Zane Grey's *Riders of the Purple Sage.*"

I stared at him in complete disbelief.

"*Riders of the Purple Sage!*" I exclaimed.

"Yes."

"Do you think I can sell those papers?"

"Sure. I make over fifty cents a week and have stuff to read," he explained.

I followed him home and he gave me a copy of the newspaper and the magazine supplement. The newspaper was thin, ill-edited, and designed to circulate among rural, white Protestant readers.

"Hurry up and start selling 'em," he urged me. "I'd like to talk to you about the stories."

I promised him that I would order a batch of them that night. I walked home through the deepening twilight, reading, lifting my eyes now and then from the print in order not to collide with strangers. I was absorbed in the tale of a renowned scientist who had rigged up a mystery room made of metal in the basement of his palatial home. Prompted by some obscure motive, he would lure his victims into this room and then throw an electric switch. Slowly, with heart-racking agony, the air would be sucked from the metal room and his victims would die, turning red, blue, then black. This was what I wanted, tales like this. I had not read enough to have developed any taste in reading. Anything that interested me satisfied me.

Now, at last, I could have my reading in the home, could have it there with the approval of Granny. She had already given me permission to sell papers. Oh, boy, how lucky it was for me that Granny could not read! She had always burned the books I had brought into the house, branding them as worldly; but she would have to tolerate these papers if she was to keep her promise to me. Aunt Addie's opinion did not count, and she never paid any attention to me anyway. In her eyes, I was dead. I told Granny that I planned to make some money by selling papers and she agreed, thinking that at last I was becoming a serious, right-thinking boy. That night I ordered the papers and waited anxiously.

The papers arrived and I scoured the Negro area, slowly building up a string of customers who bought the papers more because they knew me than from any desire to read. When I returned home at night, I would go to my room and lock the door and revel in outlandish exploits of outlandish men in faraway, outlandish cities. For the first time in my life I became aware of the life of the modern world, of vast cities, and I was claimed by it; I loved it. Though they were merely stories, I accepted them as true because I wanted to believe them, because I hungered for a different life, for something new. The cheap pulp tales enlarged my knowledge of the world more than anything I had encountered so far. To me, with my roundhouse, saloon-door, and river-levee background, they were revolutionary, my gateway to the world.

I was happy and would have continued to sell the newspaper and its magazine supplement indefinitely had it not been for the racial pride of a friend of the family. He was a tall, quiet, sober, soft-spoken black man, a carpenter by trade. One evening I called at his home with the paper. He gave me a dime, then looked at me oddly.

"You know, son," he said, "I sure like to see you make a little money each week."

"Thank you, sir," I said.

"But tell me, who told you to sell these papers?" he asked.

"Nobody."

"Where do you get them from?"

"Chicago."

"Do you ever read 'em?"

"Sure. I read the stories in the magazine supplement," I explained. "But I never read the newspaper."

He was silent a moment.

"Did a white man ask you to sell these papers?" he asked.

"No, sir," I answered, puzzled now. "Why do you ask?"

"Do your folks know you are selling these papers?"

"Yes, sir. But what's wrong?"

"How did you know where to write for these papers?" he asked, ignoring my questions.

"A friend of mine sells them. He gave me the address."

"Is this friend of yours a white man?"

"No, sir. He's colored. But why are you asking me all this?"

He did not answer. He was sitting on the steps of his front porch. He rose slowly.

"Wait right here a minute, son," he said. "I want to show you something."

Now what was wrong? The papers were all right; at least they seemed so to me. I waited, annoyed, eager to be gone on my rounds so that I could have time to get home and lie in bed and read the next installment of a thrilling horror story. The man returned with a carefully folded copy of the newspaper. He handed it to me.

"Did you see this?" he asked, pointing to a lurid cartoon.

"No, sir," I said. "I don't read the newspaper; I only read the magazine."

"Well, just look at that. Take your time and tell me what you think," he said.

It was the previous week's issue and I looked at the picture of a huge black man with a greasy, sweaty face, thick lips, flat nose, golden teeth, sitting at a polished, wide-topped desk in a swivel chair. The man had on a pair of gleaming yellow shoes and his feet were propped upon the desk. His thick lips nursed a big, black cigar that held white ashes an inch long. In the man's red-dotted tie was a dazzling horseshoe stickpin, glaring conspicuously. The man wore red suspenders and his shirt was striped silk and there were huge diamond rings on his fat black fingers. A chain of gold girded his belly and from the fob of his watch a rabbit's foot dangled. On the floor at the side of the desk was a spittoon overflowing with mucus. Across the wall of the room in which the man sat was a bold sign, reading:

The White House

Under the sign was a portrait of Abraham Lincoln, the features distorted to make the face look like that of a gangster. My eyes went to the top of the cartoon and I read:

The only dream of a nigger is to be president and to sleep with white women! Americans, do we want this in our fair land? Organize and save white womanhood!

I stared, trying to grasp the point of the picture and the captions, wondering why it all seemed so strange and yet familiar.

"Do you know what this means?" the man asked me.

"Gee, I don't know," I confessed.

"Did you ever hear of the Ku Klux Klan?" he asked me softly.

"Sure. Why?"

"Do you know what the Ku Kluxers do to colored people?"

"They kill us. They keep us from voting and getting good jobs," I said.

"Well, the paper you're selling preaches the Ku Klux Klan doctrines," he said.

"Oh, no!" I exclaimed.

"Son, you're holding it in your hands," he said.

"I read the magazine, but I never read the paper," I said vaguely, thoroughly rattled.

"Listen, son," he said. "Listen. You're a black boy and you're trying to make a few pennies. All right. I don't want to stop you from selling these papers, if you want to sell 'em. But I've read these papers now for two months and I know what they're trying to do. If you sell 'em, you're just helping white people to kill you."

"But these papers come from Chicago," I protested naïvely, feeling unsure of the entire world now, feeling that racial propaganda surely could not be published in Chicago, the city to which Negroes were fleeing by the thousands.

"I don't care where the paper comes from," he said. "Just you listen to this."

He read aloud a long article in which lynching was passionately advocated as a solution for the problem of the Negro. Even though I heard him reading it, I could not believe it.

"Let me see that," I said.

I took the paper from him and sat on the edge of the steps; in the paling light I turned the pages and read articles so brutally anti-Negro that goose pimples broke out over my skin.

"Do you like that?" he asked me.

"No, sir," I breathed.

"Do you see what you are doing?"

"I didn't know," I mumbled.

"Are you going to sell those papers now?"

"No, sir. Never again."

"They tell me that you are smart in school, and when I read those papers you were selling I didn't know what to make of it. Then I said to myself that that boy doesn't know what he's selling. Now, a lot of folks wanted to speak to you about these papers, but they were scared. They thought you were mixed up with some white Ku Kluxers and if they told you to stop you would put the Kluxers on 'em. But I said, shucks, that boy just don't know what he's doing."

I handed him his dime, but he would not take it.

"Keep the dime, son," he said. "But for God's sake, find something else to sell."

I did not try to sell any more of the papers that night; I walked home with them under my arm, feeling that some Negro would leap from a bush or fence and waylay me. How on earth could I have made so grave a mistake? The way I had erred was simple but utterly unbelievable. I had been so enthralled by reading the serial stories in the magazine supplement that I had not read a single issue of the newspaper. I decided to keep my misadventure secret, that I would tell no one that I had been unwittingly an agent for pro–Ku Klux Klan literature. I tossed the papers into a ditch and when I reached home I told Granny, in a quiet, offhand way, that the company did not want to send me any more papers because they already had too many agents in

Jackson, a lie which I thought was an understatement of the actual truth. Granny did not care one way or the other, since I had been making so little money in selling them that I had not been able to help much with household expenses.

The father of the boy who had urged me to sell the papers also found out their propagandistic nature and forbade his son to sell them. But the boy and I never discussed the subject; we were too ashamed of ourselves. One day he asked me guardedly:

"Say, are you still selling those papers?"

"Oh, no. I don't have time," I said, my eyes avoiding his.

"I'm not either," he said, pulling down the corners of his mouth. "I'm too busy."

I burned at my studies. At the beginning of the school term I read my civics and English and geography volumes through and only referred to them when in class. I solved all my mathematical problems far in advance; then, during school hours, when I was not called on to recite, I read tattered, second-hand copies of *Flynn's Detective Weekly* or the *Argosy All-Story Magazine*, or dreamed, weaving fantasies about cities I had never seen and about people I had never met.

School ended. I could not get a job that would let me rest on Granny's holy Sabbath. The long hot idle summer days palled on me. I sat at home brooding, nursing bodily and spiritual hunger. In the afternoons, after the sun had spent its force, I played ball with the neighborhood boys. At night I sat on the front steps and stared blankly at the passing people, wagons, cars . . .

On one such lazy, hot summer night Granny, my mother, and Aunt Addie were sitting on the front porch, arguing some obscure point of religious doctrine. I sat huddled on the steps, my cheeks resting sullenly in my palms, half listening to what the grownups were saying and half lost in a daydream. Suddenly the dispute evoked an idea in me and, forgetting that I had no right to speak without permission, I piped up and had my say. I must have sounded reekingly blasphemous, for Granny said, "Shut up, you!" and leaned forward promptly to chastise me with one of her casual, back-handed slaps on my mouth. But I had by now become adept at dodging blows and I nimbly ducked my head. She missed me; the force of her blow was so strong that she fell down the steps, headlong, her aged body wedged in a narrow space between the fence and the bottom step. I leaped up. Aunt Addie and my mother screamed and rushed down the steps and tried to pull Granny's body out. But they could not move her. Grandpa was called and he had to tear the fence down to rescue Granny. She was barely conscious. They put her to bed and summoned a doctor.

I was frightened. I ran to my room and locked the door, fearing that Grandpa would rend me to pieces. Had I done right or had I done wrong? If I had held still and let Granny slap me, she would not have fallen. But was it not natural to dodge a blow? I waited, trembling. But no one came to my room. The house was quiet. Was Granny dead? Hours later I unlocked the door and crept downstairs. Well, I told myself, if Granny died, I would leave home. There was nothing else to do. Aunt Addie confronted me in the hallway with burning, black eyes.

"You see what you've done to Granny," she said.

"I didn't touch her," I said. I had wanted to ask how Granny was, but my fear made me forget that.

"You were trying to kill her," Aunt Addie said.

"I didn't touch Granny, and you know it!"

"You are evil. You bring nothing but trouble!"

"I was trying to dodge her. She was trying to hit me. I had done nothing wrong . . ."

Her lips moved silently as she sought to formulate words to place me in a position of guilt.

"Why do you butt in when grown people are talking?" she demanded, finding her weapon at last.

"I just wanted to talk," I mumbled sullenly. "I sit in this house for hours and I can't even talk."

"Hereafter, you keep your mouth shut until you're spoken to," she advised me.

"But Granny oughtn't always be hitting at me like that," I said as delicately as possible.

"Boy, don't you stand there and say what Granny *ought* to do," she blazed, finding her ground of accusation. "If you don't keep your mouth shut, then *I'll* hit you!" she continued.

"I'm only trying to explain why Granny fell," I said.

"Shut up, now! Or I'll wring your neck, you fool!"

"You're another fool!" I came back at her, angry now.

She trembled with fury.

"I'll fix you this night!" she said, rushing at me.

I dodged her and ran into the kitchen and grabbed the long bread knife. She followed me and I confronted her. I was so hysterical that I was crying.

"If you touch me, I'll cut you, so help me," I said in gasps. "I'm going to leave here as soon as I can work and make a living. But as long's I'm here, you better not touch me."

We stood looking into each other's eyes, our bodies trembling with hate.

"I'm going to get you for this," she vowed in a low, serious voice. "I'll get you when you haven't got a knife."

"I'll always keep a knife for you," I told her.

"You've got to sleep at night," she whimpered with rage. "I'll get you then."

"If you touch me when I'm sleeping, I'll kill you," I told her.

She walked out of the kitchen, kicking the door open before her as she went. Aunt Addie had a habit of kicking doors; she always paused before a partly opened door and kicked it open; if the door swung in, she flung it back with her foot; or, if the door was shut, she opened it with her hand for an inch or two, then opened it the rest of the way with her foot; she acted as though she wanted to get a glimpse into the room beyond before she entered it, perhaps to see if it contained anything dreadful or unholy.

For a month after that I took a kitchen knife to bed with me each night, hiding it under my pillow so that when Aunt Addie came I could protect myself. But she never came. Perhaps she prayed.

Granny was abed for six weeks; she had wrenched her back when her slap missed me.

There were more violent quarrels in our deeply religious home than in the home of a gangster, a burglar, or a prostitute, a fact which I used to hint gently to Granny and which did my cause no good. Granny bore the standard for God, but she was always fighting. The peace that passes understanding never dwelt with us. I, too, fought; but I fought because I felt I had to keep from being crushed, to fend off continuous attack. But Granny and Aunt Addie quarreled and fought not only with me, but with each other over minor points of religious doctrine, or over some imagined infraction of what they chose to call their moral code. Wherever I found religion in my life I found strife, the attempt of one individual or group to rule another in the name of God. The naked will to power seemed always to walk in the wake of a hymn.

As summer waned I obtained a strange job. Our next-door neighbor, a janitor, decided to change his profession and become an insurance agent. He was handicapped by illiteracy and he offered me the job of accompanying him on trips into the delta plantation area to write and figure for him, at wages of five dollars a week. I made several trips with Brother Mance, as he was called, to plantation shacks, sleeping on shuck mattresses, eating salt pork and black-eyed peas for breakfast, dinner, and supper; and drinking, for once, all the milk I wanted.

I had all but forgotten that I had been born on a plantation and I was astonished at the ignorance of the children I met. I had been pitying myself for not having books to read, and now I saw children who had never read a book. Their chronic shyness made me seem bold and city-wise; a black mother would try to lure her brood into the room to shake hands with me and they would linger at the jamb of the door, peering at me with one eye, giggling hysterically. At night, seated at a crude table, with a kerosene lamp spluttering at my elbow, I would fill out insurance applications, and a sharecropper family, fresh from laboring in the fields, would stand and gape. Brother Mance would pace the floor, extolling my abilities with pen and paper. Many of the naïve black families bought their insurance from us because they felt that they were connecting themselves with something that would make their children "write 'n speak lak dat pretty boy from Jackson."

The trips were hard. Riding trains, autos, or buggies, moving from morning till night, we went from shack to shack, plantation to plantation. Exhausted, I filled out applications. I saw a bare, bleak pool of black life and I hated it; the people were alike, their homes were alike, and their farms were alike. On Sundays Brother Mance would go to the nearest country church and give his sales talk, preaching it in the form of a sermon, clapping his hands as he did so, spitting on the floor to mark off his paragraphs, and stomping his feet in the spit to punctuate his sentences, all of which captivated the black sharecroppers. After the performance the walleyed yokels would flock to Brother Mance, and I would fill out applications until my fingers ached.

I returned home with a pocketful of money that melted into the bottomless hunger of the household. My mother was proud; even Aunt Addie's hostility melted temporarily. To Granny, I had accomplished a miracle and some of my sinful qualities evaporated, for she felt that success spelled the reward of righteousness and that failure was the wages of sin. But God called Brother Mance to heaven that winter and, since the insurance company would not accept a minor as an agent, my status reverted to a worldly one; the holy household was still burdened with a wayward boy to whom, in spite of all, sin somehow insisted upon clinging.

School opened and I began the seventh grade. My old hunger was still with me and I lived on what I did not eat. Perhaps the sunshine, the fresh air, and the pot liquor from greens kept me going. Of an evening I would sit in my room reading, and suddenly I would become aware of smelling meat frying in a neighbor's kitchen and would wonder what it was like to eat as much meat as one wanted. My mind would drift into a fantasy and I would imagine myself a son in a family that had meat on the table at each meal; then I would become disgusted with my futile daydreams and would rise and shut the window to bar the torturing scent of meat.

When I came downstairs one morning and went into the dining room for my bowl of mush and lard gravy I felt at once that something seri ous was happening in the family. Grandpa, as usual, was not at the table; he always had his meals in his room. Granny nodded me to my seat; I sat and bowed my head. From under my brows I saw my mother's tight face. Aunt Addie's eyes were closed, her forehead furrowed, her lips trembling. Granny buried her face in her hands. I wanted to ask what had happened, but I knew that I would not get an answer.

Granny prayed and invoked the blessings of God for each of us, asking Him to guide us if it was His will, and then she told God that "my poor old husband lies sick this beautiful morning" and asked God, if it was His will, to heal him. That was how I learned of Grandpa's final illness. On many occasions I learned of some event, a death, a birth, or an impending visit, some happening in the neighborhood, at her church, or at some relative's home, first through Granny's informative prayers at the breakfast or dinner table.

Grandpa was a tall, black, lean man with a long face, snow-white teeth, and a head of woolly white hair. In anger he bared his teeth—a habit, Granny said, that he had formed while fighting in the trenches of the Civil War—and hissed, while his fists would clench until the veins swelled. In his rare laughs he bared his teeth in the same way, only now his teeth did not flash long and his body was relaxed. He owned a sharp pocketknife—which I had been forbidden to touch— and sat for long hours in the sun, whittling, whistling quietly, or maybe, if he was feeling well, humming some strange tune.

I had often tried to ask him about the Civil War, how he had fought, what he had felt, had he seen Lincoln, but he would never respond.

"You, git 'way from me, you young'un," was all that he would ever say.

From Granny I learned—over a course of years—that he had been wounded in the Civil War and had never received his disability pension, a fact which he hugged close to his heart with bitterness. I never heard him speak of white people; I think he hated them too much to talk of them. In the process of being discharged from the Union Army, he had gone to a white officer to seek help in filling out his papers. In filling out the papers, the white officer misspelled Grandpa's name, making him Richard Vinson instead of Richard

Wilson. It was possible that Grandpa's southern accent and his illiteracy made him mispronounce his own name. It was rumored that the white officer had been a Swede and had had a poor knowledge of English. Another rumor had it that the white officer had been a Southerner and had deliberately falsified Grandpa's papers. Anyway, Grandpa did not discover that he had been discharged in the name of Richard Vinson until years later; and when he applied to the War Department for a pension, no trace could be found of his ever having served in the Union Army under the name of Richard Wilson.

I asked endless questions about Grandpa's pension, but information was always denied me on the grounds that I was too young to know what was involved. For decades a long correspondence took place between Grandpa and the War Department; in letter after letter Grandpa would recount events and conversations (always dictating these long accounts to others); he would name persons long dead, citing their ages and descriptions, reconstructing battles in which he had fought, naming towns, rivers, creeks, roads, cities, villages, citing the names and numbers of regiments and companies with which he had fought, giving the exact day and the exact hour of the day of certain occurrences, and send it all to the War Department in Washington.

I used to get the mail early in the morning and whenever there was a long, businesslike envelope in the stack, I would know that Grandpa had got an answer from the War Department and I would run upstairs with it. Grandpa would lift his head from the pillow, take the letter from me and open it himself. He would stare at the black print for a long time, then reluctantly, distrustfully hand the letter to me.

"Well?" he would say.

And I would read him the letter—reading slowly and pronouncing each word with extreme care—telling him that his claims for a pension had not been substantiated and that his application had been rejected. Grandpa would not blink an eye, then he would curse softly under his breath.

"It's them goddamn rebels," he would hiss.

As though doubting what I had read, he would dress up and take the letter to at least a dozen of his friends in the neighborhood and ask them to read it to him; finally he would know it from memory. At last he would put the letter away carefully and begin his brooding again, trying to recall out of his past some telling fact that might help him in getting his pension. Like "K" of Kafka's novel, *The Castle,* he tried desperately to persuade the authorities of his true identity right up to the day of his death, and failed.

Often, when there was no food in the house, I would dream of the Government's sending a letter that would read something like this:

Dear Sir:

Your claim for a pension has been verified. The matter of your name has been satisfactorily cleared up. In accordance with official regulations, we are hereby instructing the Secretary of the Treasury to compile and compute and send to you, as soon as it is convenient, the total amount of all moneys past due, together with interest, for the past   years, the amount being $

We regret profoundly that you have been so long delayed in this matter. You may be assured that your sacrifice has been a boon and a solace to your country.

But no letter like that ever came, and Grandpa was so sullen most of the time that I stopped dreaming of him and his hopes. Whenever he walked into my presence I became silent, waiting for him to speak, wondering if he were going to upbraid me for something. I would relax when he left. My will to talk to him gradually died.

It was from Granny's conversations, year after year, that the meager details of Grandpa's life came to me. When the Civil War broke out, he ran off from his master and groped his way through the Confederate lines to the North. He darkly boasted of having killed "mo'n mah fair share of them damn rebels" while en route to enlist in the Union Army. Militantly resentful of slavery, he joined the Union Army to kill southern whites; he waded in icy streams; slept in mud; suffered, fought . . . Mustered out, he returned to the South and, during elections, guarded ballot boxes with his army rifle so that Negroes could vote. But when the Negro had been driven from political power, his spirit had been crushed. He was convinced that the war had not really ended, that it would start again.

And now as we ate breakfast—we ate in silence; there was never any talk at our table; Granny said that talking while eating was sinful, that God might make the food choke you—we thought of Grandpa's pension. During the days that followed letters were written, affidavits were drawn up and sworn to, conferences were held, but nothing came of it all. (It was my conviction, supported by no evidence save my own emotional fear of whites, that Grandpa had been cheated out of his pension because of his opposition to white supremacy.)

I came in from school one afternoon and Aunt Addie met me in the hallway. Her face was trembling and her eyes were red.

"Go upstairs and say good-bye to your grandpa," she said.

"What's happened?"

She did not answer. I ran upstairs and was met by Uncle Clark, who had come from Greenwood. Granny caught my hand.

"Come and say good-bye to your grandpa," she said.

She led me to Grandpa's room; he was lying fully dressed upon the bed, looking as well as he ever looked. His eyes were open, but he was so still that I did not know if he was dead or alive.

"Papa, here's Richard," Granny whispered.

Grandpa looked at me, flashed his white teeth for a fraction of a second.

"Good-bye, grandpa," I whispered.

"Good-bye, son," he spoke hoarsely. "Rejoice, for God has picked out my s-s-e . . . in-in h-heaven . . ."

His voice died. I had not understood what he had said and I wondered if I should ask him to repeat it. But Granny took my hand and led me from the room. The house was quiet; there was no crying. My mother sat silent in her rocking chair, staring out the window; now and then she would lower her face to her hands. Granny and Aunt Addie moved silently about the house. I sat mute, waiting for Grandpa to die. I was still puzzled about what he had tried to say to me; it seemed important that I should know his final words. I followed Granny into the kitchen.

"Granny, what did Grandpa say? I didn't quite hear him," I whispered.

She whirled and gave me one of her back-handed slaps across my mouth.

"Shut up! The angel of death's in the house!"

"I just wanted to know," I said, nursing my bruised lips.

She looked at me and relented.

"He said that God had picked out his seat in heaven," she said. "Now you know. So sit down and quit asking fool questions."

When I awakened the next morning my mother told me that Grandpa had "gone home."

"Get on your hat and coat," Granny said.

"What do you want me to do?" I asked.

"Quit asking questions and do what you are told," she said. I dressed for the outdoors.

"Go to Tom and tell him that Papa's gone home. Ask him to come here and take charge of things," Granny said.

Tom, her eldest son, had recently moved from Hazelhurst to Jackson and lived near the outskirts of town. Feeling that I was bearing an important message, I ran every inch of the two miles; I thought that news of a death should be told at once. I came in sight of my uncle's house with a heaving chest; I bounded up the steps and rapped on the door. My little cousin, Maggie, opened the door.

"Where's Uncle Tom?" I asked.

"He's sleeping," she said.

I ran into his room, went to his bed, and shook him.

"Uncle Tom, Granny says to come at once. Grandpa's dead," I panted.

He stared at me a long time.

"You certainly are a prize fool," he said quietly. "Don't you know that that's no way to tell a person that his father's dead?"

I stared at him, baffled, panting.

"I ran all the way out here," I gasped. "I'm out of breath. I'm sorry."

He rose slowly and began to dress, ignoring me; he did not utter a word for five minutes.

"What're you waiting for?" he asked me.

"Nothing," I said.

I walked home slowly, asking myself what on earth was the matter with me, why it was I never seemed to do things as people expected them to be done. Every word and gesture I made seemed to provoke hostility. I had never been able to talk to others, and I had to guess at their meanings and motives. I had not intentionally tried to shock Uncle Tom, and yet his anger at me seemed to outweigh his sorrow for his father. Finding no answer, I told myself that I was a fool to worry about it, that no matter what I did I would be wrong somehow as far as my family was concerned.

I was not allowed to go to Grandpa's funeral; I was ordered to stay home "and mind the house." I sat reading detective stories until the family returned from the graveyard. They told me nothing and I asked no questions. The routine of the house flowed on as usual; for me there was sleep, mush, greens, school, study, loneliness, yearning, and then sleep again.

My clothing became so shabby that I was ashamed to go to school. Many of the boys in my class were wearing their first long-pants suits. I grew so bitter that I decided to have it out with Granny; I would tell her that if she did not let me work on Saturdays I would leave home. But when I opened the subject, she would not listen. I followed her about the house, demanding the right to work on Saturday. Her answer was no and no and no.

"Then I'll quit school," I declared.

"Quit then. See how much I care," she said.

"I'll go away from here and you'll never hear from me!"

"No, you won't," she said tauntingly.

"How can I ever learn enough to get a job?" I asked her,

switching my tactics. I showed her my ragged stockings, my patched pants. "Look, I won't go to school like this! I'm not asking you for money or to do anything. I only want to work!"

"I have nothing to do with whether you go to school or not," she said. "You left the church and you are on your own. You are with the world. You're dead to me, dead to Christ."

"That old church of yours is messing up my life," I said.

"Don't you say that in this house!"

"It's true and you know it!"

"God's punishing you," she said. "And you're too proud to ask Him for help."

"I'm going to get a job anyway."

"Then you can't live here," she said.

"Then I'll leave," I said, trembling violently.

"You won't leave," she repeated.

"You think I'm joking, don't you?" I asked, determined to make her know how I felt. "I'll leave this minute!"

I ran to my room, got a battered suitcase, and began packing my ragged clothes. I did not have a penny, but I was going to leave. She came to the door.

"You little fool! Put that suitcase down!"

"I'm going where I can work!"

She snatched the suitcase out of my hands; she was trembling.

"All right," she said. "If you want to go to hell, then go. But God'll know that it was not my fault. He'll forgive me, but He won't forgive you."

Weeping, she rushed from the door. Her humanity had triumphed over her fear. I emptied the suitcase, feeling spent. I hated these emotional outbursts, these tempests of passion, for they always left me tense and weak. Now I was truly dead to Granny and Aunt Addie, but my mother smiled when I told her that I had defied them. She rose and hobbled to me on her paralytic legs and kissed me.

6

The next day at school I inquired among the students about jobs and was given the name of a white family who wanted a boy to do chores. That afternoon, as soon as school had let out, I went to the address. A tall, dour white woman talked to me. Yes, she needed a boy, an honest boy. Two dollars a week. Mornings, evenings, and all day Saturdays. Washing dishes. Chopping wood. Scrubbing floors. Cleaning the yard. I would get my breakfast and dinner. As I asked timid questions, my eyes darted about. What kind of food would I get? Was the place as shabby as the kitchen indicated?

"Do you want this job?" the woman asked.

"Yes, ma'am," I said, afraid to trust my own judgment.

"Now, boy, I want to ask you one question and I want you to tell me the truth," she said.

"Yes, ma'am," I said, all attention.

"Do you steal?" she asked me seriously.

I burst into a laugh, then checked myself.

"What's so damn funny about that?" she asked.

"Lady, if I was a thief, I'd never tell anybody."

"What do you mean?" she blazed with a red face.

I had made a mistake during my first five minutes in the white world. I hung my head.

"No, ma'am," I mumbled. "I don't steal."

She stared at me, trying to make up her mind.

"Now, look, we don't want a sassy nigger around here," she said.

"No, ma'am," I assured her. "I'm not sassy."

Promising to report the next morning at six o'clock, I walked home and pondered on what could possibly have been in the woman's mind to have made her ask me point-blank if I stole. Then I recalled hearing that white people looked upon Negroes as a variety of children, and it was only in the light of that that her question made any sense. If I had been planning to murder her, I certainly would not have told her and, rationally, she no doubt realized it. Yet habit had overcome her rationality and had made her ask me: "Boy, do you steal?" Only an idiot would have answered: "Yes, ma'am. I steal."

What would happen now that I would be among white people for hours at a stretch? Would they hit me? Curse me? If they did, I would leave at once. In all my wishing for a job I had not thought of how I would be treated, and now it loomed important, decisive, sweeping down beneath every other consideration. I would be polite, humble, saying yes sir and no sir, yes ma'am and no ma'am, but I would draw a line over which they must not step. Oh, maybe I'm just thinking up trouble, I told myself. They might like me . . .

The next morning I chopped wood for the cook stove, lugged in scuttles of coal for the grates, washed the front porch and swept the back porch, swept the kitchen, helped wait on the table, and washed the dishes. I was sweating. I swept the front walk and ran to the store to shop. When I returned the woman said:

"Your breakfast is in the kitchen."

"Thank you, ma'am."

I saw a plate of thick, black molasses and a hunk of white bread on the table. Would I get no more than this? They had had eggs, bacon, coffee . . . I picked up the bread and tried to break it; it was stale and hard. Well, I would drink the molasses. I lifted the plate and brought it to my lips and saw floating on the surface of the black liquid green and white bits of mold. Goddamn . . . I can't eat this, I told myself. The food was not even clean. The woman came into the kitchen as I was putting on my coat.

"You didn't eat," she said.

"No, ma'am," I said. "I'm not hungry."

"You'll eat at home?" she asked hopefully.

"Well, I just wasn't hungry this morning, ma'am," I lied.

"You don't like molasses and bread," she said dramatically.

"Oh, yes, ma'am, I do," I defended myself quickly, not wanting her to think that I dared criticize what she had given me.

"I don't know what's happening to you niggers nowadays," she sighed, wagging her head. She looked closely at the molasses. "It's a sin to throw out molasses like that. I'll put it up for you this evening."

"Yes, ma'am," I said heartily.

Neatly she covered the plate of molasses with another plate, then felt the bread and dumped it into the garbage. She turned to me, her face lit with an idea.

"What grade are you in school?"

"Seventh, ma'am."

"Then why are you going to school?" she asked in surprise.

"Well, I want to be a writer," I mumbled, unsure of myself; I had not planned to tell her that, but she had made me feel so utterly wrong and of no account that I needed to bolster myself.

"A what?" she demanded.

"A writer," I mumbled.

"For what?"

"To write stories," I mumbled defensively.

"You'll never be a writer," she said. "Who on earth put such ideas into your nigger head?"

"Nobody," I said.

"I didn't think anybody ever would," she declared indignantly.

As I walked around her house to the street, I knew that I would not go back. The woman had assaulted my ego; she had assumed that she knew my place in life, what I felt, what I ought to be, and I resented it with all my heart. Perhaps she was right; perhaps I would never be a writer; but I did not want her to say so.

Had I kept the job I would have learned quickly just how white people acted toward Negroes, but I was too naïve to think that there were many white people like that. I told myself that there were good white people, people with money and sensitive feelings. As a whole, I felt that they were bad, but I would be lucky enough to find the exceptions.

Fearing that my family might think I was finicky, I lied to them, telling them that the white woman had already hired a boy. At school I continued to ask about jobs and was directed to another address. As soon as school was out I made for the house. Yes, the woman said that she wanted a boy who could milk a cow, feed chickens, gather vegetables, help serve breakfast and dinner.

"But I can't milk a cow, ma'am," I said.

"Where are you from?" she asked incredulously.

"Here in Jackson," I said.

"You mean to stand there, nigger, and tell me that you live in Jackson and don't know how to milk a cow?" she demanded in surprise.

I said nothing, but I was quickly learning the reality—a Negro's reality—of the white world. One woman had assumed that I would tell her if I stole, and now this woman was amazed that I could not milk a cow, I, a nigger who dared live in Jackson . . . They were all turning out to be alike, differing only in detail. I faced a wall in the woman's mind, a wall that she did not know was there.

"I just never learned," I said finally.

"I'll show you how to milk," she said, as though glad to be charitable enough to repair a nigger's knowledge on that score. "It's easy."

The place was large; they had a cow, chickens, a garden, all of which spelled food and that decided me. I told her that I would take the job and I reported for work the next morning. My tasks were simple but many; I milked the cow under her supervision, gathered eggs, swept, and was through in time to serve breakfast. The dining-room table was set for five; there were eggs, bacon, toast, jam, butter, milk, apples . . . That seemed promising. The woman told me to bring the food in as they called for it, and I familiarized myself with the kitchen so that I could act quickly when called upon. Finally the woman came into the dining room followed by a pale young man who sat down and stared at the food.

"What the hell!" he snarled. "Every morning it's these damn eggs for breakfast."

"Listen, you sonofabitch," the woman said, sitting too, "you don't have to eat 'em."

"You might try serving some dirt," he said, and forked up the bacon.

I felt that I was dreaming. Were they like that all the time? If so, I would not stay here. A young girl came and flopped into her chair.

"That's right, you bitch," the young man said. "Knock the food right out of my goddamn mouth."

"You know what you can do," the girl said.

I stared at them so intently that I was not aware that the young man was watching me.

"Say, what in hell are you glaring at me for, you nigger bastard?" he demanded. "Get those goddamn biscuits off that stove and put 'em on the table."

"Yes, sir."

Two middle-aged men came in and sat down. I never learned who was in the family, who was related to whom, or if it was a family. They cursed each other in an amazingly offhand manner and nobody seemed to mind. As they hurled invectives, they barely looked at each other. I was tense each moment, trying to anticipate their wishes and avoid a curse, and I did not suspect that the tension I had begun to feel that morning would lift itself into the passion of my life. Perhaps I had waited too long to start working for white people; perhaps I should have begun earlier, when I was younger—as most of the other black boys had done—and perhaps by now the tension would have become an habitual condition, contained and controlled by reflex. But that was not to be my lot; I was always to be conscious of it, brood over it, carry it in my heart, live with it, sleep with it, fight with it.

The morning was physically tiring, but the nervous strain, the fear that my actions would call down upon my head a storm of curses, was even more damaging. When the time came for me to go to school, I was emotionally spent. But I clung to the job because I got enough to eat and no one watched me closely and measured out my food. I had rarely tasted eggs and I would put hunks of yellow butter into a hot skillet and hurriedly scramble three or four eggs at a time and gobble them down in huge mouthfuls so that the woman would not see me. And I would take tumblers of milk behind a convenient door and drain them in a swallow, as though they contained water.

Though the food I ate strengthened my body, I acquired another problem: I had fallen down in my studies at school. Had I been physically stronger, had not my new tensions sapped my already limited energy, I might have been able to work mornings and evenings and still carry my studies successfully. But in the middle of the day I would grow groggy; in the classroom I would feel that the teacher and the pupils were receding from me and I would know that I was drifting off to sleep. I would go to the water fountain in the corridor and let cold water run over my wrists, chilling my blood, hoping in that way to keep awake.

But the job had its boon. At the midday recess I would crowd gladly into the corner store and eat sandwiches with the boys, slamming down my own money on the counter for what I wanted, swapping descriptions of the homes of white folks in which we worked. I used to divert them with vivid word pictures of the cursing family, their brooding silences, their indifference toward one another. I told them of the food I managed to eat when the woman's back was turned, and they were filled with friendly envy.

The boys would now examine some new article of clothing I had bought; none of us allowed a week to pass without buying something new, paying fifty cents down and fifty cents per week. We knew that we were being cheated, but we never had enough cash to buy in any other way.

My mother began a rapid recovery. I was happy when she expressed the hope that someday soon we might have a home of our own. Though Granny was angry and disgusted, my mother began to attend a Methodist church in the neighborhood, and I went to Sunday school, not because my mother begged me to—which she did—but to meet and talk with my classmates.

In the black Protestant church I entered a new world; prim, brown, puritanical girls who taught in the public schools; black college students who tried to conceal their plantation origin; black boys and girls emerging self-consciously from adolescence; wobbly-bosomed black and yellow church matrons; black janitors and porters who sang proudly in the choir; subdued redcaps and carpenters who served as deacons; meek, blank-eyed black and yellow washerwomen who shouted and moaned and danced when hymns were sung; jovial, pot-bellied black bishops; skinny old maids who were constantly giving rallies to raise money; snobbery, clannishness, gossip, intrigue, petty class rivalry, and conspicuous displays of cheap clothing . . . I liked it and I did not like it; I longed to be among them, yet when with them I looked at them as if I were a million miles away. I had been kept out of their world too long ever to be able to become a real part of it.

Nevertheless, I was so starved for association with people that I allowed myself to be seduced by it all, and for a few months I lived the life of an optimist. A revival began at the church and my classmates at school urged me to attend. More because I liked them than from any interest in religion, I consented. As the services progressed night after night, my mother tried to persuade me to join, to save my soul at last, to become a member of a responsible community church. Despite the fact that I told them I could never feel any religion, the boys of my gang begged me to "come to God."

"You believe in God, don't you?" they asked.

I evaded the question.

"But this is a new day," they said, pulling down the corners of their lips. "We don't holler and moan in church no more. Come to church and be a member of the community."

"Oh, I don't know," I said.

"We don't want to push you," they said delicately, implying that if I wanted to associate with them I would have to join.

On the last night of the revival, the preacher asked all those who were members of the church to stand. A good majority of those present rose. Next the preacher called upon the Christians who were not members of any church to stand. More responded. There remained now but a few young men who, belonging to no church and professing no religion, were scattered sheepishly about the pews. Having thus isolated the sinners, the preacher told the deacons to prevail upon those who lived "in darkness to discuss the state of their souls with him." The deacons sped to their tasks and asked us to go into a room and talk with a man "chosen and anointed of God." They held our arms and smiled as they bent and talked to us. Surrounded by people I knew and liked, with my mother's eyes looking pleadingly into mine, it was hard to refuse. I followed the others into a room where the preacher stood; he smiled and shook our hands.

"Now, you young men," he began in a brisk, clipped tone, "I want all of you to know God. I'm not asking you to join the church, but it's my duty as a man of God to tell you that you are in danger. Your peril is great; you stand in the need of prayer. Now, I'm going to ask each of you a personal favor. I want you to let the members of this church send up a prayer to God for you. Now, is there any soul here so cold, so hard, so lost, that he would say no to that? Can you refuse to let the good people of this community pray for you?"

He paused dramatically and no one answered. All the techniques of his appeal were familiar to me and I sat there feeling foolish, wanting to leap through the window and go home and forget about it. But I sat still, filled more with disgust than sin.

"Would any man in this room dare fling no into God's face?" the preacher asked.

There was silence.

"Now, I'm going to ask all of you to rise and go into the church and take a seat on the front bench," he said, edging on to more definite commitments. "Just stand up," he said, lifting his hands, palms up, as though he had the power to make us rise by magic. "That's it, young man," he encouraged the first boy who rose.

I followed them and we sat like wet ducks on a bench facing the congregation. Some part of me was cursing. A low, soft hymn began.

This may be the last time, I don't know . . .

They sang it, hummed it, crooned it, moaned it, implying in sweet, frightening tones that if we did not join the church then and there we might die in our sleep that very night and go straight to hell. The church members felt the challenge and the volume of song swelled. Could they sing so terrifyingly sweet as to make us join, burst into tears and drop to our knees? A few boys rose and gave their hands to the preacher. A few women shouted and danced with joy. Another hymn began.

It ain't my brother, but it's me, Oh, Lord,
Standing in the need of prayer . . .

During the singing the preacher tried yet another ruse; he intoned mournfully, letting his voice melt into the singing, yet casting his words above it:

"How many mothers of these young men are here tonight?"

Among others, my mother rose and stood proudly.

"Now, good sweet mothers, come right down in front here," said the preacher.

Hoping that this was the night of my long-deferred salvation, my mother came forward, limping, weeping, smiling. The mothers ringed their sons around, whispering, pleading.

"Now, you good sweet mothers, symbols of Mother Mary at the tomb, kneel and pray for your sons, your only sons," the preacher chanted.

The mothers knelt. My mother grabbed my hands and I felt hot tears scalding my fingers. I tried to stifle my disgust. We young men had been trapped by the community, the tribe in which we lived and of which we were a part. The tribe, for its own safety, was asking us to be at one with it. Our mothers were kneeling in public and praying for us to give the sign of allegiance. The hymn ended and the preacher launched into a highly emotional and symbolic sermon, recounting how our mothers had given birth to us, how they had nursed us from infancy, how they had tended us when we were sick, how they had seen us grow up, how they had watched over us, how they had always known what was best for us. He then called for yet another hymn, which was hummed. He chanted above it in a melancholy tone:

"Now, I'm asking the first mother who really loves her son to bring him to me for baptism!"

Goddamn, I thought. It had happened quicker than I had expected. My mother was looking steadily at me.

"Come, son, let your old mother take you to God," she begged. "I brought you into the world, now let me help to save you."

She caught my hand and I held back.

"I've been as good a mother as I could," she whispered through her tears.

"God is hearing every word," the preacher underscored her plea.

This business of saving souls had no ethics; every human relationship was shamelessly exploited. In essence, the tribe was asking us whether we shared its feelings; if we refused to join the church, it was equivalent to saying no, to placing ourselves in the position of moral monsters. One mother led her beaten and frightened son to the preacher amid shouts of amen and hallelujah.

"Don't you love your old crippled mother, Richard?" my mother asked. "Don't leave me standing here with my empty hands," she said, afraid that I would humiliate her in public.

It was no longer a question of my believing in God; it was no longer a matter of whether I would steal or lie or murder; it was a simple, urgent matter of public pride, a matter of how much I had in common with other people. If I refused, it meant that I did not love my mother, and no man in that tight little black community had ever been crazy enough to let himself be placed in such a position. My mother pulled my arm and I walked with her to the preacher and shook his hand, a gesture that made me a candidate for baptism. There were more songs and prayers; it lasted until well after midnight. I walked home limp as a rag; I had not felt anything except sullen anger and a crushing sense of shame. Yet I was somehow glad that I had got it over with; no barriers now stood between me and the community.

"Mama, I don't feel a thing," I told her truthfully.

"Don't you worry; you'll grow into feeling it," she assured me.

And when I confessed to the other boys that I felt nothing, they too admitted that they felt nothing.

"But the main thing is to be a member of the church," they said.

The Sunday of the baptism arrived. I dressed in my best and showed up sweating. The candidates were huddled together to listen to a sermon in which the road of salvation was mapped out from the cradle to the grave. We were then called to the front of the church and lined up. The preacher, draped in white robes, dipped a small branch of a tree in a huge bowl of water and hovered above the head of the first candidate.

"I baptize thee in the name of the Father, the Son, and the Holy Ghost," he pronounced sonorously as he shook the wet branch. Drops trickled down the boy's face.

From one boy to another he went, dipping the branch each time. Finally my turn came and I felt foolish, tense; I wanted to yell for him to stop; I wanted to tell him that all this was so much nonsense. But I said nothing. The dripping branch was shaken above my head and drops of water wet my face and scalp, some of it rolling down my neck and wetting my back, like insects crawling. I wanted to squirm, but I held still. Then it was over. I relaxed. The preacher was now shaking the branch over another boy's head. I sighed. I had been baptized.

Even after receiving the "right hand of fellowship," Sunday school bored me. The Bible stories seemed slow and meaningless when compared to the bloody thunder of pulp narrative. And I was not alone in feeling this; other boys went to sleep in Sunday school. Finally the boldest of us confessed that the entire thing was a fraud and we played hooky from church.

─◈─

As summer neared, my mother suffered yet another stroke of paralysis and again I had to watch her suffer, listen to her groans, powerless to help. I used to lie awake nights and think back to the early days in Arkansas, tracing my mother's life, reliving events, wondering why she had apparently been singled out for so much suffering, meaningless suffering, and I would feel more awe than I had ever felt in church. My mind could find no answer and I would feel rebellious against all life. But I never felt humble.

Another change took place at home. We needed money badly and Granny and Aunt Addie decided that we could no longer share the entire house, and Uncle Tom and his family were invited to live upstairs at a nominal rental. The dining room and the living room were converted into bedrooms and for the first time we were squeezed for living space. We began to get on each other's nerves. Uncle Tom had taught school in country towns for thirty years and as soon as he was under the roof he proceeded to tell me what was wrong with my life. I ignored him and he resented it.

Rattling pots and pans in the kitchen would now awaken me in the mornings and I would know that Uncle Tom and his family were getting breakfast. One morning I was roused by my uncle's voice calling gently but persistently. I opened my eyes and saw the dim blob of his face peering from behind the jamb of the kitchen door.

"What time have you?" I thought he asked me, but I was not sure.

"Hunh?" I mumbled sleepily.

"What time have you got?" he repeated.

I lifted myself on my elbow and looked at my dollar watch, which lay on the chair at the bedside.

"Eighteen past five," I mumbled.

"Eighteen past five?" he asked.

"Yes, sir."

"Now, is that the right time?" he asked again.

I was tired, sleepy; I did not want to look at the watch again, but I was satisfied that, on the whole, I had given him the correct time.

"It's right," I said, snuggling back down into my pillow. "If it's a little slow or fast, it's not far wrong."

There was a short silence; I thought he had gone.

"What on earth do you mean, boy?" he asked in loud anger.

I sat up, blinking, staring into the shadows of the room, trying to see the expression on his face.

"What do I mean?" I asked, bewildered. "I mean what I said." Had I given him the wrong time? I looked again at my watch. "It's twenty past now."

"Why, you impudent black rascal!" he thundered.

I pushed back the covers of the bed, sensing trouble.

"What are you angry about?" I asked.

"I never heard a sassier black imp than you in all my life," he spluttered.

I swung my feet to the floor so that I could watch him.

"What are you talking about?" I asked. "You asked me the time and I told you."

" 'If it's a little fast or slow, it's not far wrong,' " he said, imitating me in an angry, sarcastic voice. "I've taught school for thirty years, and by God I've never had a boy say anything like that to me."

"But what's wrong with what I said?" I asked, amazed.

"Shut up!" he shouted. "Or I'll take my fist and ram it down your sassy throat! One more word out of you, and I'll get a limb and teach you a lesson."

"What's the matter with you, Uncle Tom?" I asked. "What's wrong with what I said?"

I could hear his breath whistling in his throat; I knew that he was furious.

"This day I'm going to give you the whipping some man ought to have given you long ago," he vowed.

I got to my feet and grabbed my clothes; the whole thing seemed unreal. I had been confronted so suddenly with struggle that I could not pull all the strings of the situation together at once. I did not feel that I had given him cause to say I was sassy. I had spoken to him just as I spoke to everybody. Others did not resent my words, so why should he? I heard him go out of the kitchen door and I knew that he had gone into the back yard. I pulled on my clothes and ran to the window; I saw him tearing a long, young, green switch from the elm tree. My body tightened. I was damned if he was going to beat me with it. Until a few days ago he had never lived near me, had never had any say in my rearing or lack of rearing. I was working, eating my meals out, buying my own clothes, giving what few pennies I could to Granny to help out in the house. And now a strange uncle who felt that I was impolite was going to teach me to act as I had seen the backward black boys act on the plantations, was going to teach me to grin, hang my head, and mumble apologetically when I was spoken to.

My senses reeled in protest. No, that could not be. He would not beat me. He was only bluffing. His anger would pass. He would think it over and realize that it was not worth all the bother. Dressed, I sat on the edge of the bed and waited. I heard his footsteps come onto the back porch. I felt weak all over. How long was this going to last? How long was I going to be beaten for trifles and less than trifles? I was already so conditioned toward my relatives that when I passed them I actually had a nervous tic in my muscles, and now I was going to be beaten by someone who did not like the tone of voice in which I spoke. I ran across the room and pulled out the dresser drawer and got my pack of razor blades; I opened it and took a thin blade of blue steel in each hand. I stood ready for him. The door opened. I was hoping desperately that this was not true, that this dream would end.

"Richard!" he called me in a cold, even tone.

"Yes, sir!" I answered, striving to keep my tension out of my voice.

"Come here."

I walked into the kitchen, my eyes upon him, my hands holding the razors behind my back.

"Now, Uncle Tom, what do you want with me?" I asked him.

"You need a lesson in how to live with people," he said.

"If I do need one, you're not going to give it to me," I said.

"You'll swallow those words before I'm through with you," he vowed.

"Now, listen, Uncle Tom," I said, "you're not going to whip me. You're a stranger to me. You don't support me. I don't live with you."

"You shut that foul mouth of yours and get into the back yard," he snapped.

He had not seen the razors in my hand. I ducked out the kitchen door and jumped lightly off the porch to the ground. He ran down the steps and advanced with the lifted switch.

"I've got a razor in each hand!" I warned in a low, charged voice. "If you touch me, I'll cut you! Maybe I'll get cut too, but I'll cut you, so help me God!"

He paused, staring at my lifted hands in the dawning light of morning. I held a sharp blue edge of steel tightly between thumb and forefinger of each fist.

"My God," he gasped.

"I didn't mean to hurt your feelings this morning," I told him. "You insist I did. Now, I'll be damned if I'm going to be beaten because of your hurt feelings."

"You're the worst criminal I ever saw," he exclaimed softly.

"If you want to fight, I'll fight. That's the way it'll be between us," I told him.

"You'll never amount to anything," he said, shaking his head and blinking his eyes in astonishment.

"I'm not worried about that," I said. "All I want you to do is keep away from me, now and always . . ."

"You'll end on the gallows," he predicted.

"If I do, you'll have nothing to do with it," I said.

He stared at me in silence; evidently he did not believe me, for he took a step forward to test me.

"Put those razors down," he commanded.

"I'll cut you! I'll cut you!" I said, hysteria leaping into my voice, my hands slicing out with points of steel as I backed away.

He stopped; he had never in his life faced a person more grimly determined. Now and then he blinked his eyes and shook his head.

"You fool!" he bellowed suddenly.

"I'll make you bloody if you hit me!" I warned him.

His chest heaved and his body seemed to droop.

"Somebody will yet break your spirit," he said.

"It won't be you!"

"You'll get yours someday!"

"You won't be the one to give it to me!"

"And you've just been baptized," he said heavily.

"The hell with that," I said.

We stood in the early morning light and a touch of sun broke on the horizon. Roosters were crowing. A bird chirped near-by somewhere. Perhaps the neighbors were listening. Finally Uncle Tom's face began to twitch. Tears rolled down his cheeks. His lips trembled.

"Boy, I'm sorry for you," he said at last.

"You'd better be sorry for yourself," I said.

"You think you're a man," he said, dropping his arm and letting the switch drag in the dust of the yard. His lips moved as he groped for words. "But you'll learn, and you'll learn the hard way. I wish I could be an example to you . . ."

I knew that I had conquered him, had rid myself of him mentally and emotionally; but I wanted to be sure.

"You are not an example to me; you could never be," I spat at him. "You're a *warning*. Your life isn't so hot that you can tell me what to do." He repaired chairs for a living now, since he had retired from teaching. "Do you think I want to grow up and weave the bottoms of chairs for people to sit in?"

He twitched violently, trying to control himself.

"You'll be sorry you said that," he mumbled.

He turned his tall, lean, bent body and walked slowly up the steps. I sat on the porch a long time, waiting for my emotions to ebb. Then I crept cautiously into the house, got my hat, coat, books, and went to work, went to face the whims of the white folks.

7

Summer. Bright hot days. Hunger still a vital part of my conscious-
ness. Passing relatives in the hallways of the crowded home and not
speaking. Eating in silence at a table where prayers are said. My
mother recovering slowly, but now definitely crippled for life. Will I
be able to enter school in September? Loneliness. Reading. Job
hunting. Vague hopes of going north. But what would become of
my mother if I left her in this queer house? And how would I fare in
a strange city? Doubt. Fear. My friends are buying long-pants suits
that cost from seventeen to twenty dollars, a sum as huge to me as
the Alps! This was my reality in 1924.

Word came that a near-by brickyard was hiring and I went to
investigate. I was frail, not weighing a hundred pounds. At noon I
sneaked into the yard and walked among the aisles of damp, clean-
smelling clay and came to a barrow full of wet bricks just taken
from the machine that shaped them. I caught hold of the handles of
the barrow and was barely able to lift it; it weighed perhaps four
times as much as I did. If I were only stronger and heavier!

Later I asked questions and found that the water boy was missing; I ran to the office and was hired. I walked in the hot sun lugging
a big zinc pail from one laboring gang of black men to another for a
dollar a day; a man would lift the tin dipper to his lips, take a swallow,
rinse out his mouth, spit, and then drink in long, slow gulps as sweat
dripped into the dipper. And off again I would go, chanting:

"Water!"

And somebody would yell:

"Here, boy!"

Deep into wet pits of clay, into sticky ditches, up slippery slopes I would struggle with the pail. I stuck it out, reeling at times from hunger, pausing to get my breath before clambering up a hill. At the end of the week the money sank into the endless expenses at home. Later I got a job in the yard that paid a dollar and a half a day, that of bat boy. I went between the walls of clay and picked up bricks that had cracked open; when my barrow was full, I would wheel it out onto a wooden scaffold and dump it into a pond.

I had but one fear here: a dog. He was owned by the boss of the brickyard and he haunted the clay aisles, snapping, growling. The dog had been wounded many times, for the black workers were always hurling bricks at it. Whenever I saw the animal, I would take a brick from my load and toss it at him; he would slink away, only to appear again, showing his teeth. Several of the Negroes had been bitten and had been ill; the boss had been asked to leash the dog, but he had refused. One afternoon I was wheeling my barrow toward the pond when something sharp sank into my thigh. I whirled; the dog crouched a few feet away, snarling. I had been bitten. I drove the dog away and opened my trousers; teeth marks showed deep and red.

I did not mind the stinging hurt, but I was afraid of an infection. When I went to the office to report that the boss's dog had bitten me, I was met by a tall blonde white girl.

"What do you want?" she asked.

"I want to see the boss, ma'am."

"For what?"

"His dog bit me, ma'am, and I'm afraid I might get an infection."

"Where did he bite you?"

"On my leg," I lied, shying from telling her where the bite was.

"Let's see," she said.

"No, ma'am. Can't I see the boss?"

"He isn't here now," she said, and went back to her typing.

I returned to work, stopping occasionally to examine the teeth marks; they were swelling. Later in the afternoon a tall white man wearing a cool white suit, a Panama hat, and white shoes came toward me.

"Is this the nigger?" he asked a black boy as he pointed at me.

"Yes, sir," the black boy answered.

"Come here, nigger," he called me.

I went to him.

"They tell me my dog bit you," he said.

"Yes, sir."

I pulled down my trousers and he looked.

"Humnnn," he grunted, then laughed. "A dog bite can't hurt a nigger."

"It's swelling and it hurts," I said.

"If it bothers you, let me know," he said. "But I never saw a dog yet that could really hurt a nigger."

He turned and walked away and the black boys gathered to watch his tall form disappear down the aisles of wet bricks.

"Sonofabitch!"

"He'll get his someday!"

"Boy, their hearts are hard!"

"Lawd, a white man'll do anything!"

"Break up that prayer meeting!" the white straw boss yelled.

The wheelbarrows rolled again. A boy came close to me.

"You better see a doctor," he whispered.

"I ain't got no money," I said.

Two days passed and luckily the redness and swelling went away.

Summer wore on and the brickyard closed; again I was out of work. I heard that caddies were wanted and I tramped five miles to the golf links. I was hired by a florid-faced white man at the rate of fifty cents for nine holes. I did not know the game and I lost three balls in as many minutes; it seemed that my eyes could not trace the flight of the balls. The man dismissed me. I watched the other boys do their jobs and within half an hour I had another golf bag and was following a ball. I made a dollar. I returned home, disgusted, tired, hungry, hating the sight of a golf course.

School opened and, though I had not prepared myself, I enrolled. The school was far across town and the walking distance alone consumed my breakfast of mush and lard gravy. I attended classes without books for a month, then got a job working mornings and evenings for three dollars a week.

I grew silent and reserved as the nature of the world in which I lived became plain and undeniable; the bleakness of the future affected my will to study. Granny had already thrown out hints that it was time for me to be on my own. But what had I learned so far that would help me to make a living? Nothing. I could be a porter like my father before me, but what else? And the problem of living as a Negro was cold and hard. What was it that made the hate of whites for blacks so steady, seemingly so woven into the texture of things? What kind of life was possible under that hate? How had this hate come to be? Nothing about the problems of Negroes was ever taught in the classrooms at school; and whenever I would raise these questions with the boys, they would either remain silent or turn the subject into a joke. They were vocal about the petty individual wrongs they suffered, but they possessed no desire for a knowledge of the picture as a whole. Then why was I worried about it?

Was I really as bad as my uncles and aunts and Granny repeatedly said? Why was it considered wrong to ask questions? Was I right when I resisted punishment? It was inconceivable to me that one should surrender to what seemed wrong, and most of the people I had met seemed wrong. Ought one to surrender to authority even if one believed that that authority was wrong? If the answer was yes, then I knew that I would always be wrong, because I could never do it. Then how could one live in a world in which one's mind and perceptions meant nothing and authority and tradition meant everything? There were no answers.

The eighth grade days flowed in their hungry path and I grew more conscious of myself; I sat in classes, bored, wondering, dreaming.

One long dry afternoon I took out my composition book and told myself that I would write a story; it was sheer idleness that led me to it. What would the story be about? It resolved itself into a plot about a villain who wanted a widow's home and I called it *The Voodoo of Hell's Half-Acre.* It was crudely atmospheric, emotional, intuitively psychological, and stemmed from pure feeling. I finished it in three days and then wondered what to do with it.

The local Negro newspaper! That's it . . . I sailed into the office and shoved my ragged composition book under the nose of the man who called himself the editor.

"What is that?" he asked.

"A story," I said.

"A news story?"

"No, fiction."

"All right. I'll read it," he said.

He pushed my composition book back on his desk and looked at me curiously, sucking at his pipe.

"But I want you to read it *now,*" I said.

He blinked. I had no idea how newspapers were run. I thought that one took a story to an editor and he sat down then and there and read it and said yes or no.

"I'll read this and let you know about it tomorrow," he said.

I was disappointed; I had taken time to write it and he seemed distant and uninterested.

"Give me the story," I said, reaching for it.

He turned from me, took up the book and read ten pages or more.

"Won't you come in tomorrow?" he asked. "I'll have it finished then."

I honestly relented.

"All right," I said. "I'll stop in tomorrow."

I left with the conviction that he would not read it. Now, where else could I take it after he had turned it down? The next afternoon, en route to my job, I stepped into the newspaper office.

"Where's my story?" I asked.

"It's in galleys," he said.

"What's that?" I asked; I did not know what galleys were.

"It's set up in type," he said. "We're publishing it."

"How much money will I get?" I asked, excited.

"We can't pay for manuscript," he said.

"But you sell your papers for money," I said with logic.

"Yes, but we're young in business," he explained.

"But you're asking me to *give* you my story, but you don't *give* your papers away," I said.

He laughed.

"Look, you're just starting. This story will put your name before our readers. Now, that's something," he said.

"But if the story is good enough to sell to your readers, then you ought to give me some of the money you get from it," I insisted.

He laughed again and I sensed that I was amusing him.

"I'm going to offer you something more valuable than money," he said. "I'll give you a chance to learn to write."

I was pleased, but I still thought he was taking advantage of me.

"When will you publish my story?"

"I'm dividing it into three installments," he said. "The first installment appears this week. But the main thing is this: Will you get news for me on a space rate basis?"

"I work mornings and evenings for three dollars a week," I said.

"Oh," he said. "Then you better keep that. But what are you doing this summer?"

"Nothing."

"Then come to see me before you take another job," he said. "And write some more stories."

A few days later my classmates came to me with baffled eyes, holding copies of the *Southern Register* in their hands.

"Did you really write that story?" they asked me.

"Yes."

"Why?"

"Because I wanted to."

"Where did you get it from?"

"I made it up."

"You didn't. You copied it out of a book."

"If I had, no one would publish it."

"But what are they publishing it for?"

"So people can read it."

"Who told you to do that?"

"Nobody."

"Then why did you do it?"

"Because I wanted to," I said again.

They were convinced that I had not told them the truth. We had never had any instruction in literary matters at school; the literature of the nation or the Negro had never been mentioned. My schoolmates could not understand why anyone would want to write a story; and, above all, they could not understand why I had called it *The Voodoo of Hell's Half-Acre*. The mood out of which a story was written was the most alien thing conceivable to them. They looked at me with new eyes, and a distance, a suspiciousness came between us. If I had thought anything in writing the story, I had thought that perhaps it would make me more acceptable to them, and now it was cutting me off from them more completely than ever.

At home the effects were no less disturbing. Granny came into my room early one morning and sat on the edge of my bed.

"Richard, what is this you're putting in the papers?" she asked.

"A story," I said.

"About what?"

"It's just a story, granny."

"But they tell me it's been in three times."

"It's the same story. It's in three parts."

"But what is it about?" she insisted.

I hedged, fearful of getting into a religious argument.

"It's just a story I made up," I said.

"Then it's a lie," she said.

"Oh, Christ," I said.

"You must get out of this house if you take the name of the Lord in vain," she said.

"Granny, please . . . I'm sorry," I pleaded. "But it's hard to tell you about the story. You see, granny, everybody knows that the story isn't true, but . . ."

"Then why write it?" she asked.

"Because people might want to read it."

"That's the Devil's work," she said and left.

My mother also was worried.

"Son, you ought to be more serious," she said. "You're growing up now and you won't be able to get jobs if you let people think that you're weak-minded. Suppose the superintendent of schools would ask you to teach here in Jackson, and he found out that you had been writing stories?"

I could not answer her.

"I'll be all right, mama," I said.

Uncle Tom, though surprised, was highly critical and contemptuous. The story had no point, he said. And whoever heard of a story by the title of *The Voodoo of Hell's Half-Acre?* Aunt Addie said that it was a sin for anyone to use the word "hell" and that what was wrong with me was that I had nobody to guide me. She blamed the whole thing upon my upbringing.

In the end I was so angry that I refused to talk about the story. From no quarter, with the exception of the Negro newspaper editor, had there come a single encouraging word. It was rumored that the principal wanted to know why I had used the word "hell." I felt that I had committed a crime. Had I been conscious of the full extent to which I was pushing against the current of my environment, I would have been frightened altogether out of my attempts at writing. But my reactions were limited to the attitude of the people about me, and I did not speculate or generalize.

I dreamed of going north and writing books, novels. The North symbolized to me all that I had not felt and seen; it had no relation whatever to what actually existed. Yet, by imagining a place where everything was possible, I kept hope alive in me. But where had I got this notion of doing something in the future, of going away from home and accomplishing something that would be recognized by others? I had, of course, read my Horatio Alger stories, my pulp stories, and I knew my Get-Rich-Quick Wallingford series from cover to cover, though I had sense enough not to hope to get rich; even to my naïve imagination that possibility was too remote. I knew that I lived in a country in which the aspirations of black people were limited, marked-off. Yet I felt that I had to go somewhere and do something to redeem my being alive.

I was building up in me a dream which the entire educational system of the South had been rigged to stifle. I was feeling the very thing that the state of Mississippi had spent millions of dollars to make sure that I would never feel; I was becoming aware of the thing that the Jim Crow laws had been drafted and passed to keep out of my consciousness; I was acting on impulses that southern senators in the nation's capital had striven to keep out of Negro life; I was beginning to dream the dreams that the state had said were wrong, that the schools had said were taboo.

Had I been articulate about my ultimate aspirations, no doubt someone would have told me what I was bargaining for; but nobody seemed to know, and least of all did I. My classmates felt that I was doing something that was vaguely wrong, but they did not know how to express it. As the outside world grew more meaningful, I became more concerned, tense; and my classmates and my teachers would say: "Why do you ask so many questions?" Or: "Keep quiet."

I was in my fifteenth year; in terms of schooling I was far behind the average youth of the nation, but I did not know that. In me was shaping a yearning for a kind of consciousness, a mode of being that the way of life about me had said could not be, must not be, and upon which the penalty of death had been placed. Somewhere in the dead of the southern night my life had switched onto the wrong track and, without my knowing it, the locomotive of my heart was rushing down a dangerously steep slope, heading for a collision, heedless of the warning red lights that blinked all about me, the sirens and the bells and the screams that filled the air.

8

Summer again. The old problem of hunting for a job. I told the woman for whom I was working, a Mrs. Bibbs, that I needed an all-day job that would pay me enough money to buy clothes and books for the next school term. She took the matter up with her husband, who was a foreman in a sawmill.

"So you want to work in the mill, hunh?" he asked.

"Yes, sir."

He came to me and put his hands under my arms and lifted me from the floor, as though I were a bundle of feathers.

"You're too light for our work," he said.

"But maybe I could do *something* there," I said.

"That's the problem," he said soberly. "The work's heavy and dangerous." He was silent and I knew that he considered the matter closed. That was the way things were between whites and blacks in the South; many of the most important things were never openly said; they were understated and left to seep through to one. I, in turn, said nothing; but I did not leave the room; my standing silent was a way of asking him to reconsider, telling him that I wanted ever so much to try for a job in his mill. "All right," he said finally. "Come to the mill in the morning. I'll see what I can do. But I don't think that you'll like it."

I was at the mill at dawn the next morning and saw men lifting huge logs with tackle blocks. There were scores of buzzing steel saws biting into green wood with loud whines.

"Watch out!" somebody yelled.

I looked around and saw a black man pointing above my head; I glanced up. A log was swinging toward me. I scrambled out of its path. The black man came to my side.

"What do you want here, boy?"

"Mr. Bibbs, the foreman, told me to look around. I'm looking for a job," I said.

The man gazed at me intently.

"I wouldn't try for this if I was you," he said. "If you know this game, all right. But this is dangerous stuff for a guy that's green." He held up his right hand from which three fingers were missing. "See?"

I nodded and left.

Empty days. Long days. Bright hot days. The sun heated the pavements until they felt like the top of an oven. I spent the mornings hunting for jobs and I read during the afternoons. One morning I was walking toward the center of town and passed the home of a classmate, Ned Greenley. He was sitting on his porch, looking glum.

"Hello, Ned. What's new?" I asked.

"You've heard, haven't you?" he asked.

"About what?"

"My brother, Bob?"

"No, what happened?"

Ned began to weep softly.

"They killed him," he managed to say.

"The white folks?" I asked in a whisper, guessing.

He sobbed his answer. Bob was dead; I had met him only a few times, but I felt that I had known him through his brother.

"What happened?"

"Th-they t-took him in a c-car . . . Out on a c-country road . . . Th-they shot h-him," Ned whimpered.

I had heard that Bob was working at one of the hotels in town.

"Why?"

"Th-they said he was fooling with a white prostitute there in the hotel," Ned said.

Inside of me my world crashed and my body felt heavy. I stood looking down the quiet, sun-filled street. Bob had been caught by the white death, the threat of which hung over every male black in the South. I had heard whispered tales of black boys having sex relations with white prostitutes in the hotels in town, but I had never paid any close attention to them; now those tales came home to me in the form of the death of a man I knew.

I did not search for a job that day; I returned home and sat on my porch too, and stared. What I had heard altered the look of the world, induced in me a temporary paralysis of will and impulse. The penalty of death awaited me if I made a false move and I wondered if it was worth-while to make any move at all. The things that influenced my conduct as a Negro did not have to happen to me directly; I needed but to hear of them to feel their full effects in the deepest layers of my consciousness. Indeed, the white brutality that I had not seen was a more effective control of my behavior than that which I knew. The actual experience would have let me see the realistic outlines of what was really happening, but as long as it remained something terrible and yet remote, something whose horror and blood might descend upon me at any moment, I was compelled to give my entire imagination over to it, an act which blocked the springs of thought and feeling in me, creating a sense of distance between me and the world in which I lived.

A few days later I sought out the editor of the local Negro newspaper and found that he could not hire me. I had doubts now about my being able to enter school that fall. The empty days of summer rolled on. Whenever I met my classmates they would tell me about the jobs they had found, how some of them had left town to work in summer resorts in the North. Why did they not tell me of these jobs? I demanded of them. They said that they simply had not thought of it, and as I heard the words fall from their lips my sense of isolation became doubly acute. But, after all, what would make them think of me in connection with jobs when for years I had encountered them only casually in the classroom? I had had no association with them; the religious home in which I lived, my mush-and-lard-gravy poverty had cut me off from the normal processes of the lives of black boys my own age.

One afternoon I made a discovery in the home that stunned me. I was talking to my cousin, Maggie, who was a few months younger than I, when Uncle Tom entered the room. He paused, stared at me with silent hostility, then called his daughter. I gave the matter no thought. A few moments later I rose from my chair, where I had been reading, and was on my way down the hall when I heard Uncle Tom scolding his daughter. I caught a few phrases:

"Do you want me to break your neck? Didn't I tell you to stay away from him? That boy's a dangerous fool, I tell you! Then why don't you keep away from him? And make the other children keep away from him! Ask me no questions, but do as I tell you! Keep away from him, or I'll skin you!"

And I could hear my cousin's whimpering replies. My throat grew tight with anger. I wanted to rush into the room and demand an explanation, but I held still. How long had this been going on? I thought back over the time since Uncle Tom and his family had moved into the house, and I was filled with dismay as I recalled that on scarcely any occasion had any of his children ever been alone with me. Be careful now, I told myself; don't see what isn't there . . . But no matter how carefully I weighed my memories, I could recall no innocent intimacy, no games, no playing, none of the association that usually exists between young people living in the same house. Then suddenly I was reliving that early morning when I had held Uncle Tom at bay with my razors. Though I must have seemed brutal and desperate to him, I had never thought of myself as being so, and now I was appalled at how I was regarded. It was a flash of insight which revealed to me the true nature of my relations with my family, an insight which altered the entire course of my life. I was now definitely decided upon leaving home. But I would remain until the ninth grade term had ended. There were many days when I spoke to no one in the home except my mother. My life was falling to pieces and I was acutely aware of it. I was poised for flight, but I was waiting for some event, some word, some act, some circumstance to furnish the impetus.

I returned to my job at Mrs. Bibbs's and bought my school-books; my clothing remained little better than rags. Luckily the studies in the ninth—my last year at school—were light; and, during a part of the term the teacher turned over the class to my supervision, an honor that helped me emotionally and made me hope faintly. It was even hinted that, if I kept my grades high, it would be possible for me to teach in the city school system.

During that winter my brother came home from Chicago; I was glad to see him, though we were strangers. But it was not long before I felt that the affection shown him by the family was far greater than that which I had ever had from them. Slowly my brother grew openly critical of me, taking his cue from those about him, and it hurt. My loneliness became organic. I felt walled in and I grew irritable. I associated less and less with my classmates, for their talk was now full of the schools they planned to attend when the term was over. The cold days dragged mechanically: up early and to my job, splitting wood, carrying coal, sweeping floors, then off to school and boredom.

The school term ended. I was selected as valedictorian of my class and assigned to write a paper to be delivered at one of the public auditoriums. One morning the principal summoned me to his office.

"Well, Richard Wright, here's your speech," he said with smooth bluntness and shoved a stack of stapled sheets across his desk.

"What speech?" I asked as I picked up the papers.

"The speech you're to say the night of graduation," he said.

"But, professor, I've written my speech already," I said.

He laughed confidently, indulgently.

"Listen, boy, you're going to speak to both *white* and colored people that night. What can you alone think of saying to them? You have no experience . . ."

I burned.

"I know that I'm not educated, professor," I said. "But the people are coming to hear the students, and I won't make a speech that you've written."

He leaned back in his chair and looked at me in surprise.

"You know, we've never had a boy in this school like you before," he said. "You've had your way around here. Just how you managed to do it, I don't know. But, listen, take this speech and say it. I know what's best for you. You can't afford to just say *anything* before those white people that night." He paused and added meaningfully: "The superintendent of schools will be there; you're in a position to make a good impression on him. I've been a principal for more years than you are old, boy. I've seen many a boy and girl graduate from this school, and none of them was too proud to recite a speech I wrote for them."

I had to make up my mind quickly; I was faced with a matter of principle. I wanted to graduate, but I did not want to make a public speech that was not my own.

"Professor, I'm going to say my own speech that night," I said.

He grew angry.

"You're just a young, hotheaded fool," he said. He toyed with a pencil and looked up at me. "Suppose you don't graduate?"

"But I passed my examinations," I said.

"Look, mister," he shot at me, "I'm the man who says who passes at this school."

I was so astonished that my body jerked. I had gone to this school for two years and I had never suspected what kind of man the principal was; it simply had never occurred to me to wonder about him.

"Then I don't graduate," I said flatly.

I turned to leave.

"Say, you. Come here," he called.

I turned and faced him; he was smiling at me in a remote, superior sort of way.

"You know, I'm glad I talked to you," he said. "I was seriously thinking of placing you in the school system, teaching. But, now, I don't think that you'll fit."

He was tempting me, baiting me; this was the technique that snared black young minds into supporting the southern way of life.

"Look, professor, I may never get a chance to go to school again," I said. "But I like to do things right."

"What do you mean?"

"I've no money. I'm going to work. Now, this ninth-grade diploma isn't going to help me much in life. I'm not bitter about it; it's not your fault. But I'm just not going to do things this way."

"Have you talked to anybody about this?" he asked me.

"No, why?"

"Are you sure?"

"This is the first I've heard of it, professor," I said, amazed again.

"You haven't talked to any white people about this?"

"No, sir!"

"I just wanted to know," he said.

My amazement increased; the man was afraid now for his job!

"Professor, you don't understand me." I smiled.

"You're just a young, hot fool," he said, confident again. "Wake up, boy. Learn the world you're living in. You're smart and I know what you're after. I've kept closer track of you than you think. I know your relatives. Now, if you play safe," he smiled and winked, "I'll help you to go to school, to college."

"I want to learn, professor," I told him. "But there are some things I don't want to know."

"Good-bye," he said.

I went home, hurt but determined. I had been talking to a "bought" man and he had tried to "buy" me. I felt that I had been dealing with something unclean. That night Griggs, a boy who had gone through many classes with me, came to the house.

"Look, Dick, you're throwing away your future here in Jackson," he said. "Go to the principal, talk to him, take his speech and say it. I'm saying the one he wrote. So why can't you? What the hell? What can you lose?"

"No," I said.

"Why?"

"I know only a hell of a little, but my speech is going to reflect that," I said.

"Then you're going to be blacklisted for teaching jobs," he said.

"Who the hell said I was going to teach?" I asked.

"God, but you've got a will," he said.

"It's not will. I just don't want to do things that way," I said.

He left. Two days later Uncle Tom came to me. I knew that the principal had called him in.

"I hear that the principal wants you to say a speech which you've rejected," he said.

"Yes, sir. That's right," I said.

"May I read the speech you've written?" he asked.

"Certainly," I said, giving him my manuscript.

"And may I see the one that the principal wrote?"

I gave him the principal's speech too. He went to his room and read them. I sat quiet, waiting. He returned.

"The principal's speech is the better speech," he said.

"I don't doubt it," I replied. "But why did they ask me to write a speech if I can't deliver it?"

"Would you let me work on your speech?" he asked.

"No, sir."

"Now, look, Richard, this is your future . . ."

"Uncle Tom, I don't care to discuss this with you," I said.

He stared at me, then left. The principal's speech was simpler and clearer than mine, but it did not say anything; mine was cloudy, but it said what I wanted to say. What could I do? I had half a mind not to show up at the graduation exercises. I was hating my environment more each day. As soon as school was over, I would get a job, save money, and leave.

Griggs, who had accepted a speech written by the principal, came to my house each day and we went off into the woods to practice orating; day in and day out we spoke to the trees, to the creeks, frightening the birds, making the cows in the pastures stare at us in fear. I memorized my speech so thoroughly that I could have recited it in my sleep.

The news of my clash with the principal had spread through the class and the students became openly critical of me.

"Richard, you're a fool. You're throwing away every chance you've got. If they had known the kind of fool boy you are, they would never have made you valedictorian," they said.

I gritted my teeth and kept my mouth shut, but my rage was mounting by the hour. My classmates, motivated by a desire to "save" me, pestered me until I all but reached the breaking point. In the end the principal had to caution them to let me alone, for fear I would throw up the sponge and walk out.

I had one more problem to settle before I could make my speech. I was the only boy in my class wearing short pants and I was grimly determined to leave school in long pants. Was I not going to work? Would I not be on my own? When my desire for long pants became known at home, yet another storm shook the house.

"You're trying to go too fast," my mother said.

"You're nothing but a child," Uncle Tom pronounced.

"He's beside himself," Granny said.

I served notice that I was making my own decisions from then on. I borrowed money from Mrs. Bibbs, my employer, made a down payment on a pearl-gray suit. If I could not pay for it, I would take the damn thing back after graduation.

On the night of graduation I was nervous and tense; I rose and faced the audience and my speech rolled out. When my voice stopped there was some applause. I did not care if they liked it or not; I was through. Immediately, even before I left the platform, I tried to shunt all memory of the event from me. A few of my classmates managed to shake my hand as I pushed toward the door, seeking the street. Somebody invited me to a party and I did not accept. I did not want to see any of them again. I walked home, saying to myself: The hell with it! With almost seventeen years of baffled living behind me, I faced the world in 1925.

9

My life now depended upon my finding work, and I was so anxious that I accepted the first offer, a job as a porter in a clothing store selling cheap goods to Negroes on credit. The shop was always crowded with black men and women pawing over cheap suits and dresses. And they paid whatever price the white man asked. The boss, his son, and the clerk treated the Negroes with open contempt, pushing, kicking, or slapping them. No matter how often I witnessed it, I could not get used to it. How can they accept it? I asked myself. I kept on edge, trying to stifle my feelings and never quite succeeding, a prey to guilt and fear because I felt that the boss suspected that I resented what I saw.

One morning, while I was polishing brass out front, the boss and his son drove up in their car. A frightened black woman sat between them. They got out and half dragged and half kicked the woman into the store. White people passed and looked on without expression. A white policeman watched from the corner, twirling his night stick; but he made no move. I watched out of the corner of my eyes, but I never slackened the strokes of my chamois upon the brass. After a moment or two I heard shrill screams coming from the rear room of the store; later the woman stumbled out, bleeding, crying, holding her stomach, her clothing torn. When she reached the sidewalk, the policeman met her, grabbed her, accused her of being drunk, called a patrol wagon and carted her away.

When I went to the rear of the store, the boss and his son were washing their hands at the sink. They looked at me and laughed uneasily. The floor was bloody, strewn with wisps of hair and clothing. My face must have reflected my shock, for the boss slapped me reassuringly on the back.

"Boy, that's what we do to niggers when they don't pay their bills," he said.

His son looked at me and grinned.

"Here, hava cigarette," he said.

Not knowing what to do, I took it. He lit his and held the match for me. This was a gesture of kindness, indicating that, even if they had beaten the black woman, they would not beat me if I knew enough to keep my mouth shut.

"Yes, sir," I said.

After they had gone, I sat on the edge of a packing box and stared at the bloody floor until the cigarette went out.

The store owned a bicycle which I used in delivering purchases. One day, while returning from the suburbs, my bicycle tire was punctured. I walked along the hot, dusty road, sweating and leading the bicycle by the handle bars.

A car slowed at my side.

"What's the matter there, boy?" a white man called.

I told him that my bicycle was broken and that I was walking back to town.

"That's too bad," he said. "Hop on the running board."

He stopped the car. I clutched hard at my bicycle with one hand and clung to the side of the car with the other.

"All set?"

"Yes, sir."

The car started. It was full of young white men. They were drinking. I watched the flask pass from mouth to mouth.

"Wanna drink, boy?" one asked.

The memory of my six-year-old drinking came back and filled me with caution. But I laughed, the wind whipping my face.

"Oh, no!" I said.

The words were barely out of my mouth before I felt something hard and cold smash me between the eyes. It was an empty whisky bottle. I saw stars, and fell backwards from the speeding car into the dust of the road, my feet becoming entangled in the steel spokes of the bicycle. The car stopped and the white men piled out and stood over me.

"Nigger, ain't you learned no better sense'n that yet?" asked the man who hit me. "Ain't you learned to say *sir* to a white man yet?"

Dazed, I pulled to my feet. My elbows and legs were bleeding. Fists doubled, the white man advanced, kicking the bicycle out of the way.

"Aw, leave the bastard alone. He's got enough," said one.

They stood looking at me. I rubbed my shins, trying to stop the flow of blood. No doubt they felt a sort of contemptuous pity, for one asked:

"You wanna ride to town now, nigger? You reckon you know enough to ride now?"

"I wanna walk," I said simply.

Maybe I sounded funny. They laughed.

"Well, walk, you black sonofabitch!"

Before they got back into their car, they comforted me with:

"Nigger, you sure ought to be glad it was us you talked to that way. You're a lucky bastard, 'cause if you'd said that to some other white man, you might've been a dead nigger now."

I was learning rapidly how to watch white people, to observe their every move, every fleeting expression, how to interpret what was said and what left unsaid.

Late one Saturday night I made some deliveries in a white neighborhood. I was pedaling my bicycle back to the store as fast as I could when a police car, swerving toward me, jammed me into the curbing.

"Get down, nigger, and put up your hands!" they ordered.

I did. They climbed out of the car, guns drawn, faces set, and advanced slowly.

"Keep still!" they ordered.

I reached my hands higher. They searched my pockets and

packages. They seemed dissatisfied when they could find nothing incriminating. Finally, one of them said:

"Boy, tell your boss not to send you out in white neighborhoods at this time of night."

"Yes, sir," I said.

I rode off, feeling that they might shoot at me, feeling that the pavement might disappear. It was like living in a dream, the reality of which might change at any moment.

Each day in the store I watched the brutality with growing hate, yet trying to keep my feelings from registering in my face. When the boss looked at me I would avoid his eyes. Finally the boss's son cornered me one morning.

"Say, nigger, look here," he began.

"Yes, sir."

"What's on your mind?"

"Nothing, sir," I said, trying to look amazed, trying to fool him.

"Why don't you laugh and talk like the other niggers?" he asked.

"Well, sir, there's nothing much to say or smile about," I said, smiling.

His face was hard, baffled; I knew that I had not convinced him. He whirled from me and went to the front of the store; he came back a moment later, his face red. He tossed a few green bills at me.

"I don't like your looks, nigger. Now, get!" he snapped.

I picked up the money and did not count it. I grabbed my hat and left.

I held a series of petty jobs for short periods, quitting some to work elsewhere, being driven off others because of my attitude, my speech, the look in my eyes. I was no nearer than ever to my goal of saving enough money to leave. At times I doubted if I could ever do it.

One jobless morning I went to my old classmate, Griggs, who worked for a Capitol Street jeweler. He was washing the windows of the store when I came upon him.

"Do you know where I can find a job?" I asked.

He looked at me with scorn.

"Yes, I know where you can find a job," he said, laughing.

"Where?"

"But I wonder if you can hold it," he said.

"What do you mean?" I asked. "Where's the job?"

"Take your time," he said. "You know, Dick, I know you. You've been trying to hold a job all summer, and you can't. Why? Because you're impatient. That's your big fault."

I said nothing, because he was repeating what I had already heard him say. He lit a cigarette and blew out smoke leisurely.

"Well," I said, egging him on to speak.

"I wish to hell I could talk to you," he said.

"I think I know what you want to tell me," I said.

He clapped me on the shoulder; his face was full of fear, hate, concern for me.

"Do you want to get killed?" he asked me.

"Hell, no!"

"Then, for God's sake, learn how to live in the South!"

"What do you mean?" I demanded. "Let white people tell me that. Why should you?"

"See?" he said triumphantly, pointing his finger at me. "There it is, *now!* It's in your face. You won't let people tell you things. You rush too much. I'm trying to help you and you won't let me." He paused and looked about; the streets were filled with white people. He spoke to me in a low, full tone. "Dick, look, you're black, black, *black,* see? Can't you understand that?"

"Sure. I understand it," I said.

"You don't act a damn bit like it," he spat.

He then reeled off an account of my actions on every job I had held that summer.

"How did you know that?" I asked.

"White people make it their business to watch niggers," he explained. "And they pass the word around. Now, my boss is a Yankee and he tells me things. You're marked already."

Could I believe him? Was it true? How could I ever learn this strange world of white people?

"Then tell me how must I act?" I asked humbly. "I just want to make enough money to leave."

"Wait and I'll tell you," he said.

At that moment a woman and two men stepped from the jewelry store; I moved to one side to let them pass, my mind intent upon Grigg's words. Suddenly Griggs reached for my arm and jerked me violently, sending me stumbling three or four feet across the pavement. I whirled.

"What's the matter with you?" I asked.

Griggs glared at me, then laughed.

"I'm teaching you how to get out of white people's way," he said.

I looked at the people who had come out of the store; yes, they were *white*, but I had not noticed it.

"Do you see what I mean?" he asked. "White people want you out of their way." He pronounced the words slowly so that they would sink into my mind.

"I know what you mean," I breathed.

"Dick, I'm treating you like a brother," he said. "You act around white people as if you didn't know that they were white. And they *see* it."

"Oh, Christ, I can't be a slave," I said hopelessly.

"But you've got to eat," he said.

"Yes, I got to eat."

"Then start acting like it," he hammered at me, pounding his fist in his palm. "When you're in front of white people, *think* before you act, *think* before you speak. Your way of doing things is all right among *our* people, but not for *white* people. They won't stand for it."

I stared bleakly into the morning sun. I was nearing my seventeenth birthday and I was wondering if I would ever be free of this plague. What Griggs was saying was true, but it was simply utterly impossible for me to calculate, to scheme, to act, to plot all the time. I would remember to dissemble for short periods, then I would forget and act straight and human again, not with the desire to harm anybody, but merely forgetting the artificial status of race and class. It was the same with whites as with blacks; it was my way with everybody. I sighed, looking at the glittering diamonds in the store window, the rings and the neat rows of golden watches.

"I guess you're right," I said at last. "I've got to watch myself, break myself . . ."

"No," he said quickly, feeling guilty now. Someone—a white man—went into the store and we paused in our talk. "You know, Dick, you may think I'm an Uncle Tom, but I'm not. I hate these white people, hate 'em with all my heart. But I can't show it; if I did, they'd kill me." He paused and looked around to see if there were any white people within hearing distance. "Once I heard an old drunk nigger say:

> *All these white folks dressed so fine*
> *Their ass-holes smell just like mine . . ."*

I laughed uneasily, looking at the white faces that passed me. But Griggs, when he laughed, covered his mouth with his hand and bent at the knees, a gesture which was unconsciously meant to conceal his excessive joy in the presence of whites.

"That's how I feel about 'em," he said proudly after he had finished his spasm of glee. He grew sober. "There's an optical company upstairs and the boss is a Yankee from Illinois. Now, he wants a boy to work all day in summer, mornings and evenings in winter. He wants to break a colored boy into the optical trade. You know algebra and you're just cut out for the work. I'll tell Mr. Crane about you and I'll get in touch with you."

"Do you suppose I could see him now?" I asked.

"For God's sake, take your *time!*" he thundered at me.

"Maybe that's what's wrong with Negroes," I said. "They take too much time."

I laughed, but he was disturbed. I thanked him and left. For a week I did not hear from him and I gave up hope. Then one afternoon Griggs came to my house.

"It looks like you've got a job," he said. "You're going to have a chance to learn a trade. But remember to keep your head. Remember you're black. You start tomorrow."

"What will I get?"

"Five dollars a week to start with; they'll raise you if they like you," he explained.

My hopes soared. Things were not quite so bad, after all. I would have a chance to learn a trade. And I need not give up school. I told him that I would take the job, that I would be humble.

"You'll be working for a Yankee and you ought to get along," he said.

The next morning I was outside the office of the optical company long before it opened. I was reminding myself that I must be polite, must think before I spoke, must think before I acted, must say "yes sir, no sir," that I must so conduct myself that white people would not think that I thought I was as good as they. Suddenly a white man came up to me.

"What do you want?" he asked me.

"I'm reporting for a job, sir," I said.

"O.K. Come on."

I followed him up a flight of steps and he unlocked the door of the office. I was a little tense, but the young white man's manner put me at ease and I sat and held my hat in my hand. A white girl came and began punching the typewriter. Soon another white man, thin and gray, entered and went into the rear room. Finally a tall, red-faced white man arrived, shot me a quick glance and sat at his desk. His brisk manner branded him a Yankee.

"You're the new boy, eh?"

"Yes, sir."

"Let me get my mail out of the way and I'll talk with you," he said pleasantly.

"Yes, sir."

I even pitched my voice to a low plane, trying to rob it of any suggestion or overtone of aggressiveness.

Half an hour later Mr. Crane called me to his desk and questioned me closely about my schooling, about how much mathematics I had had. He seemed pleased when I told him that I had had two years of algebra.

"How would you like to learn this trade?" he asked.

"I'd like it fine, sir. I'd like nothing better," I said.

He told me that he wanted to train a Negro boy in the optical trade; he wanted to help him, guide him. I tried to answer in a way that would let him know that I would try to be worthy of what he was doing. He took me to the stenographer and said:

"This is Richard. He's going to be with us."

He then led me into the rear room of the office, which turned out to be a tiny factory filled with many strange machines smeared with red dust.

"Reynolds," he said to a young white man, "this is Richard."

"What you saying there, boy!" Reynolds grinned and boomed at me.

Mr. Crane took me to the older man.

"Pease, this is Richard, who'll work with us."

Pease looked at me and nodded. Mr. Crane then held forth to the two white men about my duties; he told them to break me in gradually to the workings of the shop, to instruct me in the mechanics of grinding and polishing lenses. They nodded their assent.

"Now, boy, let's see how clean you can get this place," Mr. Crane said.

"Yes, sir."

I swept, mopped, dusted, and soon had the office and the shop clean. In the afternoons, when I had caught up with my work, I ran errands. In an idle moment I would stand and watch the two white men grinding lenses on the machines. They said nothing to me and I said nothing to them. The first day passed, the second, the third, a week passed and I received my five dollars. A month passed. But I was not learning anything and nobody had volunteered to help me. One afternoon I walked up to Reynolds and asked him to tell me about the work.

"What are you trying to do, get smart, nigger?" he asked me.

"No, sir," I said.

I was baffled. Perhaps he just did not want to help me. I went to Pease, reminding him that the boss had said that I was to be given a chance to learn the trade.

"Nigger, you think you're white, don't you?"

"No, sir."

"You're acting mighty like it," he said.

"I was only doing what the boss told me to do," I said.

Pease shook his fist in my face.

"This is a *white* man's work around here," he said.

From then on they changed toward me; they said good morning no more. When I was just a bit slow in performing some duty, I was called a lazy black sonofabitch. I kept silent, striving to offer no excuse for worsening of relations. But one day Reynolds called me to his machine.

"Richard, how long is your thing?" he asked me.

"What thing?" I asked.

"You know what I mean," he said. "The thing the bull uses on the cow."

I turned away from him; I had heard that whites regarded Negroes as animals in sex matters and his words made me angry.

"I heard that a nigger can stick his prick in the ground and spin around on it like a top," he said, chuckling. "I'd like to see you do that. I'd give you a dime, if you did it."

I ignored him. Mr. Pease was watching me closely; then I saw them exchange glances. My job was not leading to what Mr. Crane had said it would. I had been humble, and now I was reaping the wages of humility.

"Come here, boy," Pease said.

I walked to his bench.

"You didn't like what Reynolds just said, did you?" he asked.

"Oh, it's all right," I said smiling.

"You didn't like it. I could see it on your face," he said.

I stared at him and backed away.

"Did you ever get into any trouble?" he asked.

"No, sir."

"What would you do if you got into trouble?"

"I don't know, sir."

"Well, watch yourself and don't get into trouble," he warned.

I wanted to report these clashes to Mr. Crane, but the thought of what Pease or Reynolds would do to me if they learned that I had "snitched" stopped me. I worked through the days and tried to hide my resentment under a nervous, cryptic smile.

The climax came at noon one summer day. Pease called me to his workbench; to get to him I had to go between two narrow benches and stand with my back against a wall.

"Richard, I want to ask you something," Pease began pleasantly, not looking up from his work.

"Yes, sir."

Reynolds came over and stood blocking the narrow passage between the benches; he folded his arms and stared at me solemnly. I looked from one to the other, sensing trouble. Pease looked up and spoke slowly, so there would be no possibility of my not understanding.

"Richard, Reynolds here tells me that you called me Pease," he said.

I stiffened. A void opened up in me. I knew that this was the showdown.

He meant that I had failed to call him Mr. Pease. I looked at Reynolds; he was gripping a steel bar in his hand. I opened my mouth to speak, to protest, to assure Pease that I had never called him simply *Pease,* and that I had never had any intention of doing so, when Reynolds grabbed me by the collar, ramming my head against a wall.

"Now, be careful, nigger," snarled Reynolds, baring his teeth. "I heard you call 'im *Pease.* And if you say you didn't, you're calling me a liar, see?" He waved the steel bar threateningly.

If I had said: No, sir, Mr. Pease, I never called you *Pease,* I would by inference have been calling Reynolds a liar; and if I had said: Yes, sir, Mr. Pease, I called you *Pease,* I would have been pleading guilty to the worst insult that a Negro can offer to a southern white man. I stood trying to think of a neutral course that would resolve this quickly risen nightmare, but my tongue would not move.

"Richard, I asked you a question!" Pease said. Anger was creeping into his voice.

"I don't remember calling you *Pease*, Mr. Pease," I said cautiously. "And if I did, I sure didn't mean . . ."

"You black sonofabitch! You called me *Pease*, then!" he spat, rising and slapping me till I bent sideways over a bench.

Reynolds was up on top of me demanding:

"Didn't you call him *Pease*? If you say you didn't, I'll rip your gut string loose with this f–k–g bar, you black granny dodger! You can't call a white man a liar and get away with it!"

I wilted. I begged them not to hit me. I knew what they wanted. They wanted me to leave the job.

"I'll leave," I promised. "I'll leave right now!"

They gave me a minute to get out of the factory, and warned me not to show up again or tell the boss. Reynolds loosened his hand on my collar and I ducked out of the room. I did not see Mr. Crane or the stenographer in the office. Pease and Reynolds had so timed it that Mr. Crane and the stenographer would be out when they turned on the terror. I went to the street and waited for the boss to return. I saw Griggs wiping glass shelves in the jewelry store and I beckoned to him. He came out and I told him what had happened.

"Then what are you standing there like a fool for?" he demanded. "Won't you ever learn? Get home! They might come down!"

I walked down Capitol Street feeling that the sidewalk was unreal, that I was unreal, that the people were unreal, yet expecting somebody to demand to know what right I had to be on the streets. My wound went deep; I felt that I had been slapped out of the human race. When I reached home, I did not tell the family what had happened; I merely told them that I had quit, that I was not making enough money, that I was seeking another job.

That night Griggs came to my house; we went for a walk.

"You got a goddamn tough break," he said.

"Can you say it was my fault?" I asked.

He shook his head.

"Well, what about your goddamn philosophy of meekness?" I asked him bitterly.

"These things just happen," he said, shrugging.

"They owe me money," I said.

"That's what I came about," he said. "Mr. Crane wants you to come in at ten in the morning. Ten sharp, now, mind you, because he'll be there and those guys won't gang up on you again."

The next morning at ten I crept up the stairs and peered into the office of the optical shop to make sure that Mr. Crane was in. He was at his desk. Pease and Reynolds were at their machines in the rear.

"Come in, Richard," Mr. Crane said.

I pulled off my hat and walked into the office; I stood before him.

"Sit down," he said.

I sat. He stared at me and shook his head.

"Tell me, what happened?"

An impulse to speak rose in me and died with the realization that I was facing a wall that I would never breech. I tried to speak several times and could make no sounds. I grew tense and tears burnt my cheeks.

"Now, just keep control of yourself," Mr. Crane said.

I clenched my fists and managed to talk.

"I tried to do my best here," I said.

"I believe you," he said. "But I want to know what happened. Which one bothered you?"

"Both of 'em," I said.

Reynolds came running to the door and I rose. Mr. Crane jumped to his feet.

"Get back in there," he told Reynolds.

"That nigger's lying!" Reynolds said. "I'll kill 'im if he lies on me!"

"Get back in there or get out," Mr. Crane said.

Reynolds backed away, keeping his eyes on me.

"Go ahead," Mr. Crane said. "Tell me what happened."

Then again I could not speak. What could I accomplish by telling him? I was black; I lived in the South. I would never learn to operate those machines as long as those two white men in there stood by them. Anger and fear welled in me as I felt what I had missed; I leaned forward and clapped my hands to my face.

"No, no, now," Mr. Crane said. "Keep control of yourself. No matter what happens, keep control . . ."

"I know," I said in a voice not my own. "There's no use of my saying anything."

"Do you want to work here?" he asked me.

I looked at the white faces of Pease and Reynolds; I imagined their waylaying me, killing me. I was remembering what had happened to Ned's brother.

"No, sir," I breathed.

"Why?"

"I'm scared," I said. "They would kill me."

Mr. Crane turned and called Pease and Reynolds into the office.

"Now, tell me which one bothered you. Don't be afraid. Nobody's going to hurt you," Mr. Crane said.

I stared ahead of me and did not answer. He waved the men inside. The white stenographer looked at me with wide eyes and I felt drenched in shame, naked to my soul. The whole of my being felt violated, and I knew that my own fear had helped to violate it. I was breathing hard and struggling to master my feelings.

"Can I get my money, sir?" I asked at last.

"Just sit a minute and take hold of yourself," he said.

I waited and my roused senses grew slowly calm.

"I'm awfully sorry about this," he said.

"I had hoped for a lot from this job," I said. "I'd wanted to go to school, to college . . ."

"I know," he said. "But what are you going to do now?"

My eyes traveled over the office, but I was not seeing.

"I'm going away," I said.

"What do you mean?"

"I'm going to get out of the South," I breathed.

"Maybe that's best," he said. "I'm from Illinois. Even for me, it's hard here. I can do just so much."

He handed me my money, more than I had earned for the week. I thanked him and rose to leave. He rose. I went into the hallway and he followed me. He reached out his hand.

"It's tough for you down here," he said.

I barely touched his hand. I walked swiftly down the hall, fighting against crying again. I ran down the steps, then paused and looked back up. He was standing at the head of the stairs, shaking his head. I went into the sunshine and walked home like a blind man.

10

For weeks after that I could not believe in my feelings. My personality was numb, reduced to a lumpish, loose, dissolved state. I was a non-man, something that knew vaguely that it was human but felt that it was not. As time separated me from the experience, I could feel no hate for the men who had driven me from the job. They did not seem to be individual men, but part of a huge, implacable, elemental design toward which hate was futile. What I did feel was a longing to attack. But how? And because I knew of no way to grapple with this thing, I felt doubly cast out.

I went to bed tired and got up tired, though I was having no physical exercise. During the day I overreacted to each event, my banked emotions spilling around it. I refused to talk to anyone about my affairs, because I knew that I would only hear a justification of the ways of the white folks and I did not want to hear it. I lived carrying a huge wound, tender, festering, and I shrank when I came near anything that I thought would touch it.

But I had to work because I had to eat. My next job was that of a helper in a drugstore, and the night before I reported for work I fought with myself, telling myself that I had to master this thing, that my life depended upon it. Other black people worked, got along somehow, then I must, *must,* MUST get along until I could get my hands on enough money to leave. I would make myself fit in. Others had done it. I would do it. I had to do it.

I went to the job apprehensive, resolving to watch my every move. I swept the sidewalk, pausing when a white person was twenty feet away. I mopped the store, cautiously waiting for the white people to move out of my way in their own good time. I cleaned acres of glass shelving, changing my tempo now to work faster, holding every nuance of reality within the focus of my consciousness. Noon came and the store was crowded; people jammed to the counters for food. A white man behind the counter ran up to me and shouted:

"A jug of Coca-Cola, quick, boy!"

My body jerked taut and I stared at him. He stared at me.

"What's wrong with you?"

"Nothing," I said.

"Well, move! Don't stand there gaping!"

Even if I had tried, I could not have told him what was wrong. My sustained expectation of violence had exhausted me. My preoccupation with curbing my impulses, my speech, my movements, my manner, my expressions had increased my anxiety. I became forgetful, concentrating too much upon trivial tasks. The men began to yell at me and that made it worse. One day I dropped a jug of orange syrup in the middle of the floor. The boss was furious. He caught my arm and jerked me into the back of the drugstore. His face was livid. I expected him to hit me. I was braced to defend myself.

"I'm going to deduct that from your pay, you black bastard!" he yelled.

Words had come instead of blows and I relaxed.

"Yes, sir," I said placatingly. "It was my fault."

My tone whipped him to a frenzy.

"You goddamn right it was!" he yelled louder.

"I'm new at this," I mumbled, realizing that I had said the wrong thing, though I had been striving to say the right.

"We're only trying you out," he warned me.

"Yes, sir. I understand," I said.

He stared at me, speechless with rage. Why could I not learn to keep my mouth shut at the right time? I had said just one short sentence too many. My words were innocent enough, but they indicated, it seemed, a consciousness on my part that infuriated white people.

Saturday night came and the boss gave me my money and snapped: "Don't come back. You won't do."

I knew what was wrong with me, but I could not correct it. The words and actions of white people were baffling signs to me. I was living in a culture and not a civilization and I could learn how that culture worked only by living with it. Misreading the reactions of whites around me made me say and do the wrong things. In my dealing with whites I was conscious of the entirety of my relations with them, and they were conscious only of what was happening at a given moment. I had to keep remembering what others took for granted; I had to think out what others felt.

I had begun coping with the white world too late. I could not make subservience an automatic part of my behavior. I had to feel and think out each tiny item of racial experience in the light of the whole race problem, and to each item I brought the whole of my life. While standing before a white man I had to figure out how to perform each act and how to say each word. I could not help it. I could not grin. In the past I had always said too much, now I found that it was difficult to say anything at all. I could not react as the world in which I lived expected me to; that world was too baffling, too uncertain.

I was idle for weeks. The summer waned. Hope for school was now definitely gone. Autumn came and many of the boys who held jobs returned to school. Jobs were now numerous. I heard that hallboys were needed at one of the hotels, the hotel in which Ned's brother had lost his life. Should I go there? Would I, too, make a fatal slip? But I had to earn money. I applied and was accepted to mop long white tiled hallways that stretched around the entire perimeter of the office floors of the building. I reported each night at ten, got a huge pail of water, a bushel of soap flakes and, with a gang of moppers, I worked. All the boys were Negroes and I was happy; at least I could talk, joke, laugh, sing, say what I pleased.

I began to marvel at how smoothly the black boys acted out

the roles that the white race had mapped out for them. Most of them were not conscious of living a special, separate, stunted way of life. Yet I knew that in some period of their growing up—a period that they had no doubt forgotten—there had been developed in them a delicate, sensitive controlling mechanism that shut off their minds and emotions from all that the white race had said was taboo. Although they lived in an America where in theory there existed equality of opportunity, they knew unerringly what to aspire to and what not to aspire to. Had a black boy announced that he aspired to be a writer, he would have been unhesitatingly called crazy by his pals. Or had a black boy spoken of yearning to get a seat on the New York Stock Exchange, his friends—in the boy's own interest—would have reported his odd ambition to the white boss.

There was a pale-yellow boy who had gonorrhea and was proud of it.

"Say," he asked me one night, "you ever have the clap?"

"God, no," I said. "Why do you ask?"

"I got it," he said matter-of-factly. "I thought you could tell me something to use."

"Haven't you been to a doctor?" I asked.

"Aw, hell. Them doctors ain't no good."

"Don't be foolish," I said.

"What's the matter with you?" he demanded of me. "You talk like you'd be 'shamed of the clap."

"I would," I said.

"Hell, you ain't a man 'less you done had it three times," he said.

"Don't brag about it," I said.

"'Tain't nothing worse'n a bad cold," he said.

But I noticed that when he urinated he would grab hold of a steam pipe, a doorjamb, or a window sill and strain with tear-filled eyes and a tortured face, as though he were attempting to lift the hotel up from its foundations. I laughed to cover my disgust.

When I was through mopping, I would watch the never-ending crap games that went on in the lockers, but I could never become interested enough to participate. Gambling had never appealed to me. I could not conceive of any game holding more risks than the life I was living. Curses and sex stories sounded round the clock and blue smoke choked the air. I would sit listening for hours, wondering how on earth they could laugh so freely, trying to grasp the miracle that gave their debased lives the semblance of a human existence.

Several Negro girls were employed as maids in the hotel, some of whom I knew. One night when I was about to go home I saw a girl who lived in my direction and I fell in beside her to walk part of the distance together. As we passed the white night watchman, he slapped her playfully on her buttocks. I turned around, amazed. The girl twisted out of his reach, tossed her head saucily, and went down the hallway. I had not moved from my tracks.

"Nigger, you look like you don't like what I did," he said.

I could not move or speak. My immobility must have seemed a challenge to him, for he pulled his gun.

"Don't you like it, nigger?"

"Yes, sir," I whispered with a dry throat.

"Well, talk like it, then, goddammit!"

"Oh, yes, sir!" I said with as much heartiness as I could muster.

I walked down the hall, knowing that the gun was pointed at me, but afraid to look back. When I was out of the door, my throat felt as though it were swelling and bursting with fire. The girl was waiting for me. I walked past her. She caught up with me.

"God, how could you let him do that?" I exploded.

"It don't matter. They do that all the time," she said.

"I wanted to do something," I said.

"You woulda been a fool if you had," she said.

"But how must you feel?"

"They never get any further with us than that, if we don't want 'em to," she said dryly.

"Yes, I would've been a fool," I said, but she did not catch the point.

I was afraid to go to work the following night. What would the watchman think? Would he decide to teach me a lesson? I walked slowly through the door, wondering if he would continue his threat. His eyes looked at and through me. Evidently he considered the matter closed, or else he had had so many experiences of that kind that he had already forgotten it.

Out of my salary I had begun to save a few dollars, for my determination to leave had not lessened. But I found the saving exasperatingly slow. I pondered continuously ways of making money, and the only ways that I could think of involved transgressions of the law. No, I must not do that, I told myself. To go to jail in the South would mean the end. And there was the possibility that if I were ever caught I would never reach jail.

This was the first time in my life that I had ever consciously entertained the idea of violating the laws of the land. I had felt that my intelligence and industry could cope with all situations, and, until that time, I had never stolen a penny from anyone. Even hunger had never driven me to appropriate what was not my own. The mere idea of stealing had been repugnant. I had not been honest from deliberate motives, but being dishonest had simply never occurred to me.

Yet, all about me, Negroes were stealing. More than once I had been called a "dumb nigger" by black boys who discovered that I had not availed myself of a chance to snatch some petty piece of white property that had been carelessly left within my reach.

"How in hell you gonna git ahead?" I had been asked when I had said that one ought not steal.

I knew that the boys in the hotel filched whatever they could. I knew that Griggs, my friend who worked in the Capitol Street jewelry store, was stealing regularly and successfully. I knew that a black neighbor of mine was stealing bags of grain from a wholesale house where he worked, though he was a stanch deacon in his church and prayed and sang on Sundays. I knew that the black girls who worked in white homes stole food daily to supplement their scanty wages. And I knew that the very nature of black and white relations bred this constant thievery.

No Negroes in my environment had ever thought of organizing, no matter in how orderly a fashion, and petitioning their white employers for higher wages. The very thought would have been terrifying to them, and they knew that the whites would have retaliated with swift brutality. So, pretending to conform to the laws of the whites, grinning, bowing, they let their fingers stick to what they could touch. And the whites seemed to like it.

But I, who stole nothing, who wanted to look them straight in the face, who wanted to talk and act like a man, inspired fear in them. The southern whites would rather have had Negroes who stole, work for them than Negroes who knew, however dimly, the worth of their own humanity. Hence, whites placed a premium upon black deceit; they encouraged irresponsibility; and their rewards were bestowed upon us blacks in the degree that we could make them feel safe and superior.

My objections to stealing were not moral. I did not approve of it because I knew that, in the long run, it was futile, that it was not an effective way to alter one's relationship to one's environment. Then, how could I change my relationship to my environment? Almost my entire salary went to feed the eternally hungry stomachs at home. If I saved a dollar a week, it would take me two years to amass a hundred dollars, the amount which for some reason I had decided was necessary to stake me in a strange city. And, God knows, anything could happen to me in two years . . .

I did not know when I would be thrown into a situation where I would say the wrong word to the wrong white man and find myself in trouble. And, above all, I wanted to avoid trouble, for I feared that if I clashed with whites I would lose control of my emotions and spill out words that would be my sentence of death. Time was not on my side and I had to make some move. Often, when perplexed, I longed to be like the smiling, lazy, forgetful black boys in the noisy hotel locker rooms, with no torrential conflicts to resolve. Many times I grew weary of the secret burden I carried and longed to cast it down, either in action or in resignation. But I was not made to be a resigned man and I had only a limited choice of actions, and I was afraid of all of them.

A new anxiety was created in me by my desire to leave quickly. I had now seen at close quarters the haughty white men who made the laws; I had seen how they acted, how they regarded black people, how they regarded me; and I no longer felt bound by the laws which white and black were supposed to obey in common. I was outside those laws; the white people had told me so. Now when I thought of ways to escape from my environment I no longer felt the inner restraint that would have made stealing impossible, and this new freedom made me lonely and afraid.

My feelings became divided; in spite of myself I would dream of a locked cupboard in a near-by neighbor's house where a gun was kept. If I stole it, how much would it bring? When the yearning to leave would become strong in me, I could not keep out of my mind the image of a storehouse at a near-by Negro college that held huge cans of preserved fruits. Yet fear kept me from making any move; the idea of stealing floated tentatively in me. My inability to adjust myself to the white world had already shattered a part of the structure of my personality and had broken down the inner barriers to crime; the only thing that now stood in the way was lack of immediate opportunity, a final push of circumstance. And that came.

I was promoted to bellboy, which meant a small increase in income. But I soon learned that the substantial money came from bootlegging liquor to the white prostitutes in the hotel. The other bellboys were taking these risks, and I fell in. I learned how to walk past a white policeman with contraband upon my hip, sauntering, whistling like a nigger ought to whistle when he is innocent. The extra dollars were coming in, but slowly. How, how, how could I get my hands on more money before I was caught and sent to jail for some trivial misdemeanor? If I were going to violate the law, then I ought to get something out of it. My larcenous aims were modest. A hundred dollars would give me, temporarily, more freedom of movement than I had ever known in my life. I watched and waited, living with the thought.

While waiting for my chance to grab and run, I grew used to seeing the white prostitutes naked upon their beds, sitting nude about their rooms, and I learned new modes of behavior, new rules in how to live the Jim Crow life. It was presumed that we black boys took their nakedness for granted, that it startled us no more than a blue vase or a red rug. Our presence awoke in them no sense of shame whatever, for we blacks were not considered human anyway. If they were alone, I would steal sidelong glances at them. But if they were receiving men, not a flicker of my eyelids would show.

A huge, snowy-skinned blonde took a room on my floor. One night she rang for service and I went to wait upon her. She was in bed with a thickset man; both were nude and uncovered. She said that she wanted some liquor, and slid out of bed and waddled across the floor to get her money from the dresser drawer. Without realizing it, I watched her.

"Nigger, what in hell are you looking at?" the white man asked, raising himself upon his elbows.

"Nothing, sir," I answered, looking suddenly miles deep into the blank wall of the room.

"Keep your eyes where they belong if you want to be healthy!"

"Yes, sir."

I would have continued at the hotel until I left had not a short-cut presented itself. One of the boys at the hotel whispered to me one night that the only local Negro movie house wanted a boy to take tickets at the door.

"You ain't never been in jail, is you?" he asked me.

"Not yet," I answered.

"Then you can get the job," he said. "I'd take it, but I done six months and they know me."

"What's the catch?"

"The girl who sells tickets is using a system," he explained. "If you get the job, you can make some good gravy."

If I stole, I would have a chance to head northward quickly; if I remained barely honest, piddling with pints of bootleg liquor, I merely prolonged my stay, increased my chances of being caught, exposed myself to the possibility of saying the wrong word or doing the wrong thing and paying a penalty that I dared not think of. The temptation to venture into crime was too strong, and I decided to work quickly, taking whatever was in sight, amass a wad of money, and flee. I knew that others had tried it before me and had failed, but I was hoping to be lucky.

My chances for getting the job were good; I had no past record of stealing or violating the laws. When I presented myself to the Jewish proprietor of the movie house I was immediately accepted. The next day I reported for duty and began taking tickets. The boss man warned me:

"Now, look, I'll be honest with you if you'll be honest with me. I don't know who's honest around this joint and who isn't. But if *you* are honest, then the rest are bound to be. All tickets will pass through your hands. There can be no stealing unless you steal."

I gave him a pledge of my honesty, feeling absolutely no qualms about what I intended to do. He was white, and I could never do to him what he and his kind had done to me. Therefore, I reasoned, stealing was not a violation of my ethics, but of his; I felt that things were rigged in his favor and any action I took to circumvent his scheme of life was justified. Yet I had not convinced myself.

During the first afternoon the Negro girl in the ticket office watched me closely and I knew that she was sizing me up, trying to determine when it would be safe to break me into her graft. I waited, leaving it to her to make the first move.

I was supposed to drop each ticket that I took from a customer into a metal receptacle. Occasionally the boss would go to the ticket window and look at the serial number on the roll of unsold tickets and then compare that number with the number on the last ticket I had dropped into the receptacle. The boss continued his watchfulness for a few days, then began to observe me from across the street; finally he absented himself for long intervals.

A tension as high as that I had known when the white men had driven me from the job at the optician's returned to live in me. But I had learned to master a great deal of tension now; I had developed, slowly and painfully, a capacity to contain it within myself without betraying it in any way. Had this not been true, the mere thought of stealing, the risks involved, the inner distress would have so upset me that I would have been in no state of mind to calculate coldly, would have made me so panicky that I would have been afraid to steal at all. But my inner resistance had been blasted. I felt that I had been emotionally cast out of the world, had been made to live outside the normal processes of life, had been conditioned in feeling *against* something daily, had become accustomed to living on the side of those who watched and waited.

While I was eating supper in a near-by café one night, a strange Negro man walked in and sat beside me.

"Hello, Richard," he said.

"Hello," I said. "I don't think I know you."

"But I know *you*," he said, smiling.

Was he one of the boss's spies?

"How do you know me?" I asked.

"I'm Tel's friend," he said, naming the girl who sold the tickets at the movie.

I looked at him searchingly. Was he telling me the truth? Or was he trying to trap me for the boss? I was already thinking and feeling like a criminal, distrusting everybody.

"We start tonight," he said.

"What?" I asked, still not admitting that I knew what he was talking about.

"Don't be scared. The boss trusts you. He's gone to see some friends. Somebody's watching him and if he starts back to the movie, they'll phone us," he said.

I could not eat my food. It lay cold upon the plate and sweat ran down from my armpits.

"It'll work this way," he explained in a low, smooth tone. "A guy'll come to you and ask for a match. You give him five tickets that you'll hold out of the box, see? We'll give you the signal when to start holding out. The guy'll give the tickets to Tel; she'll resell them all at once, when a crowd is buying at the rush hour. You get it?"

I did not answer. I knew that if I were caught I would go to the chain gang. But was not my life already a kind of chain gang? What, really, did I have to lose?

"Are you with us?" he asked.

I still did not answer. He rose and clapped me on the shoulder and left. I trembled as I went back to the theater. Anything might happen, but I was used to that. Had I not felt that same sensation when I lay on the ground and the white men towered over me, telling me that I was a lucky nigger? Had I not felt it when I walked home from the optical company that morning with my job gone? Had I not felt it when I walked down the hallway of the hotel with the night watchman pointing a gun at my back? Had I not felt it all a million times before? I took the tickets with sweaty fingers. I waited. I was gambling: freedom or the chain gang. There were times when I felt that I could not breathe. I looked up and down the street; the boss was not in sight. Was this a trap? If it were, I would disgrace my family. Would not all of them say that my attitude had been leading to this all along? Would they not rake up the past and find clues that had led to my fate?

The man I had met in the café came through the door and put a ticket in my hand.

"There's a crowd at the box office," he whispered. "Save ten, not five. Start with this one."

Well, here goes, I thought. He gave me the ticket and sat looking at the moving shadows upon the screen. I held on to the ticket and my body grew tense, hot as fire; but I was used to that too. Time crawled through the cells of my brain. My muscles ached. I discovered that crime means suffering. The crowd came in and gave me more tickets. I kept ten of them tucked into my moist palm. No sooner had the crowd thinned than a black boy with a cigarette jutting from his mouth came up to me.

"Gotta match?"

With a slow movement I gave him the tickets. He went out and I kept the door cracked and watched. He went to the ticket office and laid down a coin and I saw him slip the tickets to the girl. Yes, the boy was honest. The girl shot me a quick smile and I went back inside. A few moments later the same tickets were handed to me by other customers.

We worked it for a week and after the money was split four ways, I had fifty dollars. Freedom was almost within my grasp. Ought I risk any more? I dropped the hint to Tel's friend that maybe I would quit; it was a casual hint to test him out. He grew

violently angry and I quickly consented to stay, fearing that someone might turn me in for revenge, or to get me out of the way so
that another and more pliable boy could have my place. I was dealing with cagey people and I would be cagey.

I went through another week. Late one night I resolved to
make that week the last. The gun in the neighbor's house came to
my mind, and the cans of fruit preserves in the storehouse of the
college. If I stole them and sold them, I would have enough to tide
me over in Memphis until I could get a job, work, save, and go
north. I crept from bed and found the neighbor's house empty. I
looked about; all was quiet. My heart beat so fast that it ached. I
forced a window with a screwdriver and entered and took the gun;
I slipped it in my shirt and returned home. When I took it out to
look at it, it was wet with sweat. I pawned it under an assumed
name.

The following night I rounded up two boys whom I knew to
be ready for adventure. We broke into the college storehouse and
lugged out cans of fruit preserves and sold them to restaurants.

Meanwhile I bought clothes, shoes, a cardboard suitcase, all of
which I hid at home. Saturday night came and I sent word to the
boss that I was sick. Uncle Tom was upstairs. Granny and Aunt
Addie were at church. My brother was sleeping. My mother sat in
her rocking chair, humming to herself. I packed my suitcase and
went to her.

"Mama, I'm going away," I whispered.

"Oh, no," she protested.

"I've got to, mama. I can't live this way."

"You're not running away from something you've done?"

"I'll send for you, mama. I'll be all right."

"Take care of yourself. And send for me quickly. I'm not happy
here," she said.

"I'm sorry for all these long years, mama. But I could not have
helped it."

I kissed her and she cried.

"Be quiet, mama. I'm all right."

I went out the back way and walked a quarter of a mile to the railroad tracks. It began to rain as I tramped down the crossties toward town. I reached the station soaked to the skin. I bought my ticket, then went hurriedly to the corner of the block in which the movie house stood. Yes, the boss was there, taking the tickets himself. I returned to the station and waited for my train, my eyes watching the crowd.

An hour later I was sitting in a Jim Crow coach, speeding northward, making the first lap of my journey to a land where I could live with a little less fear. Slowly the burden I had carried for many months lifted somewhat. My cheeks itched and when I scratched them I found tears. In that moment I understood the pain that accompanied crime and I hoped that I would never have to feel it again. I never did feel it again, for I never stole again; and what kept me from it was the knowledge that, for me, crime carried its own punishment.

Well, it's my life, I told myself. I'll see now what I can make of it . . .

11

I arrived in Memphis on a cold November Sunday morning, in 1925,
and lugged my suitcase down quiet, empty sidewalks through winter sunshine. I found Beale Street, the street that I had been told
was filled with danger: pickpockets, prostitutes, cutthroats, and
black confidence men. After walking several blocks, I saw a big
frame house with a sign in the window: ROOMS. I slowed, wondering if it was a rooming house or a whorehouse. I had heard of the
foolish blunders that small-town boys made when they went to big
cities and I wanted to be very cautious. I walked past the house to
the end of the block, then turned and walked slowly past it again.
Well, whatever it was, I would stay in it for a day or two, until I
found something I was certain of. I had nothing valuable in my
suitcase. My money was strapped to my body; in order for anyone
to get it, they would have to kill me.

I walked up the steps and was about to ring the bell when I saw
a big mulatto woman staring at me through the window. Oh, hell, I
thought. This *is* a whorehouse . . . I stopped. The woman smiled. I
turned around and went back down the walk. As I neared the
street, I looked back in time to see the woman's face leave the window. A moment later she appeared in the doorway.

"Come here, boy!" she called to me.

I hesitated. Goddamn, I've run into a whore right off . . .

"Come here, boy," she commanded loudly. "I'm not going to hurt you."

I turned and walked slowly toward her.

"Come inside," she said.

I stared at her a moment, then stepped into a warm hallway. The woman smiled, turned on a light, and looked at me from my head to my feet.

"How come you was walking past this house so many times?" she asked.

"I was looking for a room," I said.

"Didn't you see the sign?"

"Yes, ma'am."

"Then how come you didn't come in?"

"Well, I don't know. You see, I'm a stranger here . . ."

"Lord, and don't I know it!" She dropped heavily into a chair and went into a gale of laughter that made her big bosom shake as though it were going to fly off. "Anybody could tell that." She gasped, giggled, and grew quiet. She said: "I'm Mrs. Moss."

I told her my name.

"That's a real nice name," she said after a moment's serious thought.

I blinked. What the hell kind of place was this? And who was this woman? I stood with my suitcase in my hand, poised to leave.

"Boy, Lord, this ain't no whorehouse," she said at last. "Folks get the craziest notions about Beale Street. I own this place; this is my home. I'm a church member. I got a daughter seventeen years old, and, by God, I sure make her walk a straight chalk line. Sit down, son. You in safe hands here."

I laughed and sat.

"Where might you be from?" she asked.

"Jackson, Mississippi."

"You act mighty bright to be from there," she commented.

"There are bright people in Jackson," I said.

"If there is, I got yet to see some of 'em. Most of 'em can't talk. They just stand with their heads down, with one foot on top of the other and you have to guess at what they're trying to say."

I was at ease now. I liked her.

"My husband works in a bakery," she rattled on pleasantly, openly, as though she had known me for years. "We take in roomers to help out. We just simple people here. You can call this home, if you got a mind to. The rent's three dollars."

"That's a little high," I said.

"Then give me two dollars and a half till you get yourself a job," she said.

I accepted and she showed me my room. I set my suitcase down.

"You run off, didn't you?" she asked.

I jerked in surprise.

"How did you know?"

"Boy, your heart's like an open book," she said. "I know things. Lotta boys run off to Memphis from little towns. They think they gonna find it easy here, but they don't." She looked at me searchingly. "You drink?"

"Oh, no, ma'am."

"Didn't mean no harm, son," she said. "Just wanted to know. You can drink here, if you like. Just don't make a fool of yourself. You can bring your girl here too. Do anything you want, but be decent."

I sat on the edge of the bed and stared at her in amazement. It was on reputedly disreputable Beale Street in Memphis that I had met the warmest, friendliest person I had ever known, that I discovered that all human beings were not mean and driving, were not bigots like the members of my family.

"You can eat dinner with us when we come from church," she said.

"Thank you. I'd like to."

"Maybe you want to come to church with us?"

"Well . . ." I hedged.

"Naw, you're tired," she said, closing the door.

I lay on the bed and reveled in the delightful sensation of living out a long-sought dream. I had always flinched inwardly from the lonely terror that I had thought I would feel in a strange city, and now I had found a home with friendly people. I relaxed completely and dozed off to sleep, for I had not slept much for many nights. Later I came awake with a sudden start, remembering the fright and tension that had accompanied my foray into crime. Well, all that was gone now. I could start anew. I did not like to feel tension and fear. I wanted something else, to be human, to be caught up in something meaningful. But I must first get a job.

Late that afternoon Mrs. Moss called me for dinner and introduced me to her daughter, Bess, whom I liked at once. She was young, simple, sweet, and brown. Mrs. Moss apologized for her husband, who was still at work. Why was she treating me so kindly? It made me self-conscious. We were eating dessert when Bess spoke.

"Mama's done told me all about you," she said.

"I'm afraid that there isn't much to tell," I said.

"She said you was walking up and down in the street in front of the house, and didn't know whether to come in," Bess said, giggling. "What kind of place did you think this was?"

I hung my head and smiled. Mrs. Moss went into a storm of laughter and left the room.

"Mama says she said to herself soon's she saw you out there on that street with your suitcase, 'That boy's looking for a clean home to live in,' " Bess said. "Mama's good about knowing what folks feel."

"She seems to be," I said, helping Bess to wash the dishes.

"You can eat with us any time you like," Bess said.

"Thanks," I said. "But I couldn't do that."

"How come?" Bess asked. "We got a plenty."

"I know. But a man ought to pay his own way."

"Mama said you'd be like that," Bess said with satisfaction.

Mrs. Moss returned to the kitchen.

"Bess's going to be married soon," she announced.

"Congratulations!" I said. "Who's the lucky man?"

"Oh, I ain't got nobody yet," Bess said.

I was puzzled. Mrs. Moss laughed and nudged me.

"I say gals oughta marry young," she said. "Now, if Bess found a nice young man like *you*, Richard . . ."

"Mama!" Bess wailed, hiding her face in the dishcloth.

"I mean it," Mrs. Moss said. "Richard's a heap better'n them old ignorant nigger boys you been running after at school."

I gaped at one and then the other. What was happening here? They barely knew me; I had been in the house but a few hours.

"The minute I laid eyes on that boy in the street this morning," Mrs. Moss said, "I said to myself, 'That's the kind of boy for Bess.' "

Bess came to me and leaned her head on my shoulder. I was stunned. How on earth could she act like this?

"Mama, don't," Bess pleaded teasingly.

"I mean it," Mrs. Moss said. "Richard, I'm worried about whose hands this house is going to fall into. I ain't too long for this old world."

"Bess'll find a boy who'll love her," I said uneasily.

"I ain't so sure," Mrs. Moss said, shaking her head.

"I'm going up front," Bess said, giggling, burying her face in her hands, and running out.

Mrs. Moss came close to me and spoke confidently.

"A gal's a funny thing," she said, laughing. "They has to be tamed. Just like wild animals."

"She's all right," I said, wiping the table, thinking furiously, not wanting to become involved too deeply with the family.

"You like Bess, Richard?" Mrs. Moss asked me suddenly.

I stared at her, doubting my ears.

"I've been in the house only a couple of hours," I said hesitantly. "She's a fine girl."

"Now. I mean do you *like* her? Could you *love* her?" she asked insistently.

I stared at Mrs. Moss, wondering if something was wrong with Bess. What kind of people were these?

"You people don't know me. I didn't exist for you five hours ago," I said seriously. Then I shot at her: "I could be a robber or a burglar for all you know."

"Son, I know you," she said emphatically.

Oh, Christ, I thought. I'll have to leave this place.

"You go on up front with Bess," Mrs. Moss said.

"Look, Mrs. Moss, I'm just a poor nobody," I said.

"You got something in you I like," she said. "Money ain't everything. You got a good Christian heart and everybody ain't got that."

I winced and turned my head away. Her naïve simplicity was overwhelming. I felt as though I had been accused of something.

"I worked twenty years and bought this house myself," she went on. "I'd be happy when I died if I thought Bess had a husband like you."

"Oh, mama!" Bess shrieked with protesting laughter from the front room.

I went into a warm, cozy front room and sat on the sofa. Bess was sitting on a little bench, looking out the window. How must I act toward this girl? I did not want to be drawn into something I did not want, and neither did I wish to wound anybody's feelings.

"Don't you wanna set here with me?" Bess said.

I rose and sat with her. Neither of us spoke for a long time.

"I'm the same age as you," Bess said. "I'm seventeen."

"Do you go to school?" I asked to make conversation.

"Yes," she said. "Wanna see my books?"

"I'd like to."

She rose and brought her schoolbooks to me. I saw that she was in the fifth grade.

"I ain't so good in school," she said, tossing her head. "But I don't care."

"Well, school's kind of important, you know," I said cautiously.

"Love is the important thing," she countered strongly.

I wondered if she were demented. The behavior of the mother and the daughter ran counter to all I had ever seen or known. Mrs. Moss came into the room.

"I think I'll go out and look for a job," I said, wanting to escape them.

"On a Sunday!" Mrs. Moss exclaimed. "Wait till in the morning."

"But I can learn the streets tonight anyway," I said.

"That's really a good thought," Mrs. Moss said after a moment's reflection. "You see, Bess? That boy thinks."

I felt awkward, embarrassed, called upon to say something.

"I'll be glad to help you with your lessons, Bess," I said.

"You think you can?" she asked, doubting.

"Well, I used to take charge of classes at school last year," I said.

"Now ain't that nice?" Mrs. Moss said in a honeyed tone.

I went to my room and lay on the bed and tried to fathom out the kind of home I had come to. That they were serious, I had no doubt. Would they be angry with me when they learned that my life was a million miles from theirs? How could I avoid that? Was it wise to remain here with a seventeen-year-old girl eager for marriage and a mother equally anxious to have her marry me? What on earth had they seen in me to have made them act toward me as they had? My clothes were not good. True, I had manners, manners that had been drilled into me at home, at school, manners that had been kicked into me on jobs; but anybody could have manners. I had learned to know these people better in five hours than I had learned to know my own family in five years.

Later, after I had grown to understand the peasant mentality of Bess and her mother, I learned the full degree to which my life at home had cut me off, not only from white people but from Negroes as well. To Bess and her mother, money was important, but they did not strive for it too hard. They had no tensions, unappeasable longings, no desire to do something to redeem themselves. The main value in their lives was simple, clean, good living and when they thought they had found those same qualities in one of their race, they instinctively embraced him, liked him, and asked no questions. But such simple unaffected trust flabbergasted me. It was impossible.

I walked down Beale Street and into the heart of Memphis. My body was thin, my overcoat shabby, and each gust of wind chilled my blood. On Main Street I saw a sign in a café window:

Dish Washer Wanted

I went in and spoke to the manager and was hired to come to work the following night. The salary was ten dollars for the first week and twelve thereafter.

"Don't hire anyone else," I told him. "I'll be here."

I would get two meals at the café. But how would I eat in the daytime? I went into a store and bought a can of pork and beans and a can opener. Well, that problem was solved. I would pay two dollars and a half a week for my room and I would save the balance for my trip to Chicago. All my thoughts and movements were dictated by distant hopes.

Mrs. Moss was astonished when I told her that I had a job.

"You see, Bess," she said. "That boy's got a job his first day here. That's get-up for you. He's going somewhere. He just don't sit and gab. He moves."

Bess smiled at me. It seemed that every move I made captivated her. Mrs. Moss went upstairs to bed. I was uneasy.

"Lemme rest your coat," Bess said.

She took my coat and felt the can in the pocket.

"What you got in there?" she asked.

"Oh, nothing," I mumbled, trying to take the coat from her.

She pulled out the beans and the can opener. Her eyes widened with pity.

"Richard, you hungry, ain't you?" she asked me.

"Naw," I mumbled.

"Then let's eat some chicken," she said.

"Oh, all right," I said.

Bess ran to the stairway.

"Mama!" she called.

"Don't disturb her," I said, knowing that she was going to tell Mrs. Moss about my wanting to eat out of a can and feeling my heart fill with shame. My muscles flexed to hit her.

Mrs. Moss came down in her house robe.

"Mama, look what Richard was gonna do," Bess said, showing the can. "He was gonna eat this in his room."

"Lord, boy," Mrs. Moss said. "You don't have to do that."

"I'm used to it," I said. "I've got to save money."

"I just won't let you eat out of a can in my house," she said. "You don't have to pay me to eat. Go in the kitchen and eat. That's all."

"But I wouldn't dirty your room with the can," I said.

"It ain't that, son," Mrs. Moss said. "Why do you want to eat out of a can when you can set at the table with us?"

"I don't want to be a burden to anybody," I said.

Mrs. Moss stared at me, then hung her head and cried. I was stunned. It was incredible that what I did or the way I lived could evoke tears from anyone. Then my shame made me angry.

"You just ain't never had no home life," she said. "I'm sorry for you."

I stiffened. I did not like that. She was reaching into my inner life, where it was sore, and I did not want anyone there.

"I'm all right," I mumbled.

Mrs. Moss shook her head and went upstairs. I sighed. I was afraid that the family was getting too good a hold on me. Bess and I ate chicken, but I did not have much appetite. Bess was looking at me with melting eyes. We went back to the front room.

"I wanna get married," she whispered to me.

"You have a lot of time yet for that," I said, tense and uneasy.

"I wanna get married now. I wanna love," she said.

I had never met anyone like her, so direct, so easy in the expression of her feelings.

"Do you know what this means?" she asked me as she rose and went to a table and picked up a comb and came and stood before me.

I stared at the comb, then at her.

"What're you talking about?" I asked.

She did not answer. She smiled, then came close to me and reached out with the comb and touched my head. I drew back.

"What're you doing?"

She laughed and drew the comb through my hair. I stared at her, completely baffled.

"But my hair doesn't need combing," I said.

"I know it," she said, still combing.

"But why are you doing this?"

"Because I want to."

"What does it mean?"

She laughed again. I tried to get up and she caught hold of my arm and held me in the chair.

"You have nice hair," she said.

"It's just common nigger hair," I said.

"It's nice hair," she repeated.

"But why are you combing my hair?" I asked again.

"You know," she said.

"I don't."

"'Cause I like you," she purred.

"Is this your way of telling me that?"

"It's a custom," she said. "You just fooling me. You know that. Everybody knows that. When a girl likes a man, she combs his hair."

"You're young. Give yourself a chance," I said.

"Don't you like me?" she asked.

"I do," I said. "We're friends."

"But I want more'n a friend," she sighed.

Her simplicity frightened me. The girls I had known had been hard and calculating, those who had worked at the hotel and those whom I had met at school. We were silent for a while.

"Say, what's them books in your room?" she asked.

"Were you in my room?" I asked with soft pointedness.

"Sure," she said without batting an eye. "I looked through your suitcase."

What could I do with a girl like this? Was I dumb or was she dumb? I felt that it would be easy to have sex relations with her and I was tempted. But what would happen? Love simply did not come to me that quickly and easily. And she was talking of marriage. Could I ever talk to her about what I felt, hoped? Could she ever understand my life? What had I above sex to share with her, and what had she? But I knew that such questions did not bother her. I did not love her and did not want to marry her. The prize of the house did not tempt me. Yet I sat beside her, feeling the attraction of her body increasing and deepening for me. What if I made her pregnant? I was sure that the fear of becoming pregnant did not bother her. Perhaps she would have liked it. I had come from a home where feelings were never expressed, except in rage or religious dread, where each member of the household lived locked in his own dark world, and the light that shone out of this child's heart—for she was a child—blinded me.

She leaned over and kissed me. What the hell, I thought. Have it out with her, and if anything happens, leave . . . I kissed and petted her. She was warm, eager, childish, pliable. She threw her arms and legs about me and hugged me fiercely. I began to wonder how old she was.

"What would your mother say?" I asked in a whisper.

"She's sleeping."

"But what if she saw us?"

"I don't care."

She was crazy. Plainly she would have married me that instant, knowing no more about me than she did.

"Let's go to my room," I said.

"Naw. Mama wouldn't like that," she said.

She would let me do anything to her in her own front room, but she did not want me to do it to her in my room. It was crazy, utterly crazy.

"Mama's sleeping," she observed.

I began to suspect that she had had every boy in the block.

"You love me?" she asked in a whisper.

I stared at her, becoming more aware each minute of the terrible simplicity of her life. That was life for her, simple, direct. She just did not attach to words the same meanings I did. She caught my hands in a viselike grip. I looked at her and could not believe in her existence.

"I love you," she said.

"Don't say that," I said, then was sorry that I had said it.

"But I do love you," she said again.

Her voice had come so clearly that I could no longer doubt her. For Christ's sake, I said to myself. The girl was astoundingly simple, yet vital in a way that I had never known. What kind of life had I lived that made the reality of this girl so strange? I sat thinking of Aunt Addie, her stern face, her forbidding nature, her caution, her restraint, her keen struggle to be good and holy.

"I'd make a good wife," she said.

I disengaged my hand from hers. I looked at her and wanted either to laugh or to slap her. I was about to hurt her and I did not want to. I rose. Oh, hell . . . This girl's crazy . . . I heard her crying and I bent to her.

"Look," I whispered. "You don't know me. Let's get to know each other better."

Her eyes were beaten, baffled. Love was that simple to her; it could be turned on or off in a moment.

"You just think I'm nothing," she whimpered.

I reached out my hand to touch her, to speak to her, to try to tell her of my life, my feelings, my doubts; and she leaped to her feet.

"I hate you," she burst out in a passionate whisper and ran out of the room.

I lit a cigarette and sat for a long time. I had never dreamed that anyone would accept me so simply, so completely, without question or the least hint of personal aggrandizement. The truth was that I had—even though I had fought against it—grown to accept the value of myself that my old environment had created in me, and I had thought that no other kind of environment was possible. My life had changed too suddenly. Had I met Bess upon a Mississippi plantation, I would have expected her to act as she had. But in Memphis, on Beale Street, how could there be such hope, belief, faith in others? I wanted to go to Bess and talk to her, but I knew no words to say to her.

When I awakened the next morning and recalled Bess's naïve hopes, I was glad that I had the can of pork and beans. I did not want to face her across the breakfast table. I dressed to go out; then, with my coat and hat on, I sat on the edge of the bed and propped my feet on a chair. Taking puffs from a cigarette, I scooped the beans out of the can with my fingers and ate them. I slipped out of the house and went to the water front and sat on a knoll of earth in the cold wind and sun, looking at the boats on the Mississippi River. Tonight I would begin my new job. I knew how to save money, thanks to my long starvation in Mississippi. My heart was at peace. I was freer than I had ever been.

A black boy came up to me.

"Hy," he said.

"Hy," I said.

"What you doing these days?" he asked.

"Nothing. Waiting for night. I got a job in a café," I said.

"Shucks," he said. "I'm looking for a buddy." He was trying to act tough, but I thought that he was lonely. "I wanna hop a freight and go north."

"Why not hop one alone?" I asked.

He grinned nervously.

"Did you run off from home?" I asked.

"Yeah. Four years ago," he said.

"What have you been doing?"

"Nothing."

That should have warned me, but I was not yet wise in the ways of the world or the road.

We talked a while longer, then walked down a path toward the river's edge, skirting high weeds. The boy stopped suddenly and pointed.

"What's that?"

"Looks like a can of some sort," I said.

I saw a huge can partially screened by high weeds. We went to it and found that it was full of something heavy. I pulled out the stopper and smelt it.

"This stuff is liquor," I said.

The boy smelt it and his eyes widened.

"Reckon we can sell it?" he asked.

"But whose is it?" I asked.

"Gee, I wish I could sell this stuff," he said.

"Maybe somebody's watching," I suggested.

We looked about, but no one was in sight.

"This belongs to a bootlegger," I said.

"Let's see if we can sell it," he said.

"I wouldn't take that can out of here," I said. "The cops might see us."

"I need money," the boy said. "This'll help me on the road."

We agreed to look for a white buyer. We went into the streets and looked over the white men who passed. Finally we spotted one sitting alone in his car. We went up to him.

"Mister," the boy said, "we found a big can of liquor over there in the weeds. You want to buy it?"

The man screwed up his eyes and studied us.

"Is it good liquor?" he asked.

"I don't know," I said. "Go and see it."

"You niggers ain't lying to me, are you?" he asked suspiciously.

"Come on. I'll show it to you," I said.

We led the white man to the liquor; he unstoppered it and smelt it, then tasted the wetness on the cork.

"Holy cats," he said. He looked at us. "Did you really find this here?"

"Oh, yes, sir," we said.

"If you two niggers are lying, I'll kill both of you," he breathed.

"We're telling the truth," I said.

The other boy stood awkwardly and looked on. I wondered why he did not say anything. Some vague thought was trying to worm its way into my dense, naïve, childlike mind. But it did not come clear and I brushed it away.

"You boys bring this can to my car," the white man said.

I was afraid. But the other boy was eager and willing. With the white man encouraging us, we lugged the can to his car and put it into the back upon the floor.

"Here," the white man said, extending a five-dollar bill to the boy. The car drove off and I could see the white man looking about anxiously, fearing a trap; or so it seemed to me.

"Gee, let's get this changed," the boy said.

"All right," I said. "We'll split it."

The boy pointed across the street.

"There's a store over there," he said. "I'll run over and get change."

"O.K.," I said, angel-like.

I sat on a sloping embankment and waited. He ran off in the direction of the store, but I was so confident that I did not even watch him. I felt amused. I was going to get two and one-half dollars for finding a cache of liquor. I was a hijacker already. Last night a girl had thrown herself at me. And all this had happened within forty-eight hours of my leaving home. I wanted to laugh out loud. Things could happen to one when one was not at home. I looked up, waiting for the boy to return. But I did not see him. He's sure taking his time, I thought, pushing down other ideas that were trying to bubble into my mind. I waited longer, then rose and went quickly to the store and peered through the window. The boy was not inside. I went in and asked the proprietor if a boy had been in.

"Yeah," he said. "A nigger boy came in here, looked around, then went out of the back door. He went like a light. Did he have something of yours?"

"Yes," I said.

"Well, you'll never see that nigger again," the man said.

I walked along the streets in the winter sun, thinking: Well, that's good enough for you, you fool. You had no business monkeying in that liquor business anyway. Then I stopped in my tracks. *They had been together!* The white man and the black boy had seen me loitering in the vicinity of their liquor and had thought I was a hijacker; and they had used me in disposing of their liquor.

Last night I had found a naïve girl. This morning I had been a naïve boy.

12

While wandering aimlessly about the streets of Memphis, gaping at the tall buildings and the crowds, killing time, eating bags of popcorn, I was struck by an odd and sudden idea. If I had attempted to work for an optical company in Jackson and had failed, why should I not try to work for an optical company in Memphis? Memphis was not a small town like Jackson; it was urban and I felt that no one would hold the trivial trouble I had had in Jackson against me.

I looked for the address of a company in a directory and walked boldly into the building, rode up in the elevator with a fat, round, yellow Negro of about five feet in height. At the fifth floor I stepped into an office. A white man rose to meet me.

"Pull off your hat," he said.

"Oh, yes, sir," I said, jerking off my hat.

"What do you want?"

"I was wondering if you needed a boy," I said. "I worked for an optical company for a short while in Jackson."

"Why did you leave?" he asked.

"I had a little trouble there," I said honestly.

"Did you steal something?"

"No, sir," I said. "A white boy there didn't want me to learn the optical trade and ran me off the job."

"Come and sit down."

I sat and recounted the story from beginning to end.

"I'll write Mr. Crane," he said. "But you won't get a chance to learn the optical trade here. That's not our policy."

I told him that I understood and accepted his policy. I was hired at eight dollars per week and promised a raise of a dollar a week until my wages reached ten. Though this was less than I had been offered for the café job, I accepted it. I liked the open, honest way in which the man talked to me; and, too, the place seemed clean, brisk, businesslike.

I was assigned to run errands and wash eyeglasses after they had come from the rouge-smeared machines. Each evening I had to take sacks of packages to the post office for mailing. It was light work and I was fast on my feet. At noon I would forgo my lunch hour and run errands for the white men who were employed in the shop. I would buy their lunches, take their suits out to have them pressed, pay their light, telephone, and gas bills, and deliver notes for them to their stenographer girl friends in near-by office buildings. The first day I made a dollar and a half in tips. I deposited the money I had left from my trip and resolved to live off my tips.

I was now rapidly learning to contain the tension I felt in my relations with whites, and the people in Memphis had an air of relative urbanity that took some of the sharpness off the attitude of whites toward Negroes. There were about a dozen white men in the sixth-floor shop where I spent most of my time; they varied from Ku Klux Klanners to Jews, from theosophists to just plain poor whites. Although I could detect disdain and hatred in their attitudes, they never shouted at me or abused me. It was fairly easy to contemplate the race issue in the shop without reaching those heights of fear that devastated me. A measure of objectivity entered into my observations of white men and women. Either I could stand more mental strain than formerly or I had discovered deep within me ways of handling it.

When I returned to Mrs. Moss's that Monday night, she was surprised that I had changed my plans and had taken a new job. I showed her my bankbook and told her my plan for saving money and bringing my mother to Memphis. As I talked to her I tried to tell from her manner if Bess had said anything about what had happened between us, but Mrs. Moss was bland and motherly as always.

Bess avoided me, refusing to speak when we were alone together; but when her mother was present, she was polite. A few days later Mrs. Moss came to me with a baffled look in their eyes.

"What's happened between you and Bess?" she asked.

"Nothing," I lied, burning with shame.

"She don't seem to like you no more," she said. "I wanted you-all to kinda hit it off." She looked at me searchingly. "Don't you like her none?"

I could not answer or look at her; I wondered if she had told Bess to give herself to me.

"Well," she drawled, sighing, "I guess folks just have to love each other naturally. You can't make 'em." Tears rolled down her cheeks. "Bess'll find somebody."

I felt sick, filled with a consciousness of the woman's helplessness, of her naïve hope. Time and again she told me that Bess loved me, wanted me. She even suggested that I "try Bess and see if you like her. Ain't no harm in that." And her words evoked in me a pity for her that had no name.

Finally it became unbearable. One night I returned home from work and found Mrs. Moss sitting by the stove in the hall, nodding. She blinked her eyes and smiled.

"How're you, son?" she asked.

"Pretty good," I said.

"Ain't you and Bess got to be friends or something yet?"

"No, ma'am," I said softly.

"How come you don't like Bess?" she demanded.

"Oh, I don't know." I was becoming angry.

"It's 'cause she ain't so bright?"

"No, ma'am. Bess's bright," I lied.

"Then how come?"

I still could not tell her.

"You and Bess could have this house for your home," she went on. "You-all could bring up your children here."

"But people have to find their own way to each other," I said.

"Young folks ain't got no sense these days," she said at last. "If somebody had fixed things for me when I was a gal, I sure would've taken it."

"Mrs. Moss," I said, "I think I'd better move."

"Move then!" she exploded. "You ain't got no sense!"

I went to my room and began to pack. A knock came at the door. I opened it. Mrs. Moss stood in the doorway, weeping.

"Son, forgive me," she said. "I didn't mean it. I wouldn't hurt you for nothing. You just like a son to me."

"That's all right," I said. "But I'd better move."

"No!" she wailed. "Then you ain't forgive me! When a body asks forgiveness, they means it!"

I stared. Bess appeared in the doorway.

"Don't leave, Richard," she said.

"We won't bother you no more," Mrs. Moss said.

I wilted, baffled, sorry, ashamed. Mrs. Moss took Bess's hand and led her away.

I centered my attention now upon making enough money to send for my mother and brother. I saved each penny I came by, stinting myself on food, walking to work, eating out of paper bags, living on a pint of milk and two sweet rolls for breakfast, a hamburger and peanuts for lunch, and a can of beans which I would eat at night in my room. I was used to hunger and I did not need much food to keep me alive.

I now had more money than I had ever had before, and I began patronizing secondhand bookstores, buying magazines and books. In this way I became acquainted with periodicals like *Harper's Magazine,* the *Atlantic Monthly,* and the *American Mercury.* I would buy them for a few cents, read them, then resell them to the bookdealer.

Once Mrs. Moss questioned me about my reading.

"What you reading all them books for, boy?"

"I just like to."

"You studying for law?"

"No, ma'am."

"Well, I reckon you know what you doing," she said.

Though I did not have to report for work until nine o'clock

each morning, I would arrive at eight and go into the lobby of the downstairs bank—where I knew the Negro porter—and read the early edition of the Memphis *Commercial Appeal,* thereby saving myself five cents each day, which I spent for lunch. After reading, I would watch the black porter perform his morning ritual: he would get a mop, bucket, soap flakes, water, then would pause dramatically, roll his eyes to the ceiling and sing out:

"Lawd, today! Ahm still working for white folks!"

And he would mop until he sweated. He hated his job and talked incessantly of leaving to work in the post office.

The most colorful of the Negro boys on the job was Shorty, the round, yellow, fat elevator operator. He had tiny, beady eyes that looked out between rolls of flesh with a hard but humorous stare. He had the complexion of a Chinese, a short forehead, and three chins. Psychologically he was the most amazing specimen of the southern Negro I had ever met. Hardheaded, sensible, a reader of magazines and books, he was proud of his race and indignant about its wrongs. But in the presence of whites he would play the role of a clown of the most debased and degraded type.

One day he needed twenty-five cents to buy his lunch.

"Just watch me get a quarter from the first white man I see," he told me as I stood in the elevator that morning.

A white man who worked in the building stepped into the elevator and waited to be lifted to his floor. Shorty sang in a low mumble, smiling, rolling his eyes, looking at the white man roguishly.

"I'm hungry, Mister White Man. I need a quarter for lunch."

The white man ignored him. Shorty, his hands on the controls of the elevator, sang again:

"I ain't gonna move this damned old elevator till I get a quarter, Mister White Man."

"The hell with you, Shorty," the white man said, ignoring him and chewing on his black cigar.

"I'm hungry, Mister White Man. I'm dying for a quarter," Shorty sang, drooling, drawling, humming his words.

"If you don't take me to my floor, you will die," the white man said, smiling a little for the first time.

"But this black sonofabitch sure needs a quarter," Shorty sang, grimacing, clowning, ignoring the white man's threat.

"Come on, you black bastard, I got to work," the white man said, intrigued by the element of sadism involved, enjoying it.

"It'll cost you twenty-five cents, Mister White Man; just a quarter, just two bits," Shorty moaned.

There was silence. Shorty threw the lever and the elevator went up and stopped about five feet shy of the floor upon which the white man worked.

"Can't go no more, Mister White Man, unless I get my quarter," he said in a tone that sounded like crying.

"What would you do for a quarter?" the white man asked, still gazing off.

"I'll do anything for a quarter," Shorty sang.

"What, for example?" the white man asked.

Shorty giggled, swung around, bent over, and poked out his broad, fleshy ass.

"You can kick me for a quarter," he sang, looking impishly at the white man out of the corners of his eyes.

The white man laughed softly, jingled some coins in his pocket, took out one and thumped it to the floor. Shortly stooped to pick it up and the white man bared his teeth and swung his foot into Shorty's rump with all the strength of his body. Shorty let out a howling laugh that echoed up and down the elevator shaft.

"Now, open this door, you goddamn black sonofabitch," the white man said, smiling with tight lips.

"Yeeeess, siiiiir," Shorty sang; but first he picked up the quarter and put it into his mouth. "This monkey's got the peanuts," he chortled.

He opened the door and the white man stepped out and looked back at Shorty as he went toward his office.

"You're all right, Shorty, you sonofabitch," he said.

"I know it!" Shorty screamed, then let his voice trail off in a gale of wild laughter.

I witnessed this scene or its variant at least a score of times and

I felt no anger or hatred, only disgust and loathing. Once I asked him:

"How in God's name can you do that?"

"I needed a quarter and I got it," he said soberly, proudly.

"But a quarter can't pay you for what he did to you," I said.

"Listen, nigger," he said to me, "my ass is tough and quarters is scarce."

I never discussed the subject with him after that.

Other Negroes worked in the building: an old man whom we called Edison; his son, John; and a night janitor who answered to the name of Dave. At noon, when I was not running errands, I would join the rest of the Negroes in a little room at the front of the building overlooking the street. Here, in this underworld pocket of the building, we munched our lunches and discussed the ways of white folks toward Negroes. When two or more of us were talking, it was impossible for this subject not to come up. Each of us hated and feared the whites, yet had a white man put in a sudden appearance we would have assumed silent, obedient smiles.

To our minds the white folks formed a kind of superworld: what was said by them during working hours was rehashed and weighed here; how they looked; what they wore; what moods they were in; who had outdistanced whom in business; who was replacing whom on the job; who was getting fired and who was getting hired. But never once did we openly say that we occupied none but subordinate positions in the building. Our talk was restricted to the petty relations which formed the core of life for us.

But under all our talk floated a latent sense of violence; the whites had drawn a line over which we dared not step and we accepted that line because our bread was at stake. But within our boundaries we, too, drew a line that included our right to bread regardless of the indignities or degradations involved in getting it. If a white man had sought to keep us from obtaining a job, or enjoying the rights of citizenship, we would have bowed silently to his power. But if he had sought to deprive us of a dime, blood might have been split. Hence, our daily lives were so bound up

with trivial objectives that to capitulate when challenged was tantamount to surrendering the right to life itself. Our anger was like the
anger of children, passing quickly from one petty grievance to
another, from the memory of one slight wrong to another.

"You know what the bastard Olin said to me this morning?"
John would ask, biting into a juicy hamburger.

"What?" Shorty would ask.

"Well, I brought him his change from paying his gas bill and he
said: 'Put it here in my pocket; my hands are dirty,' " John said.
"Hunh . . . I just laid the money on the bench besides him. I ain't
no personal slave to him and I'll be damned if I'll put his *own*
money in his *own* pocket."

"Hell, you're right," Shorty would say.

"White folks just don't think," old man Edison would say.

"You sure got to watch 'em," Dave, the night janitor, would
say. (He would have slept in the room on a cot after his night's
cleaning; he would be ready now to keep a date with some girl
friend.)

"Falk sent me to have his suit pressed," I would say. "He didn't
give me a penny. Told me he would remember it on payday."

"Ain't that some nerve?" John would say.

"You can't eat his memories," Shorty would say.

"But you got to keep on doing them favors," old man Edison
would say. "If you don't, they won't like you."

"I'm going north one of these days," Shorty would say.

We would all laugh, knowing that Shorty would never leave,
that he depended too much upon the whites for the food he ate.

"What would you do up north?" I would ask Shorty.

"I'd pass for Chinese," Shorty would say.

And we would laugh again. The lunch hour would pass and we
would go back to work, but there would be in our faces not one
whit of the sentiment we had felt during the hour of discussion.

One day I went to the optical counter of a department store to
deliver a pair of eyeglasses. The counter was empty of customers
and a tall, florid-faced white man looked at me curiously. He was

unmistakably a Yankee, for his physical build differed sharply from that of the lanky Southerner.

"Will you please sign for this, sir?" I asked, presenting the account book and the eyeglasses.

He picked up the book and the glasses, but his eyes were still upon me.

"Say, boy, I'm from the North," he said quietly.

I held very still. Was this a trap? He had mentioned a tabooed subject and I wanted to wait until I knew what he meant. Among the topics that southern white men did not like to discuss with Negroes were the following: American white women; the Ku Klux Klan; France, and how Negro soldiers fared while there; French-women; Jack Johnson; the entire northern part of the United States; the Civil War; Abraham Lincoln; U. S. Grant; General Sherman; Catholics; the Pope; Jews; the Republican party; slavery; social equality; Communism; Socialism; the 13th, 14th, and 15th Amendments to the Constitution; or any topic calling for positive knowledge or manly self-assertion on the part of the Negro. The most accepted topics were sex and religion. I did not look at the man or answer. With one sentence he had lifted out of the silent dark the race question and I stood on the edge of a precipice.

"Don't be afraid of me," he went on. "I just want to ask you one question."

"Yes, sir," I said in a waiting, neutral tone.

"Tell me, boy, are you hungry?" he asked seriously.

I stared at him. He had spoken one word that touched the very soul of me, but I could not talk to him, could not let him know that I was starving myself to save money to go north. I did not trust him. But my face did not change its expression.

"Oh, no, sir," I said, managing a smile.

I was hungry and he knew it; but he was a white man and I felt that if I told him I was hungry I would have been revealing something shameful.

"Boy, I can see hunger in your face and eyes," he said.

"I get enough to eat," I lied.

"Then why do you keep so thin?" he asked me.

"Well, I suppose I'm just that way, naturally," I lied.

"You're just scared, boy," he said.

"Oh, no, sir," I lied again.

I could not look at him. I wanted to leave the counter, yet he was a white man and I had learned not to walk abruptly away from a white man when he was talking to me. I stood, my eyes looking away. He ran his hand into his pocket and pulled out a dollar bill.

"Here, take this dollar and buy yourself some food," he said.

"No, sir," I said.

"Don't be a fool," he said. "You're ashamed to take it. God, boy, don't let a thing like that stop you from taking a dollar and eating."

The more he talked the more it became impossible for me to take the dollar. I wanted it, but I could not look at it. I wanted to speak, but I could not move my tongue. I wanted him to leave me alone. He frightened me.

"Say something," he said.

All about us in the store were piles of goods; white men and women went from counter to counter. It was summer and from a high ceiling was suspended a huge electric fan that whirred. I stood waiting for the white man to give me the signal that would let me go.

"I don't understand it," he said through his teeth. "How far did you go in school?"

"Through the ninth grade, but it was really the eighth," I told him. "You see, our studies in the ninth grade were more or less a review of what we had in the eighth grade."

Silence. He had not asked me for this long explanation, but I had spoken at length to fill up the yawning, shameful gap that loomed between us; I had spoken to try to drag the unreal nature of the conversation back to safe and sound southern ground. Of course, the conversation was real; it dealt with my welfare, but it had brought to the surface of day all the dark fears I had known all my life. The Yankee white man did not know how dangerous his words were.

(There are some elusive, profound, recondite things that men find hard to say to other men; but with the Negro it is the little things of life that become hard to say, for these tiny items shape his destiny. A man will seek to express his relation to the stars; but when a man's consciousness has been riveted upon obtaining a loaf of bread, that loaf of bread is as important as the stars.)

Another white man walked up to the counter and I sighed with relief.

"Do you want the dollar?" the man asked.

"No, sir," I whispered.

"All right," he said. "Just forget it."

He signed the account book and took the eyeglasses. I stuffed the book into my bag and turned from the counter and walked down the aisle, feeling a physical tingling along my spine, knowing that the white man knew I was really hungry. I avoided him after that. Whenever I saw him I felt in a queer way that he was my enemy, for he knew how I felt and the safety of my life in the South depended upon how well I concealed from all whites what I felt.

One summer morning I stood at a sink in the rear of the factory washing a pair of eyeglasses that had just come from the polishing machines whose throbbing shook the floor upon which I stood. At each machine a white man was bent forward, working intently. To my left sunshine poured through a window, lighting up the rouge smears and making the factory look garish, violent, dangerous. It was nearing noon and my mind was drifting toward my daily lunch of a hamburger and a bag of peanuts. It had been a routine day, a day more or less like the other days I had spent on the job as errand boy and washer of eyeglasses. I was at peace with the world, that is, at peace in the only way in which a black boy in the South can be at peace with a world of white men.

Perhaps it was the mere sameness of the day that soon made it different from the other days; maybe the white men who operated the machines felt bored with their dull, automatic tasks and hankered for some kind of excitement. Anyway, I presently heard footsteps behind me and turned my head. At my elbow stood a young white man, Mr. Olin, the immediate foreman under whom I worked. He was smiling and observing me as I cleaned emery dust from the eyeglasses.

"Boy, how's it going?" he asked.

"Oh, fine, sir!" I answered with false heartiness, falling quickly into that nigger-being-a-good-natured-boy-in-the-presence-of-a-white-man pattern, a pattern into which I could now slide easily; although I was wondering if he had any criticism to make of my work.

He continued to hover wordlessly at my side. What did he want? It was unusual for him to stand there and watch me; I wanted to look at him, but was afraid to.

"Say, Richard, do you believe that I'm your friend?" he asked me.

The question was so loaded with danger that I could not reply at once. I scarcely knew Mr. Olin. My relationship to him had been the typical relationship of Negroes to southern whites. He gave me orders and I said, "Yes, sir," and obeyed them. Now, without warning, he was asking me if I thought that he was my friend; and I knew that all southern white men fancied themselves as friends of niggers. While fishing for an answer that would say nothing, I smiled.

"I mean," he persisted, "do you think I'm your friend?"

"Well," I answered, skirting the vast racial chasm between us, "I hope you are."

"I am," he said emphatically.

I continued to work, wondering what motives were prompting him. Already apprehension was rising in me.

"I want to tell you something," he said.

"Yes, sir," I said.

"We don't want you to get hurt," he explained. "We like you round here. You act like a good boy."

"Yes, sir," I said. "What's wrong?"

"You don't deserve to get into trouble," he went on.

"Have I done something that somebody doesn't like?" I asked, my mind frantically sweeping over all my past actions, weighing them in the light of the way southern white men thought Negroes should act.

"Well, I don't know," he said and paused, letting his words sink meaningfully into my mind. He lit a cigarette. "Do you know Harrison?"

He was referring to a Negro boy of about my own age who worked across the street for a rival optical house. Harrison and I knew each other casually, but there had never been the slightest trouble between us.

"Yes, sir," I said. "I know him."

"Well, be careful," Mr. Olin said. "He's after you."

"After me? For what?"

"He's got a terrific grudge against you," the white man explained. "What have you done to him?"

The eyeglasses I was washing were forgotten. My eyes were upon Mr. Olin's face, trying to make out what he meant. Was this something serious? I did not trust the white man, and neither did I trust Harrison. Negroes who worked on jobs in the South were usually loyal to their white bosses; they felt that that was the best way to ensure their jobs. Had Harrison felt that I had in some way jeopardized his job? Who was my friend: the white man or the black boy?

"I haven't done anything to Harrison," I said.

"Well, you better watch that nigger Harrison," Mr. Olin said in a low, confidential tone. "A little while ago I went down to get a Coca-Cola and Harrison was waiting for you at the door of the building with a knife. He asked me when you were coming down. Said he was going to get you. Said you called him a dirty name. Now, we don't want any fighting or bloodshed on the job."

I still doubted the white man, yet thought that perhaps Harrison had really interpreted something I had said as an insult.

"I've got to see that boy and talk to him," I said, thinking out loud.

"No, you'd better not," Mr. Olin said. "You'd better let some of us white boys talk to him."

"But how did this start?" I asked, still doubting but half believing.

"He just told me that he was going to get even with you, going to cut you and teach you a lesson," he said. "But don't you worry. Let me handle this."

He patted my shoulder and went back to his machine. He was an important man in the factory and I had always respected his word. He had the authority to order me to do this or that. Now, why would he joke with me? White men did not often joke with Negroes, therefore what he had said was serious. I was upset. We black boys worked long hard hours for what few pennies we earned and we were edgy and tense. Perhaps that crazy Harrison was really after me. My appetite was gone. I had to settle this thing. A white man had walked into my delicately balanced world and had tipped it and I had to right it before I could feel safe. Yes, I would go directly to Harrison and ask what was the matter, what I had said that he resented. Harrison was black and so was I; I would ignore the warning of the white man and talk face to face with a boy of my own color.

At noon I went across the street and found Harrison sitting on a box in the basement. He was eating lunch and reading a pulp magazine. As I approached him, he ran his hand into his pocket and looked at me with cold, watchful eyes.

"Say, Harrison, what's this all about?" I asked, standing cautiously four feet from him.

He looked at me a long time and did not answer.

"I haven't done anything to you," I said.

"And I ain't got nothing against you," he mumbled, still watchful. "I don't bother nobody."

"But Mr. Olin said that you came over to the factory this morning, looking for me with a knife."

"Aw, naw," he said, more at ease now. "I ain't been in your factory all day." He had not looked at me as he spoke.

"Then what did Mr. Olin mean?" I asked. "I'm not angry with you."

"Shucks, I thought *you* was looking for me to cut me," Harrison explained. "Mr. Olin, he came over here this morning and said you was going to kill me with a knife the moment you saw me. He said you was mad at me because I had insulted you. But I ain't said nothing about you." He still had not looked at me. He rose.

"And I haven't said anything about you," I said.

Finally he looked at me and I felt better. We two black boys, each working for ten dollars a week, stood staring at each other, thinking, comparing the motives of the absent white man, each asking himself if he could believe the other.

"But why would Mr. Olin tell me things like that?" I asked.

Harrison dropped his head; he laid his sandwich aside.

"I . . . I . . ." he stammered and pulled from his pocket a long, gleaming knife; it was already open. "I was just waiting to see what you was gonna do to me . . ."

I leaned weakly against a wall, feeling sick, my eyes upon the sharp steel blade of the knife.

"You were going to cut me?" I asked.

"If you had cut me, I was gonna cut you first," he said. "I ain't taking no chances."

"Are you angry with me about something?" I asked.

"Man, I ain't mad at nobody," Harrison said uneasily.

I felt how close I had come to being slashed. Had I come suddenly upon Harrison, he would have thought I was trying to kill him and he would have stabbed me, perhaps killed me. And what did it matter if one nigger killed another?

"Look here," I said. "Don't believe what Mr. Olin says."

"I see now," Harrison said. "He's playing a dirty trick on us."

"He's trying to make us kill each other for nothing."

"How come he wanna do that?" Harrison asked.

I shook my head. Harrison sat, but still played with the open knife. I began to doubt. Was he really angry with me? Was he waiting until I turned my back to stab me? I was in torture.

"I suppose it's fun for white men to see niggers fight," I said, forcing a laugh.

"But you might've killed me," Harrison said.

"To white men we're like dogs or cocks," I said.

"I don't want to cut you," Harrison said.

"And I don't want to cut you," I said.

Standing well out of each other's reach, we discussed the problem and decided that we would keep silent about our conference. We would not let Mr. Olin know that we knew that he was egging us to fight. We agreed to ignore any further provocations. At one o'clock I went back to the factory. Mr. Olin was waiting for me, his manner grave, his face serious.

"Did you see that Harrison nigger?" he asked.

"No, sir," I lied.

"Well, he still has that knife for you," he said.

Hate tightened in me. But I kept a dead face.

"Did you buy a knife yet?" he asked me.

"No, sir," I answered.

"Do you want to use mine?" he asked. "You've got to protect yourself, you know."

"No, sir. I'm not afraid," I said.

"Nigger, you're a fool," he spluttered. "I thought you had some sense! Are you going to just let that nigger cut your heart out? His boss gave *him* a knife to use against *you!* Take this knife, nigger, and stop acting crazy!"

I was afraid to look at him; if I had looked at him I would have had to tell him to leave me alone, that I knew he was lying, that I knew he was no friend of mine, that I knew if anyone had thrust a knife through my heart he would simply have laughed. But I said nothing. He was the boss and he could fire me if he did not like me. He laid an open knife on the edge of his workbench, about a foot from my hand. I had a fleeting urge to pick it up and give it to him, point first into his chest. But I did nothing of the kind. I picked up the knife and put it into my pocket.

"Now, you're acting like a nigger with some sense," he said.

As I worked Mr. Olin watched me from his machine. Later when I passed him he called me.

"Now, look here, boy," he began. "We told that Harrison nigger to stay out of this building, and leave you alone, see? But I can't protect you when you go home. If that nigger starts at you when you are on your way home, you stab him before he gets a chance to stab you, see?"

I avoided looking at him and remained silent.

"Suit yourself, nigger," Mr. Olin said. "But don't say I didn't warn you."

I had to make my round of errands to deliver eyeglasses and I stole a few minutes to run across the street to talk to Harrison. Harrison was sullen and bashful, wanting to trust me, but afraid. He told me that Mr. Olin had telephoned his boss and had told him to tell Harrison that I had planned to wait for him at the back entrance of the building at six o'clock and stab him. Harrison and I found it difficult to look at each other; we were upset and distrustful. We were not really angry at each other; we knew that the idea of murder had been planted in each of us by the white men who employed us. We told ourselves again and again that we did not agree with the white men; we urged ourselves to keep faith in each other. Yet there lingered deep down in each of us a suspicion that maybe one of us was trying to kill the other.

"I'm not angry with you, Harrison," I said.

"I don't wanna fight nobody," Harrison said bashfully, but he kept his hand in his pocket on his knife.

Each of us felt the same shame, felt how foolish and weak we were in the face of the domination of the whites.

"I wish they'd leave us alone," I said.

"Me too," Harrison said.

"There are a million black boys like us to run errands," I said. "They wouldn't care if we killed each other."

"I know it," Harrison said.

Was he acting? I could not believe in him. We were toying with the idea of death for no reason that stemmed from our own lives, but because the men who ruled us had thrust the idea into our minds. Each of us depended upon the whites for the bread we ate, and we actually trusted the whites more than we did each other. Yet there existed in us a longing to trust men of our own color. Again Harrison and I parted, vowing not to be influenced by what our white boss men said to us.

The game of egging Harrison and me to fight, to cut each other, kept up for a week. We were afraid to tell the white men that we did not believe them, for that would have been tantamount to calling them liars or risking an argument that might have ended in violence being directed against us.

One morning a few days later Mr. Olin and a group of white men came to me and asked me if I was willing to settle my grudge with Harrison with gloves, according to boxing rules. I told them that, though I was not afraid of Harrison, I did not want to fight him and that I did not know how to box. I could feel now that they knew I no longer believed them.

When I left the factory that evening, Harrison yelled at me from down the block. I waited and he ran toward me. Did he want to cut me? I backed away as he approached. We smiled uneasily and sheepishly at each other. We spoke haltingly, weighing our words.

"Did they ask you to fight me with gloves?" Harrison asked.

"Yes," I told him. "But I didn't agree."

Harrison's face became eager.

"They want us to fight four rounds for five dollars apiece," he said. "Man, if I had five dollars, I could pay down on a suit. Five dollars is almost half a week's wages for me."

"I don't want to," I said.

"We won't hurt each other," he said.

"But why do a thing like that for white men?"

"To get that five dollars."

"I don't need five dollars that much."

"Aw, you're a fool," he said. Then he smiled quickly.

"Now, look here," I said. "Maybe you *are* angry with me . . ."

"Naw, I'm not." He shook his head vigorously.

"I don't want to fight for white men. I'm no dog or rooster."

I was watching Harrison closely and he was watching me closely. Did he really want to fight me for some reason of his own? Or was it the money? Harrison stared at me with puzzled eyes. He stepped toward me and I stepped away. He smiled nervously.

"I need that money," he said.

"Nothing doing," I said.

He walked off wordlessly, with an air of anger. Maybe he will stab me now, I thought. I got to watch that fool . . .

For another week the white men of both factories begged us to fight. They made up stories about what Harrison had said about me; and when they saw Harrison they lied to him in the same way. Harrison and I were wary of each other whenever we met. We smiled and kept out of arm's reach, ashamed of ourselves and of each other.

Again Harrison called to me one evening as I was on my way home.

"Come on and fight," he begged.

"I don't want to and quit asking me," I said in a voice louder and harder than I had intended.

Harrison looked at me and I watched him. Both of us still carried the knives that the white men had given us.

"I wanna make a payment on a suit of clothes with that five dollars," Harrison said.

"But those white men will be looking at us, laughing at us," I said.

"What the hell," Harrison said. "They look at you and laugh at you every day, nigger."

It was true. But I hated him for saying it. I ached to hit him in his mouth, to hurt him.

"What have we got to lose?" Harrison asked.

"I don't suppose we have anything to lose," I said.

"Sure," he said. "Let's get the money. We don't care."

"And now they know that we know what they tried to do to us," I said, hating myself for saying it. "And they hate us for it."

"Sure," Harrison said. "So let's get the money. You can use five dollars, can't you?"

"Yes."

"Then let's fight for 'em."

"I'd feel like a dog."

"To them, both of us are dogs," he said.

"Yes," I admitted. But again I wanted to hit him.

"Look, let's fool them white men," Harrison said. "We won't hurt each other. We'll just pretend, see? We'll show 'em we ain't dumb as they think, see?"

"I don't know."

"It's just exercise. Four rounds for five dollars. You scared?"

"No."

"Then come on and fight."

"All right," I said. "It's just exercise. I'll fight."

Harrison was happy. I felt that it was all very foolish. But what the hell. I would go through with it and that would be the end of it. But I still felt a vague anger that would not leave.

When the white men in the factory heard that we had agreed to fight, their excitement knew no bounds. They offered to teach me new punches. Each morning they would tell me in whispers that Harrison was eating raw onions for strength. And—from Harrison— I heard that they told him I was eating raw meat for strength. They offered to buy me my meals each day, but I refused. I grew ashamed of what I had agreed to do and wanted to back out of the fight, but I was afraid that they would be angry if I tried to. I felt that if white men tried to persuade two black boys to stab each other for no reason save their own pleasure, then it would not be difficult for them to aim a wanton blow at a black boy in a fit of anger, in a passing mood of frustration.

The fight took place one Saturday afternoon in the basement of a Main Street building. Each white man who attended the fight dropped his share of the pot into a hat that sat on the concrete floor. Only white men were allowed in the basement; no women or Negroes were admitted. Harrison and I were stripped to the waist. A bright electric bulb glowed above our heads. As the gloves were tied on my hands, I looked at Harrison and saw his eyes watching me. Would he keep his promise? Doubt made me nervous.

We squared off and at once I knew that I had not thought sufficiently about what I had bargained for. I could not pretend to fight. Neither Harrison nor I knew enough about boxing to deceive even a child for a moment. Now shame filled me. The white men were smoking and yelling obscenities at us.

"Crush that nigger's nuts, nigger!"

"Hit that nigger!"

"Aw, fight, you goddamn niggers!"

"Sock 'im in his f–k–g piece!"

"Make 'im bleed!"

I lashed out with a timid left. Harrison landed high on my head and, before I knew it, I had landed a hard right on Harrison's mouth and blood came. Harrison shot a blow to my nose. The fight was on, was on against our will. I felt trapped and ashamed. I lashed out even harder, and the harder I fought the harder Harrison fought. Our plans and promises now meant nothing. We fought four hard rounds, stabbing, slugging, grunting, spitting, cursing, crying, bleeding. The shame and anger we felt for having allowed ourselves to be duped crept into our blows and blood ran into our eyes, half blinding us. The hate we felt for the men whom we had tried to cheat went into the blows we threw at each other. The white men made the rounds last as long as five minutes and each of us was afraid to stop and ask for time for fear of receiving a blow that would knock us out. When we were on the point of collapsing from exhaustion, they pulled us apart.

I could not look at Harrison. I hated him and I hated myself. I clutched my five dollars in my fist and walked home. Harrison and I avoided each other after that and we rarely spoke. The white men attempted to arrange other fights for us, but we had sense enough to refuse. I heard of other fights being staged between other black boys, and each time I heard those plans falling from the lips of the white men in the factory I eased out of earshot. I felt that I had done something unclean, something for which I could never properly atone.

13

One morning I arrived early at work and went into the bank lobby where the Negro porter was mopping. I stood at a counter and picked up the Memphis *Commercial Appeal* and began my free reading of the press. I came finally to the editorial page and saw an article dealing with one H. L. Mencken. I knew by hearsay that he was the editor of the *American Mercury,* but aside from that I knew nothing about him. The article was a furious denunciation of Mencken, concluding with one, hot, short sentence: Mencken is a fool.

I wondered what on earth this Mencken had done to call down upon him the scorn of the South. The only people I had ever heard denounced in the South were Negroes, and this man was not a Negro. Then what ideas did Mencken hold that made a newspaper like the *Commercial Appeal* castigate him publicly? Undoubtedly he must be advocating ideas that the South did not like. Were there, then, people other than Negroes who criticized the South? I knew that during the Civil War the South had hated northern whites, but I had not encountered such hate during my life. Knowing no more of Mencken than I did at that moment, I felt a vague sympathy for him. Had not the South, which had assigned me the role of a non-man, cast at him its hardest words?

Now, how could I find out about this Mencken? There was a huge library near the riverfront, but I knew that Negroes were not allowed to patronize its shelves any more than they were the parks and playgrounds of the city. I had gone into the library several times to get books for the white men on the job. Which of them would now help me to get books? And how could I read them without causing concern to the white men with whom I worked? I had so far been successful in hiding my thoughts and feelings from them, but I knew that I would create hostility if I went about this business of reading in a clumsy way.

I weighed the personalities of the men on the job. There was Don, a Jew; but I distrusted him. His position was not much better than mine and I knew that he was uneasy and insecure; he had always treated me in an offhand, bantering way that barely concealed his contempt. I was afraid to ask him to help me to get books; his frantic desire to demonstrate a racial solidarity with the whites against Negroes might make him betray me.

Then how about the boss? No, he was a Baptist and I had the suspicion that he would not be quite able to comprehend why a black boy would want to read Mencken. There were other white men on the job whose attitudes showed clearly that they were Kluxers or sympathizers, and they were out of the question.

There remained only one man whose attitude did not fit into an anti-Negro category, for I had heard the white men refer to him as a "Pope lover." He was an Irish Catholic and was hated by the white Southerners. I knew that he read books, because I had got him volumes from the library several times. Since he, too, was an object of hatred, I felt that he might refuse me but would hardly betray me. I hesitated, weighing and balancing the imponderable realities.

One morning I paused before the Catholic fellow's desk.

"I want to ask you a favor," I whispered to him.

"What is it?"

"I want to read. I can't get books from the library. I wonder if you'd let me use your card?"

He looked at me suspiciously.

"My card is full most of the time," he said.

"I see," I said and waited, posing my question silently.

"You're not trying to get me into trouble, are you, boy?" he asked, staring at me.

"Oh, no, sir."

"What book do you want?"

"A book by H. L. Mencken."

"Which one?"

"I don't know. Has he written more than one?"

"He has written several."

"I didn't know that."

"What makes you want to read Mencken?"

"Oh, I just saw his name in the newspaper," I said.

"It's good of you to want to read," he said. "But you ought to read the right things."

I said nothing. Would he want to supervise my reading?

"Let me think," he said. "I'll figure out something."

I turned from him and he called me back. He stared at me quizzically.

"Richard, don't mention this to the other white men," he said.

"I understand," I said. "I won't say a word."

A few days later he called me to him.

"I've got a card in my wife's name," he said. "Here's mine."

"Thank you, sir."

"Do you think you can manage it?"

"I'll manage fine," I said.

"If they suspect you, you'll get in trouble," he said.

"I'll write the same kind of notes to the library that you wrote when you sent me for books," I told him. "I'll sign your name."

He laughed.

"Go ahead. Let me see what you get," he said.

That afternoon I addressed myself to forging a note. Now, what were the names of books written by H. L. Mencken? I did not know any of them. I finally wrote what I thought would be a foolproof note: *Dear Madam: Will you please let this nigger boy*—I used the word "nigger" to make the librarian feel that I could not possibly be the author of the note—*have some books by H. L. Mencken?* I forged the white man's name.

I entered the library as I had always done when on errands for whites, but I felt that I would somehow slip up and betray myself. I doffed my hat, stood a respectful distance from the desk, looked as unbookish as possible, and waited for the white patrons to be taken care of. When the desk was clear of people, I still waited. The white librarian looked at me.

"What do you want, boy?"

As though I did not possess the power of speech, I stepped forward and simply handed her the forged note, not parting my lips.

"What books by Mencken does he want?" she asked.

"I don't know, ma'am," I said, avoiding her eyes.

"Who gave you this card?"

"Mr. Falk," I said.

"Where is he?"

"He's at the work, at the M—— Optical Company," I said. "I've been in here for him before."

"I remember," the woman said. "But he never wrote notes like this."

Oh, God, she's suspicious. Perhaps she would not let me have the books? If she had turned her back at that moment, I would have ducked out the door and never gone back. Then I thought of a bold idea.

"You can call him up, ma'am," I said, my heart pounding.

"You're not using these books, are you?" she asked pointedly.

"Oh, no, ma'am. I can't read."

"I don't know what he wants by Mencken," she said under her breath.

I knew now that I had won; she was thinking of other things and the race question had gone out of her mind. She went to the shelves. Once or twice she looked over her shoulder at me, as though she was still doubtful. Finally she came forward with two books in her hand.

"I'm sending him two books," she said. "But tell Mr. Falk to come in next time, or send me the names of the books he wants. I don't know what he wants to read."

I said nothing. She stamped the card and handed me the

books. Not daring to glance at them, I went out of the library, fearing that the woman would call me back for further questioning. A block away from the library I opened one of the books and read a title: *A Book of Prefaces*. I was nearing my nineteenth birthday and I did not know how to pronounce the word "preface." I thumbed the pages and saw strange words and strange names. I shook my head, disappointed. I looked at the other book; it was called *Prejudices*. I knew what that word meant; I had heard it all my life. And right off I was on guard against Mencken's books. Why would a man want to call a book *Prejudices*? The word was so stained with all my memories of racial hate that I could not conceive of anybody using it for a title. Perhaps I had made a mistake about Mencken? A man who had prejudices must be wrong.

When I showed the books to Mr. Falk, he looked at me and frowned.

"That librarian might telephone you," I warned him.

"That's all right," he said. "But when you're through reading those books, I want you to tell me what you get out of them."

That night in my rented room, while letting the hot water run over my can of pork and beans in the sink, I opened *A Book of Prefaces* and began to read. I was jarred and shocked by the style, the clear, clean, sweeping sentences. Why did he write like that? And how did one write like that? I pictured the man as a raging demon, slashing with his pen, consumed with hate, denouncing everything American, extolling everything European or German, laughing at the weaknesses of people, mocking God, authority. What was this? I stood up, trying to realize what reality lay behind the meaning of the words . . . Yes, this man was fighting, fighting with words. He was using words as a weapon, using them as one would use a club. Could words be weapons? Well, yes, for here they were. Then, maybe, perhaps, I could use them as a weapon? No. It frightened me. I read on and what amazed me was not what he said, but how on earth anybody had the courage to say it.

Occasionally I glanced up to reassure myself that I was alone in the room. Who were these men about whom Mencken was talking so passionately? Who was Anatole France? Joseph Conrad? Sinclair

Lewis, Sherwood Anderson, Dostoevski, George Moore, Gustave Flaubert, Maupassant, Tolstoy, Frank Harris, Mark Twain, Thomas Hardy, Arnold Bennett, Stephen Crane, Zola, Norris, Gorky, Bergson, Ibsen, Balzac, Bernard Shaw, Dumas, Poe, Thomas Mann, O. Henry, Dreiser, H. G. Wells, Gogol, T. S. Eliot, Gide, Baudelaire, Edgar Lee Masters, Stendhal, Turgenev, Huneker, Nietzsche, and scores of others? Were these men real? Did they exist or had they existed? And how did one pronounce their names?

I ran across many words whose meanings I did not know, and I either looked them up in a dictionary or, before I had a chance to do that, encountered the word in a context that made its meaning clear. But what strange world was this? I concluded the book with the conviction that I had somehow overlooked something terribly important in life. I had once tried to write, had once reveled in feeling, had let my crude imagination roam, but the impulse to dream had been slowly beaten out of me by experience. Now it surged up again and I hungered for books, new ways of looking and seeing. It was not a matter of believing or disbelieving what I read, but of feeling something new, of being affected by something that made the look of the world different.

As dawn broke I ate my pork and beans, feeling dopey, sleepy. I went to work, but the mood of the book would not die; it lingered, coloring everything I saw, heard, did. I now felt that I knew what the white men were feeling. Merely because I had read a book that had spoken of how they lived and thought, I identified myself with that book. I felt vaguely guilty. Would I, filled with bookish notions, act in a manner that would make the whites dislike me?

I forged more notes and my trips to the library became frequent. Reading grew into a passion. My first serious novel was Sinclair Lewis's *Main Street*. It made me see my boss, Mr. Gerald, and identify him as an American type. I would smile when I saw him lugging his golf bags into the office. I had always felt a vast distance separating me from the boss, and now I felt closer to him, though still distant. I felt now that I knew him, that I could feel the very limits of his narrow life. And this had happened because I had read a novel about a mythical man called George F. Babbitt.

The plots and stories in the novels did not interest me so much as the point of view revealed. I gave myself over to each novel without reserve, without trying to criticize it; it was enough for me to see and feel something different. And for me, everything was something different. Reading was like a drug, a dope. The novels created moods in which I lived for days. But I could not conquer my sense of guilt, my feeling that the white men around me knew that I was changing, that I had begun to regard them differently.

Whenever I brought a book to the job, I wrapped it in newspaper—a habit that was to persist for years in other cities and under other circumstances. But some of the white men pried into my packages when I was absent and they questioned me.

"Boy, what are you reading those books for?"

"Oh, I don't know, sir."

"That's deep stuff you're reading, boy."

"I'm just killing time, sir."

"You'll addle your brains if you don't watch out."

I read Dreiser's *Jennie Gerhardt* and *Sister Carrie* and they revived in me a vivid sense of my mother's suffering; I was overwhelmed. I grew silent, wondering about the life around me. It would have been impossible for me to have told anyone what I derived from these novels, for it was nothing less than a sense of life itself. All my life had shaped me for the realism, the naturalism of the modern novel, and I could not read enough of them.

Steeped in new moods and ideas, I bought a ream of paper and tried to write; but nothing would come, or what did come was flat beyond telling. I discovered that more than desire and feeling were necessary to write and I dropped the idea. Yet I still wondered how it was possible to know people sufficiently to write about them? Could I ever learn about life and people? To me, with my vast ignorance, my Jim Crow station in life, it seemed a task impossible of achievement. I now knew what being a Negro meant. I could endure the hunger. I had learned to live with hate. But to feel that there were feelings denied me, that the very breath of life itself was beyond my reach, that more than anything else hurt, wounded me. I had a new hunger.

In buoying me up, reading also cast me down, made me see what was possible, what I had missed. My tension returned, new, terrible, bitter, surging, almost too great to be contained. I no longer *felt* that the world about me was hostile, killing; I *knew* it. A million times I asked myself what I could do to save myself, and there were no answers. I seemed forever condemned, ringed by walls.

I did not discuss my reading with Mr. Falk, who had lent me his library card; it would have meant talking about myself and that would have been too painful. I smiled each day, fighting desperately to maintain my old behavior, to keep my disposition seemingly sunny. But some of the white men discerned that I had begun to brood.

"Wake up there, boy!" Mr. Olin said one day.

"Sir!" I answered for the lack of a better word.

"You act like you've stolen something," he said.

I laughed in the way I knew he expected me to laugh, but I resolved to be more conscious of myself, to watch my every act, to guard and hide the new knowledge that was dawning within me.

If I went north, would it be possible for me to build a new life then? But how could a man build a life upon vague, unformed yearnings? I wanted to write and I did not even know the English language. I bought English grammars and found them dull. I felt that I was getting a better sense of the language from novels than from grammars. I read hard, discarding a writer as soon as I felt that I had grasped his point of view. At night the printed page stood before my eyes in sleep.

Mrs. Moss, my landlady, asked me one Sunday morning:

"Son, what is this you keep on reading?"

"Oh, nothing. Just novels."

"What you get out of 'em?"

"I'm just killing time," I said.

"I hope you know your own mind," she said in a tone which implied that she doubted if I had a mind.

I knew of no Negroes who read the books I liked and I wondered if any Negroes ever thought of them. I knew that there were

Negro doctors, lawyers, newspapermen, but I never saw any of them. When I read a Negro newspaper I never caught the faintest echo of my preoccupation in its pages. I felt trapped and occasionally, for a few days, I would stop reading. But a vague hunger would come over me for books, books that opened up new avenues of feeling and seeing, and again I would forge another note to the white librarian. Again I would read and wonder as only the naïve and unlettered can read and wonder, feeling that I carried a secret, criminal burden about with me each day.

That winter my mother and brother came and we set up house-keeping, buying furniture on the installment plan, being cheated and yet knowing no way to avoid it. I began to eat warm food and to my surprise found that regular meals enabled me to read faster. I may have lived through many illnesses and survived them, never suspecting that I was ill. My brother obtained a job and we began to save toward the trip north, plotting our time, setting tentative dates for departure. I told none of the white men on the job that I was planning to go north; I knew that the moment they felt I was thinking of the North they would change toward me. It would have made them feel that I did not like the life I was living, and because my life was completely conditioned by what they said or did, it would have been tantamount to challenging them.

I could calculate my chances for life in the South as a Negro fairly clearly now.

I could fight the southern whites by organizing with other Negroes, as my grandfather had done. But I knew that I could never win that way; there were many whites and there were but few blacks. They were strong and we were weak. Outright black rebellion could never win. If I fought openly I would die and I did not want to die. News of lynchings were frequent.

I could submit and live the life of a genial slave, but that was impossible. All of my life had shaped me to live by my own feelings and thoughts. I could make up to Bess and marry her and inherit the house. But that, too, would be the life of a slave; if I did that, I would crush to death something within me, and I would hate myself as much as I knew the whites already hated those who had submitted. Neither could I ever willingly present myself to be kicked, as Shorty had done. I would rather have died than do that.

I could drain off my restlessness by fighting with Shorty and Harrison. I had seen many Negroes solve the problem of being black by transferring their hatred of themselves to others with a black skin and fighting them. I would have to be cold to do that, and I was not cold and I could never be.

I could, of course, forget what I had read, thrust the whites out of my mind, forget them; and find release from anxiety and longing in sex and alcohol. But the memory of how my father had conducted himself made that course repugnant. If I did not want others to violate my life, how could I voluntarily violate it myself?

I had no hope whatever of being a professional man. Not only had I been so conditioned that I did not desire it, but the fulfillment of such an ambition was beyond my capabilities. Well-to-do Negroes lived in a world that was almost as alien to me as the world inhabited by whites.

What, then, was there? I held my life in my mind, in my consciousness each day, feeling at times that I would stumble and drop it, spill it forever. My reading had created a vast sense of distance between me and the world in which I lived and tried to make a living, and that sense of distance was increasing each day. My days and nights were one long, quiet, continuously contained dream of terror, tension, and anxiety. I wondered how long I could bear it.

14

The accidental visit of Aunt Maggie to Memphis formed a practical basis for my planning to go north. Aunt Maggie's husband, the "uncle" who had fled from Arkansas in the dead of night, had deserted her; and now she was casting about for a living. My mother, Aunt Maggie, my brother, and I held long conferences, speculating on the prospects of jobs and the cost of apartments in Chicago. And every time we conferred, we defeated ourselves. It was impossible for all four of us to go at once; we did not have enough money.

Finally sheer wish and hope prevailed over common sense and facts. We discovered that if we waited until we were prepared to go, we would never leave, we would never amass enough money to see us through. We would have to gamble. We finally decided that Aunt Maggie and I would go first, even though it was winter, and prepare a place for my mother and brother. Why wait until next week or next month? If we were going, why not go at once?

Next loomed the problem of leaving my job cleanly, smoothly, without arguments or scenes. How could I present the fact of leaving to my boss? Yes, I would pose as an innocent boy; I would tell him that my aunt was taking me and my paralyzed mother to Chicago. That would create in his mind the impression that I was not asserting my will; it would block any expression of dislike on his part for my act. I knew that southern whites hated the idea of

Negroes leaving to live in places where the racial atmosphere was different.

It worked as I had planned. When I broke the news of my leaving two days before I left—I was afraid to tell it sooner for fear that I would create hostility on the part of the whites with whom I worked—the boss leaned back in his swivel chair and gave me the longest and most considerate look he had ever given me.

"Chicago?" he repeated softly.

"Yes, sir."

"Boy, you won't like it up there," he said.

"Well, I have to go where my family is, sir," I said.

The other white office workers paused in their tasks and listened. I grew self-conscious, tense.

"It's cold up there," he said.

"Yes, sir. They say it is," I said, keeping my voice in a neutral tone.

He became conscious that I was watching him and he looked away, laughing uneasily to cover his concern and dislike.

"Now, boy," he said banteringly, "don't you go up there and fall into that lake."

"Oh, no, sir," I said, smiling as though there existed the possibility of my falling accidentally into Lake Michigan.

He was serious again, staring at me. I looked at the floor.

"You think you'll do any better up there?" he asked.

"I don't know, sir."

"You seem to've been getting along all right down here," he said.

"Oh, yes, sir. If it wasn't for my mother's going, I'd stay right here and work," I lied as earnestly as possible.

"Well, why not stay? You can send her money," he suggested.

He had trapped me. I knew that staying now would never do. I could not have controlled my relations with the whites if I had remained after having told them that I wanted to go north.

"Well, I want to be with my mother," I said.

"You want to be with your mother," he repeated idly. "Well, Richard, we enjoyed having you with us."

"And I enjoyed working here," I lied.

There was silence; I stood awkwardly, then moved to the door. There was still silence; white faces were looking strangely at me. I went upstairs, feeling like a criminal. The word soon spread through the factory and the white men looked at me with new eyes. They came to me.

"So you're going north, hunh?"

"Yes, sir. My family's taking me with 'em."

"The North's no good for your people, boy."

"I'll try to get along, sir."

"Don't believe all the stories you hear about the North."

"No, sir. I don't."

"You'll come back here where your friends are."

"Well, sir. I don't know."

"How're you going to act up there?"

"Just like I act down here, sir."

"Would you speak to a white girl up there?"

"Oh, no, sir. I'll act there just like I act here."

"Aw, no, you won't. You'll change. Niggers change when they go north."

I wanted to tell him that I was going north precisely to change, but I did not.

"I'll be the same," I said, trying to indicate that I had no imagination whatever.

As I talked I felt that I was acting out a dream. I did not want to lie, yet I had to lie to conceal what I felt. A white censor was standing over me and, like dreams forming a curtain for the safety of sleep, so did my lies form a screen of safety for my living moments.

"Boy, I bet you've been reading too many of them damn books."

"Oh, no, sir."

I made my last errand to the post office, put my bag away, washed my hands, and pulled on my cap. I shot a quick glance about the factory; most of the men were working late. One or two looked up. Mr. Falk, to whom I had returned my library card, gave me a quick, secret smile. I walked to the elevator and rode down with Shorty.

"You lucky bastard," he said bitterly.

"Why do you say that?"

"You saved your goddamn money and now you're gone."

"My problems are just starting," I said.

"You'll never have any problems as hard as the ones you had here," he said.

"I hope not," I said. "But life is tricky."

"Sometimes I get so goddamn mad I want to kill everybody," he spat in a rage.

"You can leave," I said.

"I'll never leave this goddamn South," he railed. "I'm always saying I am, but I won't . . . I'm lazy. I like to sleep too goddamn much. I'll die here. Or maybe they'll kill me."

I stepped from the elevator into the street, half expecting someone to call me back and tell me that it was all a dream, that I was not leaving.

This was the culture from which I sprang. This was the terror from which I fled.

PART TWO

THE HORROR
AND THE GLORY

Sometimes I wonder, huh,
Wonder if other people wonder, huh,
Sometimes I wonder, huh,
Wonder if other people wonder, huh,
Just like I do, oh, my Lord, just like I do!

—NEGRO FOLK SONG

15

⚬⚭⚬

My first glimpse of the flat black stretches of Chicago depressed and dis-
mayed me, mocked all my fantasies. Chicago seemed an unreal city
whose mythical houses were built of slabs of black coal wreathed in
palls of gray smoke, houses whose foundations were sinking slowly
into the dank prairie. Flashes of steam showed intermittently on the
wide horizon, gleaming translucently in the winter sun. The din of
the city entered my consciousness, entered to remain for years to
come. The year was 1927.

What would happen to me here? Would I survive? My expecta-
tions were modest. I wanted only a job. Hunger had long been my
daily companion. Diversion and recreation, with the exception of
reading, were unknown. In all my life—though surrounded by
many people—I had not had a single satisfying, sustained relationship with another human being and, not having had any, I did not
miss it. I made no demands whatever upon others.

The train rolled into the depot. Aunt Maggie and I got off and
walked slowly through the crowds into the station. I looked about
to see if there were signs saying: FOR WHITE—FOR COLORED. I saw
none. Black people and white people moved about, each seemingly
intent upon his private mission. There was no racial fear. Indeed,
each person acted as though no one existed but himself. It was
strange to pause before a crowded newsstand and buy a newspaper
without having to wait until a white man was served. And yet,

because everything was so new, I began to grow tense again, although it was a different sort of tension than I had known before. I knew that this machine-city was governed by strange laws and I wondered if I would ever learn them.

As we waited for a streetcar to take us to Aunt Cleo's home for temporary lodging, I looked northward at towering buildings of steel and stone. There were no curves here, no trees; only angles, lines, squares, bricks and copper wires. Occasionally the ground beneath my feet shook from some faraway pounding and I felt that this world, despite its massiveness, was somehow dangerously fragile. Streetcars screeched past over steel tracks. Cars honked their horns. Clipped speech sounded about me. As I stood in the icy wind, I wanted to talk to Aunt Maggie, to ask her questions, but her tight face made me hold my tongue. I was learning already from the frantic light in her eyes the strain that the city imposed upon its people. I was seized by doubt. Should I have come here? But going back was impossible. I had fled a known terror, and perhaps I could cope with this unknown terror that lay ahead.

The streetcar came. Aunt Maggie motioned for me to get on and pushed me toward a seat in which a white man sat looking blankly out the window. I sat down beside the man and looked straight ahead of me. After a moment I stole a glance at the white man out of the corners of my eyes; he was still staring out the window, his mind fastened upon some inward thought. I did not exist for him; I was as far from his mind as the stone buildings that swept past in the street. It would have been illegal for me to sit beside him in the part of the South that I had come from.

The car swept past soot-blackened buildings, stopping at each block, jerking again into motion. The conductor called street names in a tone that I could not understand. People got on and off the car, but they never glanced at one another. Each person seemed to regard the other as a part of the city landscape. The white man who sat beside me rose and I turned my knees aside to let him pass, and another white man sat beside me and buried his face in a newspaper. How could that possibly be? Was he conscious of my blackness?

We went to Aunt Cleo's address and found that she was living in a rented room. I had imagined that she lived in an apartment and I was disappointed. I rented a room from Aunt Cleo's landlady and decided to keep it until I got a job. I was baffled. Everything seemed makeshift, temporary. I caught an abiding sense of insecurity in the personalities of the people around me. I found Aunt Cleo aged beyond her years. Her husband, a product of a southern plantation, had, like my father, gone off and left her. Why had he left? My aunt could not answer. She was beaten by the life of the city, just as my mother had been beaten. Wherever my eyes turned they saw stricken, frightened black faces trying vainly to cope with a civilization that they did not understand. I felt lonely. I had fled one insecurity and had embraced another.

When I rose the next morning the temperature had dropped below zero. The house was as cold to me as the southern streets had been in winter. I dressed, doubling my clothing. I ate in a restaurant, caught a streetcar and rode south, rode until I could see no more black faces on the sidewalks. I had now crossed the boundary line of the Black Belt and had entered that territory where jobs were perhaps to be had from white folks. I walked the streets and looked into shop windows until I saw a sign in a delicatessen: PORTER WANTED.

I went in and a stout white woman came to me.

"Vat do you vant?" she asked.

The voice jarred me. She's Jewish, I thought, remembering with shame the obscenities I used to shout at Jewish storekeepers in Arkansas.

"I thought maybe you needed a porter," I said.

"Meester 'Offman, he eesn't here yet," she said. "Vill you vait?"

"Yes, ma'am."

"Seet down."

"No, ma'am. I'll wait outside."

"But eet's cold out zhere," she said.

"That's all right," I said.

She shrugged. I went to the sidewalk. I waited for half an hour in the bitter cold, regretting that I had not remained in the warm store, but unable to go back inside. A bald, stoutish white man went into the store and pulled off his coat. Yes, he was the boss man . . . I went in.

"Zo you vant a job?" he asked.

"Yes, sir," I answered, guessing at the meaning of his words.

"Vhere you vork before?"

"In Memphis, Tennessee."

"My brudder-in-law vorked in Tennessee vonce," he said.

I was hired. The work was easy, but I found to my dismay that I could not understand a third of what was said to me. My slow southern ears were baffled by their clouded, thick accents. One morning Mrs. Hoffman asked me to go to a neighboring store—it was owned by a cousin of hers—and get a can of chicken à la king. I had never heard the phrase before and I asked her to repeat it.

"Don't you know nosing?" she demanded of me.

"If you would write it down for me, I'd know what to get," I ventured timidly.

"I can't vite!" she shouted in a sudden fury. "Vat kinda boy ees you?"

I memorized the separate sounds that she had uttered and went to the neighboring store.

"Mrs. Hoffman wants a can of Cheek Keeng Awr Lar Keeng," I said slowly, hoping that he would not think I was being offensive.

"All vight," he said, after staring at me a moment.

He put a can into a paper bag and gave it to me; outside in the street I opened the bag and read the label: Chicken à La King. I cursed, disgusted with myself. I knew those words. It had been her thick accent that had thrown me off. Yet I was not angry with her for speaking broken English; my English, too, was broken. But why could she not have taken more patience? Only one answer came to my mind. I was black and she did not care. Or so I thought . . . I was persisting in reading my present environment in the light of my old one. I reasoned thus: Though English was my native tongue and America my native land, she, an alien, could operate a store and earn a living in a neighborhood where I could not even live. I reasoned further that she was aware of this and was trying to protect her position against me.

(It was not until I had left the delicatessen job that I saw how grossly I had misread the motives and attitudes of Mr. Hoffman and his wife. I had not yet learned anything that would have helped me to thread my way through these perplexing racial relations. Accepting my environment at its face value, trapped by my own emotions, I kept asking myself what had black people done to bring this crazy world upon them?

(The fact of the separation of white and black was clear to me; it was its effect upon the personalities of people that stumped and dismayed me. I did not feel that I was a threat to anybody; yet, as soon as I had grown old enough to think I had learned that my entire personality, my aspirations had long ago been discounted; that, in a measure, the very meaning of the words I spoke could not be fully understood.

(And when I contemplated the area of No Man's Land into which the Negro mind in America had been shunted I wondered if there had ever existed in all human history a more corroding and devastating attack upon the personalities of men than the idea of racial discrimination. In order to escape the racial attack that went to the roots of my life, I would have gladly accepted any way of life but the one in which I found myself. I would have agreed to live under a system of feudal oppression, not because I preferred feudalism but because I felt that feudalism made use of a limited part of a man, defined him, his rank, his function in society. I would have consented to live under the most rigid type of dictatorship, for I felt that dictatorships, too, defined the use of men, however degrading that use might be.

(While working in Memphis I had stood aghast as Shorty had offered himself to be kicked by the white men; but now, while working in Chicago, I was learning that perhaps even a kick was better than uncertainty . . . I had elected, in my fevered search for honorable adjustment to the American scene, not to submit and in doing so I had embraced the daily horror of anxiety, of tension, of eternal disquiet. I could now sympathize with—though I could never bring myself to approve—those tortured blacks who had given up and had gone to their white tormentors and had said: "Kick me, if that's all there is for me; kick me and let me feel at home, let me have peace!"

(Color hate defined the place of black life as below that of white life; and the black man, responding to the same dreams as the white man, strove to bury within his heart his awareness of this difference because it made him lonely and afraid. Hated by whites and being an organic part of the culture that hated him, the black man grew in turn to hate in himself that which others hated in him. But pride would make him hide his self-hate, for he would not want whites to know that he was so thoroughly conquered by them that his total life was conditioned by their attitude; but in the act of hiding his self-hate, he could not help but hate those who evoked his self-hate in him. So each part of his day would be consumed in a war with himself, a good part of his energy would be spent in keeping control of his unruly emotions, emotions which he had not wished to have, but could not help having. Held at bay by the hate of others, preoccupied with his own feelings, he was continuously at war with reality. He became inefficient, less able to see and judge the objective world. And when he reached that state, the white people looked at him and laughed and said:

("Look, didn't I tell you niggers were that way?"

(To solve this tangle of balked emotion, I loaded the empty part of the ship of my personality with fantasies of ambition to keep it from toppling over into the sea of senselessness. Like any other American, I dreamed of going into business and making money; I dreamed of working for a firm that would allow me to advance until I reached an important position; I even dreamed of organizing secret groups of blacks to fight all whites . . . And if the blacks would not agree to organize, then they would have to be fought. I would end up again with self-hate, but it was now a self-hate that was projected outward upon other blacks. Yet I knew—with that part of my mind that the whites had given me—that none of my dreams was possible. Then I would hate myself for allowing my mind to dwell upon the unattainable. Thus the circle would complete itself.

(Slowly I began to forge in the depths of my mind a mechanism that repressed all the dreams and desires that the Chicago streets, the newspapers, the movies were evoking in me. I was going through a second childhood; a new sense of the limit of the possible was being born in me. What could I dream of that had the barest possibility of coming true? I could think of nothing. And, slowly, it was upon exactly that nothingness that my mind began to dwell, that constant sense of wanting without having, of being hated without reason. A dim notion of what life meant to a Negro in America was coming to consciousness in me, not in terms of external events, lynchings, Jim Crowism, and the endless brutalities, but in terms of crossed-up feeling, of psyche pain. I sensed that Negro life was a sprawling land of unconscious suffering, and there were but few Negroes who knew the meaning of their lives, who could tell their story.)

Word reached me that an examination for postal clerk was impending and at once I filed an application and waited. As the date for the examination drew near, I was faced with another problem. How could I get a free day without losing my job? In the South it would have been an unwise policy for a Negro to have gone to his white boss and asked for time to take an examination for another job. It would have implied that the Negro did not like to work for the white boss, that he felt he was not receiving just consideration and, inasmuch as most jobs that Negroes held in the South involved a personal, paternalistic relationship, he would have been risking an argument that might have led to violence.

I now began to speculate about what kind of man Mr. Hoffman was, and I found that I did not know him; that is, I did not know his basic attitude toward Negroes. If I asked him, would he be sympathetic enough to allow me time off with pay? I needed the money. Perhaps he would say: "Go home and stay home if you don't like this job"? I was not sure of him. I decided, therefore, that I had better not risk it. I would forfeit the money and stay away without telling him.

The examination was scheduled to take place on a Monday; I

.d been working steadily and I would be too tired to do my best if
I took the examination without the benefit of rest. I decided to stay
away from the shop Saturday, Sunday, and Monday. But what could
I tell Mr. Hoffman? Yes, I would tell him that I had been ill. No,
that was too thin. I would tell him that my mother had died in
Memphis and that I had gone down to bury her. That lie might
work.

I took the examination and when I came to the store on
Tuesday, Mr. Hoffman was astonished, of course.

"I didn't sink you vould ever come back," he said.

"I'm awfully sorry, Mr. Hoffman."

"Vat happened?"

"My mother died in Memphis and I had to go down and bury
her," I lied.

He looked at me, then shook his head.

"Rich, you lie," he said.

"I'm not lying," I lied stoutly.

"You vanted to do somesink, zo you zayed ervay," he said,
shrugging.

"No, sir. I'm telling you the truth," I piled another lie upon
the first one.

"No. You lie. You disappoint me," he said.

"Well, all I can do is tell you the truth," I lied indignantly.

"Vy didn't you use the phone?"

"I didn't think of it," I told a fresh lie.

"Rich, if your mudder die, you vould tell me," he said.

"I didn't have time. Had to catch the train," I lied yet again.

"Vhere did you get the money?"

"My aunt gave it to me," I said, disgusted that I had to lie and
lie again.

"I don't vant a boy vat tells lies," he said.

"I don't lie," I lied passionately to protect my lies.

Mrs. Hoffman joined in and both of them hammered at me.

"Ve know. You come from ze Zouth. You feel you can't tell us
ze truth. But ve don't bother you. Ve don't feel like people in ze
Zouth. Ve treat you nice, don't ve?" they asked.

"Yes, ma'am," I mumbled.

"Zen vy lie?"

"I'm not lying," I lied with all my strength.

I became angry because I knew that they knew that I was lying. I had lied to protect myself, and then I had to lie to protect my lie. I had met so many white faces that would have violently disapproved of my taking the examination that I could not have risked telling Mr. Hoffman the truth. But how could I now tell him that I had lied because I was so unsure of myself? Lying was bad, but revealing my own sense of insecurity would have been worse. It would have been shameful and I did not like to feel ashamed.

Their attitudes had proved utterly amazing. They were taking time out from their duties in the store to talk to me, and I had never encountered anything like that from whites before. A southern white man would have said: "Get to hell out of here!" or "All right, nigger. Get to work." But no white people had ever stood their ground and probed at me, questioned me at such length. It dawned upon me that they were trying to treat me as an equal, which made it even more impossible for me ever to tell them that I had lied, why I had lied. I felt that if I confessed I would give them a moral advantage over me that would be unbearable.

"All vight, zday and vork," Mr. Hoffman said. "I know you're lying, but I don't care, Rich."

I wanted to quit. He had insulted me. But I liked him in spite of myself. Yes, I had done wrong, but how on earth could I have known the kind of people I was working for? Perhaps Mr. Hoffman would have gladly consented for me to take the examination, but my hopes had been far weaker than my powerful fears.

Working with them from day to day and knowing that they knew I had lied from fear crushed me. I knew that they pitied me and pitied the fear in me. I resolved to quit and risk hunger rather than stay with them. I left the job that following Saturday, not telling them that I would not be back, not possessing the heart to say good-bye. I just wanted to go quickly and have them forget that I had ever worked for them.

—∞—

er an idle week, I got a job as a dishwasher in a North Side café that had just opened. My boss, a white woman, directed me in unpacking barrels of dishes, setting up new tables, painting, and so on. I had charge of serving breakfast; in the late afternoons I carted trays of food to patrons in the hotel who did not want to come down to eat. My wages were fifteen dollars a week; the hours were long, but I ate my meals on the job.

The cook was an elderly Finnish woman with a sharp, bony face. There were several white waitresses. I was the only Negro in the café. The waitresses were a hard, brisk lot and I was keenly aware of how their attitudes contrasted with those of southern white girls. They had not been taught to keep a gulf between me and themselves; they were relatively free of the heritage of racial hate.

One morning as I was making coffee, Cora came forward with a tray loaded with food and squeezed against me to draw a cup of coffee.

"Pardon me, Richard," she said.

"Oh, that's all right," I said in an even tone.

But I was aware that she was a white girl and that her body was pressed closely against mine, an incident that had never happened to me before in my life, an incident charged with the memory of dread. But she was not conscious of my blackness or of what her actions would have meant in the South. And had I not been born in the South, her trivial act would have been as unnoticed by me as it was by her. As she stood close to me, I could not help thinking that if a southern white girl had wanted to draw a cup of coffee, she would have commanded me to step aside so that she might not come in contact with me. The work of the hot and busy kitchen would have had to cease for the moment so that I could have taken my tainted body far enough away to allow the southern white girl a chance to get a cup of coffee. There lay a deep, emotional safety in knowing that the white girl who was now leaning carelessly against me was not thinking of me, had no deep, vague, irrational fright that made her feel that I was a creature to be avoided at all costs.

One summer morning a white girl came late to work and

rushed into the pantry where I was busy. She went into the women's room and changed her clothes; I heard the door open and a second later I was surprised to hear her voice:

"Richard, quick! Tie my apron!"

She was standing with her back to me and the strings of her apron dangled loose. There was a moment of indecision on my part, then I took the two loose strings and carried them around her body and brought them again to her back and tied them in a clumsy knot.

"Thanks a million," she said grasping my hand for a split second, and was gone.

I continued my work, filled with all the possible meanings that that tiny, simple, human event could have meant to any Negro in the South where I had spent most of my hungry days.

I did not feel any admiration for the girls, nor any hate. My attitude was one of abiding and friendly wonder. For the most part I was silent with them, though I knew that I had a firmer grasp of life than most of them. As I worked I listened to their talk and perceived its puzzled, wandering, superficial fumbling with the problems and facts of life. There were many things they wondered about that I could have explained to them, but I never dared.

During my lunch hour, which I spent on a bench in a near-by park, the waitresses would come and sit beside me, talking at random, laughing, joking, smoking cigarettes. I learned about their tawdry dreams, their simple hopes, their home lives, their fear of feeling anything deeply, their sex problems, their husbands. They were an eager, restless, talkative, ignorant bunch, but casually kind and impersonal for all that. They knew nothing of hate and fear, and strove instinctively to avoid all passion.

I often wondered what they were trying to get out of life, but I never stumbled upon a clue, and I doubt if they themselves had any notion. They lived on the surface of their days; their smiles were surface smiles, and their tears were surface tears. Negroes lived a truer and deeper life than they, but I wished that Negroes, too, could live as thoughtlessly, serenely as they. The girls never talked of their feelings; none of them possessed the insight or the emotional

...ipment to understand themselves or others. How far apart in culture we stood! All my life I had done nothing but feel and cultivate my feelings; all their lives they had done nothing but strive for petty goals, the trivial material prizes of American life. We shared a common tongue, but my language was a different language from theirs.

It was in the psychological distance that separated the races that the deepest meaning of the problem of the Negro lay for me. For these poor, ignorant white girls to have understood my life would have meant nothing short of a vast revolution in theirs. And I was convinced that what they needed to make them complete and grown-up in their living was the inclusion in their personalities of a knowledge of lives such as I lived and suffered containedly.

(As I, in memory, think back now upon those girls and their lives I feel that for white America to understand the significance of the problem of the Negro will take a bigger and tougher America than any we have yet known. I feel that America's past is too shallow, her national character too superficially optimistic, her very morality too suffused with color hate for her to accomplish so vast and complex a task. Culturally the Negro represents a paradox: Though he is an organic part of the nation, he is excluded by the entire tide and direction of American culture. Frankly, it is felt to be right to exclude him, and it is felt to be wrong to admit him freely. Therefore if, within the confines of its present culture, the nation ever seeks to purge itself of its color hate, it will find itself at war with itself, convulsed by a spasm of emotional and moral confusion. If the nation ever finds itself examining its real relation to the Negro, it will find itself doing infinitely more than that; for the anti-Negro attitude of whites represents but a tiny part—though a symbolically significant one—of the moral attitude of the nation. Our too-young and too-new America, lusty because it is lonely, aggressive because it is afraid, insists upon seeing the world in terms of good and bad, the holy and the evil, the high and the low, the white and the black; our America is frightened of fact, of history, of processes, of necessity. It hugs the easy way of damning those whom it cannot understand, of excluding those who look different, and it salves its conscience with a self-draped cloak of righteousness. Am I damning my native land? No; for I, too, share these faults of character! And I really do not think that America, adolescent and cocksure, a stranger to suffering and travail, an enemy of passion and sacrifice, is ready to probe into its most fundamental beliefs.

(I know that not race alone, not color alone, but the daily values that give meaning to life stood between me and those white girls with whom I worked. Their constant outward-looking, their mania for radios, cars, and a thousand other trinkets made them dream and fix their eyes upon the trash of life, made it impossible for them to learn a language which could have taught them to speak of what was in their or others' hearts. The words of their souls were the syllables of popular songs.

(The essence of the irony of the plight of the Negro in America, to me, is that he is doomed to live in isolation while those who condemn him seek the basest goals of any people on the face of the earth. Perhaps it would be possible for the Negro to become reconciled to his plight if he could be made to believe that his sufferings were for some remote, high, sacrificial end; but sharing the culture that condemns him, and seeing that a lust for trash is what blinds the nation to his claims, is what sets storms to rolling in his soul.)

Though I had fled the pressure of the South, my outward conduct had not changed. I had been schooled to present an unalteringly smiling face and I continued to do so despite the fact that my environment allowed more open expression. I hid my feelings and avoided all relationships with whites that might cause me to reveal them.

One afternoon the boss lady entered the kitchen and found me sitting on a box reading a copy of the *American Mercury*.

"What on earth are you reading?" she demanded.

I was at once on guard, though I knew I did not have to be.

"Oh, just a magazine," I said.

"Where did you get it?" she asked.

"Oh, I just found it," I lied; I had bought it.

"Do you understand it?" she asked.

"Yes, ma'am."

"Well," she exclaimed, "the colored dishwasher reads the *American Mercury!*"

She walked away, shaking her head. My feelings were mixed. I was glad that she had learned that I was not completely dumb, yet I felt a little angry because she seemed to think it odd for dishwashers to read magazines. Thereafter I kept my books and magazines wrapped in newspaper so that no one would see them, reading them at home and on the streetcar to and from work.

Tillie, the Finnish cook, was a tall, ageless, red-faced, raw-boned woman with long, snow-white hair which she balled in a knot at the nape of her neck. She cooked expertly and was superbly efficient. One morning as I passed the sizzling stove I thought I heard Tillie cough and spit. I paused and looked carefully to see where her spittle had gone, but I saw nothing; her face, obscured by steam, was bent over a big pot. My senses told me that Tillie had coughed and spat into that pot, but my heart told me that no human being could possibly be so filthy. I decided to watch her. An hour or so later I heard Tillie clear her throat with a grunt, saw her cough, and spit into the boiling soup. I held my breath; I did not want to believe what I had seen.

Should I tell the boss lady? Would she believe me? I watched Tillie for another day to make sure that she was spitting into the food. She was; there was no doubt of it. But who would believe me if I told them what was happening? I was the only black person in the café. Perhaps they would think that I hated the cook? I stopped eating my meals there and bided my time.

The business of the café was growing rapidly and a Negro girl was hired to make salads. I went to her at once.

"Look, can I trust you?" I asked.

"What are you talking about?" she asked.

"I want you to say nothing, but watch that cook."

"For what?"

"Now, don't get scared. Just watch the cook."

She looked at me as though she thought I was crazy; and,

frankly, I felt that perhaps I ought not to say anything to anybody.

"What do you mean?" she demanded.

"All right," I said. "I'll tell you. That cook spits in the food."

"What are you saying?" she asked aloud.

"Keep quiet," I said.

"Spitting?" she asked me in a whisper. "Why would she do that?"

"I don't know. But watch her."

She walked away from me with a funny look in her eyes. But half an hour later she came rushing to me, looking ill, sinking into a chair.

"Oh, God, I feel awful!"

"Did you see it?"

"She *is* spitting in the food!"

"What ought we do?" I asked.

"Tell the lady," she said.

"She wouldn't believe me," I said.

She widened her eyes as she understood. We were black and the cook was white.

"But I can't work here if she's going to do that," she said.

"Then you tell her," I said.

"She wouldn't believe me either," she said.

She rose and ran to the women's room. When she returned she stared at me. We were two Negroes and we were silently asking ourselves if the white boss lady would believe us if we told her that her expert white cook was spitting in the food all day long as it cooked upon the stove.

"I don't know," she wailed in a whisper and walked away.

I thought of telling the waitresses about the cook, but I could not get up enough nerve. Many of the girls were friendly with Tillie. Yet I could not let the cook spit in the food all day. That was wrong by any human standard of conduct. I washed dishes, thinking, wondering; I served breakfast, thinking, wondering; I served meals in the apartments of patrons upstairs, thinking, wondering. Each time I picked up a tray of food I felt like retching. Finally the Negro salad girl came to me and handed me her purse and hat.

"I'm going to tell her and quit, goddamn," she said.

"I'll quit too, if she doesn't fire her," I said.

"Oh, she won't believe me," she wailed in agony.

"You tell her. You're a woman. She might believe you."

Her eyes welled with tears and she sat for a long time; then she rose and went abruptly into the dining room. I went to the door and peered. Yes, she was at the desk, talking to the boss lady. She returned to the kitchen and went into the pantry; I followed her.

"Did you tell her?" I asked.

"Yes."

"What did she say?"

"She said I was crazy."

"Oh, God!" I said.

"She just looked at me with those gray eyes of hers," the girl said. "Why would Tillie do that?"

"I don't know," I said.

The boss lady came to the door and called the girl; both of them went into the dining room. Tillie came over to me; a hard, cold look was in her eyes.

"What's happening here?" she asked.

"I don't know," I said, wanting to slap her across the mouth.

She muttered something and went back to the stove, coughed, spat into a bubbling pot. I left the kitchen and went into the back areaway to breathe. The boss lady came out.

"Richard," she said.

Her face was pale. I was smoking a cigarette and I did not look at her.

"Is this true?"

"Yes, ma'am."

"It couldn't be. Do you know what you're saying?"

"Just watch her," I said.

"I don't know," she moaned.

She looked crushed. She went back into the dining room, but I saw her watching the cook through the doors. I watched both of them, the boss lady and the cook, praying that the cook would spit again. She did. The boss lady came into the kitchen and stared at

Tillie, but she did not utter a word. She burst into tears and ran back into the dining room.

"What's happening here?" Tillie demanded.

No one answered. The boss lady came out and tossed Tillie her hat, coat, and money.

"Now, get out of here, you dirty dog!" she said.

Tillie stared, then slowly picked up her hat, coat, and the money; she stood a moment, wiped sweat from her forehead with her hand, then spat, this time on the floor. She left.

Nobody was ever able to fathom why Tillie liked to spit into the food.

Brooding over Tillie, I recalled the time when the boss man in Mississippi had come to me and had tossed my wages to me and said:

"Get out, nigger! I don't like your looks."

And I wondered if a Negro who did not smile and grin was as morally loathsome to whites as a cook who spat into the food . . .

I worked at the café all spring and in June I was called for temporary duty in the post office. My confidence soared; if I obtained an appointment as a regular clerk, I could spend at least five hours a day writing.

I reported at the post office and was sworn in as a temporary clerk. I earned seventy cents an hour and I went to bed each night now with a full stomach for the first time in my life. When I worked nights, I wrote during the day; when I worked days, I wrote during the night.

But the happiness of having a job did not keep another worry from rising to plague me. Before I could receive a permanent appointment I would have to take a physical examination and the weight requirement was one hundred and twenty-five pounds and I—with my long years of semistarvation—barely tipped the scales at a hundred and ten. Frantically I turned all of my spare money into food and ate. But my skin and flesh would not respond to the food. Perhaps I was not eating the right diet? Perhaps my chronic anxiety kept my weight down. I drank milk, ate steak, but it did not give

an extra ounce of flesh. I visited a doctor who told me that
ere was nothing wrong with me except malnutrition, that I must
eat and sleep long hours. I did and my weight remained the same. I
knew now that my job was temporary and that when the time came
for my appointment I would have to resume my job hunting again.

While I crammed my stomach I read Stein's *Three Lives*,
Crane's *The Red Badge of Courage*, and Dostoevski's *The Possessed*,
all of which revealed new realms of feeling. But the most important
discoveries came when I veered from fiction proper into the field of
psychology and sociology. I ran through volumes that bore upon
the causes of my conduct and the conduct of my family. I studied
tables of figures relating population density to insanity, relating
housing to disease, relating school and recreational opportunities
to crime, relating various forms of neurotic behavior to environment, relating racial insecurities to the conflicts between whites and
blacks . . .

I still had no friends, casual or intimate, and felt the need for
none. I had developed a self-sufficiency that kept me distant from
others, emotionally and psychologically. Occasionally I went to
house-rent parties, parties given by working-class families to raise
money to pay the landlord, the admission to which was a quarter or
a half dollar. At these affairs I drank home-brewed beer, ate
spaghetti and chitterlings, laughed and talked with black, southern-
born girls who worked as domestic servants in white middle-class
homes. But with none of them did my relations rest upon my deepest feelings. I discussed what I read with no one, and to none did I
confide. Emotionally, I was withdrawn from the objective world;
my desires floated loosely within the walls of my consciousness,
contained and controlled.

As a protective mechanism, I developed a terse, cynical mode
of speech that rebuffed those who sought to get too close to me.
Conversation was my way of avoiding expression; my words were
reserved for those times when I sat down alone to write. My face
was always a deadpan or a mask of general friendliness; no word or
event could jar me into a gesture of enthusiasm or despair. A slowly,
hesitantly spoken "Yeah" was my general verbal reaction to almost

everything I heard. "That's pretty good," said with a slow nod of the head, was my approval. "Aw, naw," muttered with a cold smile, was my rejection. Even though I reacted deeply, my true feelings raced along underground, hidden.

I did not act in this fashion deliberately; I did not prefer this kind of relationship with people. I wanted a life in which there was a constant oneness of feeling with others, in which the basic emotions of life were shared, in which common memory formed a common past, in which collective hope reflected a national future. But I knew that no such thing was possible in my environment. The only ways in which I felt that my feelings could go outward without fear of rude rebuff or searing reprisal was in writing or reading, and to me they were ways of living.

Aunt Maggie had now rented an apartment in which I shared a rear room. My mother and brother came and all three of us slept in that one room; there was no window, just four walls and a door. My excessive reading puzzled Aunt Maggie; she sensed my fiercely indrawn nature and she did not like it. Being of an open, talkative disposition, she declared that I was going about the business of living wrongly, that reading books would not help me at all. But nothing she said had any effect. I had long ago hardened myself to criticism.

"Boy, are you reading for law?" my aunt would demand.

"No."

"Then why are you reading all the time?"

"I like to."

"But what do you get out of it?"

"I get a great deal out of it."

And I knew that my words sounded wild and foolish in my environment, where reading was almost unknown, where the highest item of value was a dime or a dollar, an apartment or a job; where, if one aspired at all, it was to be a doctor or a lawyer, a shopkeeper or a politician. The most valued pleasure of the people I knew was a car, the most cherished experience a bottle of whisky, the most sought-after prize somebody else's wife. I had no sense of being inferior or superior to the people about me; I merely felt that they had had no chance to learn to live differently. I never criticized them or praised them, yet they felt in my neutrality a deeper rejection of them than if I had cursed them.

Repeatedly I took stabs at writing, but the results were so poor that I would tear up the sheets. I was striving for a level of expression that matched those of the novels I read. But I always somehow failed to get onto the page what I thought and felt. Failing at sustained narrative, I compromised by playing with single sentences and phrases. Under the influence of Stein's *Three Lives,* I spent hours and days pounding out disconnected sentences for the sheer love of words.

I would write:

"The soft melting hunk of butter trickled in gold down the stringy grooves of the split yam."

Or:

"The child's clumsy fingers fumbled in sleep, feeling vainly for the wish of its dream."

"The old man huddled in the dark doorway, his bony face lit by the burning yellow in the windows of distant skyscrapers."

My purpose was to capture a physical state or movement that carried a strong subjective impression, an accomplishment which seemed supremely worth struggling for. If I could fasten the mind of the reader upon words so firmly that he would forget words and be conscious only of his response, I felt that I would be in sight of knowing how to write narrative. I strove to master words, to make them disappear, to make them important by making them new, to make them melt into a rising spiral of emotional stimuli, each greater than the other, each feeding and reinforcing the other, and all ending in an emotional climax that would drench the reader with a sense of a new world. That was the single aim of my living.

Autumn came and I was called for my physical examination for the position of regular postal clerk. I had not told my mother or brother or aunt that I knew I would fail. On the morning of the examination I drank two quarts of buttermilk, ate six bananas, but it did not hoist the red arrow of the government scales to the required mark of one hundred and twenty-five pounds. I went home and sat disconsolately in my back room, hating myself, wondering where I could find another job. I had almost got my hands upon a decent job and had lost it, had let it slip through my fingers. Waves of self-doubt rose to haunt me. Was I always to hang on the fringes of life? What I wanted was truly modest, and yet my past, my diet, my hunger, had snatched it from before my eyes. But these self-doubts did not last long; I dulled the sense of loss through reading, reading, writing and more writing.

The loss of my job did not evoke in me any hostility toward the system of rules that had barred my first grasp at the material foundations of American life. I felt that it was unfair that my lack of a few pounds of flesh should deprive me of a chance at a good job, but I had long ago emotionally rejected the world in which I lived and my reaction was: Well, this is the system by which people want the world to run whether it helps them or not. To me, my losing was only another manifestation of that queer, material way of American living that computed everything in terms of the concrete: weight, color, race, fur coats, radios, electric refrigerators, cars, money . . . It seemed that I simply could not fit into a materialistic life.

The living arrangement of my mother, brother, and Aunt Maggie—now that I had no promise of being a postal clerk—quickly deteriorated. In Aunt Maggie's eyes I was a plainly marked failure and she feared that perhaps she would have to feed me. The emotional atmosphere in the cramped quarters became tense, ugly, petty, bickering. Fault was found with my reading and writing; it was claimed that I was swelling the electric bill. Though I had saved almost no money, I decided to rent an apartment. Aunt Cleo was living in a rented room and I invited her to share the apartment with me, my mother, and brother, and she consented. We moved into a tiny, dingy two-room den in whose kitchen a wall bed fitted snugly into a corner near the stove. The place was alive with vermin and the smell of cooking hung in the air day and night.

I asked for my job back at the café and the boss lady allowed me to return; again I served breakfast, washed dishes, carted trays of food up into the apartments. Another postal examination was scheduled for spring and to that end I made eating an obsession. I ate when I did not want to eat, drank milk when it sickened me. Slowly my starved body responded to food and overcame the lean years of Mississippi, Arkansas, and Tennessee, counteracting the flesh-sapping anxiety of fear-filled days.

I spent my nights reading Proust's *A Remembrance of Things Past,* admiring the lucid, subtle but strong prose, stupefied by its dazzling magic, awed by the vast, delicate, intricate, and psychological structure of the Frenchman's epic of death and decadence. But it crushed me with hopelessness, for I wanted to write of the people in my environment with an equal thoroughness, and the burning example before my eyes made me feel that I never could.

My ability to endure tension had now grown amazingly. From the accidental pain of southern years, from anxiety that I had sought to avoid, from fear that had been too painful to bear, I had learned to like my unintermittent burden of feeling, had become habituated to acting with all of my being, had learned to seek those areas of life, those situations, where I knew that events would complement my own inner mood. I was conscious of what was happening to me; I knew that my attitude of watchful wonder had usurped all other feelings, had become the meaning of my life, an integral part of my personality; that I was striving to live and measure all things by it. Having no claims upon others, I bent the way the wind blew, rendering unto my environment that which was my environment's, and rendering unto myself that which I felt was mine.

It was a dangerous way to live, far more dangerous than violating laws or ethical codes of conduct; but the danger was for me and me alone. Had I not been conscious of what I was doing, I could have easily lost my way in the fogbound regions of compelling fantasy. Even so, I floundered, staggered; but somehow I always groped my way back to that path where I felt a tinge of warmth from an unseen light.

Hungry for insight into my own life and the lives about me, knowing my fiercely indrawn nature, I sought to fulfill more than my share of all obligations and responsibilities, as though offering libations of forgiveness to my environment. Indeed, the more my emotions claimed my attention, the sharper—as though in ultimate self-defense—became my desire to measure accurately the reality of the objective world so that I might more than meet its demands. At twenty years of age the mold of my life was set, was hardening into a pattern, a pattern that was neither good nor evil, neither right nor wrong.

16

In the spring I took the postal examination again. Time had some-what repaired the ravages of hunger and I was able to meet the required physical weight. We moved to a larger apartment. My increased pay made better food possible. I was happy in my own way.

Working nights, I spent my days in experimental writing, filling endless pages with stream-of-consciousness Negro dialect, trying to depict the dwellers of the Black Belt as I felt and saw them. My reading in sociology had enabled me to discern many strange types of Negro characters, to identify many modes of Negro behavior; and what moved me above all was the frequency of mental illness, that tragic toll that the urban environment exacted of the black peasant. Perhaps my writing was more an attempt at understanding than self-expression. A need that I did not comprehend made me use words to create religious types, criminal types, the warped, the lost, the baffled; my pages were full of tension, frantic poverty, and death.

But something was missing in my imaginative efforts; my flights of imagination were too subjective, too lacking in reference to social action. I hungered for a grasp of the framework of con-temporary living, for a knowledge of the forms of life about me, for eyes to see the bony structures of personality, for theories to light up the shadows of conduct.

While sorting mail in the post office, I met a young Irish chap whose sensibilities amazed me. We would take a batch of mail in our fingers and, while talking in low monotones out of the sides of our mouths, toss them correctly into their designated holes and suddenly our hands would be empty and we would have no memory of having worked. Most of the clerks could work in this automatic manner. The Irish chap and I had read a lot in common and we laughed at the same sacred things. He was as cynical as I was regarding uplift and hope, and we were proud of having escaped what we called the "childhood disease of metaphysical fear." I was introduced to the Irish chap's friends and we formed a "gang" of Irish, Jewish, and Negro wits who poked fun at government, the masses, statesmen, and political parties. We assumed that all people were good to the degree to which they amused us, or to the extent to which we could make them objects of laughter. We ridiculed all ideas of protest, of organized rebellion or revolution. We felt that all businessmen were thoroughly stupid and that no other group was capable of rising to challenge them. We sneered at voting, for we felt that the choice between one political crook and another was too small for serious thought. We believed that man should live by hard facts alone, and we had so long ago put God out of our minds that we did not even discuss Him.

During this cynical period I met a Negro literary group on Chicago's South Side; it was composed of a dozen or more boys and girls, all of whom possessed academic learning, economic freedom, and vague ambitions to write. I found them more formal in manner than their white counterparts; they wore stylish clothes and were finicky about their personal appearance. I had naïvely supposed that I would have much in common with them, but I found them preoccupied with twisted sex problems. Coming from a station in life which they no doubt would have branded "lower class," I could not understand why they were so all-absorbed with sexual passion. I was encountering for the first time the full-fledged Negro Puritan invert—the emotionally sick—and I discovered that their ideas were but excuses for sex, leads to sex, hints at sex, substitutes for sex. In speech and action they strove to act as un-Negro as possible, denying the racial and material foundations of their lives, accepting their class and racial status in ways so oblique that one had the impression that no difficulties existed for them. Though I had never had any assignments from a college professor, I had made much harder and more prolonged attempts at self-expression than any of them. Swearing love for art, they hovered on the edge of Bohemian life. Always friendly, they could never be anybody's friend; always reading, they could really never learn; always boasting of their passions, they could never really feel and were afraid to live.

The one group I met during those exploring days whose lives enthralled me was the Garveyites, an organization of black men and women who were forlornly seeking to return to Africa. Theirs was a passionate rejection of America, for they sensed with that directness of which only the simple are capable that they had no chance to live a full human life in America. Their lives were not cluttered with ideas in which they could only half believe; they could not create illusions which made them think they were living when they were not; their daily lives were too nakedly harsh to permit of camouflage. I understood their emotions, for I partly shared them.

The Garveyites had embraced a totally racialistic outlook which endowed them with a dignity that I had never seen before in Negroes. On the walls of their dingy flats were maps of Africa and India and Japan, pictures of Japanese generals and admirals, portraits of Marcus Garvey in gaudy regalia, the faces of colored men and women from all parts of the world. I gave no credence to the ideology of Garveyism; it was, rather, the emotional dynamics of its adherents that evoked my admiration. Those Garveyites I knew could never understand why I liked them but would never follow them, and I pitied them too much to tell them that they could never achieve their goal, that Africa was owned by the imperial powers of Europe, that their lives were alien to the mores of the natives of Africa, that they were people of the West and would forever be so until they either merged with the West or perished. It was when the Garveyites spoke fervently of building their own country, of someday living within the boundaries of a culture of their own making, that I sensed the passionate hunger of their lives, that I caught a glimpse of the potential strength of the American Negro.

Rumors of unemployment came, but I did not listen to them. I heard of the organizational efforts of the Communist party among the Negroes of the South Side, but Communist activities were too remote to strike my mind with any degree of vividness. Whenever I met a person whom I suspected of being a Communist, I talked to him affably but from an emotional distance. I sensed that something terrible was beginning to happen in the world, but I tried to shut it out of my mind by reading and writing.

When the time came for my appointment as a regular clerk, I was told that no appointments would be made for the time being. The volume of mail dropped. My hours of work dwindled. My paychecks grew small. Food became scarce at home. The hunger I thought I had left behind returned. One winter afternoon, in 1929, en route to work from the library, I passed a newsstand on which papers blazed:

Stocks Crash—Billions Fade

Most of what I had seen in newspapers had never concerned me, so why should this? Newspapers reported the doings in a life I did not share. But the volume of mail fell so low that I worked but one or two nights a week. In the post-office canteen the boys stood about and talked.

"The cops beat up some demonstrators today."

"The Reds had a picket line around the City Hall."

"Wall Street's cracking down on the country."

"Surplus production's throwing millions out of work."

"There're more than two million unemployed."

"They don't count. They're always out of work."

"Read Karl Marx and get the answer, boys."

"There'll be a revolution if this keeps up."

"Hell, naw. Americans are too dumb to make a revolution."

The post-office job ended and again I was out of work. I could no longer think that the tides of economics were not my concern.

But how could I have had any possible say in how the world had been run? I had grown up in complete ignorance of what created jobs. Having been thrust out of the world because of my race, I had accepted my destiny by not being curious about what shaped it.

The following summer I was again called for temporary duty in the post office, and the work lasted into the winter. Aunt Cleo succumbed to a severe cardiac condition and, hard on the heels of her illness, my brother developed stomach ulcers. To rush my worries to a climax, my mother also became ill. I felt that I was maintaining a private hospital. Finally the post-office work ceased altogether and I haunted the city for jobs. But when I went into the streets in the morning I saw sights that killed my hope for the rest of the day. Unemployed men loitered in doorways with blank looks in their eyes, sat dejectedly on front steps in shabby clothing, congregated in sullen groups on street corners, and filled all the empty benches in the parks of Chicago's South Side.

Luck of a sort came when a distant cousin of mine, who was a superintendent in a Negro burial society, offered me a position on his staff as an agent. The thought of selling insurance policies to ignorant Negroes disgusted me.

"Well, if you don't sell them, somebody else will," my cousin told me. "You've got to eat, haven't you?"

During that year I worked for several burial and insurance societies that operated among Negroes, and I received a new kind of education. I found that the burial societies, with some exceptions, were mostly "rackets." Some of them conducted their businesses legitimately, but there were many that exploited the ignorance of their black customers.

I was paid under a system that netted me fifteen dollars for every dollar's worth of new premiums that I placed upon the company's books, and for every dollar's worth of old premiums that lapsed I was penalized fifteen dollars. In addition, I was paid a commission of ten per cent on total premiums collected, but during the depression it was extremely difficult to persuade a black family to buy a policy carrying even a dime premium. I considered myself lucky if, after subtracting lapses from new business, there remained fifteen dollars that I could call my own.

This "gambling" method of remuneration was practiced by some of the burial companies because of the tremendous "turnover" in policyholders, and the companies had to have a constant stream of new business to keep afloat. Whenever a black family moved or suffered a slight reverse in fortune, it usually let its policy lapse and later bought another policy from some other company.

Each day now I saw how the Negro in Chicago lived, for I visited hundreds of dingy flats filled with rickety furniture and ill-clad children. Most of the policyholders were illiterate and did not know that their policies carried clauses severely restricting their benefit payments, and, as an insurance agent, it was not my duty to tell them.

After tramping the streets and pounding on doors to collect premiums, I was dry, strained, too tired to read or write. I hungered for relief and, as a salesman of insurance to many young black girls, I found it. There were many comely black housewives who, trying desperately to keep up their insurance payments, were willing to make bargains to escape paying a ten-cent premium. I had a long, tortured affair with one girl by paying her ten-cent premium each week. She was an illiterate black child with a baby whose father she did not know. During the entire period of my relationship with her, she had but one demand to make of me: She wanted me to take her to a circus. Just what significance circuses had for her, I was never able to learn.

After I had been with her one morning—in exchange for the dime premium—I sat on the sofa in the front room and began to read a book I had with me. She came over shyly.

"Lemme see that," she said.

"What?" I asked.

"That book," she said.

I gave her the book; she looked at it intently. I saw that she was holding it upside down.

"What's in here you keep reading?" she asked.

"Can't you really read?" I asked.

"Naw," she giggled. "You know I can't read."

"You can read *some*," I said.

"Naw," she said.

I stared at her and wondered just what a life like hers meant in the scheme of things, and I came to the conclusion that it meant absolutely nothing. And neither did my life mean anything.

"How come you looking at me that way for?" she asked.

"Nothing."

"You don't talk much."

"There isn't much to say."

"I wished Jim was here," she sighed.

"Who's Jim?" I asked, jealous. I knew that she had other men, but I resented her mentioning them in my presence.

"Just a friend," she said.

I hated her then, then hated myself for coming to her.

"Do you like Jim better than you like me?" I asked.

"Naw. Jim just likes to talk."

"Then why do you be with me, if you like Jim better?" I asked, trying to make an issue and feeling a wave of disgust because I wanted to.

"You all right," she said, giggling. "I like you."

"I could kill you," I said.

"What?" she exclaimed.

"Nothing," I said, ashamed.

"Kill me, you said? You crazy, man," she said.

"Maybe I am," I muttered, angry that I was sitting beside a human being to whom I could not talk, angry with myself for coming to her, hating my wild and restless loneliness.

"You oughta go home and sleep," she said. "You tired."

"What do you ever think about?" I demanded harshly.

"Lotta things."

"What, for example?"

"You," she said, smiling.

"You know I mean just one dime to you each week," I said.

"Naw, I thinka lotta you."

"Then what do you think?"

"'Bout how you talk when you talk. I wished I could talk like you," she said seriously.

"Why?" I taunted her.

"When you gonna take me to a circus?" she demanded suddenly.

"You ought to be in a circus," I said.

"I'd like it," she said, her eyes shining.

I wanted to laugh, but her words sounded so sincere that I could not laugh.

"There's no circus in town," I said.

"I bet there is and you won't tell me 'cause you don't wanna take me," she said, pouting.

"But there's no circus in town, I tell you!"

"When will one come?"

"I don't know."

"Can't you read it in the papers?" she asked.

"There's nothing in the papers about a circus."

"There is," she said. "If I could read, I'd find it."

I laughed and she was hurt.

"There *is* a circus in town," she said stoutly.

"There's no circus in town," I said. "But if you want to learn to read, then I'll teach you."

She nestled at my side, giggling.

"See that word?" I said, pointing.

"Yeah."

"That's an 'and,' " I said.

She doubled, giggling.

"What's the matter?" I asked.

She rolled on the floor, giggling.

"What's so funny?" I demanded.

"You," she giggled. "You so funny."

I rose.

"The hell with you," I said.

"Don't you go and cuss me now," she said. "I don't cuss you."

"I'm sorry," I said.

I got my hat and went to the door.

"I'll see you next week?" she asked.

"Maybe," I said.

When I was on the sidewalk, she called to me from a window.

"You promised to take me to a circus, remember?"

"Yes." I walked close to the window. "What is it you like about a circus?"

"The animals," she said simply.

I felt that there was a hidden meaning, perhaps, in what she had said; but I could not find it. She laughed and slammed the window shut.

Each time I left her I resolved not to visit her again. I could not talk to her; I merely listened to her passionate desire to see a circus. She was not calculating; if she liked a man, she just liked him. Sex relations were the only relations she had ever had; no others were possible with her, so limited was her intelligence.

Most of the other agents also had their bought girls and they were extremely anxious to keep other agents from tampering with them. One day a new section of the South Side was given to me as a part of my collection area and the agent from whom the territory had been taken suddenly became very friendly with me.

"Say, Wright," he asked, "did you collect from Ewing at Champlain Avenue yet?"

"Yes," I answered, after consulting my book.

"How did you like her?" he asked, staring at me.

"She's a good-looking number," I said.

"You had anything to do with her yet?" he asked.

"No, but I'd like to," I said, laughing.

"Look," he said. "I'm a friend of yours."

"Since when?" I countered.

"No, I'm really a friend," he said.

"What's on your mind?"

"Listen, that gal's sick," he said seriously.

"What do you mean?"

"She's got the clap," he said. "Keep away from her. She'll lay with anybody."

"Gee, I'm glad you told me," I said.

"You had your eye on her, didn't you?" he asked.

"Yes, I did," I said.

"Leave her alone," he said. "She'll get you down."

That night I told my cousin what the agent had said about Miss Ewing. My cousin laughed.

"That gal's all right," he said. "That agent's been fooling around with her. He told you she had a disease so that you'd be scared to bother her. He was protecting her from you."

That was the way the black women were regarded by the black agents. Some of the agents were vicious; if they had claims to pay to a sick black woman and if the woman was able to have sex relations with them, they would insist upon it, using the claim money as a bribe. If the woman refused, they would report to the office that the woman was a malingerer. The average black woman would submit because she needed the money badly.

As an insurance agent, it was necessary for me to take part in one swindle. It appears that the burial society had originally issued a policy that was—from their point of view—too liberal in its provisions, and the officials decided to exchange the policies then in the hands of their clients for other policies carrying stricter clauses; of course, this had to be done in a manner that would not allow the policyholder to know that his policy was being switched, that he was being swindled. I did not like it, but there was only one thing I could do to keep from being a party to it: I could quit and starve. But I did not feel that being honest was worth the price of starvation.

The swindle worked in this way. In my visits to the homes of policyholders to collect premiums, I was accompanied by the superintendent who claimed to the policyholder that he was making a routine inspection. The policyholder, usually an illiterate black woman, would dig up her policy from the bottom of a trunk or a chest and hand it to the superintendent. Meanwhile I would be marking the woman's premium book, an act which would distract her from what the superintendent was doing. The superintendent would exchange the old policy for a new one which was identical in color, serial number, and beneficiary, but which carried much smaller payments. It was dirty work and I wondered how I could stop it. And when I could think of no safe way I would curse myself and the victims and forget about it. (The black owners of the burial societies were leaders in the Negro communities and were respected by whites.)

As I went from house to house collecting money, I saw black men mounted upon soapboxes at street corners, bellowing about bread, rights, and revolution. I liked their courage, but I doubted their wisdom. The speakers claimed that Negroes were angry, that they were about to rise and join their white fellow workers to make a revolution. I was in and out of many Negro homes each day and I knew that the Negroes were lost, ignorant, sick in mind and body. I saw that a vast distance separated the agitators from the masses, a distance so vast that the agitators did not know how to appeal to the people they sought to lead.

Some mornings I found leaflets on my steps telling of China, Russia, and Germany; on some days I witnessed as many as five thousand jobless Negroes, led by Communists, surging through the streets. I would watch them with an aching heart, firmly convinced that they were being duped; but if I had been asked to give them another solution for their problems, I would not have known how.

It became a habit of mine to visit Washington Park of an afternoon after collecting a part of my premiums, and I would wander through crowds of unemployed Negroes, pausing here and there to sample the dialectic or indignation of Communist speakers. What I heard and saw baffled and angered me. The Negro Communists were deliberately careless in their personal appearance, wearing their shirt collars turned in to make V's at their throats, wearing their caps—they wore caps because Lenin had worn caps—with the visors turned backward, tilted upward at the nape of their necks. Many of their mannerisms, pronunciations, and turns of speech had been consciously copied from white Communists whom they had recently met. While engaged in conversation, they stuck their thumbs in their suspenders or put their left hands into their shirt bosoms or hooked their thumbs into their back pockets as they had seen Lenin or Stalin do in photographs. Though they did not know it, they were naïvely practicing magic; they thought that if they acted like the men who had overthrown the czar, then surely they ought to be able to win their freedom in America.

In speaking they rolled their "r's" in Continental style, pronouncing "party" as "parrrtee," stressing the last syllable, having picked up the habit from white Communists. "Comrades" became "cumrrrades," and "distribute," which they had known how to pronounce all their lives, was twisted into "distrrribuuute," with the accent on the last instead of the second syllable, a mannerism which they copied from Polish Communist immigrants who did not know how to pronounce the word. Many sensitive Negroes agreed with the Communist program but refused to join their ranks because of the shabby quality of those Negroes whom the Communists had already admitted to membership.

When speaking from the platform, the Negro Communists, eschewing the traditional gestures of the Negro preacher—as though they did not possess the strength to develop their own style of Communist preaching—stood straight, threw back their heads, brought the edge of the right palm down hammerlike into the outstretched left palm in a series of jerky motions to pound their points home, a mannerism that characterized Lenin's method of speaking. When they walked, their stride quickened; all the peasant hesitancy of their speech vanished as their voices became clipped, terse. In debate they interrupted their opponents in a tone of voice that was an octave higher, and if their opponents raised their voices to be heard, the Communists raised theirs still higher until shouts rang out over the park. Hence, the only truth that prevailed was that which could be shouted and quickly understood.

Their emotional certainty seemed buttressed by access to a fund of knowledge denied to ordinary men, but a day's observation of their activities was sufficient to reveal all their thought processes. An hour's listening disclosed the fanatical intolerance of minds sealed against new ideas, new facts, new feelings, new attitudes, new hints at ways to live. They denounced books they had never

read, people they had never known, ideas they could never understand, and doctrines whose names they could not pronounce.
Communism, instead of making them leap forward with fire in
their hearts to become masters of ideas and life, had frozen them at
an even lower level of ignorance than had been theirs before they
met Communism.

When Hoover threatened to drive the bonus marchers from
Washington, one Negro Communist speaker said:

"If he drives the bonus marchers out of Washington, the people will rise up and make a revolution!"

I went to him, determined to get at what he really meant.

"You know that even if the United States Army actually kills
the bonus marchers, there'll be no revolution," I said.

"You don't know the indignation of the masses!" he exploded.

"But you don't seem to know what it takes to make a revolution," I explained. "Revolutions are rare occurrences."

"You underestimate the masses," he told me.

"No, I know the masses of Negroes very well," I said. "But I
don't believe that a revolution is pending. Revolutions come
through concrete historical processes . . ."

"You're an intellectual," he said, smiling disdainfully.

A few days later, after Hoover had had the bonus marchers driven from Washington at the point of bayonets, I accosted him:

"What about that revolution you predicted if the bonus
marchers were driven out?" I asked.

"The prerequisite conditions did not exist," he shrugged and
muttered.

I left him, wondering why he felt it necessary to make so many
ridiculous overstatements. I could not refute the general Communist analysis of the world; the only drawback was that their
world was just too simple for belief. I liked their readiness to act,
but they seemed lost in folly, wandering in a fantasy. For them there
was no yesterday or tomorrow, only the living moment of today;
their only task was to annihilate the enemy that confronted them in
any manner possible.

At times their speeches, glowing with rebellion, were downright offensive to lowly, hungry Negroes. Once a Negro Communist speaker, inveighing against religion, said:

"There ain't no goddamn God! If there is, I hereby challenge Him to strike me dead!"

He paused dramatically before his vast black audience for God to act, but God declined. He then pulled out his watch.

"Maybe God didn't hear me!" he yelled. "I'll give Him two more minutes!" Then, with sarcasm: "Mister God, kill me!"

He waited, looking mockingly at his watch. The audience laughed uneasily.

"I'll tell you where to find God," the speaker went on in a hard, ranting voice. "When it rains at midnight, take your hat, turn it upside down on a floor in a dark room, and you'll have God!"

I had to admit that I had never heard atheism of so militant a nature; but the Communist speaker seemed to be amusing and frightening the people more than he was convincing them.

"If there is a God up there in that empty sky," the speaker roared on, "I'll reach up there and grab Him by His beard and jerk Him down here on this hungry earth and cut His throat!" He wagged his head. "Now, let God dare me!"

The audience was shocked into silence for a moment, then it yelled with delight. I shook my head and walked away. That was not the way to destroy people's outworn beliefs . . . They were acting like irresponsible children . . .

I was now convinced that they did not know the complex nature of Negro life, did not know how great was the task to which they had set themselves. They had rejected the state of things as they were, and that seemed to me to be the first step toward embracing a creative attitude toward life. I felt that it was not until one wanted the world to be different that one could look at the world with will and emotion. But these men had rejected what was before their eyes without quite knowing what they had rejected and why.

I felt that the Negro could not live a full, human life under the conditions imposed upon him by America; and I felt, too, that America, for different reasons, could not live a full, human life. It seemed to me, then, that if the Negro solved his problem, he would be solving infinitely more than his problem alone. I felt certain that the Negro could never solve his problem until the deeper problem of American civilization had been faced and solved. And because the Negro was the most cast-out of all the outcast people in America, I felt that no other group in America could tackle this problem of what our American lives meant so well as the Negro could.

But, as I listened to the Communist Negro speakers, I wondered if the Negro, blasted by three hundred years of oppression, could possibly cast off his fear and corruption and rise to the task. Could the Negro ever possess himself, learn to know what had happened to him in relation to the aspirations of Western society? It seemed to me that for the Negro to try to save himself he would have to forget himself and try to save a confused, materialistic nation from its own drift toward self-destruction. Could the Negro accomplish this miracle? Could he take up his bed and walk?

Election time was nearing and a Negro Republican precinct captain asked me to help him round up votes. I had no interest in the candidates, but I needed the money. I went from door to door with the precinct captain and discovered that the whole business was one long process of bribery, that people voted for three dollars, for the right to continue their illicit trade in sex or alcohol. On election day I went into the polling booth and drew the curtain behind me and unfolded my ballots. As I stood there the sordid implications of politics flashed through my mind. "Big Bill" Thompson headed the local Republican machine and I knew that he was using the Negro vote to control the city hall; in turn, he was engaged in vast political deals of which the Negro voters, political innocents, had no notion. With my pencil I wrote in a determined scrawl across the face of the ballots:

I Protest This Fraud

I knew that my gesture was futile. But I wanted somebody to know that out of that vast sea of ignorance in the Black Belt there was at least one person who knew the game for what it was. I collected my ten dollars and went home.

The depression deepened and I could not sell insurance to hungry Negroes. I sold my watch and scouted for cheaper rooms; I found a rotting building and rented an apartment in it. The place was dismal; plaster was falling from the walls; the wooden stairs sagged. When my mother saw it, she wept. I felt bleak. I had not done what I had come to the city to do.

One morning I rose and my mother told me that there was no food for breakfast. I knew that the city had opened relief stations, but each time I thought of going into one of them I burned with shame. I sat for hours, fighting hunger, avoiding my mother's eyes. Then I rose, put on my hat and coat, and went out. As I walked toward the Cook County Bureau of Public Welfare to plead for bread, I knew that I had come to the end of something.

17

When I reached the relief station, I felt that I was making a public confession of my hunger. I sat waiting for hours, resentful of the mass of hungry people about me. My turn finally came and I was questioned by a middle-class Negro woman who asked me for a short history of my life. As I waited again I became aware of something happening in the room. The black men and women were mumbling quietly among themselves; they had not known one another before they had come here, but now their timidity and shame were wearing off and they were exchanging experiences. Before this they had lived as individuals, each somewhat afraid of the other, each seeking his own pleasure, each stanch in that degree of Americanism that had been allowed him. But now life had tossed them together, and they were learning to know the sentiments of their neighbors for the first time; their talking was enabling them to sense the collectivity of their lives, and some of their fear was passing.

Did the relief officials realize what was happening? No. If they had, they would have stopped it. But they saw their "clients" through the eyes of their profession, saw only what their "science" allowed them to see. As I listened to the talk I could see black minds shedding many illusions. These people now knew that the past had betrayed them, had cast them out; but they did not know what the future would be like, did not know what they wanted. Yes,

some of the things that the Communists said were true; they maintained that there came times in history when a ruling class could no
longer rule, and I sat looking at the beginnings of anarchy. To permit the birth of this new consciousness in these people was proof
that those who ruled did not quite know what they were doing,
assuming that they were trying to save themselves and their class.
Had they understood what was happening, they would never have
allowed millions of perplexed and defeated people to sit together
for long hours and talk, for out of their talk was rising a new realization of life. And once this new conception of themselves had
formed, no power on earth could alter it.

I left the relief station with the promise that food would be sent
to me, but I also left with a knowledge that the relief officials had
not wanted to give to me. I had felt the possibility of creating a new
understanding of life in the minds of people rejected by the society
in which they lived, people to whom the Chicago *Daily Tribune*
referred contemptuously as the "idle" ones, as though these people
had deliberately sought their present state of helplessness.

Who would give these people a meaningful way of life?
Communist theory defined these people as the molders of the
future of mankind, but the Communist speeches I had heard in the
park had mocked that definition. These people, of course, were not
ready for a revolution; they had not abandoned their past lives by
choice, but because they simply could not live the old way any
longer. Now, what new faith would they embrace? The day I
begged bread from the city officials was the day that showed me I
was not alone in my loneliness, society had cast millions of others
with me. But how could I be with them? How many understood
what was happening? My mind swam with questions that I could
not answer.

I was slowly beginning to comprehend the meaning of my
environment; a sense of direction was beginning to emerge from
the conditions of my life. I began to feel something more powerful
than I could express. My speech and manner changed. My cynicism
slid from me. I grew open and questioning. I wanted to know.

(If I were a member of the class that rules, I would post men in all the neighborhoods of the nation, not to spy upon or club rebellious workers, not to break strikes or disrupt unions; but to ferret out those who no longer respond to the system in which they live. I would make it known that the real danger does not stem from those who seek to grab their share of wealth through force, or from those who try to defend their property through violence, for both of these groups, by their affirmative acts, support the values of the system in which they live. The millions that I would fear are those who do not dream of the prizes that the nation holds forth, for it is in them, though they may not know it, that a revolution has taken place and is biding its time to translate itself into a new and strange way of life.

(I feel that the Negroes' relation to America is symbolically peculiar, and from the Negroes' ultimate reactions to their trapped state a lesson can be learned about America's future. Negroes are told in a language they cannot possibly misunderstand that their native land is not their own; and when they, acting upon impulses which they share with whites, try to assert a claim to their birthright, whites retaliate with terror, never pausing to consider the consequences should the Negroes give up completely. They never dream that they would face a situation far more terrifying if they were confronted by Negroes who made no claims at all than by those who are buoyed by social aggressiveness. My knowledge of how Negroes react to their plight makes me declare that no man can possibly be individually guilty of treason, that an insurgent act is but a man's desperate answer to those who twist his environment so that he cannot fully share the spirit of his native land. Treason is a crime of the state.)

Christmas came and I was once more called to the post office for temporary work. Again I met the Irish chap and we discussed world happenings, the vast armies of unemployed, the rising tide of radical action. I now detected a change in the attitudes of the whites I met; their privations were making them regard Negroes with new eyes, and for the first time I was invited to their homes.

When the work in the post office ended, I was assigned by the relief system as an orderly to a medical research institute in one of the largest and wealthiest hospitals in Chicago. I cleaned operating rooms, dog, rat, mice, cat, and rabbit pens, and fed guinea pigs. Four of us Negroes worked there and we occupied an underworld position, remembering that we must restrict ourselves—when not engaged upon some task—to the basement corridors so that we would not mingle with white nurses, doctors, or visitors.

The sharp line of racial division drawn by the hospital authorities came to me the first morning when I walked along an underground corridor and saw two long lines of women coming toward me. A line of white girls marched past, clad in starched uniforms that gleamed white; their faces were alert, their steps quick, their bodies lean and shapely, their shoulders erect, their faces lit with the light of purpose. And after them came a line of black girls, old, fat, dressed in ragged gingham, walking loosely, carrying tin cans of soap powder, rags, mops, brooms . . . I wondered what law of the universe kept them from being mixed? The sun would not have stopped shining had there been a few black girls in the first line, and the earth would not have stopped whirling on its axis had there been a few white girls in the second line. But the two lines I saw graded status in purely racial terms.

Of the three Negroes who worked with me, one was a boy of about my own age, Bill, who was either sleepy or drunk most of the time. Bill straightened his hair and I suspected that he kept a bottle hidden somewhere in the piles of hay which we fed to the guinea pigs. He did not like me and I did not like him, though I tried harder than he to conceal my dislike. We had nothing in common except that we were both black and lost. While I contained my frustration, he drank to drown his. Often I tried to talk to him, tried in simple words to convey to him some of my ideas, and he would listen in sullen silence. Then one day he came to me with an angry look on his face.

"I got it," he said.

"You've got what?" I asked.

"This old race problem you keep talking about," he said.

"What about it?"

"Well, it's this way," he explained seriously. "Let the government give every man a gun and five bullets, then let us all start over again. Make it just like it was in the beginning. The ones who come out on top, white or black, let them rule."

His simplicity terrified me. I had never met a Negro who so irredeemably brutalized. I stopped pumping my ideas into Bill's brain for fear that the fumes of alcohol might send him reeling toward some fantastic fate.

The two other Negroes were elderly and had been employed in the institute for fifteen years or more. One was Brand, a short, black, morose bachelor; the other was Cooke, a tall, yellow, spectacled fellow who spent his spare time keeping track of world events through the Chicago *Daily Tribune*. Brand and Cooke hated each other for a reason that I was never able to determine, and they spent a good part of each day quarreling.

When I began working at the institute, I recalled my adolescent dream of wanting to be a medical research worker. Daily I saw young Jewish boys and girls receiving instruction in chemistry and medicine that the average black boy or girl could never receive. When I was alone, I wandered and poked my fingers into strange chemicals, watched intricate machines trace red and black lines upon ruled paper. At times I paused and stared at the walls of the rooms, at the floors, at the wide desks at which the white doctors sat; and I realized—with a feeling that I could never quite get used to—that I was looking at the world of another race.

My interest in what was happening in the institute amused the three other Negroes with whom I worked. They had no curiosity about "white folks' things," while I wanted to know if the dogs being treated for diabetes were getting well; if the rats and mice in whom cancer had been induced showed any signs of responding to treatment. I wanted to know the principle that lay behind the Aschheim-Zondek tests that were made with rabbits, the Wasser-mann tests that were made with guinea pigs. But when I asked a timid question I found that even Jewish doctors had learned to imitate the sadistic method of humbling a Negro that the native-born whites had cultivated.

"If you know too much, boy, your brains might explode," a doctor said one day.

Each Saturday morning I assisted a young Jewish doctor in slitting the vocal cords of a fresh batch of dogs from the city pound. The object was to devocalize the dogs so that their howls would not disturb the patients in the other parts of the hospital. I held each dog as the doctor injected nembutal into its veins to make it unconscious; then I held the dog's jaws open as the doctor inserted the scalpel and severed the vocal cords. Later, when the dogs came to, they would lift their heads to the ceiling and gape in a soundless wail. The sight became lodged in my imagination as a symbol of silent suffering.

To me nembutal was a powerful and mysterious liquid, but when I asked questions about its properties I could not obtain a single intelligent answer. The young Jewish doctor simply ignored me with:

"Come on. Bring the next dog. I haven't got all day."

One Saturday morning, after I had held the dogs for their vocal cords to be slit, the doctor left the nembutal on a bench. I picked it up, uncorked it, and smelt it. It was odorless. Suddenly Brand ran to me with a stricken face.

"What're you doing?" he asked.

"I was smelling this stuff to see if it had any odor," I said.

"Did you really smell it?" he asked me.

"Yes."

"Oh, God!" he exclaimed.

"What's the matter?" I asked.

"You shouldn't've done that!" he shouted.

"Why?"

He grabbed my arm and jerked me across the room.

"Come on!" he yelled, snatching open the door.

"What's the matter?" I asked.

"I gotta get you to a doctor 'fore it's too late," he gasped.

Had my foolish curiosity made me inhale something dangerous?

"But . . . Is it poisonous?"

"Run, boy!" he said, pulling me. "You'll fall dead."

Filled with fear, with Brand pulling my arm, I rushed out of the room, raced across a rear areaway, into another room, then down a long corridor. I wanted to ask Brand what symptoms I must expect, but we were running too fast. Brand finally stopped, gasping for breath. My heart beat wildly and my blood pounded in my head. Brand then dropped to the concrete floor, stretched out on his back and yelled with laughter, shaking all over. He beat his fists against the concrete; he moaned, giggled.

I tried to master my outrage, wondering if some of the white doctors had told him to play the joke. He rose and wiped tears from his eyes, still laughing. I walked away from him. He knew that I was angry and he followed me.

"Don't get mad," he gasped through his laughter.

"Go to hell," I said.

"I couldn't help it," he giggled. "You looked at me like you'd believe anything I said. Man, you was scared . . ."

He leaned against the wall, laughing again, stomping his feet. I was angry, for I felt that he would spread the story. I knew that Bill and Cooke never ventured beyond the safe bounds of Negro living, and they would never blunder into anything like this. And if they heard about this, they would laugh for months.

"Brand, if you mention this, I'll kill you," I swore.

"You ain't mad?" he asked, laughing, staring at me through tears.

Sniffing, Brand walked ahead of me. I followed him back into the room that housed the dogs. All day, while at some task, he would pause and giggle, then smother it with his hand, looking at me out of the corner of his eyes, shaking his head. He laughed at me for a week. I kept my temper and let him amuse himself. I finally found out the properties of nembutal by consulting medical books, but I never told Brand.

One summer morning, just as I began work, a young Jewish boy came to me with a stop watch in his hand.

"Dr. _____ wants me to time you when you clean a room," he

said. "We're trying to make the institute more efficient."

"I'm doing my work and getting through on time," I said.

"This is the boss's order," he said.

"Why don't you work for a change?" I blurted, angry.

"Now, look," he said. "*This* is my work. Now *you* work."

I got mop and pail, sprayed a room with disinfectant, and scrubbed at coagulated blood and hardened dog, rat, and rabbit feces. The normal temperature of a room was ninety, but as the sun beat down upon the skylights, the temperature rose above a hundred. Stripped to my waist, I slung the mop, moving steadily like a machine, hearing the Jewish boy press the button on the stop watch as I finished cleaning a room. I worked from seven in the morning until noon, and I was limp, washed-out.

"Well, how is it?" I asked.

"It took you seventeen minutes to clean that last room," he said. "That ought to be the time for each room."

"But that room was not very dirty," I said.

"You have seventeen rooms to clean," he went on as though I had not spoken. "Seventeen times seventeen make four hours and forty-nine minutes." He wrote upon a little pad. "After lunch, clean the five flights of stone stairs. I timed a boy who scrubbed one step and multiplied that time by the number of steps. You ought to be through at six."

"Suppose I want relief?" I asked.

"You'll manage," he said and left.

Never had I felt so much the slave as when I scoured those stone steps each afternoon. Working against time, I would wet five steps, sprinkle soap powder, then a white doctor or a nurse would come and, instead of avoiding the soppy steps, walk on them and track the dirty water onto the steps that I had already cleaned. To obviate this, I cleaned but two steps at a time, a distance over which a ten-year-old child could step. But it did no good. The white people still plopped their feet down into the dirty water and muddied the other clean steps. If I ever really hotly hated unthinking whites, it was then. Not once during my entire stay at the institute did a single white person show enough courtesy to avoid a wet step. I

would be on my knees, scrubbing, sweating, pouring out what limited energy my body could wring from my meager diet, and I
would hear feet approaching. I would pause and curse with tense
lips:

"These sonofabitches are going to dirty these steps again, goddamn their souls to hell!"

Sometimes a sadistically observant white man would notice
that he had tracked dirty water up the steps, and he would look
back down at me and smile and say:

"Boy, we sure keep you busy, don't we?"

And I would not be able to answer.

The feud that went on between Brand and Cooke continued.
Although they were working daily in a building where scientific history was being made, the light of curiosity was never in their eyes.
They were conditioned to their racial "place," had learned to see
only a part of the whites and the white world; and the whites, too,
had learned to see only a part of the lives of the blacks and their
world.

Perhaps Brand and Cooke, lacking interests that could absorb
them, fuming like children over trifles, simply invented their hate of
each other in order to have something to feel deeply about. Or perhaps there was in them a vague psyche pain stemming from their
chronically frustrating way of life, a pain whose cause they did not
know; and, like those devocalized dogs, they would whirl and snap
at the air when their old pain struck them. Anyway, they argued
about the weather, sports, sex, war, race, politics, and religion; neither of them knew the subjects they debated, but it seemed that the
less they knew the better they could argue.

The tug of war between the two elderly men reached a climax
one winter day at noon. It was incredibly cold and an icy gale swept
up and down the Chicago streets with blizzard force. The door of
the animal-filled room was locked, for we always insisted that we be
allowed one hour in which to eat and rest. Bill and I were sitting on
wooden boxes, eating our lunches out of paper bags. Brand was
washing his hands at the sink. Cooke was sitting on a rickety stool,
munching an apple and reading the Chicago *Daily Tribune*.

Now and then a devocalized dog lifted his nose to the ceiling and howled soundlessly. The room was filled with many rows of high steel tiers. Perched upon each of these tiers were layers of steel cages containing the dogs, rats, mice, rabbits, and guinea pigs. Each cage was labeled in some indecipherable scientific jargon. Along the walls of the room were long charts with zigzagging red and black lines that traced the success or failure of some experiment. The lonely piping of guinea pigs floated unheeded about us. Hay rustled as a rabbit leaped restlessly about in its pen. A rat scampered around in its steel prison. Cooke tapped the newspaper for attention.

"It says here," Cooke mumbled through a mouthful of apple, "that this is the coldest day since 1888."

Bill and I sat unconcerned. Brand chuckled softly.

"What in hell you laughing about?" Cooke demanded of Brand.

"You can't believe what that damn *Tribune* says," Brand said.

"How come I can't?" Cooke demanded. "It's the world's greatest newspaper."

Brand did not reply; he shook his head pityingly and chuckled again.

"Stop that damn laughing at me!" Cooke said angrily.

"I laugh as much as I wanna," Brand said. "You don't know what you talking about. The *Herald-Examiner* says it's the coldest day since 1873."

"But the *Trib* oughta know," Cooke countered. "It's older'n that *Examiner.*"

"That damn *Trib* don't know nothing!" Brand drowned out Cooke's voice.

"How in hell you know?" Cooke asked with rising anger.

The argument waxed until Cooke shouted that if Brand did not shut up he was going to "cut his black throat."

Brand whirled from the sink, his hands dripping soapy water, his eyes blazing.

"Take that back," Brand said.

"I take nothing back! What you wanna do about it?" Cooke taunted.

The two elderly Negroes glared at each other. I wondered if the quarrel was really serious, or if it would turn out harmlessly as so many others had done.

Suddenly Cooke dropped the Chicago *Daily Tribune* and pulled a long knife from his pocket; his thumb pressed a button and a gleaming steel blade leaped out. Brand stepped back quickly and seized an ice pick that was stuck in a wooden board above the sink.

"Put that knife down," Brand said.

"Stay 'way from me, or I'll cut your throat," Cooke warned.

Brand lunged with the ice pick. Cooke dodged out of range. They circled each other like fighters in a prize ring. The cancerous and tubercular rats and mice leaped about their cages. The guinea pigs whistled in fright. The diabetic dogs bared their teeth and barked soundlessly in our direction. The Aschheim-Zondek rabbits flopped their ears and tried to hide in the corners of their pens. Cooke now crouched and sprang forward with the knife. Bill and I jumped to our feet, speechless with surprise. Brand retreated. The eyes of both men were hard and unblinking; they were breathing deeply.

"Say, cut it out!" I called in alarm.

"Them damn fools is really fighting," Bill said in amazement.

Slashing at each other, Brand and Cooke surged up and down the aisles of steel tiers. Suddenly Brand uttered a bellow and charged into Cooke and swept him violently backward. Cooke grasped Brand's hand to keep the ice pick from sinking into his chest. Brand broke free and charged Cooke again, sweeping him into an animal-filled steel tier. The tier balanced itself on its edge for an indecisive moment, then toppled.

Like kingpins, one steel tier lammed into another, then they all crashed to the floor with a sound as of the roof falling. The whole aspect of the room altered quicker than the eye could follow. Brand and Cooke stood stock-still, their eyes fastened upon each other, their pointed weapons raised; but they were dimly aware of the havoc that churned about them.

The steel tiers lay jumbled; the doors of the cages swung open.

Rats and mice and dogs and rabbits moved over the floor in wild panic. The Wassermann guinea pigs were squealing as though judgment day had come. Here and there an animal had been crushed beneath a cage.

All four of us looked at one another. We knew what this meant. We might lose our jobs. We were already regarded as black dunces, and if the doctors saw this mess they would take it as final proof. Bill rushed to the door to make sure that it was locked. I glanced at the clock and saw that it was 12:30. We had one half hour of grace.

"Come on," Bill said uneasily. "We got to get this place cleaned."

Brand and Cooke stared at each other, both doubting.

"Give me your knife, Cooke," I said.

"Naw! Take Brand's ice pick *first*," Cooke said.

"The hell you say!" Brand said. "Take his knife *first!*"

A knock sounded at the door.

"Sssshh," Bill said.

We waited. We heard footsteps going away. We'll all lose our jobs, I thought.

Persuading the fighters to surrender their weapons was a difficult task, but at last it was done and we could begin to right things. Slowly Brand stooped and tugged at one end of a steel tier. Cooke stooped to help him. Both men seemed to be acting in a dream. Soon, however, all four of us were working frantically, watching the clock.

As we labored we conspired to keep the fight a secret; we agreed to tell the doctors—if any should ask—that we had not been in the room during our lunch hour; we felt that that lie would explain why no one had unlocked the door when the knock had come.

We righted the tiers and replaced the cages; then we were faced with the impossible task of sorting the cancerous rats and mice, the diabetic dogs, the Aschheim-Zondek rabbits, and the Wassermann guinea pigs. Whether we kept our jobs or not depended upon how shrewdly we could cover up all evidence of the fight. It was pure guesswork, but we had to try to put the animals back into the correct cages. We knew that certain rats or mice went into certain cages, but we did not know *what* rat or mouse went into *what* cage. We did not know a tubercular mouse from a cancerous mouse; the white doctors had made sure that we would not know. They had never taken time to answer a single question; though we worked in the institute, we were as remote from the meaning of the experiments as if we lived in the moon. The doctors had laughed at what they felt was our childlike interest in the fate of the animals.

First we sorted the dogs; that was fairly easy, for we could remember the size and color of most of them. But the rats and mice and guinea pigs baffled us completely.

We put our heads together and pondered, down in the underworld of the great scientific institute. It was a strange scientific conference; the fate of the entire medical research institute rested in our ignorant, black hands.

We remembered the number of rats, mice, or guinea pigs—we had to handle them several times each day—that went into a given cage, and we supplied the number helter-skelter from those animals that we could catch running loose on the floor. We discovered that many rats, mice, and guinea pigs were missing; they had been killed in the scuffle. We solved that problem by taking healthy stock from other cages and putting them into cages with sick animals. We repeated this process until we were certain that, numerically at least, all the animals with which the doctors were experimenting were accounted for.

The rabbits came last. We broke the rabbits down into two general groups: those that had fur on their bellies and those that did not. We knew that all those rabbits that had shaven bellies—our scientific knowledge adequately covered this point because it was our job to shave the rabbits—were undergoing Aschheim-Zondek tests. But in what pen did a given rabbit belong? We did not know. I solved the problem very simply. I counted the shaven rabbits; they numbered seventeen. I counted the pens labeled "Aschheim-Zondek," then proceeded to drop a shaven rabbit into each pen at random. And again we were numerically successful. At least white America had taught us how to count . . .

Lastly we carefully wrapped all the dead animals in newspapers and hid their bodies in a garbage can.

At a few minutes to one the room was in order; that is, the kind of order that we four Negroes could figure out. I unlocked the door and we sat waiting, whispering, vowing secrecy, wondering what the reaction of the doctors would be.

Finally a doctor came, gray-haired, white-coated, spectacled, efficient, serious, taciturn, bearing a tray upon which sat a bottle of mysterious fluid and a hypodermic needle.

"My rats, please."

Cooke shuffled forward to serve him. We held our breath. Cooke got the cage which he knew the doctor always called for at that hour and brought it forward. One by one, Cooke took out the rats and held them as the doctor solemnly injected the mysterious fluid under their skins.

"Thank you, Cooke," the doctor murmured.

"Not at all, sir," Cooke mumbled with a suppressed gasp.

When the doctor had gone we looked at one another, hardly daring to believe that our secret would be kept. We were so anxious that we did not know whether to curse or laugh. Another doctor came.

"Give me A-Z rabbit number 14."

"Yes, sir," I said.

I brought him the rabbit and he took it upstairs to the operating room. We waited for repercussions. None came.

All that afternoon the doctors came and went. I would run into the room—stealing a few seconds from my step scrubbing—and ask what progress was being made and would learn that the doctors had detected nothing. At quitting time we felt triumphant.

"They won't never know," Cooke boasted in a whisper.

I saw Brand stiffen. I knew that he was aching to dispute Cooke's optimism, but the memory of the fight he had just had was so fresh in his mind that he could not speak.

Another day went by and nothing happened. Then another day. The doctors examined the animals and wrote in their little black books, in their big black books, and continued to trace red and black lines upon the charts.

A week passed and we felt out of danger. Not one question had been asked.

Of course, we four black men were much too modest to make our contribution known, but we often wondered what went on in the laboratories after that secret disaster. Was some scientific hypothesis, well on its way to validation and ultimate public use, discarded because of unexpected findings on that cold winter day? Was some tested principle given a new and strange refinement because of fresh, remarkable evidence? Did some brooding research worker—those who held stop watches and slopped their feet carelessly in the water of the steps I tried so hard to keep clean—get a wild, if brief, glimpse of a new scientific truth? Well, we never heard . . .

I brooded, of course, upon whether I should have gone to the director's office and told him what had happened, but each time I thought of it I remembered that the director had been the man who had ordered the boy to stand over me while I was working and time my movements with a stop watch. He did not regard me as a human being. I did not share his world. I earned thirteen dollars a week and I had to support four people with it, and should I risk that thirteen dollars by acting idealistically? Brand and Cooke would have hated me and would have eventually driven me from the job had I "told" on them. The hospital kept us four Negroes, as though we were close kin to the animals we tended, huddled together down in the underworld corridors of the hospital, separated by a vast psychological distance from the significant processes of the rest of the hospital—just as America had kept us locked in the dark underworld of American life for three hundred years—and we had made our own code of ethics, values, loyalty.

18

One Thursday night I received an invitation from a group of white boys I had known in the post office to meet in a South Side hotel and argue the state of the world. About ten of us gathered and ate salami sandwiches, drank beer, and talked. I was amazed to discover that many of them had joined the Communist party. I challenged them by reciting the antics of the Negro Communists I had seen in the parks, and I was told that those antics were "tactics" and were all right. I was dubious.

Then one Thursday night Sol, a Jewish chap, startled us by announcing that he had had a short story accepted by a little magazine called the *Anvil*, edited by Jack Conroy, and that he had joined a revolutionary artists' organization, the John Reed Club. Sol repeatedly begged me to attend the meetings of the club, but I always found an easy excuse for refusing.

"You'd like them," Sol said.

"I don't want to be organized," I said.

"They can help you to write," he said.

"Nobody can tell me how or what to write," I said.

"Come and see," he urged. "What have you to lose?"

I felt that Communists could not possibly have a sincere interest in Negroes. I was cynical and I would rather have heard a white man say that he hated Negroes, which I could have readily believed, than to have heard him say that he respected Negroes, which would have made me doubt him. I did not think that there existed many whites who, through intellectual effort, could lift themselves out of the traditions of their times and see the Negro objectively.

One Saturday night, sitting home idle, not caring to visit the girls I had met on my former insurance route, bored with reading, I decided to appear at the John Reed Club in the capacity of an amused spectator. I rode to the Loop and found the number. A dark stairway led upwards; it did not look welcoming. What on earth of importance could transpire in so dingy a place? Through the windows above me I saw vague murals along the walls. I mounted the stairs to a door that was lettered:

The Chicago John Reed Club

I opened it and stepped into the strangest room I had ever seen. Paper and cigarette butts lay on the floor. A few benches ran along the walls, above which were vivid colors depicting colossal figures of workers carrying streaming banners. The mouths of the workers gaped in wild cries; their legs were sprawled over cities.

"Hello."

I turned and saw a white man smiling at me.

"A friend of mine, who's a member of this club, asked me to visit here. His name is Sol _____," I told him.

"You're welcome here," the white man said. "We're not having an affair tonight. We're holding an editorial meeting. Do you paint?" He was slightly gray and he had a mustache.

"No," I said. "I try to write."

"Then sit in on the editorial meeting of our magazine, *Left Front*," he suggested.

"I know nothing of editing," I said.

"You can learn," he said.

I stared at him, doubting.

"I don't want to be in the way here," I said.

"My name's Grimm," he said.

I told him my name and we shook hands. He went to a closet and returned with an armful of magazines.

"Here are some back issues of the *Masses*," he said. "Have you ever read it?"

"No," I said.

"Some of the best writers in America publish in it," he explained. He also gave me copies of a magazine called *International Literature*. "There's stuff here from Gide, Gorky . . ."

I assured him that I would read them. He took me to an office and introduced me to a Jewish boy who was to become one of the nation's leading painters, to a chap who was to become one of the eminent composers of his day, to a writer who was to create some of the best novels of his generation, to a young Jewish boy who was destined to film the Nazi invasion of Czechoslovakia. I was meeting men and women whom I would know for decades to come, who were to form the first sustained relationships in my life.

I sat in a corner and listened while they discussed their magazine, *Left Front*. Were they treating me courteously because I was a Negro? I must let cold reason guide me with these people, I told myself. I was asked to contribute something to the magazine, and I said vaguely that I would consider it. After the meeting I met an Irish girl who worked for an advertising agency, a girl who did social work, a schoolteacher, and the wife of a prominent university professor. I had once worked as a servant for people like these and I was skeptical. I tried to fathom their motives, but I could detect no condescension in them.

I went home full of reflection, probing the sincerity of the strange white people I had met, wondering how they *really* regarded Negroes. I lay on my bed and read the magazines and was amazed to find that there did exist in this world an organized search for the truth of the lives of the oppressed and the isolated. When I had begged bread from the officials, I had wondered dimly if the outcasts could become united in action, thought, and feeling. Now I knew. It was being done in one-sixth of the earth already. The revolutionary words leaped from the printed page and struck me with tremendous force.

It was not the economics of Communism, nor the great power

of trade unions, nor the excitement of underground politics that claimed me; my attention was caught by the similarity of the experiences of workers in other lands, by the possibility of uniting scattered but kindred peoples into a whole. My cynicism—which had been my protection against an America that had cast me out—slid from me and, timidly, I began to wonder if a solution of unity was possible. My life as a Negro in America had led me to feel—though my helplessness had made me try to hide it from myself—that the problem of human unity was more important than bread, more important than physical living itself; for I felt that without a common bond uniting men, without a continuous current of shared thought and feeling circulating through the social system, like blood coursing through the body, there could be no living worthy of being called human.

I hungered to share the dominant assumptions of my time and act upon them. I did not want to feel, like an animal in a jungle, that the whole world was alien and hostile. I did not want to make individual war or individual peace. So far I had managed to keep humanly alive through transfusions from books. In my concrete relations with others I had encountered nothing to encourage me to believe in my feelings. It had been by denying what I saw with my eyes, disputing what I felt with my body, that I had managed to keep my identity intact. But it seemed to me that here at last in the realm of revolutionary expression was where Negro experience could find a home, a functioning value and role. Out of the magazines I read came a passionate call for the experiences of the disinherited, and there were none of the lame lispings of the missionary in it. It did not say: "Be like us and we will like you, maybe." It said: "If you possess enough courage to speak out what you are, you will find that you are not alone." It urged life to believe in life.

I read on into the night; then, toward dawn, I swung from bed and inserted paper into the typewriter. Feeling for the first time that I could speak to listening ears, I wrote a wild, crude poem in free verse, coining images of black hands playing, working, holding bayonets, stiffening finally in death . . . I read it and felt that in a clumsy way it linked white life with black, merged two streams of common experience.

I heard someone poking about the kitchen.

"Richard, are you ill?" my mother called.

"No. I'm reading."

My mother opened the door and stared curiously at the pile of magazines that lay upon my pillow.

"You're not throwing away money buying those magazines, are you?" she asked.

"No. They were given to me."

She hobbled to the bed on her crippled legs and picked up a copy of the *Masses* that carried a lurid May Day cartoon. She adjusted her glasses and peered at it for a long time.

"My God in heaven," she breathed in horror.

"What's the matter, mama?"

"What is this?" she asked, extending the magazine to me, pointing to the cover. "What's wrong with that man?"

With my mother standing at my side, lending me her eyes, I stared at a cartoon drawn by a Communist artist; it was the figure of a worker clad in ragged overalls and holding aloft a red banner. The man's eyes bulged; his mouth gaped as wide as his face; his teeth showed; the muscles of his neck were like ropes. Following the man was a horde of nondescript men, women, and children, waving clubs, stones, and pitchforks.

"What are those people going to do?" my mother asked.

"I don't know," I hedged.

"Are these Communist magazines?"

"Yes."

"And do they want people to act like this?"

"Well . . ." I hesitated.

My mother's face showed disgust and moral loathing. She was a gentle woman. Her ideal was Christ upon the Cross. How could I tell her that the Communist party wanted her to march in the streets, chanting, singing?

"What do Communists think people are?" she asked.

"They don't quite mean what you see there," I said, fumbling with my words.

"Then what do they mean?"

"This is symbolic," I said.

"Then why don't they speak out what they mean?"

"Maybe they don't know how."

"Then why do they print this stuff?"

"They don't quite know how to appeal to people yet," I admitted, wondering whom I could convince of this if I could not convince my mother.

"That picture's enough to drive a body crazy," she said, dropping the magazine, turning to leave, then pausing at the door. "You're not getting mixed up with those people?"

"I'm just reading, mama," I dodged.

My mother left and I brooded upon the fact that I had not been able to meet her simple challenge. I looked again at the cover of the *Masses* and I knew that the wild cartoon did not reflect the passions of the common people. I reread the magazine and was convinced that much of the expression embodied what the *artists* thought would appeal to others, what they thought would gain recruits. They had a program, an ideal, but they had not yet found a language.

Here, then, was something that I could do, reveal, say. The Communists, I felt, had oversimplified the experience of those whom they sought to lead. In their efforts to recruit masses, they had missed the meaning of the lives of the masses, had conceived of people in too abstract a manner. I would make voyages, discoveries, explorations with words and try to put some of that meaning back. I would address my words to two groups: I would tell Communists how common people felt, and I would tell common people of the self-sacrifice of Communists who strove for unity among them.

That following Thursday night, when I joined my friends at the hotel for beer, I pulled out my crude verses and laid them on the table. Sol read them.

"This can be published," he said.

"That's not the point," I said. "What do they mean to you?"

"This is the vision of the disinherited," he said.

"If you're going to publish these to recruit me into the party, then nothing doing," I said.

"They'll be published whether you join or not," he said.

I told the group of my mother's reaction to the *Masses* cartoon.

"She'll have to learn the symbolism of the revolution," somebody said.

"But why can't Communism speak a language she understands?" I asked.

There was a lot of argument that went nowhere.

Still suspicious, my eyes watching for the slightest anti-Negro gesture, I attended the next meeting of the club. In the end I had to admit that they were glad to have me with them. But I still doubted their motives. Were they trying to get my head bashed in a picket line so that they could capitalize on the publicity? Or did the discipline of the club demand that they be friendly with me? If that was true, then those who did not want a Negro in the club could resign. But no one made a move to resign. How had these people, denying profit and home and God, made that hurdle that even the churches of America had not been able to make?

The editor of *Left Front* accepted two of my crude poems for publication, sent two of them to Jack Conroy's *Anvil,* and sent another to the *New Masses,* the successor of the *Masses.* Doubts still lingered in my mind.

"Don't send them if you think they aren't good enough," I said.

"They're good enough," he said.

"Are you doing this to get me to join up?" I asked.

"No," he said. "Your poems are crude, but good for us. You see, we're all new in this. We write articles about Negroes, but we never see any Negroes. We need your stuff."

I sat through several meetings of the club and was impressed by the scope and seriousness of its activities. The club was demanding that the government create jobs for unemployed artists; it planned and organized art exhibits; it raised funds for the publication of *Left Front;* and it sent scores of speakers to trade-union meetings. The members were fervent, democratic, restless, eager, self-sacrificing. I was convinced, and my response was to set myself the task of making Negroes know what Communists were. While mopping the operating rooms of the medical research institute, I got the notion of writing a series of biographical sketches of Negro Communists. I told no one of my intentions, and I did not know how fantastically naïve my ambition was.

I had attended but a few meetings before I realized that a bitter factional fight was in progress between two groups of members of the club. But when I tried to learn the nature of the fight, no one would tell me anything. Sharp arguments rose at every meeting. I noticed that a small group of painters actually led the club and dominated its policies. The group of writers that centered about *Left Front* resented the leadership of the painters. Being primarily interested in *Left Front*, I sided in simple loyalty with the writers. Then came a strange development. The *Left Front* group declared that the incumbent leadership did not reflect the wishes of the club. A special meeting was called and a motion was made to reelect an executive secretary. When nominations were made for the office, my name was included. I declined the nomination, telling the members that I was too ignorant of their aims to be seriously considered. The debate lasted all night. A vote was taken in the early hours of morning by a show of hands, and I was elected. I had been a member of the club for less than two months and did not fully understand the purposes of the organization.

Later I learned what had happened: the writers of the club had decided to "use" me to oust the painters, who were party members, from the leadership of the club. Without my knowledge and consent, they confronted the members of the party with a Negro, knowing that it would be difficult for Communists to refuse to vote for a man representing the largest single racial minority in the nation, inasmuch as Negro equality was one of the main tenets of Communism.

Though I was not a Communist, cynical rivalry had put me in charge of one of the party's leading cultural organizations. At once I offered my resignation, but the members would not hear of it. I could not determine if they were acting sincerely. I was afraid that the defeated secretary, being white, would resent losing to a Negro, but his conduct showed nothing but friendliness.

As the club's leader, I soon learned the nature of the fight. The Communists had secretly organized a "fraction" in the club; that is, a small portion of the club's members were secret members of the Communist party. They would meet outside of the club, decide what policies the club should follow; and when they put forth their proposals in open meetings, the sheer strength of their arguments usually persuaded nonparty members to vote with them. The crux of the fight was that the non-party members resented the excessive demands made upon the club by the local party authorities through the fraction. For example, the fraction demanded that the *Daily Worker* and the *New Masses,* official periodicals of the Communist party, be put on sale at all meetings. The nonparty group declared that this would limit the club's membership to those who already believed in Communism.

The demands of the local party authorities for money, speakers, and poster painters were so great that the publication of *Left Front* was in danger. Many young writers had joined the club because of their hope of publishing in *Left Front,* and when the Communist party sent word through the fraction that the magazine should be dissolved, the writers rejected the decision, an act which was interpreted as hostility toward party authority.

I pleaded with the party members for a more liberal program for the club. Feelings waxed violent and bitter. Then the showdown came. I was informed that if I wanted to continue as secretary of the club I would have to join the Communist party. I stated that I favored a policy that allowed for the development of writers and artists. My policy was accepted. I signed the membership card.

As the club's leader, I strove to keep the quarrels within limits by striking a series of compromises: for example, the sale of the *Daily Worker* was withdrawn, but the sale of the *New Masses* was continued. My position was in the "middle"; the fraction urged me to collect money from the members for the Communist party, and the members urged me to fight for the continuance of *Left Front,* which had been branded as "useless" by the Communist party. Trying to please everybody, I pleased nobody. The club's energies were sapped by internal strife. Bills piled up. Rent fell past due. I wanted the club to continue at all hazards; my feelings were intensely personal. The club was my first contact with the modern world. I had lived so utterly isolated a life that the club filled for me a need that could not be imagined by the white members who were becoming disgusted with it, whose normal living had given them what I was so desperately trying to get.

One night a Jewish chap appeared at one of our meetings and introduced himself as Comrade Young of Detroit. He told us that he was a member of the Communist party, a member of the Detroit John Reed Club, that he planned to make his home in Chicago. He was a short, friendly, black-haired, well-read fellow with hanging lips and bulging eyes. Shy of forces to execute the demands of the Communist party, we welcomed him. But I could not make out Young's personality; whenever I asked him a simple question, he looked off and stammered a confused answer. I decided to send his references to the Communist party for checking and forthwith named him for membership in the club. He's okay, I thought. Just a queer artist . . .

After the meeting Comrade Young confronted me with a problem. He had no money, he said, and asked if he could sleep temporarily on the club's premises. Believing him loyal, I gave him permission. Straightway Young became one of the most ardent members of our organization, admired by all. His paintings—which I did not understand—impressed our best artists. No report about Young had come from the Communist party, but since Young seemed a conscientious worker, I did not think the omission serious in any case.

At a meeting one night Young asked that his name be placed upon the agenda; when his time came to speak, he rose and launched into one of the most violent and bitter political attacks upon Swann, one of our best young artists, in the club's history. We were aghast. Young accused Swann of being a traitor to the workers, an opportunist, a collaborator with the police, and an adherent of Trotsky. Naturally most of the club's members assumed that Young, a member of the party, was voicing the ideas of the party. Surprised and baffled, I moved that Young's statement be referred to the executive committee for decision. Swann rightfully protested; he declared that he had been attacked in public and would answer in public.

It was voted that Swann should have the floor. He refuted Young's wild charges, but the majority of the club's members were bewildered, did not know whether to believe him or not. We all liked Swann, did not believe him guilty of any misconduct; but we did not want to offend the party. A verbal battle ensued. Finally the members who had been silent in deference to the party rose and demanded of me that the foolish charges against Swann be withdrawn. Again I moved that the matter be referred to the executive committee, and again my proposal was voted down. The membership had now begun to distrust the party's motives. They were afraid to let an executive committee, the majority of whom were party members, pass upon the charges made by party member Young.

Three meetings were consumed in bitter debate. Between meetings we urged Young to tell us who had given him the authority to castigate Swann, and Young hinted darkly that he was acting under the orders of either the Central Committee of the Communist party or the Communist International. And we were naturally impressed. Who were we to question the decisions of political bodies so highly placed? I sympathized with Swann, but was afraid to say a word in his behalf for fear that I, too, would be charged.

A delegation of members asked me if I had anything to do with Young's charges. I was so hurt and humiliated that I disavowed all relations with Young. Determined to end the farce, I cornered Young and demanded to know who had given him authority.

"I've been asked to rid the club of traitors," he said.

"But Swann isn't a traitor," I said.

"We must have a purge," he said, his eyes bulging, his face quivering with passion.

I admitted his great revolutionary fervor, but I felt that his zeal was a trifle excessive. The situation became worse. A delegation of members informed me that if the charges against Swann were not withdrawn, they would resign in a body. I was frantic. I wrote to the Communist party to ask why orders had been issued to punish Swann, and a reply came back that no such orders had been issued. Then what was Young up to? Who was prompting him? I finally begged the club to let me place the matter before the leaders of the Communist party for decision. After a violent debate, my proposal was accepted.

One night ten of us met in an office of a leader of the party to hear Young restate his charges against Swann. The party leader, aloof and amused, gave Young the signal to begin. Young unrolled a sheaf of papers and declaimed a list of political charges that excelled in viciousness his previous charges. An instinct warned me that something was wrong, but I could not make out what it was. I stared at Young, feeling that he was making a dreadful mistake, but fearing him because he had, by his own account, the sanction of high political authority. When Young had finished, the party leader asked:

"Will you allow me to read these charges?"

"Of course," said Young, surrendering a copy of his indictment. "You may keep that copy. I have ten carbons."

"Why did you make so many carbons?" the leader asked.

"I didn't want anyone to steal them," Young said.

"If this man's charges against me are taken seriously," Swann said, "I'll resign and publicly denounce the club."

"You see!" Young yelled. "He's with the police!"

I was sick. The meeting ended with a promise from the party leader to read the charges carefully and render a verdict as to whether Swann should be placed on trial or not. I was convinced that something was wrong, but I could not figure it out. One afternoon I went to the club to have a long talk with Young; but when I arrived, he was not there. Nor was he there the next day. For a week I sought Young in vain. What had become of the man? I asked about him far and wide, but could get no word. Meanwhile the club's members asked his whereabouts and they would not believe me when I told them that I did not know. Was he ill? Had he been picked up by the police?

Somebody suggested that we search Young's luggage which was still in the club's back room. One afternoon Comrade Grimm and I sneaked into the club's headquarters and opened Young's luggage. What we saw amazed and puzzled us. First of all, there was a scroll of paper twenty yards long—one page pasted to another—which had drawings depicting the history of the human race from a Marxist point of view. The first page was titled:

A Pictorial Record of Man's Economic Progress

"This is terribly ambitious," I said.

"He's very studious," Grimm said.

There were long dissertations written in long hand; some were political and others dealt with the history of art. Finally we found a letter with a Detroit return address and I promptly wrote asking news of our esteemed member. A few days later a letter came which said in part:

Dear Sir:

In reply to your letter of the   , we beg to inform you that Mr. Young, who was a patient in our institution and who escaped from our custody a few months ago, has been apprehended and returned to this institution for mental treatment.

I was thunderstruck. Was this true? Undoubtedly it was. Then what kind of club did we run that a lunatic could step into it and help run it? Were we all so mad that we could not detect a madman when we saw one? I called a meeting of a few of the most trusted members of the club and laid the matter before them. They were dumfounded. We swore ourselves to secrecy and decided to suppress the matter. We agreed that we had made a terrible mistake.

But, of course, we had no power to restrain the other members from asking questions. Swann hammered at us from meeting to meeting.

"Where is Comrade Young? Is he sick? Is he dead? Is he in jail? Did the Communist party order him to stay away from the club?"

And to these questions I could but lie:

"I've had no word from Comrade Young. As soon as any is received, I'll inform the club."

Meanwhile I made a motion that all charges against Swann be dropped, which was done. I offered Swann an apology but, as the leader of the Chicago John Reed Club, I was a completely sober and chastened Communist.

19

I had read widely in revolutionary literature, had observed many Communists, white and black, and had learned to know the daily hazards they faced and the sacrifices they made. I now wanted to give time to writing the book of biographical sketches I had planned. I did not know Negro Communists as well as I wanted to, and when, on many occasions, I had sought to question them about their feelings, their work, and their actions, they had been reticent. My zeal made me forget these rebuffs, for I was sure that an atmosphere of trust would be created as soon as I had explained my project to them.

The Communist party fraction in the John Reed Club instructed me to ask my party cell—or "unit," as it was called—to assign me to full duty in the work of the club. I was instructed to give my unit a report of my activities, writing, organizing, speaking. I agreed to do this and wrote a report.

A unit, membership in which is obligatory for all Communists, is the party's basic form of organization. Unit meetings are held on certain nights which are kept secret for fear of police raids. Nothing treasonable transpires at these meetings; but, once one is a Communist, one does not have to be guilty of wrongdoing to attract the attention of the police. At these meetings members pay their dues, are given party tasks, are instructed in the party's interpretation of world events.

I went to my first unit meeting—which was held in the Black Belt of the South Side—and introduced myself to the Negro organizer.

"Welcome, comrade," he said, grinning. "We're glad to have a writer with us."

"I'm not much of a writer," I said.

The meeting started. About twenty Negroes were gathered. The time came for me to make my report and I took out my notes and told them how I had come to join the party, what few stray items I had published, what my duties were in the John Reed Club. I finished and waited for comment. There was silence. I looked about. Most of the comrades sat with bowed heads. Then I was surprised to catch a twitching smile on the lips of a Negro woman. Minutes passed. The Negro woman lifted her head and looked at the organizer. The organizer smothered a smile. Then the woman broke into unrestrained laughter, bending forward and burying her face in her hands. I stared. Had I said something funny?

"What's the matter?" I asked.

The giggling became general. The unit organizer, who had been dallying with his pencil, looked up.

"It's all right, comrade," he said. "We're glad to have a writer in the party."

There was more smothered laughter. Some of the more intelligent ones were striving to keep deadpan faces. What kind of people were these? I had made a serious report and now I heard giggles.

"I did the best I could," I said uneasily. "I realize that writing is not basic or important. But, given time, I think I can make a contribution."

"We know you can, comrade," the black organizer said.

His tone was more patronizing than that of a southern white man. I grew angry. I thought I knew these people, but evidently I did not. I wanted to take issue with their attitude, but caution urged me to talk it over with others first. I left the meeting baffled.

During the following days I learned through discreet questioning that I had seemed a fantastic element to the black Communists. I was shocked to hear that I, who had been only to grammar

school, had been classified as an *intellectual*. What was an intellectual? I had never heard the word used in the sense in which it was
applied to me. I had thought that they might refuse me on the
grounds that I was not politically advanced; I had thought they
might place me on probation; I had thought they might say I
would have to be investigated. But they had simply laughed. And I
began to realize why so few sensitive Negroes had had the gall to
come as close to them as I had.

I learned, to my dismay, that the black Communists in my unit
had commented upon my shined shoes, my clean shirt, and the tie I
had worn. Above all, my manner of speech had seemed an alien
thing to them.

"He talks like a book," one of the Negro comrades had said.

And that was enough to condemn me forever as bourgeois.

The more I learned of the Negro Communists the more I
found that they were not vicious, that they had no intention to
hurt. They just did not know anything and did not want to learn
anything. They felt that all questions had been answered, and anyone who asked new ones or tried to answer old ones was dangerous. The word "writer" was enough to make a black Chicago
Communist feel that the man to whom the word applied had gone
wrong.

I discovered that it was not wise to be seen reading books that
were not endorsed by the Communist party. On one occasion I was
asked to show a book that I carried under my arm. The comrade
looked at it and shook his head.

"What're you reading this for?" he asked.

"It's interesting," I said.

"Reading bourgeois books can only confuse you, comrade," he
said, returning the book.

"You seem convinced that I'm easily confused," I said.

"You know," he said, his voice dropping to a low, confidential
tone, "many comrades go wrong by reading the books of the bour-
geoisie. The party in the Soviet Union had trouble with people like
that."

"Didn't Lenin read bourgeois books?" I asked.

"But you're not Lenin," he shot at me.

"Are there some books reserved for some people to read, while others cannot read them?" I asked.

"Comrade, you do not understand," he said.

An invisible wall was building slowly between me and the people with whom I had cast my lot. Well, I would show them that all men who wrote books were not their enemies. I would communicate the meaning of their lives to people whom they could not reach; then, surely, my intentions would merit their confidence. I dismissed the warning about the Soviet Union's trouble with intellectuals. I felt that it simply did not apply to me. The problem I faced seemed a much simpler one. I had to win the confidence of people who had been misled so often that they were afraid of anybody who differed from themselves. Yet deep down I feared their militant ignorance.

In my party work I met a Negro Communist, Ross, who was under indictment for "inciting to riot." I decided to use him in my series of biographical sketches. His trial was pending and he was organizing support in his behalf. Ross was typical of the effective, street agitator. Southern-born, he had migrated north and his life reflected the crude hopes and frustrations of the peasant in the city. Distrustful but aggressive, he was a bundle of the weaknesses and virtues of a man struggling blindly between two societies, of a man living on the margin of a culture. I felt that if I could get his story I would make known some of the difficulties inherent in the adjustment of a folk people to an urban environment; I would make his life more intelligible to others than it was to himself. I would reclaim his disordered days and cast them into a form that people could grasp, see, understand, and accept.

I approached Ross and explained my plan. He was agreeable. He invited me to his home, introduced me to his Jewish wife, his young son, his friends. I talked to Ross for hours, explaining what I was about, cautioning him not to relate anything that he did not want to divulge.

"I'm after the things that made you a Communist," I said.

It was arranged that I was to visit Ross each morning and take notes for two hours. At last, I thought, I would reveal dramas of hope, fear, love, and hate that existed in these humble people. I would make these lives merge with the lives of the mass of mankind. I knew I could. My life had prepared me for this.

Word spread in the Communist party that I was taking notes on the life of Ross and strange things began to happen. A quiet black Communist came to my home one night and called me out to the street to speak to me in private. He made a prediction about my future that frightened me.

"Intellectuals don't fit well into the party, Wright," he said solemnly.

"But I'm not an intellectual," I protested. "I sweep the streets for a living." I had just been assigned by the relief system to sweep the streets for thirteen dollars a week.

"That doesn't make any difference," he said. "We've kept records of the trouble we've had with intellectuals in the past. It's estimated that only 13 per cent of them remain in the party."

"Why do they leave, since you insist upon calling me an intellectual?" I asked.

"Most of them drop out of their own accord," he said.

"Well, I'm not dropping out," I said.

"Some are expelled," he hinted gravely.

"For what?"

"General opposition to the party's policies," he said.

"But I'm not opposing anything in the party."

"But you have to prove yourself."

"What do you mean?"

"You'll have to prove your revolutionary loyalty."

"That's what I'm trying to do through writing."

"That's not the way to do it," he said. "You must act."

"How?"

"The party has a way of testing people."

"Well, talk. What is this?"

"How do you react to police?"

"I don't react to them," I said. "I've never been bothered by them."

"Do you know Evans?" he asked, referring to a local, militant Negro Communist.

"Yes. I've seen him; I've met him."

"Did you notice that he was injured?"

"Yes. His head was bandaged."

"He got that wound from the police in a demonstration," he explained. "That's proof of revolutionary loyalty."

"Do you mean that I must get whacked over the head by cops to prove that I'm sincere?" I asked.

"I'm not suggesting anything," he said. "I'm explaining."

"That's a primitive way to measure sincerity," I gasped.

"It's a practical way," he said.

"Look, suppose a cop whacks me over the head and I suffer a brain concussion. Suppose I'm nuts after that? Can I write then? What will I have proven?"

He did not answer. He shook his head.

"The Soviet Union has had to shoot a lot of intellectuals," he said.

"Good God!" I exclaimed. "Do you know what you're saying? You're not in Russia. You're standing on a sidewalk in Chicago. You talk like a man lost in a fantasy."

He said nothing. I did not know that the notes I was taking of Ross's life were being discussed by the local Communist leaders, that my motives were already being questioned; and no doubt my rash words did not help any.

"You've heard of Trotsky, haven't you?" he asked.

"Yes."

"Do you know what happened to him?"

"He was banished from the Soviet Union," I said.

"Do you know why?"

"Well," I stammered, trying not to reveal my ignorance of politics, for I had not followed the details of Trotsky's fight against the Communist party of the Soviet Union, "it seems that after a decision had been made, he broke that decision by organizing against the party."

"It was for counterrevolutionary activity," he snapped impatiently; I learned afterwards that my answer had not been satisfactory, had not been couched in the acceptable phrases of bitter, anti-Trotsky denunciation.

"I understand," I said. "But I've never read Trotsky. What's his stand on minorities?"

"Why ask me?" he asked. "I don't read Trotsky."

"Look," I asked, "if you found me reading Trotsky, what would that mean to you?"

"You have no need to read Trotsky," he said.

"Don't you think I can read Trotsky and not be influenced to follow him?" I asked.

"Comrade, you don't understand," he said in an annoyed tone.

That ended the conversation. But that was not the last time I was to hear the phrase: "Comrade, you don't understand." I had not been aware of holding wrong ideas. I had not read any of Trotsky's works; indeed, the very opposite had been true. It had been Stalin's *The National and Colonial Question* that had captured my interest.

Stalin's book showed how diverse minorities could be welded into unity, and I regarded it as a most politically sensitive volume that revealed a new way of looking upon lost and beaten peoples. Of all the developments in the Soviet Union, the method by which scores of backward peoples had been led to unity on a national scale was what had enthralled me. I had read with awe how the Communists had sent phonetic experts into the vast regions of Russia to listen to the stammering dialects of peoples oppressed for centuries by the czars. I had made the first total emotional commitment of my life when I read how the phonetic experts had given these tongueless people a language, newspapers, institutions. I had read how these forgotten folk had been encouraged to keep their old cultures, to see in their ancient customs meanings and satisfactions as deep as those contained in supposedly superior ways of living. And I had exclaimed to myself how different this was from the way in which Negroes were sneered at in America.

Then what was the meaning of the warning I had received from the black Communist? Why was it that I was a suspected man because I wanted to reveal the vast physical and spiritual ravages of Negro life, the profundity latent in these rejected people, the dramas as old as man and the sun and the mountains and the seas that were transpiring in the poverty of black America? What was the danger in showing the kinship between the sufferings of the Negro and the sufferings of other people?

I sat one morning in Ross's home with his wife and child. I was scribbling furiously upon my yellow sheets of paper. The doorbell rang and Ross's wife admitted a black Communist, one Ed Green. He was tall, taciturn, soldierly, square-shouldered. I was introduced to him and he nodded stiffly.

"What's happening here?" he asked bluntly.

Ross explained my project to him, and as Ross talked I could see Ed Green's face darken. He had not sat down and when Ross's wife offered him a chair, he did not hear her.

"What're you going to do with these notes?" he asked me.

"I hope to weave them into stories," I said.

"What're you asking the party members?"

"About their lives in general."

"Who suggested this to you?" he asked.

"Nobody. I thought of it myself."

"Were you ever a member of any other political group?"

"I worked with the Republicans once," I said.

"I mean, revolutionary organizations?" he asked.

"No. Why do you ask?"

"What kind of work do you do?"

"I sweep the streets for a living."

"How far did you go in school?"

"Through the grammar grades."

"You talk like a man who went further than that," he said.

"Why would I lie to you about my education?" I asked.

"I don't know," he said, looking directly at me.

"I've read books. I taught myself."

"You know about Ross's indictment?" he asked.

"Yes."

"I don't know," he said, looking off.

"What do you mean?" I asked. "What's wrong?"

"To whom have you shown this material?"

"I've shown it to no one yet."

What was the meaning of his questions? Naïvely I thought that he himself would make a good model for a biographical sketch.

"I'd like to interview you next," I said.

"I'm not interested," he snapped.

His manner was so rough that I did not urge him. He called Ross into a rear room. I sat feeling that I was guilty of something. In a few minutes Ed Green returned, stared at me wordlessly, then marched out.

"Who does he think he is?" I asked Ross.

"He's a member of the Central Committee," Ross said.

"But why does he act like that?"

"Oh, he's always like that," Ross said uneasily.

There was a long silence.

"He's wondering what you're doing with this material," Ross said finally.

I looked at him. He, too, had been captured by suspicion. He was trying to hide the fear in his face.

"You don't have to tell me anything you don't want to," I said.

That seemed to soothe him for a moment. But the seed of doubt had already been planted. I felt dizzy. Was I mad? Or were these people mad?

"You see, Dick," Ross's wife said, "Ross's under an indictment. Ed Green is the representative of the International Labor Defense for the South Side. It's his duty to keep track of the people he's trying to defend. He wanted to know if Ross has given you anything that could be used against him in court."

I was speechless.

"What does he think I am?" I demanded.

There was no answer.

"You lost people!" I cried and banged my fist on the table.

Ross was shaken and ashamed.

"Aw, Ed Green's just supercautious," he mumbled.

"Ross," I asked, "do you trust me?"

"Oh, yes," he said uneasily.

We two black men sat in the same room looking at each other in fear. Both of us were hungry. Both of us depended upon public charity to eat and for a place to sleep. Yet we had more doubt in our hearts of each other than of the men who had cast the mold of our lives.

Self-consciously we went on with the work, but something was gone out of it. Did they think I was gathering material for the police? How could I make them understand what I was trying to do? I found that when I talked to them in abstract terms, my ideas were not understood. The irony of it was that I, who had all but to steal books to read, had been branded as an intellectual by the one group that claimed it was dedicated to educating the oppressed and informing them with a vision of life. I was doubted by those who shared more of my life than any others could possibly share of it.

I could not doubt the sincerity of Ed Green. His was a long and militant record in the Communist party. Then why was he suspicious of me? And, if he doubted me, whom could he ever trust? If I was an intellectual, then what was a Negro doctor, lawyer, teacher? The thing just did not make sense. Yet there it was . . .

Ed Green was afterwards killed in action while fighting for the Spanish Loyalists. He knew how to die better than he knew how to live. He was organically capable of only the most elementary reactions. His fear-haunted life made him suspicious of everything that did not look as he looked, that did not act as he acted, that did not talk as he talked, that did not feel as he felt. His existence both gladdened and frightened me. I was glad that he was militant, but I was frightened when I pondered upon what he could do with his militancy. The only people he could move to believe in him were those who shared his own world of fear, and all the world that lay beyond his terribly restricted vision was enemy ground.

I wanted to make the lives of these men known through the images already accepted as the common coin of communication. I wanted to make them know that they had allies, that more people than they knew, and in ways they did not understand, were their friends, and that I was their friend. I wanted to voice the words in them that they could not say, to be a witness for their living. And they were wondering if I were in league with the police!

I had embraced their aims with the freest impulse I had ever known. I, the chary cynic, the man who had felt that no idea on earth was worthy of self-sacrifice, had publicly identified myself with them, and now their suspicion of me hit me with a terrific impact, froze me within. I groped in the noon sun. What was I after? they wanted to know. And when I tried to explain, I always, it seemed, said the wrong things. There were no concrete charges that they could bring against me. They were simply afraid of that which was not familiar. They were more fearful of my ideas than they would have been had I held a gun on them; they could have taken the gun away from me and shot me with it, but they did not know what to do with ideas.

I talked with white Communists about my experiences with black Communists, and I could not make them understand what I was talking about. White Communists had idealized all Negroes to the extent that they did not see the same Negroes I saw. And the more I tried to explain my ideas the more they, too, began to suspect that I was somehow dreadfully wrong. Words lost their usual meanings. Simple motives took on sinister colors. Attitudes underwent quick and startling transformations. Ideas turned into their opposites while you were talking to a person you thought you knew. I began to feel an emotional isolation that I had not known in the depths of the hate-ridden South.

I continued to take notes on Ross's life, but each successive morning found him more reticent. I pitied him and did not argue with him, for I knew that persuasion would not nullify his fears. Instead I sat and listened to him and his friends tell tales of southern Negro experience, noting them down in my mind, not daring to ask questions for fear they would become alarmed. In spite of their fears, I became quite drenched in the details of their lives. I gave up the idea of the biographical sketches and settled finally upon writing a series of short stories, using the material I had got from Ross and his friends, building upon it, inventing. I wove a tale of a group of black boys trespassing upon the property of a white man and the lynching that followed. The story was published in an anthology under the title of *Big Boy Leaves Home,* but its appearance came too late to influence the Communists who were questioning the use to which I was putting their lives.

My fitful work assignments from the relief officials ceased and I looked for work that did not exist. I borrowed money to ride to and fro on the club's business. I found a cramped attic for my mother and aunt and brother behind some railroad tracks. At last the relief authorities placed me in the South Side Boys' Club and my wages were just enough to provide a deficient diet.

Then political problems rose to plague me. Ross, whose life I had tried to write, was charged by the Communist party with "antileadership tendencies," "class collaborationist attitudes," and "ideological factionalism," phrases so fanciful that I gaped when I heard them. And it was rumored that I, too, would face similar charges. It was known that I had visited Ross, had taken notes on his life, and it was believed that I had been politically influenced by him, though in what way was not stated. As before, the more I tried to explain the guiltier I seemed in the eyes of my comrades. I had taken part in the formation of none of the policies of the Communist party, had expressed no opinion regarding its leadership or work. But the rumors of my disaffection persisted.

One night a group of black comrades came to my house and warned me against believing in Ross's ideas. When I assured them that I did not share Ross's views, they ordered me to stay away from him.

"But why?" I demanded.

"He's an unhealthy element," they said. "Can't you accept a decision?"

"Is this a decision of the Communist party?"

"Yes," they said.

"If I were guilty of something, I'd feel bound to keep your decision," I said. "But I've done nothing."

"Comrade, you don't understand," they said. "Members of the party do not violate the party's decisions."

"But your decision does not apply to me," I said. "I'll be damned if I'll act as if it does."

"Your attitude does not merit our trust," they said.

I was angry.

"Look," I exploded, rising and sweeping my arms at the bleak attic in which I lived, "what is it here that frightens you? You know where I work! You know what I earn! You know my friends! Now, what in God's name is wrong?"

They left with mirthless smiles which implied that I would soon know what was wrong.

But there was relief from these shadowy political bouts. I found my work in the South Side Boys' Club deeply engrossing. Each day black boys between the ages of eight and twenty-five came to swim, draw, and read. They were a wild and homeless lot, culturally lost, spiritually disinherited, candidates for the clinics, morgues, prisons, reformatories, and the electric chair of the state's death house. For hours I listened to their talk of planes, women, guns, politics, and crime. Their figures of speech were as forceful and colorful as any ever used by English-speaking people. I kept pencil and paper in my pocket to jot down their word-rhythms and reactions. These boys did not fear people to the extent that every man looked like a spy. The Communists who doubted my motives did not know these boys, their twisted dreams, their all-too-clear destinies; and I doubted if I would ever be able to convey to them the tragedy I saw here.

Wrestling with words gave me my moments of deepest meaning. The short story, *Big Boy Leaves Home,* had posed a question: What quality of will must a Negro possess to live and die with dignity in a country that denied his humanity? There took shape in my mind—as though an answer was trying to grope its way out of the depths of me—the tale of a flood, *Down by the Riverside.* I waded into it, feeling my way, trying to find the answer to my question. But it dissatisfied me when I had finished it; so, casting it aside, I tried to say the same thing in yet another way in *Long Black Song.*

But that did not catch the quality of the experience I was looking for.

Party duties broke into my efforts at expression. The club decided upon a conference of all the left-wing writers in the Middle West. I supported the idea and argued that the conference should deal with craft problems. My arguments were rejected. The conference, the club decided, would deal with political questions. I asked for a definition of what was expected from the writers, books or political activity. Both, was the answer. Write a few hours a day and march on the picket line the other hours. I pointed out that the main concern of a revolutionary artist was to produce revolutionary art, and that the future of the club was in doubt if a clear policy could not be found.

The conference convened with a leading Communist attending as adviser. The question debated was: What did the Communist party expect from the club? The answer of the Communist leader ran from organizing to writing novels. I argued that either a man organized or he wrote novels. The party leader said that both must be done. The attitude of the party leader prevailed and *Left Front*, for which I had worked so long, was voted out of existence.

The party leader demanded that writers be assigned the task of producing pamphlets for the use of trade unions. I contended that it would be a mistake for the Communist party to persuade writers to abandon imaginative work to write pamphlets. I explained the advantages that could be derived from the long-term artistic products of the club's writers, and pointed out that these more durable products would outweigh all the pamphleteering. This, too, was rejected by vote. I then appealed for an organizational structure that would include provisions for artistic work of all types, hoping in this way to eliminate constant quarrels over tactics and strategy. But all my proposals were voted down.

I knew now that the club was nearing its end, and I rose and stated my gloomy conclusions, recommending that the club dissolve. My "defeatism," as it was called, brought upon my head the sharpest disapproval of the party leader. The conference ended with the passing of a multitude of resolutions dealing with China, India, Germany, Japan, and conditions afflicting various parts of the earth. But not one idea regarding writing had emerged.

The ideas I had expounded at the conference were linked with the suspicions I had roused among the Negro Communists on the South Side, and the Communist party was now certain that it had a dangerous enemy in its midst. It was whispered that I was trying to lead a secret group in opposition to the party. I had learned that denial of accusations was useless. It was now painful to meet a Communist, for I did not know what his attitude would be.

Following the conference, a national John Reed Club congress was called. It convened in the summer of 1934 with left-wing writers attending from all states. But, as the sessions got under way, there was a sense of looseness, bewilderment, and dissatisfaction among the writers, most of whom were young, eager, and on the verge of doing their best work. No one knew what was expected of him, and out of the congress came no unifying idea. Through conversations I learned that the members of the New York John Reed Club were in despair at the way in which the congress was drifting, but they took care to conceal their disapproval. This puzzled me, for I felt that the problem should be brought into the open for discussion. But I was glad to hear the New York Communists express horror at the brutal way in which the Chicago Communists made demands upon the Chicago John Reed Club membership. One astonished New York comrade declared:

"A Chicago Communist is a walking terror!"

As the congress drew to a close, I attended a caucus to plan the future of the clubs. Ten of us met in a Loop hotel room and, to my amazement, the leaders of the club's national board confirmed my criticisms of the manner in which the clubs had been conducted. I was excited. Now, I thought, the clubs will be given a new lease on life. Writers would now be free to make their political contributions in the form of their creative work.

Then I was stunned when I heard a nationally known Communist announce a decision to dissolve the clubs. Why? I asked. Because the clubs do not serve the new People's Front policy, I was told. That can be remedied; the clubs can be made healthy and broad, I said. No; a bigger and better organization must be launched, one in which the leading writers of the nation could be included, they said. I was informed that the People's Front policy was now the correct vision of life and that the clubs could no longer exist. I asked what was to become of the young writers whom the Communist party had implored to join the clubs and who were ineligible for the new group, and there was no answer. This thing is cold! I exclaimed to myself. To effect a swift change in policy, the Communist party was dumping one organization, scattering its members, then organizing a new scheme with entirely new people!

I had sacrificed energy to recruit writers who subscribed to a revolutionary point of view, and now my feelings fought against the waste and meaninglessness to which my efforts were being reduced. This was the first time I had sat with a Communist policy-making body; I had had the illusion that each man would have his say and, out of the facts presented, a decision would be made. I was naïve. I had merely been called in to give my approval to a decision previously made. It angered me.

I found myself arguing alone against the majority opinion and then I made still another amazing discovery. I saw that even those who agreed with me would not support me. At that meeting I learned that when a man was informed of the wish of the party he submitted, even though he knew with all the strength of his brain that the wish was not a wise one, was one that would ultimately harm the party's interests. I had heard Communists discuss discipline in the abstract, but when I saw it in its concrete form it tore my feelings.

It was not courage that made me oppose the party. I simply did not know any better. It was inconceivable to me, though bred in the lap of southern hate, that a man could not have his say. I had spent a third of my life traveling from the place of my birth to the North just to talk freely, to escape the pressure of fear. And now I was facing fear again, though I had no notion that I was slowly adding fagots to a flame that would soon blaze over my head with all the violence of the assault I had sustained when I had naïvely thought I could learn the optical trade in Mississippi.

(The artist and the politician stand at opposite poles. The artist enhances life by his prolonged concentration upon it, while the politician emphasizes the impersonal aspect of life by his attempts to fit men into groups. The artist's enhancement of life may emphasize, at certain times, those aspects that a politician can use. But the politician, at other times, eager to do good for man, may sneer at the artist because the art product cannot be used by him. Hence, the two groups of men, driving in the same direction, committed to the same vision, often find themselves locked in a struggle more desperate than either of them wanted, while their mutual enemies gape at the spectacle in amazement.

(Why did not we writers leave the realm of politics and organize ourselves? We simply did not know how. We were hostile toward our environment and we did not know how other American writers had met such problems. Totally at odds with our culture, we wanted nothing less than to make anew; and, for our examples, we looked toward Russia, Germany, and France. Out of step with our times, it was but natural for us to respond to the Communist party, which said: "Your rebellion is right. Come with us and we will support your vision with militant action."

(Indeed, we felt that we were lucky. Why cower in towers of ivory and squeeze out private words when we had only to speak and millions listened? Our writing was translated into French, German, Russian, Chinese, Spanish, Japanese . . . Who had ever, in all human history, offered to young writers an audience so vast? True, our royalties were small or less than small, but that did not matter.

(We wrote what we felt. Confronted with a picture of a revolutionary and changing world, there spilled out of our hearts our reaction to that world, our hope, our anger at oppression, our dreams of a new life; it spilled without coercion, without the pleading of anyone.)

Before the congress adjourned, it was decided that another congress of American writers would be called in New York the following summer, 1935. I was lukewarm to the proposal and tried to make up my mind to stand alone, write alone. I was already afraid that the stories I had written would not fit into the new, official mood. Must I discard my plot-ideas and seek new ones? No. I could not. My writing was my way of seeing, my way of living, my way of feeling; and who could change his sight, his notion of direction, his senses?

My relationship with Communists reached a static phase. I shunned them and they shunned me. Buddy Nealson, a member of the Communist International, had arrived in Chicago to assume charge of Negro work. This man, it was rumored, was the party's theoretician on the Negro Question, and word reached me that he had launched a campaign to rid the Communist party of all its "Negro Trotskyite elements." Of all the Negro Communists I knew, I tried to determine who could be called a Trotskyite, and I could think of none. None of the black Communists I knew possessed the intellectual capacity to formulate a Trotskyite position in politics. Most of them were illiterate migrants from southern plantations and they had never been vitally interested in politics until they had entered the Communist party. Nevertheless, the drive against Negro Trotskyism went on, though I was too remote from it to know what was happening.

The spring of 1935 came and the plans for the writers' congress went on apace. For some obscure reason—it might have been to "save" me—I was urged by the local Communists to attend and I was named as a delegate. I got time off from my job at the South Side Boys' Club and, along with several other delegates, hitchhiked to New York.

Long used to the flat western prairie, I was startled by my first view of New York. We came in along the Hudson River and I stared at the sweep of clean-kept homes and grounds. But where was the smoke pall? The soot? Grain elevators? Factories? Stack-pipes? The flashes of steam on the horizon? The people on the sidewalks seemed better dressed than the people of Chicago. Their eyes were bold and impersonal. They walked with a quicker stride and seemed intent upon reaching some destination in a great hurry.

We arrived in the early evening and registered for the congress sessions. The opening mass meeting was being held at Carnegie Hall.

I asked about housing accommodations and the New York John Reed Club members, all white members of the Communist party, looked embarrassed. I waited while one white Communist called another white Communist to one side and discussed what could be done to get me, a black Chicago Communist, housed. During the trip I had not thought of myself as a Negro; I had been mulling over the problems of the young left-wing writers I knew. Now, as I stood watching one white comrade talk frantically to another about the color of my skin, I felt disgusted. The white comrade returned.

"Just a moment, comrade," he said to me. "I'll get a place for you."

"But haven't you places already?" I asked. "Matters of this sort are ironed out in advance."

"Yes," he admitted in an intimate tone. "We have some addresses here, but we don't know the people. You understand?"

"Yes, I understand," I said, gritting my teeth.

"But just wait a second," he said, touching my arm to reassure me. "I'll find something."

"Listen, don't bother," I said, trying to keep anger out of my voice.

"Oh, no," he said, shaking his head determinedly. "This is a problem and I'll solve it."

"It oughtn't to be a problem," I could not help saying.

"Oh, I didn't mean that," he caught himself quickly.

Goddamn, I cursed under my breath. Several people standing near-by observed the white Communist trying to find a black Communist a place to sleep. I burned with shame. A few minutes later the white Communist returned, frantic-eyed, sweating.

"Did you find anything?" I asked.

"No, not yet," he said, panting. "Just a moment. I'm going to call somebody I know. Say, give me a nickel for the phone."

"Forget it," I said. My legs felt like water. "I'll find a place. But I'd like to put my suitcase somewhere until after the meeting tonight."

"Do you really think you can find a place?" he asked, trying to keep a note of desperate hope out of his voice.

"Of course, I can," I said.

He was still uncertain. He wanted to help me, but he did not know how. He locked my bag in a closet and I stepped to the side-walk wondering where Harlem was, wondering where I would sleep that night. Before I had left Chicago I had thought of a thou-sand arguments to present for the retention of the John Reed Clubs, but now the retention of those clubs did not seem impor-tant. I stood on the sidewalks of New York with a black skin, practi-cally no money, and I was not absorbed with the burning questions of the left-wing literary movement in the United States, but with the problem of how to get a bath. I presented my credentials at Carnegie Hall. The building was jammed with people. As I listened to the militant speeches, I found myself wondering why in hell I had come.

I went to the sidewalk and stood studying the faces of the peo-ple. The white Communist, who had been scouting for a room in which I could sleep, ran up to me.

"Did you find a place yet?"

"No," I answered.

"Well, here's a name and address," he said proudly. "Go there and they'll put you up for tonight."

"Thanks," I said, glad to have a place to flop.

When the meeting ended, I retrieved my bag from the club and found the address in a dark alley of Greenwich Village. I knocked at the door. A white man opened it, took one quick look at my face, then pushed the door almost shut again, as though in desperate defense of himself and his home.

"What do you want?" the words spilled out of him.

I asked for the name of the person written on the slip of paper I had.

"They aren't here," he said.

"When will they return?" I asked.

"I don't know," he spluttered, inching the door to.

I walked away. How could I sleep in a home where the sight of my face struck fear into people? I returned to the club and saw a few of the white comrades standing about the sidewalk. I crossed to the opposite side of the street to avoid them. I approached a news-stand merchant. It was nearing three o'clock.

"Where is Harlem?" I asked.

He stared at me. I lost my temper.

"For God's sake!" I exploded. "I'm a stranger here. I'm asking you where Harlem is!"

He blinked and pointed vaguely.

"That way," he said.

His directions did not help me. I walked on. I met a Chicago club member.

"Didn't you find a place yet?" he asked.

"No," I said. "I'd like to try one of the hotels, but, God, I'm in no mood to argue with a hotel clerk about my color."

"Oh, goddamn, wait a minute," he said.

I waited as he scooted off. He returned in a few moments with a big heavy white woman. He introduced us.

"You can sleep in my place, tonight," she said.

I walked with her to her apartment and she introduced me to her husband. I thanked them for their hospitality and went to sleep on a cot in the kitchen. I got up at six, dressed, tapped on their door and bade them good-bye. I went to the sidewalk, sat on a bench, took out pencil and paper and tried to jot down notes for the argument I wanted to make in defense of the John Reed Clubs. But again the problem of the clubs did not seem important. What did seem important was: Could a Negro ever live halfway like a human being in this goddamn country?

That day I sat through the congress sessions, but what I heard did not touch me. That night I found my way to Harlem and walked pavements filled with black life. I was amazed, when I asked passers-by, to learn that there were practically no hotels for Negroes in Harlem. I kept walking. Finally I saw a tall, clean hotel; black people were passing the doors and no white people were in sight. Confidently I entered and was surprised to see a white clerk behind the desk. I hesitated.

"I'd like a room," I said.

"Not here," he said.

"But isn't this Harlem?" I asked.

"Yes, but this hotel is for white only," he said.

"Where is a hotel for colored?"

"You might try the Y," he said.

"In what direction is it?"

"Keep walking that way," he said, pointing.

Half an hour later I found the Negro Young Men's Christian Association, that bulwark of Jim Crowism for young black men, got a room, took a bath, and slept for twelve hours. When I awakened, I did not want to go to the congress. I lay in bed thinking: I've got to go it alone . . . I've got to learn how again . . .

I dressed and attended the meeting that was to make the final decision to dissolve the clubs. It started briskly. A New York Communist writer summed up the history of the clubs and made a motion for their dissolution. Debate started and I rose and explained what the clubs had meant to young writers and begged for their continuance. I sat down amid silence. Debate was closed. The vote was called. The room filled with uplifted hands to dissolve. Then there came a call for those who disagreed and my hand went up alone. I knew that my stand would be interpreted as one of opposition to the Communist party, but I thought: The hell with it . . .

New York held no further interest and the next morning I left for home.

With the clubs now dissolved, I was free of all party relations. I avoided unit meetings for fear of being subjected to discipline. Occasionally a Negro Communist—defying the code that enjoined him to shun suspect elements—came to my home and informed me of the current charges that Communists were bringing against one another. To my astonishment I heard that Buddy Nealson had branded me a "smuggler of reaction."

"Why does he call me that?" I asked.

"He says that you are a petty bourgeois degenerate," I was told.

"What does that mean?"

"He says that you are corrupting the party with your ideas," I was told.

"How?"

There was no answer. I decided that my relationship with the party was about over; I would have to leave it. The attacks were growing worse, and my refusal to react incited Nealson into coining more absurd phrases. I was termed a "bastard intellectual," an "incipient Trotskyite"; it was claimed that I possessed an "antileadership attitude" and that I was manifesting "seraphim tendencies," the latter phrase meaning that one has withdrawn from the struggle of life and considers oneself an infallible angel.

I could not dismiss these charges lightly, for a frantic, hysterical hunt was going on then in the ranks of the party for Trotskyites. In the Soviet Union men were being shot for Trotskyism. I used to lie awake nights wondering what would happen to me if I lived in the Soviet Union.

Working all day and writing half the night brought me down with a severe chest ailment. I was in constant pain, scarcely able to breathe. I lay reviewing the life I had lived in the party and I found it distasteful. I realized that I had not been objective in my quixotic fight to save the clubs. I had been fighting as much for myself as for them. But was that wrong? Again I resolved to leave the party, for the emotional cost of membership was too high.

While I was ill, a knock came at my door one morning. My mother admitted Ed Green, the man who had demanded to know what use I planned to make of the material I was collecting from the comrades. I stared at him as I lay abed and I knew that he considered me a clever and sworn enemy of the party. Bitterness welled up in me.

"What do you want?" I asked bluntly. "You see I'm ill."

"I have a message from the party for you," he said.

I had not said good day, and he had not offered to say it. He had not smiled, and neither had I. He looked curiously at my bleak room.

"This is the home of a bastard intellectual," I cut at him.

He stared without blinking. I could not endure his standing there so stone-like. Common decency made me say:

"Sit down."

His shoulders stiffened.

"I'm in a hurry." He spoke like an army officer.

"What do you want to tell me?"

"Do you know Buddy Nealson?" he asked.

"No," I said. "But I've heard of him."

I was suspicious. Was this a political trap? They had hurled baseless accusations at me and I felt that there could be no ground of trust between us. Was he trying to discover if I knew someone whom, politically, I should not know? But, after all, Buddy Nealson was a member of the Communist International. But what if Buddy Nealson had suddenly been accused of something and Ed Green was here trying to find out if I knew him?

"What about Buddy Nealson?" I asked, committing myself to nothing until I knew the kind of reality I was grappling with.

"He wants to see you," Ed Green said.

I breathed easier. I could not meet Communists now without feeling a degree of fear.

"What about?" I asked, still suspicious.

"He wants to talk with you about your party work," he said.

"I'm ill and can't see him until I'm well," I said.

Ed Green stood for a fraction of a second, then turned on his heel and marched out of the room.

Ought I see Buddy Nealson? He was the man who had formulated the Communist position for the American Negro; he had made speeches in the Kremlin; he had spoken before Stalin himself. Then perhaps he could explain many of the aspects of Communism that had baffled me. Anyway, I resolved to confront him and ask him some direct, simple questions and hear what he had to say.

When my chest healed, I sought an appointment with Buddy Nealson. He was a short, black man with an ever-ready smile, thick lips, a furtive manner, and a greasy, sweaty look. His bearing was nervous, self-conscious; he seemed always to be hiding some deep irritation. He spoke in short, jerky sentences, hopping nimbly from thought to thought, as though his mind worked in a free, associational manner. He suffered from asthma and would snort at unexpected intervals. Now and then he would punctuate his flow of words by taking a nip from a bottle of whisky. He had traveled half around the world and his talk was pitted with vague allusions to European cities. I met him in his apartment, listened to him intently, observed him minutely, for I knew that I was facing one of the leaders of World Communism.

"Hello, Wright," he snorted. "I've heard about you."

As we shook hands he burst into a loud, seemingly causeless laugh; and as he guffawed I could not tell whether his mirth was directed at me or was meant to hide his uneasiness.

"I hope what you've heard about me is good," I parried.

"Sit down," he laughed again, waving me to a chair. "Yes, they tell me you write . . ."

"I try to," I said.

"You can write," he snorted. "I read that article you wrote for the *New Masses* about Joe Louis. Good stuff . . . First political treatment of sports we've yet had. Ha-ha . . ."

"I'm trying to reveal the meaning of Negro experience," I said.

"We need a man like you," he said flatteringly.

I waited. I had thought that I would encounter a man of ideas, but he was not that. Then perhaps he was a man of action? But that was not indicated either. As we talked, I tried to grasp the frame of reference of his words, so that I would know how to talk to him.

"They tell me that you are a friend of Ross's," he shot at me.

I paused before answering. He had not asked me directly, but had hinted in a neutral, teasing way. Mentally I prodded myself into remembering that I was speaking to a member of the Communist International. Ross, I had been told, was slated for expulsion on the grounds that he was "antileadership"; and if a member of the Communist International was asking me if I were a friend of a man about to be expelled, he was indirectly asking me if I were loyal or not.

"Ross is not particularly a friend of mine," I said frankly. "But I know him well; in fact, quite well."

"If he isn't your friend, how do you happen to know him so well?" he asked, laughing to soften the hard threat of his question.

"I was writing an account of his life and I know him as well, perhaps, as anybody," I told him.

"I heard about that," he said. "Wright . . . Ha-ha . . . Say, let me call you Dick, hunh?"

"Go ahead," I said.

"Dick," he said, "Ross is a nationalist." He paused to let the weight of his accusation sink in. He meant that Ross's militancy was extreme. "We Communists don't dramatize Negro nationalism," he said in a voice that laughed, accused, and drawled.

"What do you mean?" I asked.

"We're not advertising Ross," he spoke directly now.

"We're talking about two different things," I said. "You seem worried about my making Ross popular because he is your political opponent. But I'm not concerned about Ross's politics at all. The man struck me as one who typified certain traits of the Negro migrant. I've already sold a story based upon an incident in his life."

Nealson became excited.

"What was the incident?" he asked.

"Some trouble he got into when he was thirteen years old," I said.

His face looked blank for a second, then he laughed.

"Oh, I thought it was political," he said, shrugging.

"But I'm telling you that you are wrong about that," I explained. "I'm not trying to fight you with my writing. I've no political ambitions. I'm not trying to hurt or help any particular comrade. You must believe that. I'm trying to depict Negro life."

"Have you finished writing about Ross?" he asked.

"No," I said. "I dropped the idea. Our party members were suspicious of me and were afraid to talk."

He laughed.

"You've got to know us better, Dick," he grinned. "I hold a high position in the party. I'll straighten out this misunderstanding."

"I'm not looking for a patron," I said.

"I don't mean that," he said, grinning, snorting. "Here, Dick, hava drink."

"No, thank you."

"Don't you drink?"

"Sometimes."

There are men with whom one can drink and there are men with whom one cannot drink. Nealson was one of the men with whom I could not drink. He drank and put the bottle back; he shot me a quick, self-conscious glance. I was tense, but rigidly controlled.

"Dick," he began, "we're short of forces. We're facing a grave crisis."

"The party's always facing a crisis," I said.

His smile left and he stared at me.

"You're not cynical, are you, Dick?" he asked.

"No," I said. "But it's the truth. Each week, each month there's a crisis."

"You're a funny guy," he said, laughing, snorting again. "But we've got a job to do. We're altering our work. Fascism's the danger, the danger now to all people."

"I understand," I said.

"You were in New York not long ago," he said unexpectedly.

"Yes."

"Did you talk with any of the party leaders?"

"No."

"You said nothing to anyone about your work here?"

I stared at him. Was he trying to find out whether I had taken up any of his accusations with the national leadership of the party? Was he trying to determine whether I had influential enough political connections to make trouble for him?

"I told you that I have no political ambitions," I said.

"Yes," he said. "They say that you didn't want the clubs dissolved."

"No, I didn't," I said truthfully. "I felt that the ground was being cut from under the feet of the party's best writers."

"We've got to defeat the Fascists," he said, snorting from asthma, switching his line of thought. "We've discussed you and know your abilities. We want you to work with us. We've got to

crash out of our narrow way of working and get our message to
the church people, students, club people, professionals, middle
class . . ."

"I've been called names," I said softly. "Is that crashing out of
the narrow way?"

"Forget that," he said, laughing.

He had not denied the name-calling. That meant that, if I did
not obey him, the name-calling would begin again.

"I don't know if I fit into things," I said openly.

"We want to trust you with an important assignment," he said.

"What do you want me to do?"

"We want you to organize a committee against the high cost of
living . . ."

"The high cost of living?" I exclaimed. "What do I know about
such things?"

"It's easy. You can learn," he said.

I was in the midst of writing a novel and he was calling me
from it to tabulate the price of groceries. He doesn't think much of
what I'm trying to do, I thought.

"Comrade Nealson," I said, "a writer who hasn't written anything
worth-while is a most doubtful person. Now, I'm in that category. Yet
I think I can write. I don't want to ask for special favors, but I'm in the
midst of a book which I hope to complete in six months or so. Let me
convince myself that I'm wrong about my hankering to write and then
I'll be with you all the way."

"The party can't wait," he said. "You'll find time to write."

"I work every day for a living," I said, remembering that he
was being paid by the party to talk to me.

"Look, we want to make you a mass leader," he said.

"But suppose I'm not that kind of material?"

He laughed. Not one word that I had said had been seriously
considered by him. Our talk was a game; he was trying to outwit
me. The feelings of others meant nothing to him.

"Dick," he said, turning in his chair and waving his hand as
though to brush away an insect that was annoying him, "you've got
to get to the masses of people . . ."

"You've seen some of my work," I said. "Isn't it just barely good enough to warrant my being given a chance?"

"The party can't deal with your feelings," he said.

"Maybe I don't belong in the party," I stated it in full.

"Oh, no! Don't say that," he said, snorting. He looked at me. "You're blunt."

"I put things the way I feel them," I said. "I want to start in right with you. I've had too damn much crazy trouble in the party."

He laughed and lit a cigarette.

"Dick," he said, shaking his head, "the trouble with you is that you've been around with those white artists on the North Side too much . . . You even talk like 'em. You've got to know your own people . . ."

"I think I know them," I said, realizing that I could never really talk with him. "I've been inside of three-fourths of the Negroes' homes on the South Side . . ."

"But you've got to work with 'em," he said.

"I was working with Ross until I was suspected of being a spy," I said.

There was silence. The doorbell rang and he admitted his wife, a dark, attractive, European white woman who carried a book under her arm. She came forward with a wide smile. Nealson introduced us.

"What are you reading?" I asked.

"A Dracula mystery story," she said, eagerly exhibiting her book. "You know, Dick, you and I ought to build Negro culture on the South Side."

"I'm asking Nealson for that chance right now," I said, wondering what connection there could be between a Dracula mystery and Negro culture.

"I want him to organize against high prices," Nealson told his wife. "But he's writing a book . . ."

"That oughtn't interfere with his book," she said, sliding easily into a verbal solution of my problem.

"I work in the day," I said.

"Oh, you'll find time," she said lightly.

She left the room and there was silence. The next word was due to come from the member of the Communist International.

"Dick," he spoke seriously now, "the party has decided that you are to accept this task."

I was silent. I knew the meaning of what he had said. A decision was the highest injunction that a Communist could receive from his party, and to break a decision was to break the effectiveness of the party's ability to act. In principle I heartily agreed with this, for I knew that it was impossible for working people to forge instruments of political power until they had achieved unity of action. Oppressed for centuries, divided, hopeless, corrupted, misled, they were cynical—as I had once been—and the Communist method of unity had been found historically to be the only means of achieving discipline. In short, Nealson had asked me directly if I were a Communist or not. I wanted to be a Communist, but my kind of Communist. I wanted to shape people's feelings, awaken their hearts. But I could not tell Nealson that; he would only have snorted.

"I'll organize the committee and turn it over to someone else," I suggested.

"You don't want to do this, do you?" he asked.

"No," I said firmly.

"You worked willingly enough to organize white writers," he cut at me.

"I was organizing people I understood," I said.

"What would you like to do on the South Side, then?"

"I'd like to organize Negro artists," I said.

"But the party doesn't need that now," he said.

I rose, knowing that he had no intention of letting me go after I had organized the committee. I wanted to tell him that I was through, but I was not ready to bring matters to a head. I went out, angry with myself, angry with him, angry with the party. Well, I had not broken the decision, but neither had I accepted it wholly. I had dodged, trying to save time for writing, time to think.

Again I urged myself to quit, but I could not do it. I knew that

Nealson was not a leader. His mind was too rigid, too limited. I had not discerned in him any understanding of life or politics. His approach had been to offer me a drink, and when that had failed he had threatened; he had tried flattery, and when that had failed he had hinted at expulsion. If I had been wrong, he certainly had not convinced me. In the end I resolved to work a month, then confront him with my original compromise.

My task consisted in attending meetings until the late hours of the night, taking part in discussions, or lending myself generally along with other Communists in leading the people of the South Side. We debated the housing situation, the best means of forcing the city to authorize open hearings on conditions among Negroes. I gritted my teeth as the daily value of pork chops was tabulated, longing to be at home with my writing. I felt that pork chops were a fundamental item in life, but I preferred that someone else chart their rise and fall in price.

Nealson was cleverer than I and he confronted me before I had a chance to confront him. I was summoned one night to meet Nealson and a "friend." When I arrived at a South Side hotel I was introduced to a short, yellow man who carried himself like Napoleon. He wore glasses, kept his full lips pursed as though he were engaged in perpetual thought. He swaggered when he walked. He spoke slowly, precisely, trying to charge each of his words with more meaning than the words were able to carry. He talked of trivial things in lofty tones. He said that his name was Smith, that he was from Washington, that he planned to launch a national organization among Negroes to federalize all existing Negro institutions so as to achieve a broad unity of action. The three of us sat at a table, facing one another. There were no smiles now. I knew that another and last offer was about to be made to me, and if I did not accept it, there would be open warfare.

"Wright, how would you like to go to Switzerland?" Smith asked with dramatic suddenness.

"I'd like it," I said. "But I'm tied up with work now."

"You can drop that," Nealson said. "This is important."

"What would I do in Switzerland?" I asked.

"You'll go as a youth delegate," Smith said. "From there you can go to the Soviet Union."

"Much as I'd like to, I'm afraid I can't make it," I said honestly. "I simply cannot drop the writing I'm doing now."

We sat looking at one another, smoking silently.

"Has Nealson told you how I feel?" I asked Smith.

Smith did not answer. He stared at me a long time, then spat: "Wright, you're a fool!"

I rose. Smith turned away from me. A breath more of anger and I would have driven my fist into his face. Nealson laughed sheepishly, snorting.

"Was that necessary?" I asked, trembling.

I stood recalling how, in my boyhood, I would have fought until blood ran had anyone said anything like that to me. But I was a man now and master of my rage, able to control the surging emotions. I put on my hat and walked to the door. Keep cool, I said to myself. Don't let this get out of hand . . .

"This is good-bye," I said.

I walked home. My mind was made up. I would attend the next unit meeting and announce my withdrawal, telling the comrades that I still adhered to the ideological program of the party, but that I did not want to be bound any longer by the party's decisions.

I attended the next unit meeting and asked for a place on the agenda, which was readily granted. Nealson was there. Evans was there. Ed Green was there. When my time came to speak, I rose and said:

"Comrades, for the past two years I've worked daily with most of you. Despite this, I have for some time found myself in a difficult position in the party. What has caused this difficulty is a long story which I do not care to recite now; it would serve no purpose. But I tell you honestly that I think I've found a solution of my difficulty. I am proposing here tonight that my membership be dropped from the party rolls. No ideological differences impel me to say this. I simply do not wish to be bound any longer by the party's decisions. I would like to retain my membership in those organizations in which the party has influence, and I shall comply with the party's program in those organizations. I hope that my words will be accepted in the spirit in which they are said. Perhaps sometime in the future I would like to meet and talk with the leaders of the party as to what tasks I can best perform."

I sat down amid a profound silence. The Negro secretary of the meeting looked frightened, glancing at Nealson, Evans, and Ed Green.

"Is there any discussion on Comrade Wright's statement?" the secretary asked finally.

"I move that discussion on Wright's statement be deferred," Nealson said.

A quick vote confirmed Nealson's motion. I looked about the silent room, then reached for my hat and rose.

"I would like to go now," I said.

No one said anything. I walked to the door and out into the night and a heavy burden seemed to lift from my shoulders. I was free. And I had done it in a decent and forthright manner. I had not been bitter. I had not raked up a single recrimination. I had attacked no one. I had disavowed nothing. I remembered, as I walked the night streets, how I had stolen money from the movie house in Jackson, Mississippi; how I had forced the window and had stolen the gun; how I had broken into the college storehouse and had stolen cans of fruit preserves; I remembered how I had lied to my boss man in Memphis when I had wanted to leave my job and come to Chicago; how I had lied to Mr. Hoffman; how I had forged notes to the library in Memphis when I had wanted books to read . . . But I had changed; I had none of that fear, none of those wild impulses now. I had merely confronted my comrades, stated what I felt, and had let it go at that.

The Communist party could not say that I was an enemy, that I had attacked them. A Trotskyite or a man bent upon wrecking or disrupting the work of the Communist party would have remained within the organization so as better to quarrel, obstruct. But I had only asked to be free, had accused no one, and had denounced nothing. Perhaps, I told myself, when the Communist party has grown up, when it can work without tactics of terror, threat, invective, intimidation, suspicion, I would go back . . .

Aw, God . . . How naïve I was! I was young and brimming with confidence. I felt that my strength was unlimited. I had neatly solved a problem that had been worrying me for a long time, and now I thought that I could turn my energies to writing and justify myself. I did not know that night how little I understood the political party to which I had belonged. But I soon learned, learned how simple were my motives, how trusting was my attitude, how wide and innocent were my eyes, as round and open and dew-wet as morning-glories . . .

The next night two Negro Communists called at my home. They pretended to be ignorant of what had happened at the unit meeting. Patiently I explained what had occurred.

"Your story does not agree with what Nealson says," they said, revealing the motive of their visit.

"And what does Nealson say?" I asked.

"He says that you are in league with a Trotskyite group, and that you made an appeal for other party members to follow you in leaving the party . . ."

"What?" I gasped. "That's not true. I asked that my membership be dropped. I raised no political issues." What did this mean? I sat pondering. "Look, maybe I ought to make my break with the party clean. If Nealson's going to act this way, I'll resign . . ."

"You can't resign," they told me.

"What do you mean?" I demanded.

"No one can resign from the Communist party," they said.

I looked at them and laughed.

"You're talking crazy," I said.

"Nealson would expel you publicly, cut the ground from under your feet if you resigned," they said. "People would think that something was wrong if someone like you quit here on the South Side."

I was angry. Was the party so weak and uncertain of itself that it could not accept what I had said at the unit meeting? Who thought up such tactics? Then, suddenly, I understood. These were the secret, underground tactics of the political movement of the Communists under the czars of Old Russia! The Communist party felt that it had to assassinate me morally merely because I did not want to be bound by its decisions. I saw now that my comrades were acting out a fantasy that had no relation whatever to the reality of their environment.

"Tell Nealson that if he fights me, then, by God, I'll fight him," I said. "If he leaves this damn thing where it is, then all right. If he thinks I won't fight him publicly, he's crazy!"

I was not able to know if my statement reached Nealson, but there was no public outcry against me. But in the ranks of the party itself a storm broke loose and I was branded a traitor, an unstable personality, and one whose faith had failed.

What a weird experience I had had! At no time had I felt at home in the Communist party. I had always felt that the possibility was there, but always I was not quite sure of the motives of the people with whom I worked and they never seemed quite sure of mine. My comrades had known me, my family, my friends; they, God knows, had known my aching poverty. But they had never been able to conquer their fear of the individual way in which I acted and lived, an individuality which life had seared into my blood and bones.

I now avoided the comrades as much as possible, and, as I was losing touch with the party, many other young Negroes of the South Side were entering it for the first time. The expansion of the party's activity under the People's Front policy offered many opportunities to young Negroes who, because of race and status, had led cramped lives. The invitation to go to Switzerland as a youth delegate, which I had refused, was accepted by a young Negro who had fought the Communist party and all its ideas until he had seen a chance to take a trip to Europe.

I was transferred by the relief authorities from the South Side Boys' Club to the Federal Negro Theater to work as a publicity agent. There were days when I was acutely hungry for the incessant analyses that went on among the comrades, but whenever I heard news of the party's inner life, it was of charges and countercharges, reprisals and counterreprisals. I was glad to be out of it. All its energies, it seemed, were absorbed in factional fights, hair-splitting political definitions.

The Federal Negro Theater, for which I was doing publicity, had run a series of ordinary plays, all of which had been revamped to "Negro style," with jungle scenes, spirituals, and all. For example, the skinny white woman who directed it, an elderly missionary type, would take a play whose characters were white, whose theme dealt with the Middle Ages, and recast it in terms of southern Negro life with overtones of African backgrounds. Contemporary plays dealing realistically with Negro life were spurned as being controversial. There were about forty Negro actors and actresses in the theater, lolling about, yearning, disgruntled, not knowing what to do with themselves.

What a waste of talent, I thought. Here was an opportunity for the production of a worth-while Negro drama and no one was aware of it. I studied the situation, then laid the matter before white friends of mine who held influential positions in the Works Progress Administration. I asked them to replace the white woman—including her quaint aesthetic notions—with someone who knew the Negro and the theater. They promised me that they would act.

Within a month the white woman director had been transferred. We moved from the South Side to the Loop and were housed in a first-rate theater. I successfully recommended Charles DeSheim, a talented Jew, as director. DeSheim and I held long talks during which I outlined what I thought could be accomplished. I urged that our first offering should be a bill of three one-act plays, including Paul Green's *Hymn to the Rising Sun,* a grim, poetical, powerful one-acter dealing with chain gang conditions in the South.

I was happy. At last I was in a position to make suggestions and have them acted upon. I was convinced that we had a rare chance to build a genuine Negro theater. I convoked a meeting and introduced DeSheim to the Negro company, telling them that he was a man who knew the theater, who would lead them toward serious dramatics. DeSheim made a speech wherein he said that he was not at the theater to direct it, but to help the Negroes to direct it. He spoke so simply and eloquently that they rose and applauded him.

I then proudly passed out copies of Paul Green's *Hymn to the Rising Sun* to all members of the company. DeSheim assigned reading parts. I sat down to enjoy adult Negro dramatics. But something went wrong. The Negroes stammered and faltered in their lines. Finally they stopped reading altogether. DeSheim looked frightened. One of the Negro actors rose.

"Mr. DeSheim," he began, "we think this play is indecent. We don't want to act in a play like this before the American public. I don't think any such conditions exist in the South. I lived in the South and I never saw any chain gangs. Mr. DeSheim, we want a play that will make the public love us."

I could not believe my ears. I had assumed that the heart of the Negro actor was pining for adult expression in the American theater, that he was ashamed of the stereotypes of clowns, mammies, razors, dice, watermelon, and cotton fields . . . Now they were protesting against dramatic realism! I tried to defend the play and I was heckled down.

"What kind of play do you want?" DeSheim asked them.

They did not know. I went to the office and looked up their records and found that most of them had spent their lives playing cheap vaudeville. I had thought that they played vaudeville because the legitimate theater was barred to them, and now it turned out that they wanted none of the legitimate theater, that they were scared spitless at the prospects of appearing in a play that the public might not like, even though they did not understand that public and had no way of determining its likes or dislikes.

I felt—but only temporarily—that perhaps the whites were right, that Negroes were children and would never grow up. DeSheim informed the company that he would produce any play they liked, and they sat like frightened mice, possessing no words to make known their vague desires.

When I arrived at the theater a few mornings later, I was horrified to find that the company had drawn up a petition demanding the ousting of DeSheim. I was asked to sign the petition and I refused.

"Don't you know your friends?" I asked them.

They glared at me. I called DeSheim to the theater and we went into a frantic conference.

"What must I do?" he asked.

"Take them into your confidence," I said. "Let them know that it is their right to petition for a redress of their grievances."

DeSheim thought my advice sound and, accordingly, he assembled the company and told them that they had a right to petition against him if they wanted to, but that he thought any misunderstandings that existed could be settled smoothly.

"Who told you that we were getting up a petition?" a black man demanded.

DeSheim looked at me and stammered wordlessly.

"There's an Uncle Tom in the theater!" a black girl yelled.

After the meeting a delegation of Negro men came to my office and took out their pocketknives and flashed them in my face.

"You get the hell off this job before we cut your belly button out!" they said.

I tried to talk to them, but could not. That day a huge, fat, black woman, a blues singer, found an excuse to pass me as often as possible and she hissed under her breath in a menacing singsong:

"Lawd, Ah sho hates a white man's nigger."

I telephoned my white friends in the Works Progress Administration:

"Transfer me at once to another job, or I'll be murdered."

Within twenty-four hours DeSheim and I were given our papers. We shook hands and went our separate ways.

I was transferred to a white experimental theatrical company as a publicity agent and I resolved to keep my ideas to myself, or, better, to write them down and not attempt to translate them into reality. I dodged the Negro theatrical world and kept rigorously clear of all members of the Communist party. Whenever I met any of my erst-while comrades, they refused to acknowledge my existence in accordance with a party principle that made it imperative that all "traitors be isolated from the working class."

One evening a group of Negro Communists called at my home and asked to speak to me in strict secrecy. I took them into my room and locked the door.

"Dick," they began abruptly, "the party wants you to attend a meeting Sunday."

"Why?" I asked. "I'm no longer a member."

"That's all right. They want you to be present," they said.

"Communists don't speak to me on the street," I said. "Now, why do you want me at a meeting?"

They hedged. They did not want to tell me.

"If you can't tell me, then I can't come," I said.

They whispered among themselves and finally decided to take me into their confidence.

"Dick, Ross is going to be tried," they said.

"For what?"

They recited a long list of political offenses of which they alleged that he was guilty.

"But what has this got to do with me?"

"If you come, you'll find out," they said.

"I'm not that naïve," I said, smiling. I was suspicious now. Were they trying to lure me to a trial and expel me? "This trial might turn out to be mine . . ."

They swore that they had no intention of placing me on trial, that the party merely wanted me to observe Ross's trial so that I might learn what happened to "enemies of the working class."

"But I'm not your enemy," I said.

"We want to save you," they said.

"Save me from what?" I asked. "I'm not lost."

"We have your welfare at heart," they said.

"Then why did you-all lie and call me a Trotskyite?"

"Nealson lost his head," they said. "When you left the party, he had to hit at you some way."

"Why do you spend your time in these crazy witch hunts?" I asked them. "You claim to be fighting oppression, but you spend more of your time fighting each other than in fighting your avowed enemies." As I spoke to them I recalled the time when my mother had slapped me when I had asked her—in the far-off days of Arkansas—why my "uncle" had run away from the white people, why he had not fought back; my mother had given me a ringing slap—fear had made her do it. And I felt that it was the fear of their enemies that made Communists—unconsciously compensating for their fear—fight one another so doggedly and persistently. But I did not tell them that; they would not have understood. "Look, Ross is a minor street agitator. Forget him. And in two weeks he'd be no issue at all."

"We're going to make an example out of Ross," they told me. "His trial will be an education for the working class, and for you, too, if you'll come."

As they talked, my old love of witnessing something new came over me. I wanted to see this trial, but I did not want to risk being placed on trial myself.

"Listen," I told them. "I'm not guilty of Nealson's charges. If I showed up at this trial, it would seem that I am."

"No, it won't. Please come."

"All right. But, listen . . . If I'm tricked, I'll fight. You hear? I don't trust Nealson. I'm not a politician and I cannot anticipate all the funny moves of a man who spends his waking hours plotting."

Ross's trial took place that following Sunday afternoon. Comrades stood inconspicuously on guard about the meeting hall, at the doors, down the street, and along the hallways. When I appeared, I was ushered in quickly. I was tense. It was a rule that once you had entered a meeting of this kind you could not leave until the meeting was over; it was feared that you might go to the police and denounce them all.

Acting upon the loftiest of impulses, filled with love for those who suffer, urged toward fellowship with the rebellious, committed to sacrifice, why was it that there existed among Communists so much hate, suspicion, bitterness, and internecine strife? I stood in

the midst of people I loved and I was afraid of them. I felt profoundly that they were traveling in the right direction, yet if their
having power to rule had depended merely upon my lifting my
right hand, I would have been afraid to do so. My heart throbbed
and I whispered to myself: God, I love these people, but I'm glad
that they're not in power, or they'd shoot me!

No one spoke to me. Some of the party leaders shot me hostile
glances and looked away. Why had I been called in to witness this
trial? I sat with jumpy nerves, impatient for the trial to get under
way. Despite my fear, I was keenly curious. But I was determined
not to participate in any way, for that would have surely, by implica-
tion, incriminated me in a network of guilt which I did not share.

Ross, the accused, sat alone at a table in the front of the hall,
his face distraught. I felt sorry for him, yet I could not escape feeling that he enjoyed this. For him, this was perhaps the highlight of
an otherwise bleak existence.

I was for these people. Being a Negro, I could not help it. They
did not hate Negroes. They had no racial prejudices. Many of the
white men in the hall were married to Negro women, and many of
the Negro men were married to white women. Jews, Germans,
Russians, Spaniards, all races and nationalities were represented
without any distinctions whatever.

Racial hate had been the bane of my life, and here before my
eyes was concrete proof that it could be abolished. Yet a new hate
had come to take the place of the rankling racial hate. It was irrational that Communists should hate what they called "intellectuals," or anybody who tried to think for himself. I had fled men who
did not like the color of my skin, and now I was among men who
did not like the tone of my thoughts.

In trying to grasp why Communists hated intellectuals, my
mind was led back again to the accounts I had read of the Russian
Revolution. There had existed in Old Russia millions of poor, ignorant people who were exploited by a few, educated, arrogant noble-
men, and it became natural for the Russian Communists to associate betrayal with intellectualism. But there existed in the Western
world an element that baffled and frightened the Communist party:

the prevalence of self-achieved literacy. Even a Negro, entrapped by ignorance and exploitation—as I had been—could, if he had the will and the love for it, learn to read and understand the world in which he lived. And it was these people that the Communists could not understand. The American Communists, enjoying legality, were using the methods forged by the underground Russian Bolshevik fire, and therefore had to have their followers willing to accept all explanations of reality, even when the actual situation did not call for it.

The heritage of free thought,—which no man could escape if he read at all,—the spirit of the Protestant ethic which one suckled, figuratively, with one's mother's milk, that self-generating energy that made a man feel, whether he realized it or not, that he had to work and redeem himself through his own acts, all this was forbidden, taboo. And yet this was the essence of that cultural heritage which the Communist party had sworn to carry forward, whole and intact, into the future. But the Communist party did not recognize the values that it had sworn to save when it saw them; the slightest sign of any independence of thought or feeling, even if it aided the party in its work, was enough to make one suspect, to brand one as a dangerous traitor.

The trial began in a quiet, informal manner. The comrades acted like a group of neighbors sitting in judgment upon one of their kind who had stolen a chicken. Anybody could ask and get the floor. There was absolute freedom of speech. Yet the meeting had an amazingly formal structure of its own, a structure that went as deep as the desire of men to live together.

A member of the Central Committee of the Communist party rose and gave a description of the world situation. He spoke without emotion and piled up hard facts. He painted a horrible but masterful picture of Fascism's aggression in Germany, Italy, and Japan.

I accepted the reason why the trial began in this manner. It was imperative that there be postulated against what or whom Ross's crimes had been committed. Therefore there had to be established in the minds of all present a vivid picture of mankind under oppression. And it was a true picture. Perhaps no organization on earth, save the Communist party, possessed so detailed a knowledge of how workers lived, for its sources of information stemmed directly from the workers themselves.

The next speaker discussed the role of the Soviet Union as the world's lone workers' state, how the Soviet Union was hemmed in by enemies, how the Soviet Union was trying to industrialize itself, what sacrifices she was making to help the workers of the world to steer a path toward peace through the idea of collective security.

The facts presented so far were as true as any facts could be in this uncertain world. Yet not one word had been said of the accused, who sat listening like any other member. The time had not yet come to include him and his crimes in this picture of global struggle. An absolute had first to be established in the minds of the comrades so that they could measure the success or failure of their deeds by it. There was no mysticism, no invoking of God, merely a passionate identification of all present with a will to right wrongs. It was a simple, elemental morality. Communism had found a moral code that could control the conduct of men, yet it was a code that stemmed from practical living, and not from the injunctions of the supernatural.

Still another speaker rose and described the domestic situation in the United States and linked it with the world scene. This was done in a leisurely, painstaking manner; yet the people in the hall were charged with passion; a sense of human destiny lived; an atmosphere of human frailty was present.

Finally a speaker came forward and spoke of Chicago's South Side, its Negro population, their sufferings, and handicaps, linking all that, also, to the world struggle. Then still another speaker followed and described the tasks of the Communist party of the South Side. At last, the world, the national, and the local pictures had been fused into one overwhelming drama of moral struggle in which everybody in the hall was participating. This presentation had lasted for more than three hours, but it had enthroned a new sense of reality in the hearts of those present, a sense of man on earth. With the exception of the church and its myths and legends, there was no agency in the world so capable of making men feel the earth and the people upon it as the Communist party.

I knew, as I watched, that I was looking at the future of mankind, that this way of living would finally win out. I knew that in no other way could the emotional capacities, the passional nature of men be so deeply tapped. In no other system yet devised could man so clearly reveal his destiny on earth, a destiny to rise and grapple with the world in which he lives, to wring from it the satisfactions he feels he must have. I knew, as I watched and listened, that but few people understood the essence of Communism, its passional dynamics; but a few knew that Communism was more important than any of its individual parties, than the sum of all its tactics, strategies, theories, mistakes, and tragedies. I knew that once this system became entrenched on earth, for good or bad, it could not fail, that all Europe and her armies could not destroy the Soviet Union, that the spirit of self-sacrifice that Communism engendered in men would astound the world.

And these people had asked me to come and listen to another man being tried so that I might know what was in store for me if I went wrong. I was with them. Could I not rise up and tell them? But, even as I thought of it, I knew they would not be able to know when I was telling the truth. My kind of helping was something frightening to them. If I talked, I would only incriminate myself further.

I had wanted to tell others what these men felt. I understood their impulses, the long years' privation and hurt out of which they had come to Communism. I knew that I did not know as much politics as Buddy Nealson, as the members of the Central Committee, or the members of the Communist International. Politics was not my game; the human heart was my game, but it was only in the realm of politics that I could see the depths of the human heart. I had wanted to make others see what was in the Communist heart, what the Communists were after; but I was on trial by proxy, condemned by them.

Toward evening the direct charges against Ross were made, not by the leaders of the party but by Ross's friends, those who knew him best! It was crushing. Ross wilted. His emotions could not withstand the weight of the moral pressure. No one was terrorized into giving information against him. They gave it willingly, citing dates, conversations, scenes. The black mass of Ross's wrongdoing emerged slowly and irrefutably. He could not deny it. No one could.

They did not place me on trial because they did not know how to give names to what they feared in me. I had not fought them as Ross had; I had not challenged a single policy of theirs. It was my way of thinking and feeling that they feared. The conditions under which I had to work were what baffled them. Writing had to be done in loneliness and Communism had declared war upon human loneliness. Alone, they said, a man was weak; united with others, he was strong. Therefore, they habitually feared a man who stood alone. Communism spelt the unity of human life, and when a Communist, newly risen from his oppressed isolation and feeling strange and lonely because of it, saw another man seeking seclusion, he became afraid of him. The Communism I looked upon was impatient of extended processes, of results that could not be obtained overnight, of an act that could not be performed within a day. This was how America had embraced Communism; this was America's first green fruit of materialistic rebellion.

The moment came for Ross to defend himself. I had been told that he had arranged for friends of his to testify in his behalf, but he called upon no one. He stood, trembling; he tried to talk and his words would not come. The hall was as still as death. Guilt was written in every pore of his black skin. His hands shook. He held onto the edge of the table to keep on his feet. His personality, his sense of himself, had been obliterated. Yet he could not have been so humbled unless he had shared and accepted the vision that had crushed him, the common vision that bound us all together.

"Comrades," he said in a low, charged voice, "I'm guilty of all the charges, all of them . . ."

His voice broke in a sob. No one prodded him. No one tortured him. No one threatened him. He was free to go out of the hall and never see another Communist. But he did not want to. He could not. The vision of a communal world had sunk down into his soul and it would never leave him until life left him. He talked on, outlining how he had erred, how he would reform.

I knew, as I sat there, that there were many people who thought they knew life who had been skeptical of the Moscow trials. But they could not have been skeptical had they witnessed this astonishing trial. Ross had not been doped; he had been awakened. It was not a fear of the Communist party that had made him confess, but a fear of the punishment that he would exact of himself that made him tell of his wrongdoings. The Communists had talked to him until they had given him new eyes with which to see his own crime. And then they sat back and listened to him tell how he had erred. He was one with all the members there, regardless of race or color; his heart was theirs and their hearts were his; and when a man reaches that state of kinship with others, that degree of oneness, or when a trial has made him kin after he has been sundered from them by wrongdoing, then he must rise and say, out of a sense of the deepest morality in the world:

"I'm guilty. Forgive me."

This, to me, was a spectacle of glory; and yet, because it had condemned me, because it was blind and ignorant, I felt that it was a spectacle of horror. The blindness of their limited lives—lives truncated and impoverished by the oppression they had suffered long before they had ever heard of Communism—made them think that I was with their enemies. American life had so corrupted their consciousness that they were unable to recognize their friends when they saw them. I knew that if they had held state power I would have been declared guilty of treason and my execution would have followed. And I knew that they felt, with all the strength of their black blindness, that they were right.

I could not stay until the end. I was anxious to get out of the hall and into the streets and shake free from the gigantic tension that had hold of me. I rose and went to the door; a comrade shook his head, warning me that I could not leave until the trial had ended.

"You can't leave now," he said.

"I'm going out of here," I said, my anger making my voice sound louder than I intended.

We glared at each other. Another comrade came running up. I stepped forward. The comrade who had rushed up gave the signal for me to be allowed to leave. They did not want violence, and neither did I. They stepped aside.

I went into the dark Chicago streets and walked home through the cold, filled with a sense of sadness. Once again I told myself that I must learn to stand alone. I did not feel so wounded by their rejection of me that I wanted to spend my days bleating about what they had done. Perhaps what I had already learned to feel in my childhood saved me from that futile path. I lay in bed that night and said to myself: I'll be for them, even though they are not for me.

The next morning a Negro Communist came to my house before I was out of bed. He sat and would not look at me.

"What do you want, Harold?" I asked.

"I don't know how to say what I want to say," he said.

"Say it anyhow. I can stand anything now."

"Gee, I'm sorrier than I've ever been in all my life," he cried. "I didn't know what they were going to do . . ."

"Do you mean that?" I asked.

"God, yes!"

"Thanks. I'm no enemy of the party."

"It was horrible," he said.

"There was a glimpse of glory in it, too," I said.

"What?"

"Nothing," I said.

He left. He was the only Communist who had enough courage to speak to me.

20

From the Federal Experimental Theater I was transferred to the Federal Writers' Project, and I tried to earn my bread by writing guidebooks. Many of the writers on the project were members of the Communist party and they kept their revolutionary vows that restrained them from speaking to "traitors of the working class." I sat beside them in the office, ate next to them in restaurants, and rode up and down in the elevators with them, but they always looked straight ahead, wordlessly.

After working on the project for a few months, I was made acting supervisor of essays and straightway I ran into political difficulties. One morning the administrator of the project called me into his office.

"Wright, who are your friends on this project?" he asked.

"I don't know," I said. "Why?"

"Well, you ought to find out soon," he said.

"What do you mean?"

"Some people are asking for your removal on the grounds that you are incompetent," he said.

"Who are they?"

He named several of my erstwhile comrades. Yes, it had come to that. They were trying to take the bread out of my mouth, and I agreed with them too much to want to fight back.

"What do you propose to do about their complaints?" I asked.

"Nothing," he said, laughing. "I think I understand what's happening here. I'm not going to let them drive you off this job."

I thanked him and rose to go to the door. Something in his words had not sounded right. I turned and faced him.

"*This* job?" I repeated. "What do you mean?"

"You mean to say that you don't know?" he asked.

"Know what? What are you talking about?"

"Why did you leave the Federal Negro Theater?"

"I had trouble there. They drove me off the job, the Negroes did."

"And you don't think that they had any encouragement?" he asked me ironically.

I sat again. This was deadly. I gaped at him.

"You needn't fear here," he said. "You work, write . . ."

"It's hard to believe that," I murmured.

"Forget it," he said.

I returned to my desk and stared at the Communists who sat near me. I was not angry. I was sorry. How far can they go acting like this? I wondered. I knew that if they had succeeded in getting me fired they would have considered it a triumph of proletarian tactics. Why could they not forget me? I was opposing no policy of theirs. I was not speaking or writing against them. But the worst was yet to come.

One day at noon I closed my desk and went down in the elevator. When I reached the first floor of the building, I saw a picket line moving to and fro in the streets. Many of the men and women carrying placards were old friends of mine, and they were chanting for higher wages for Works Progress Administration artists and writers. It was not the kind of picket line that one was not supposed to cross, and as I started away from the door I heard my name shouted:

"There's Wright, that goddamn Trotskyite!"

"That sonofabitch Wright is with 'em, too!"

"We know you, you bastard!"

"Wright's a traitor, too!"

For a moment it seemed that I ceased to live. I had now

reached that point where I was cursed aloud in the busy streets of America's second largest city. It shook me as nothing else had.

I decided upon a bold, open, and friendly move. I had to put a stop to this hounding of me. I would go directly to the head of the local Communist party and have it out with him, talk to him, explain things. I implored a friend of mine to use what influence he had to obtain an appointment for me with the secretary of the party.

Weeks passed and finally word came that I had an appointment, not with the secretary, but with the secretary's secretary, a girl, Alma Zetkin. I sighed and accepted it.

When I walked into the headquarters of the Communist party, I was ushered into Alma Zetkin's presence. She was plump, blonde, blue-eyed, with big braids of hair circling her head. She was shuffling a pile of papers in her hand. She did not look up.

"I've an appointment to see you," I said. "But I'd like to see Bernard, the party secretary."

"What do you want with him?" she asked, not lifting her head, her eyes glued to the papers in her hand.

"I want to discuss my party affiliation with him," I said.

"He cannot see you about such matters," she said.

"With whom can I talk?"

"I can listen to what you have to say," she said.

She was cold, distant; I knew that she had already made up her mind, that a decision had already been made about me.

"There're a lot of misunderstandings that I'd like to clear up," I said, forcing the words out of me, for I knew now that my errand was futile.

"What are they?" she asked, still not looking at me.

Quietly I outlined the story, sticking to bare facts, feeling that I was talking to a stone wall. When I had finished, she said:

"We can't help you with that problem."

"What do you mean?"

"If you can't get along with your comrades on the South Side, what do you expect us to do about it?" she snapped, her eyes flashing blue and cold and hard.

"They're not people with whom one can talk," I said. "I'm called a Trotskyite. WHY?"

"Are you a Trotskyite?" she asked, looking at me full now.

"No, and why would you think I was one?" I asked.

She laughed silently and turned to her papers again.

"Well, what have you to say?" I asked.

"There's nothing we can do for you here," she said.

I stood silent for a moment. I had had my answer. Yet the answer did not seem sensible, intelligible. I had not solved anything. I looked at her; she was still intent upon the papers.

"Good-bye," I said, turning and walking toward the door.

She did not answer. I paused at the door and stared at her again; she was still gazing at the papers. I went out.

That night I tossed sleepless, trying to imagine what had been in Alma Zetkin's mind, what she had been told, what were her motives. And my mind could find nothing but improbable answers. Had she been warned that I must under no circumstances be given encouragement? If so, why? Even Ross, who had actively fought the party within the ranks of the party, was still a member in good standing. But I, whom they had officially accused of nothing, was an open enemy in their eyes.

Nothing that I could think of could explain the reality I saw. My mind was like an ulcer whenever it touched upon what had happened to my relations with the party. I asked myself why a million times, and there were no answers.

Days passed. I continued on my job, where I functioned as the shop chairman of the union which I had helped to organize, though my election as shop chairman had been bitterly opposed by the party. In their efforts to nullify my influence in the union, my old comrades were willing to kill the union itself.

As May Day of 1936 approached, it was voted by the union membership that we should march in the public procession. On the morning of May Day I received printed instructions as to the time and place where our union contingent would assemble to join the parade. At noon I hurried to the spot and found that the parade was already in progress. In vain I searched for the banners of my union local. Where were they? I went up and down the streets, asking for the location of my local.

"Oh, that local's gone fifteen minutes ago," a Negro told me. "If you're going to march, you'd better fall in somewhere."

I thanked him and walked through the milling crowds. Suddenly I heard my name called. I turned. To my left was the Communist party's South Side section, lined up and ready to march.

"Come here!" an old party friend called me.

I walked over to him.

"Aren't you marching today?" he asked me.

"I missed my union local," I told him.

"What the hell," he said. "March with us."

"I don't know," I said, remembering my last visit to the head-quarters of the party, and my status as an "enemy."

"This is May Day," he said. "Get into the ranks."

"You know the trouble I've had," I said.

"That's nothing," he said. "Everybody's marching today."

"I don't think I'd better," I said, shaking my head.

"Goddamn, are you scared?" he asked. "This is *May Day*."

He caught my right arm and pulled me into line beside him. I stood talking to him, asking him about his work, about common friends.

"Get out of our ranks!" a voice barked in my ears.

I turned. A white Communist, a leader of the district of the Communist party, Cy Perry, a slender, close-cropped fellow, stood glaring at me.

"I . . . It's May Day and I want to march," I said.

"Get out!" he shouted.

"I was invited here," I said.

I turned to the Negro Communist who had invited me into the ranks. I did not want public violence. I looked at my friend. He turned his eyes away. He was afraid. I did not know what to do.

"You asked me to march here," I said to him.

He did not answer.

"Tell him that you did invite me," I said, pulling his sleeve.

"I'm asking you for the last time to get out of our ranks!" Cy Perry shouted.

I did not move. I had intended to, but I was beset by so many impulses that I could not act. Another white Communist came to assist Perry. Perry caught hold of my collar and pulled at me. I resisted. They held me fast. I struggled to free myself.

"Turn me loose!" I said.

Hands lifted me bodily from the sidewalk; I felt myself being pitched headlong through the air. I saved myself from landing on my head by clutching a curbstone with my hands. Slowly I rose and stood. Perry and his assistant were glaring at me. The rows of white and black Communists were looking at me with cold eyes of non-recognition. I could not quite believe what had happened, even though my hands were smarting and bleeding. I had suffered a public physical assault by two white Communists with black Communists looking on. I could not move from the spot. I was empty of any idea about what to do. But I did not feel belligerent. I had outgrown my childhood. I did not know how much time elapsed as I stood there, numb, astonished; but, suddenly, the vast ranks of the Communist party began to move. Scarlet banners with the hammer and sickle emblem of world revolution were lifted, and they fluttered in the May breeze. Drums beat. Voices were chanting. The tramp of many feet shook the earth. A long line of set-faced men and women, white and black, flowed past me.

I followed the procession to the Loop and went into Grant Park Plaza and sat upon a bench. I was not thinking; I could not think. But an objectivity of vision was being born within me. A surging sweep of many odds and ends came together and formed an attitude, a perspective. They're blind, I said to myself. Their enemies have blinded them with too much oppression. I lit a cigarette and I heard a song floating out over the sunlit air.

Arise, you pris'ners of starvation!

I remembered the stories I had written, the stories in which I had assigned a role of honor and glory to the Communist party and

I was glad that they were down in black and white, were finished. For I knew in my heart that I would never be able to write that way again, would never be able to feel with that simple sharpness about life, would never again express such passionate hope, would never again make so total a commitment of faith.

Arise, you wretched of the earth . . .

The days of my past, of my youth, were receding from me like a rolling tide, leaving me alone upon high, dry ground, leaving me with a quieter and deeper consciousness.

For justice thunders condemnation . . .

My thoughts seemed to be coming from somewhere within me, as by a power of their own: It's going to take a long and bloody time, a lot of stumbling and a lot of falling, before they find the right road.

They will have to grope about blindly in the sunshine, butting their heads against every mistake, bruising their bodies against every illusion, making a million futile errors and suffering for them, bleeding for them, until they learn how to live, I thought.

Somehow man had been sundered from man and, in his search for a new unity, for a new wholeness, for oneness again, he would have to blunder into a million walls to find merely that he could not go in certain directions. No one could tell him. He would have to learn by marching down history's bloody road. He would have to purchase his wisdom of life with sacred death. He would have to pay dearly to learn just a little.

But perhaps that is the way it has always been with man . . .

A better world's in birth . . .

The procession still passed. Banners still floated. Voices of hope still chanted.

I headed toward home alone, really alone now, telling myself that in all the sprawling immensity of our mighty continent the least-known factor of living was the human heart, the least-sought goal of being was a way to live a human life. Perhaps, I thought, out of my tortured feelings I could fling a spark into this darkness. I would try, not because I wanted to but because I felt that I had to if I were to live at all.

I sat alone in my narrow room, watching the sun sink slowly in the chilly May sky. I was restless. I rose to get my hat; I wanted to visit some friends and tell them what I felt, to talk. Then I sat down. Why do that? My problem was here, here with me, here in this room, and I would solve it here alone or not at all. Yet, I did not want to face it; it frightened me. I rose again and went out into the streets. Halfway down the block I stopped, undecided. Go back . . . I returned to my room and sat again, determined to look squarely at my life.

Well, what had I got out of living in the city? What had I got out of living in the South? What had I got out of living in America? I paced the floor, knowing that all I possessed were words and dim knowledge that my country had shown me no examples of how to live a human life. All my life I had been full of a hunger for a new way to live . . .

I heard a trolley lumbering past over steel tracks in the early dusk and I knew that underpaid, bewildered black men and women were returning to their homes from serving their white masters. In the front room of my apartment our radio was playing, pouring a white man's voice into my home, a voice that hinted of a coming war that would consume millions of lives.

Yes, the whites were as miserable as their black victims, I thought. If this country can't find its way to a human path, if it can't inform conduct with a deep sense of life, then all of us, black as well as white, are going down the same drain . . .

I picked up a pencil and held it over a sheet of white paper, but my feelings stood in the way of my words. Well, I would wait, day and night, until I knew what to say. Humbly now, with no vaulting dream of achieving a vast unity, I wanted to try to build a bridge of words between me and that world outside, that world which was so distant and elusive that it seemed unreal.

I would hurl words into this darkness and wait for an echo, and if an echo sounded, no matter how faintly, I would send other words to tell, to march, to fight, to create a sense of the hunger for life that gnaws in us all, to keep alive in our hearts a sense of the inexpressibly human.

Chronology

1908

Born Richard Nathaniel Wright, September 4, on Rucker's Plantation, a farm near Roxie, Mississippi, 22 miles east of Natchez, first child of Nathan Wright, an illiterate sharecropper, and Ella Wilson Wright, a schoolteacher. (All four grandparents had been born in slavery. Father was born shortly before 1880, the son of Nathaniel Wright, a freed slave who farmed a plot of land he had been given at the end of the Civil War. Maternal grandfather, Richard Wilson, born March 21, 1847, served in the United States Navy in 1865, then became disillusioned because of a bureaucratic error that deprived him of his pension. Maternal grandmother, Margaret Bolton Wilson, of Irish, Scottish, American Indian, and African descent, was virtually white in appearance. A house slave before the Emancipation, she later became a midwife nurse, a devoted Seventh-Day Adventist, and the strict head of her Natchez household, which included eight surviving children. Mother, born 1883, married Nathan Wright in 1907 despite her parents' disapproval, and then gave up school teaching to work on the farm.)

1910

Brother Leon Alan, called Alan, born September 24.

1911–12

Unable to care for her children while working on the farm, mother takes Wright and his brother to live with Wilson family in Natchez. Father rejoins family and finds work in a sawmill. Wright accidentally sets fire to grandparents' house.

1913–14

Family moves to Memphis, Tennessee, by steamboat. Father deserts family to live with another woman, leaving them impoverished. Mother finds work as a cook.

1915–16

Wright enters school at Howe Institute, Memphis, in September 1915. Mother falls seriously ill in early 1916. Grandmother comes to care for family. After grandmother returns home, mother puts Wright and his brother in the Settlement House, Methodist orphanage in Memphis, where they stay for over a month. Spends relatively pleasant summer at 1107 Lynch Street in Jackson, Mississippi, where maternal grandparents now live, before going with mother and brother to Elaine, Arkansas, to live with his favorite aunt, Maggie (his mother's younger sister), and her husband, Silas Hoskins, a saloonkeeper.

1917–18

After Hoskins is murdered by whites who want his prosperous liquor business, terrified family flees to West Helena, Arkansas, then returns to Jackson with Aunt Maggie to live with the Wilsons. After several months they go back to West Helena, where mother and aunt find work cooking and cleaning for whites. Aunt Maggie leaves with her lover, "Professor" Matthews, a fugitive from the law (they eventually settle in Detroit).

1918–19

Wright enters local school in fall 1918. Mother's health deteriorates early in 1919 and Wright is forced to leave school to earn money. Delivers wood and laundry and carries lunches to railroad workers. Family moves frequently because of lack of rent money; Wright gathers stray pieces of coal along railroad tracks to heat their home. Mother suffers paralyzing stroke, and grandmother comes to bring the family back to Jackson. Aunt Maggie helps care for mother, then takes Leon Alan back to Detroit with her; other aunts and uncles help pay for mother's treatment.

1919–20

Wright moves into home of aunt and uncle, Clark and Jody Wilson, in nearby Greenwood, Mississippi, where he is able to attend school. Finds household calm and orderly but his aunt and uncle cold and unsympathetic, and is terrified by episodes of sleepwalking. Returns to grandparents' home in Jackson. Mother begins to show signs of recovery from paralysis, then has relapse caused by a cerebral blood clot that leaves her virtually crippled. Her illness impoverishes the family, already hurt by the rheumatism that makes Grandfather Wilson unable to work.

1920–21

Enters Seventh-Day Adventist school taught by his youngest aunt, Addie. Only nine years older than Wright, she is a rigid disciplinarian often at odds with him. Wright rebels against the rules and practices of the religion, including its diet, which forbids eating pork. Finds himself opposed to his family in general, except for his mother, who is too sick to help him.

1921–22

Enters the fifth grade of the Jim Hill School in Jackson, two years behind his age group. Does well, quickly gains in confidence, and is soon promoted to the sixth grade. Begins friendships, some of them lasting into his adulthood, with a number of other students, including Dick Jordan, Joe Brown, Perry Booker, D. C. Blackburn, Lewis Anderson, Sarah McNeamer, and Essie Lee Ward. Takes job as a newsboy, which gives him the chance to read material forbidden at home because of religious prohibitions. Family life continues to be difficult, although his mother's health improves slightly. Travels briefly during summer in the Mississippi Delta region as "secretary-accountant" to an insurance agent, W. Mance. The trip allows him to know better the rural South, but he is dismayed by the illiteracy and lack of education he encounters among blacks.

1922–23

Enters the seventh grade. Grandfather Wilson dies November 8. After many arguments, grandmother reluctantly lets Wright take jobs after school and on Saturday (the Seventh-Day Adventist sabbath). Runs errands and performs small chores, mainly for whites. For the first time has enough money to buy school books, food to combat his chronic hunger, and clothing. Baptized in the Methodist Church, mainly to please his mother. Avidly reads pulp magazines, dime novels, and books and magazines discarded by others. Uncle Thomas Wilson, his wife, and their two daughters come to live with the family in spring 1923. Mother's health worsens. Wright works during the summer at a brickyard and as a caddy at a golf course.

1923–24

Enters eighth grade at the Smith Robertson Junior High School, Jackson (a former slave, Smith Robertson had become a successful local barber and a community leader; the school, built in 1894, was the first black institution of its kind in Jackson). Until he can afford a bicycle, Wright walks several miles daily to and from the school. Makes new friends at school, including Wade Griffin, Varnie Reed, Arthur Leaner, and Minnie Farish. Begins working for the Walls, a white family he finds kindly (will serve them for two years). Later remembers writing his first short story, "The Voodoo of Hell's Half-Acre," in late winter (story is reported to have been published in the spring as "Hell's Half-Acre" in the Jackson *Southern Register*, a black weekly newspaper; no copies are known to be extant). Brother Leon Alan returns from Detroit. Wright is initially pleased, but their relationship soon disappoints him. Works for the American Optical Company, cleaning workshop and making deliveries.

1924–25

Enters ninth grade at Smith Robertson Junior High School, and graduates on May 29, 1925, as valedictorian. Rejects graduation speech prepared for him by the principal and instead delivers his own, "The Attributes of Life." Works as a delivery boy, sales clerk, hotel hallboy and bellboy, and in a movie theater. Begins classes in fall at newly founded Lanier High School, but quits a few weeks later to earn money. Leaves Jackson for Memphis, Tennessee, where he boards with a family at 570 Beale Street.

1926

Works for low pay as a dishwasher and delivery boy and at the Merry Optical Company. Reads widely in *Harper's, Atlantic Monthly,* the *American Mercury,* and other magazines. Moves to 875 Griffith Place.

1927

Joined by mother, who is still in poor health, and brother; they take an apartment together at 370 Washington Street. After reading an editorial highly critical of H. L. Mencken, long noted as a critic of the white South, Wright seeks out Mencken's *Prejudices* and *A Book of Prefaces* and is particularly impressed by Mencken's iconoclasm and use of "words as weapons." These books serve as guides to further reading, including works by Theodore Dreiser, Sinclair Lewis, Sherwood Anderson, the elder Alexandre Dumas, Frank Harris, and O. Henry. Aunt Maggie, who has been deserted by "Professor" Matthews, joins family in the fall. In December, Wright and Maggie, who hopes to open a beauty salon, move to the South Side of Chicago, while mother and Leon Alan return to Jackson. Sees his aunt Cleopatra ("Sissy"), but is disappointed to find that she lives in a rooming house, not an apartment, and moves into a rooming house with Aunt Maggie.

1928

Works as delivery boy in a delicatessen, then as a dishwasher. Wright finds Chicago stimulating and less racially oppressive than the South, but is often dismayed by the pace and disarray of urban life. Passes written examination for the postal service in the spring, then begins work in the summer as a temporary employee at 65 cents an hour. Rents an apartment with Aunt Maggie and is joined by mother and brother. In the fall Wright fails the postal service medical examination required for a permanent position because of chronic undernourishment and returns to dishwashing. Disputes over money and his reading cause tension with Aunt Maggie. Wright takes another apartment for family and invites his aunt Cleopatra to move in with them.

1929

After undertaking a crash diet to increase his weight, Wright passes the physical examination and is hired by the central post office at Clark Street and Jackson Boulevard as a substitute clerk and mail sorter. Moves with family to four rooms at 4831 Vincennes Avenue, which allows him to read and write in relative comfort. Dislikes the post office bureaucracy, but becomes friendly with many fellow workers, both black and white. Among his friends are schoolmates from the South, including Essie Lee Ward, Arthur Leaner, and Joe Brown. Writes steadily and attends meetings of a local black literary group, but feels distant from its middle-class members. Attracted by the Universal Negro Improvement Association, a group inspired by Marcus Garvey, but does not join it.

1930

Volume of mail drops in decline following the 1929 Wall Street crash; Wright has his working hours cut back before losing his job altogether. South Side sinks into economic depression. Works temporarily for post office in the summer. Mother suffers a relapse, aunt Cleopatra has a heart attack, and brother develops stomach ulcers. Begins work on "Cesspool," novel about black life in Chicago. Enrolls in tenth grade at Hyde Park Public School, but soon drops out.

1931

Reads books recommended by friend William Harper (who will later own a bookstore on the South Side). Wright is particularly impressed by Dreiser and Joseph Conrad, and continues to write. Short story "Superstition" is published in April *Abbott's Monthly Magazine*, a black journal (magazine fails before Wright is paid). Through a distant relative, finds job as a funeral insurance agent for several burial societies. Also works as an assistant to a black Republican precinct captain during the mayoral campaign, and at the post office in December. Becomes interested in views of Communist orators and organizers, especially those in the League of Struggle for Negro Rights.

1932

Sells insurance policies door-to-door and works briefly as an assistant to a Democratic precinct captain. Family moves to slum apartment as Wright is increasingly unable to sell policies to blacks impoverished by the Depression. Asks for and receives relief assistance from the Cook County Bureau of Public Welfare, which finds him a temporary job as a street cleaner. Works at the post office during the Christmas season.

1933

Digs ditches in the Cook County Forest Preserves, then works at Michael Reese Hospital, caring for animals used in medical research. Recruited by fellow post office worker Abraham Aaron to join the newly formed Chicago branch of the John Reed Club, a national literary organization sponsored by the Communist party. Welcomed and encouraged by the almost entirely white membership of the club, Wright begins to read and study *New Masses* and *International Literature,* the organ of the International League of Revolutionary Writers. Writes and submits revolutionary poems ("I Have Seen Black Hands," "A Red Love Note") to *Left Front,* the magazine of the midwestern John Reed Clubs. Elected executive secretary of the Chicago John Reed Club and organizes a successful lecture series which allows him to meet a variety of intellectuals. Gives lecture at open forum on "The Literature of the Negro."

1934

Hoping to consolidate his position in the John Reed Club, Wright joins the Communist party; is also impressed by the party's opposition to racial discrimination. Publishes poetry in *Left Front, Anvil,* and *New Masses.* Becomes a member of the editorial board of *Left Front.* Enjoys literary and social friendships with Bill Jordan, Abraham Chapman, Howard Nutt, Laurence Lipton, Nelson Algren, Joyce Gourfain, and Jane Newton. Grandmother Wilson comes to Chicago to join the family; they move to apartment at 4804 St. Lawrence Avenue, near the railroad tracks. Mother's paralysis returns after attack of encephalitis. Wright is laid off by the hospital in the summer, and again works as a street sweeper and ditch digger before being hired to supervise a youth club organized to counter juvenile delinquency among blacks on the South Side. Attends Middle West Writers' Congress in August and the national congress of John Reed Clubs in September. Dismayed by party decision to cease publication of *Left Front* and to dissolve the John Reed Clubs in 1935 as part of its Popular Front strategy. Meets Jack Conroy, editor of *Anvil.* Reading in Chicago by this time includes Henry James (especially the Prefaces to the New York

Edition), Gertrude Stein (notably her *Three Lives,* with its portrait of a black character, Melanctha Herbert), Faulkner, T. S. Eliot, Sherwood Anderson, Dos Passos, O'Neill, Stephen Crane, Dreiser, Whitman, Poe, D. H. Lawrence, Conrad, Galsworthy, Hardy, Dickens, George Moore, Carlyle, Swift, Shakespeare, Tolstoy, Dostoevsky, Turgenev, Chekhov, Proust, Dumas, and Balzac. Lectures on the career of Langston Hughes to the Indianapolis John Reed Club in November and contributes fee to new publication *Midland Left.*

1935

Publishes leftist poetry in *Midland Left,* a short-lived journal, *New Masses* ("Red Leaves of Red Books" and "Spread Your Sunshine"), and *International Literature* ("A Red Slogan"). Family moves to 2636 Grove Avenue. Begins submitting novel "Cesspool" to publishers (later retitled *Lawd Today!* by Wright; it is rejected repeatedly over the next two years, then published posthumously as *Lawd Today* in 1963 by Walker and Company). Wright attends the first American Writers' Congress, held in New York in April. Speaks on "The Isolation of the Negro Writer," meets Chicago novelist James T. Farrell, and becomes one of fifty members of the national council of the newly formed League of American Writers. Works on story "Big Boy Leaves Home." Publishes "Between the World and Me," poem about lynching, in July–August *Partisan Review.* Falls seriously ill with attack of pneumonia during the summer. Article "Avant-Garde Writing" wins second prize in contest sponsored by two literary magazines but is never published. First piece of journalism, "Joe Louis Uncovers Dynamite," describing the reaction of Chicago blacks to the Louis–Max Baer fight, published in *New Masses.* Grandmother Wilson dies. Family, with Wright still virtually its sole support, moves to 3743 Indiana Avenue. Wright is hired by the Federal Writers' Project (part of the Works Progress Administration) to help research the history of Illinois and of the Negro in Chicago for the Illinois volume in the American Guide Series. Discusses influence of Hemingway with fellow writers in federal project.

1936

Publishes "Transcontinental," a six-page radical poem influenced by Whitman and Louis Aragon, in January *International Literature.* Becomes a principal organizer of the Communist party–sponsored National Negro Congress (successor to the League of Struggle for Negro Rights), held in Chicago in February, and reports on it for *New Masses.* Transferred in spring to the Federal Theatre Project, where he serves as literary adviser and press agent for the Negro Federal Theatre of Chicago and becomes involved in dramatic productions. Finishes two one-act plays based in part on a section of his unpublished novel. In April, Wright takes a leading role in the new South Side Writers' Group (members will include Arna Bontemps, Frank Marshall Davis, Theodore Ward, Fenton Johnson, Horace Cayton, and Margaret Walker). Takes an active role in the Middle West Writers' Congress, held in Chicago June 14–15. Because of what he later describes as a Communist plot against him on the Federal Theatre Project assignment, Wright returns to the Writers' Project, where he becomes a group coordinator. Story "Big Boy Leaves Home" appears in anthology *The New Caravan* in November and receives critical attention and praise in mainstream newspapers and journals.

1937

Publishes poem "We of the Streets" in April *New Masses* and story "Silt" in the August number. Breaks with the Communist party in Chicago, basically over the question of his freedom as a writer. Brother finds job with the Works Progress Administration and assumes some responsibility for support of the family. Wright ranks first in postal service examination in Chicago, but turns down offer in May of permanent position at approximately $2,000 a year in order to move to New York City to pursue career as a writer. Stays briefly with artist acquaintances in Greenwich Village, then moves to Harlem; by mid-June he has a furnished room in the Douglass Hotel at 809 St. Nicholas Avenue. Attends Second American Writers' Congress as a delegate and serves as a session president; stresses the need for writers to think of themselves as writers first and not as laborers. Becomes Harlem editor of the Communist newspaper *Daily Worker* and writes over 200 articles for it during the year, including pieces on blues singer Leadbelly and the continuing Scottsboro Boys controversy. With Dorothy West and Marian Minus, helps launch magazine *New Challenge*, designed to present black life "in relationship to the struggle against war and Fascism." Wright publishes "The Ethics of Living Jim Crow—An Autobiographical Sketch" in *American Stuff: WPA Writers' Anthology* (essay is later included in the second edition of *Uncle Tom's Children* and incorporated into *Black Boy*). In November, publishes influential essay "Blueprint for Negro Writing" in *New Challenge*, criticizing past black literature and urging a Marxist-influenced approach that would transcend nationalism. Lacking party support, *New Challenge* fails after one number. Befriends 23-year-old Ralph Ellison. Wright's second novel, "Tarbaby's Dawn," about a black adolescent in the South, is rejected by publishers (it remains unpublished). Learns that story "Fire and Cloud" has won first prize ($500) among 600 entries in *Story Magazine* contest. Wright joins the New York Federal Writers' Project (will write the Harlem section for *New York Panorama* and work on "The Harlems" in *The New York City Guide*).

1938

Rents furnished room at 139 West 143rd Street. Engages Paul Reynolds, Jr., as literary agent. Reynolds makes arrangements to place *Uncle Tom's Children: Four Novellas* ("Big Boy Leaves Home," "Down by the Riverside," "Long Black Song," and "Fire and Cloud") with editor Edward Aswell at Harper and Brothers, beginning Wright's long association with Aswell and Harper; book is published in March and is widely praised. Sends Aswell outline of novel about a black youth in Chicago. Announces plans to marry daughter of his Harlem landlady in May, but then cancels wedding, telling friends that a medical examination had revealed that the young woman has congenital syphilis. Moves into home of friends from Chicago, Jane and Herbert Newton, at 175 Carleton Avenue in Brooklyn. Story "Bright and Morning Star" appears in May *New Masses*. Writes about the second Joe Louis–Max Schmeling fight in the June *Daily Worker* and July *New Masses*. In June, replaces Horace Gregory on the editorial board of the literature section of *New Masses*. Works steadily on new novel; often writes in Fort Greene Park in the mornings, and discusses his progress with Jane Newton. Asks Margaret Walker to send him newspaper accounts of the case of Robert Nixon, a young Chicago black man accused of murder (executed in August 1939). Moves in the fall with the Newtons to 522 Gates Avenue. Congressman Martin Dies, chairman of the House Special Committee on Un-American Activities, denounces "The Ethics of Living Jim Crow" during an investigation of the Federal Writers' Project. Finishes first draft of novel, now titled *Native Son,* in October and receives $400 advance from Harper in November. "Fire and Cloud" wins the O. Henry Memorial Award ($200). Travels to Chicago in November to research settings and events used in *Native Son.* Moves with Newtons to 87 Lefferts Place.

1939

Meets Ellen Poplar (b. 1912), daughter of Polish Jewish immigrants and a Communist party organizer in Brooklyn. Completes revised version of novel in February and shows it to Reynolds. Awarded Guggenheim Fellowship ($2,500) in March and resigns from the Federal Writers' Project in May. Discusses black American writing with Langston Hughes, Alain Locke, Countee Cullen, and Warren Cochrane during meeting of Harlem Cultural Congress. After Newtons' landlord evicts them, Wright moves to Douglass Hotel at 809 St. Nicholas Avenue in May, renting room next to Theodore Ward, a friend from Chicago. Becomes close to Ellen Poplar and considers marrying her, but also sees Dhima Rose Meadman, a modern-dance teacher of Russian Jewish ancestry. Plays active role at Third American Writers' Congress. Finishes *Native Son* on June 10. Ward drama- tizes "Bright and Morning Star." The story is included in Edward O'Brien's *Best American Short Stories, 1939* and *Fifty Best American Short Stories (1914–1939)*. Begins work on new novel, "Little Sister." Marries Dhima Rose Meadman in August in Episcopal church on Convent Avenue, with Ralph Ellison serving as best man. Lives with his wife, her two-year- old son by an earlier marriage, and his mother-in-law in large apartment on fashionable Hamilton Terrace in Harlem. Attends Festival of Negro Culture held in Chicago in September. Moves to Crompond, New York, to work on "Little Sister" (it is never completed).

1940

Visits Chicago in February and buys house for his family on Vincennes Avenue. Has lunch in Chicago with W.E.B. Du Bois, Langston Hughes, and Arna Bontemps. *Native Son* published by Harper and Brothers March 1 and is offered by the Book-of-the-Month Club as one of its two main selections. In three weeks it sells 215,000 copies. Wright delivers talk "How 'Bigger' Was Born" at Columbia University on March 12 (later published as a pamphlet by Harper, then added to future printings of *Native Son*). *Native Son* is banned in Birmingham, Alabama, libraries. Takes his first airplane flight when he accompanies *Life* magazine photog- raphers to Chicago for an article on the South Side; tours the area with sociologist Horace Cayton, beginning long friendship (article is later can- celed). Sails in April for Veracruz, Mexico, with wife, her son, mother-in- law, and wife's pianist. Rents ten-room villa in the Miraval Colony in Cuernavaca. Takes lessons in Spanish and studies the guitar. Reunited with Herbert Kline, friend from the Chicago John Reed Club, who is filming documentary *The Forgotten Village* with John Steinbeck; Wright travels with them through the countryside and takes an interest in the filming. Signs contract with John Houseman and Orson Welles for stage produc- tion of *Native Son*. Marriage becomes strained. Wright leaves Mexico in June and travels through the South alone. Visits his father, a poor and bro- ken farm laborer, in Natchez, but is unable to make anything other than a token reconciliation with him. Goes to Chapel Hill, North Carolina, to begin collaboration with Paul Green on stage adaptation of *Native Son*. Meets producer John Houseman and drives to New York with him. Travels to Chicago to do research for book on black American life featuring photographs selected by Edwin Rosskam. Wright and Langston Hughes are guests of honor at reception given by Jack Conroy and Nelson Algren to launch magazine *New Anvil*. Returns to Chapel Hill in July to continue work with Paul Green. Elected vice-president of the League of American Writers. Harper reissues story collection as *Uncle Tom's Children: Five Long Stories* with "Bright and Morning Star" added and "The Ethics of Living Jim Crow" as an introduction. Starts divorce proceedings. Moves in with the Newtons, now at 343 Grand Avenue in Brooklyn; in the autumn Ellen Poplar moves into the Newton house. In September Wright is elected a vice-president of American Peace Mobilization, a Communist-sponsored group opposed to American involvement in World War II. Works with Houseman on revising stage version of *Native Son* (both Wright and Houseman think that Green has diverged too much from the novel); Houseman agrees that Orson Welles, who is finishing *Citizen Kane,* should direct. Story "Almos' a Man" appears in *O. Henry Award Prize Stories of 1940.*

1941

In January the National Association for the Advancement of Colored People awards Wright the Spingarn Medal, given annually to the black American judged to have made the most notable achievement in the preceding year. Rehearsals for *Native Son* begin in February. Marries Ellen Poplar in Coytesville, New Jersey, on March 12. They move to 473 West 140th Street. *Native Son,* starring Canada Lee, opens at St. James Theatre on March 24 after a benefit performance for the NAACP. Reviews are generally favorable, though the play is attacked in the Hearst papers, which are hostile to Welles following *Citizen Kane.* Production runs in New York until June 15. Welles' striking but costly staging causes production to lose some money, but it recovers during successful tour of Pittsburgh, Boston, Chicago, Milwaukee, Detroit, St. Louis, and Baltimore. Wright asks the governor of New Jersey to parole Clinton Brewer, a black man imprisoned since 1923 for murdering a young woman, arguing that Brewer, who had taught himself music composition, has rehabilitated himself (Brewer is released July 8; Wright had previously sent one of his pieces to his friend, record producer and talent scout John Hammond, who arranged for Count Basie to record it). Begins novel "Black Hope" (never completed). Introduces Ellen to his family in Chicago during visit in April. Signs appeal of forty members of the League of American Writers against American intervention in the war that appears in *New Masses* May 27, and publishes "Not My People's War" in *New Masses* June 17. After Germany invades the Soviet Union, June 22, American Peace Mobilization changes its name to American People's Mobilization. Wright travels to

Houston with Horace Cayton and John Hammond to accept Spingarn award from NAACP convention on June 27. Delivers enthusiastically received speech, in which his criticism of Roosevelt administration racial policies is muted in response to Communist party pressure. Lectures at Writers' Schools sponsored by the League of American Writers. Wrights move to 11 Revere Place, Brooklyn, in July. At John Hammond's request, Wright writes "Note on Jim Crow Blues" as a preface to the blues singer Josh White's *Southern Exposure,* an album of three recordings attacking segregation. Hammond then produces recording of Paul Robeson singing Wright's blues song "King Joe," accompanied by the Count Basie orchestra. *12 Million Black Voices: A Folk History of the Negro in the United States,* with photographs selected by Edwin Rosskam (one taken by Wright), published by Viking Press in October to enthusiastic reviews. Wright reads *Dark Legend,* a psychoanalytic study of matricide by psychiatrist Frederic Wertham, then writes to Wertham about Clinton Brewer, who had murdered another young woman within months of his release. Wertham intervenes in the case and helps save Brewer from execution (Wright and Wertham begin close friendship, and Wright becomes increasingly interested in psychoanalysis). Finishes draft of novel "The Man Who Lived Underground." Signs petition "Communication to All American Writers" in December 16 *New Masses,* supporting America's entry into the war after the December 7 Japanese attack on Pearl Harbor.

1942

Mother and Aunt Maggie rejoin Addie in Jackson, Mississippi (brother remains in Chicago, though house on Vincennes Avenue is sold two years later). Daughter Julia, Wright's first child, born April 15. Wrights move in summer to 7 Middagh Street, a 19th-century house near the Brooklyn Bridge shared by George Davis, Carson McCullers, and other writers and artists. Excerpts from "The Man Who Lived Underground" appear in *Accent.* As the sole support of his family, Wright is classified 3-A and not drafted. Unsuccessfully tries to secure a special commission in the psychological warfare or propaganda services of the army. *Native Son* returns to Broadway in October (runs until January 1943). Publishes "What You Don't Know Won't Hurt You," article describing some of his experiences as a hospital janitor in Chicago, in December *Harper's Magazine.* Breaks quietly with the Communist party over its unwillingness to confront wartime racial discrimination and its continuing attempts to control his writing.

1943

Accompanied by Horace Cayton, Wright goes to Fisk University, Nashville, in April to deliver talk on his experiences with racism. Strong reaction from the audience leads Wright to begin autobiography *American Hunger.* Neighbors and associates are interviewed by the Federal Bureau of Investigation. (Files obtained under the Freedom of Information Act in the 1970s show that the FBI began an investigation in December 1942 to determine if *12 Million Black Voices* was prosecutable under the sedition statutes. Although the sedition investigation is concluded in 1943, the FBI will continue to monitor Wright's activities, chiefly through the use of informers, for the remainder of his life.) Wrights move in August to 89 Lefferts Place in Brooklyn Heights. Helps organize the Citizens' Emergency Conference for Interracial Unity in response to widespread riots in Harlem following the wounding of a black soldier by white police in August. Finishes *American Hunger* in December.

1944
Writes film scenario "Melody Limited," about group of black singers during Reconstruction (scenario is never produced). Becomes friends with C. L. R. James, a Trinidad-born historian and Trotskyist, with whom he plans a book, "The Negro Speaks," and a journal, "American Pages" (neither of these projects appear), and his wife, Constance Webb. Writes series of radio programs on the life of a black family for producer Leston Huntley and is frustrated when Huntley is unable to place the series, in part because of criticism by middle-class blacks. Attends party held in honor of Theodore Dreiser on June 2, where Wright and Dreiser discuss the influence of life in Chicago on their attitudes. Deepens friendship with Dorothy Norman, New York *Post* editorial writer and editor of *Twice a Year,* who introduces him to existentialist philosophy and literature. Book-of-the-Month Club tells Harper that it will accept only the first section of *American Hunger,* describing Wright's experiences in the South; Wright agrees to this arrangement. Changes title to *Black Boy.* (Second section, telling of Wright's life in Chicago, is published as *American Hunger* by Harper & Row in 1977.) Wrights vacation in August outside Ottawa and in the nearby Gatineau country in Quebec. Excerpts from second section of autobiography appear as "I Tried to Be a Communist" in *Atlantic Monthly,* August–September, making public Wright's break with the Communist party. He is denounced by various party organs, including *New Masses* and the *Daily Worker.* Helps the Chicago poet Gwendolyn Brooks to place her first book, *A Street in Bronzeville.* Expanded version of "The Man Who Lived Underground" is published as a novella in *Cross Section.*

1945
To circumvent racial discrimination, Wrights form the "Richelieu Realty Co." and use their lawyer as an intermediary in buying a house at 13

Charles Street in Greenwich Village. (Residence is delayed by their waiting for a Communist tenant hostile to Wright to leave and by redecorating.) Reviews books for *P.M.* newspaper; his highly favorable review of Gertrude Stein's *Wars I Have Seen* leads to correspondence with her. *Black Boy: A Record of Childhood and Youth* published by Harper and Brothers in March to enthusiastic reviews. The book is number one on the bestseller list from April 29 to June 6 and stirs controversy when it is denounced as obscene in the U.S. Senate by Democrat Theodore Bilbo of Mississippi. Takes part in several radio programs, including the nationally influential "Town Meeting," where he argues the negative on the question "Are We Solving America's Race Problem?" In the summer, Wrights vacation on island off Quebec City, and Wright lectures at the Bread Loaf writers' school in Middlebury, Vermont. Writes long introduction to *Black Metropolis,* a sociological study of black Chicago by Horace Cayton and St. Clair Drake. Befriending a number of younger writers, white and black, Wright helps the 20-year-old James Baldwin win a Eugene F. Saxton Foundation Fellowship. Publishes a favorable review of Chester Himes's first novel, *If He Hollers Let Him Go,* and lends Himes $1,000. In the fall, Wrights move to an apartment at 82 Washington Place in Greenwich Village to be closer to a school for Julia. Wright undertakes four-month lecture tour but stops after six weeks because of exhaustion.

1946

Serves as honorary pallbearer at funeral on January 12 of poet Countee Cullen, attending service at Salem Methodist Church in Harlem and burial at Woodlawn Cemetery in the Bronx. By January 19, *Black Boy* has sold 195,000 copies in the Harper trade edition and 351,000 through the Book-of-the-Month Club, making it the fourth best-selling nonfiction title of 1945. Wright, his psychiatrist friend Dr. Frederic Wertham, and others found the Lafargue Clinic, a free psychiatric clinic in Harlem. Meets Jean-Paul Sartre in New York. Receives invitation to visit France, but requests for a passport meet with opposition. Wright goes to Washington for an interview and enlists the aid of Dorothy Norman (who appoints him co-editor of *Twice a Year*), Gertrude Stein, and French cultural attaché, anthropologist Claude Lévi-Strauss, who sends him an official invitation from the French government to visit Paris for a month. Wright leaves New York on May 1. In Paris, welcomed by Gertrude Stein and by almost all the important French literary societies and circles. (Stein dies on July 27 after operation for cancer.) Meets Simone de Beauvoir and André Gide, whose *Travels in the Congo* has impressed Wright, as well as Léopold Sédar Senghor of Senegal, Aimé Césaire of Martinique, and others in the *Négritude* movement. Assists Senghor, Césaire, and Alioune Diop of Senegal in founding the magazine *Présence Africaine* and attends its first board meeting at the Brasserie Lipp. Donates a manuscript to an auction for benefit of experimental dramatist Antonin Artaud. "The Man Who Killed a Shadow" published in French in *Les Lettres Françaises* (first appears in English in 1949 in magazine *Zero*). Leaves Paris in late December and travels to London.

1947

Meets the Trinidad-born intellectual George Padmore and dines with members of the Coloured Writers' Association, including its president, Cedric Dover, author of *Half Caste,* and the colored South African journalist and novelist Peter Abrahams. Returns to New York in January. Moves with family into their Charles Street house in Greenwich Village. Helps to welcome Simone de Beauvoir to New York in the spring. Refuses offer from Hollywood producer to film *Native Son* with character Bigger Thomas changed to a white man. Wright's works are being translated into French, Italian, German, Dutch, and Czech. Decides to return to Europe permanently with his family, partially in response to the racial hostility they are encountering in New York. Sells Greenwich Village house in June. Vacations at a cottage at Wading River, Long Island, owned by a friend. Buys an Oldsmobile sedan to take to Europe. Wright, his wife, and daughter reach Paris in August. They rent rooms from a friend, Odette Licutier, in her apartment on the rue de Lille, then move into an apartment at 166 avenue de Neuilly. Albin Michel publishes French translation of *Native Son* in autumn.

1948

Begins to read more deeply in existentialism, including Heidegger and Husserl. Sees much of Sartre and Simone de Beauvoir. Wright is particularly impressed by Camus' *The Stranger,* and begins work on an existentialist novel, eventually titled *The Outsider.* Gallimard translation of *Black Boy* wins French Critics' Award. Wright establishes friendships with the Reverend Clayton Williams, pastor of the American Church, and with Harry Goldberg of the American Library. Becomes unofficial spokesman for African-American colony in Paris, which includes James Baldwin. Visits Italy for the publication there of *Native Son.* Meets with Carlo Levi and Ignazio Silone, who later introduces him to Arthur Koestler in Paris. Interviewed by his Italian translator, Fernanda Pivano, Wright says he likes to read *Metamorphosis, Moby-Dick, Ulysses,* and *The Sound and the Fury.* Travels through Belgium to London, where he sees a performance of *Native Son* and renews friendship with George Padmore, who stirs Wright's interest in the question of colonialism in Africa. Moves with family to 14 rue Monsieur le Prince in the Latin Quarter in May. Ellen returns to New York in June to select furniture and other possessions for their new life in France. Wright is beset by recurring sinus problems and influenza. His tonsils are removed. Aids Sartre and Camus in the leadership of the Rassemblement Démocratique Révolutionnaire (RDR), an organization of intellectuals critical of both the Soviet Union and the United States. Wright plays prominent role in its writers' congress, held in Paris on December 13, delivering lengthy speech (translated by Simone de Beauvoir). Spends $6,000 to buy Paul Green's share of film rights to *Native Son* in hopes of making screen version with French director Pierre Chenal.

1949

Daughter Rachel born January 17 at the American Hospital. Wright travels again to Rome and to Switzerland, for the publication of *Black Boy*. In April, James T. Farrell and Nelson Algren visit him in Paris. Suspects socialist David Rousset of trying to shift the RDR toward a more pro-American, anti-Soviet stance. Refuses to attend large RDR rally held on April 30 (organization soon splits and dissolves). In May, visits London to consult with Richard Crossman, who is including "I Tried to Be a Communist" with similar essays by Koestler, Gide, Silone, Stephen Spender, and Louis Fischer in collection *The God That Failed* (published later in year, book is widely reviewed). Continues work on his existentialist novel. Assists George Plimpton and others in launching of *Paris Review.* James Baldwin's essay "Everybody's Protest Novel," attacking Stowe's *Uncle Tom's Cabin* but including criticism of *Native Son,* sours relationship between Wright and Baldwin. Wright writes screenplay for *Native Son,* adding several dream sequences to the story, then revises it with Chenal. After Canada Lee withdraws from project because of new commitments and worsening health, Wright undertakes to play the main role of Bigger Thomas. Sails for the United States in August, briefly visiting New York before going to Chicago for filming of exteriors for *Native Son.* Sees old friends Horace Cayton, St. Clair Drake, and others. Leaves New York in September for Argentina, where film is being made (Chenal had worked there during World War II, and political pressure had blocked access to French studios). Makes brief stops in Trinidad, Brazil, and Uruguay before arriving in Buenos Aires in October. Loses 35 pounds in preparation for the role by following strict diet and exercise program. Continues working on screenplay with Chenal.

1950

Production is delayed by financial problems. Wright finds atmosphere of Argentine life under the Perón dictatorship oppressive. Filming ends in June. Wright leaves Buenos Aires in July. Stops briefly in Brazil and Trinidad, spends two weeks in Haiti, then returns to Paris by way of New

York, where he visits Frederic Wertham and the Lafargue Clinic. In Paris, begins work on screenplay about Toussaint L'Ouverture of Haiti. Works with Aimé Césaire on "Revelation of Negro Art," an exhibition that includes works from the Musée de l'Homme and song and dance performances at the Cité Universitaire. Vacations in the fall in the Swiss and French Alps, visiting Basel, Zurich, and the Aoste Valley, where he is a jury member with Paul Eluard, Louis Bromfield, and others for international San Vicente literary prize. Founds and becomes president of the Franco-American Fellowship, intended to protest official American policies and oppose racial discrimination by American companies and organizations active in France. Fellowship members take precautions when meeting in anticipation of surveillance by the American government (files released in the 1970s show that the Fellowship was monitored by informers employed by the Central Intelligence Agency and the FBI).

1951

Lectures in Turin, Genoa, and Rome in January. *Sangre Negra* (the film version of *Native Son*) opens to acclaim in Buenos Aires on March 30. American distributor cuts almost 30 minutes from film under pressure from New York state censors (original length was approximately 105 minutes); shortened version opens in New York on June 16 to unfavorable reviews. (Several states ban the film, but it is shown in Beverly Hills and, in spring 1952, in Mississippi, where members of Wright's family see it.) A partially restored print is warmly received at the Venice Film Festival in August. The Milan press praises Wright's acting; in general, his performance is deemed sincere but awkward, especially by American critics who compare it with Canada Lee's stage version. Wright visits the sociologist Gunnar Myrdal in Geneva, beginning a long friendship. With Jean Cocteau, inaugurates the Cercle International du Théâtre et du Cinéma. *New Story Magazine* accepts excerpts from Jean Genet's *Our Lady of the Flowers* on Wright's recommendation. Baldwin's essay "Many Thousands Gone," an explicit attack on Wright in *Partisan Review* (November–December), leads to painful break between the writers. Submits screenplay about refugees forced to choose between sides in the Cold War to the French Association of Film Writers.

1952

Travels to England in February. Spends several months in London and Catford, Surrey, completing the first full version of *The Outsider*. Vacations with his family in Corrèze at the end of August and continues to revise and cut novel. Refuses suggestion by John Fischer, his new Harper editor, that he come to the United States for the publication of his book, citing the risk that he would be subpoenaed by an anti-Communist congressional investigating committee. Begins work in December on a novel about a white psychopathic murderer, based in part on his experience with Clinton Brewer.

1953

Begins correspondence with Frantz Fanon. *The Outsider* published by Harper and Brothers in March. Reviews are mixed; sales are initially brisk but eventually disappointing in comparison to *Native Son* and *Black Boy*. Wright composes an introduction to *In the Castle of My Skin,* first novel by the young Barbados writer George Lamming. Friendship with Sartre cools as Sartre moves closer to Communism. Wright's circle of friends remains wide, including Americans such as Chester Himes and William Gardner Smith, but he begins to withdraw from official organizations and to avoid formal gatherings. He is a regular at favorite cafés such as the Monaco and Tournon, where he entertains a steady stream of visitors from America, including Elmer Carter, Dorothy Norman, Nelson Algren, E. Franklin Frazier, and Louis Wirth. Discusses treatment of Algerians in France with Ben Burns, editor of *Ebony* magazine, during his visit. Wright tells Burns that he avoids criticizing French policies for fear of being deported. Ellen Wright begins work as a literary agent with Hélène Bokanowski, a prolific translator of Wright's work. From June to August, Wright travels in the Gold Coast (then a British colony with limited self-government, after 1957 the independent country of Ghana) to collect material for a book on Africa. Boat stops briefly in Freetown, Sierra Leone, en route to Takoradi; from there travels by road 170 miles to Accra, his main stop. Meets Prime Minister Kwame Nkrumah and other members of the pro-independence Convention People's Party, as well as Osei Agyeman Prempeh II, king of the Ashanti, and other traditional leaders. Excursions take him from Accra to Cape Coast, Christianborg, and Prampram; visits slave-trading fortresses and dungeons. Travels almost 3,000 miles in a chauffeur-driven car, touring the interior through Koforidua to Mampong, and the Secondi-Takoradi to Kumasi regions. In general, Wright is fascinated by Africans but is reinforced in his sense of self as a Western intellectual. Visits England to discuss his impressions with George and Dorothy Padmore before returning to Paris in September to begin work on book about his trip. Undergoes surgery for hernia.

1954

Revises book on Africa. Decides to write an account of Spanish life and culture. Drives his Citroen almost 4,000 miles between August 15 and September 9 on a route that includes Barcelona, Valencia, Saragossa, Guadalajara, Madrid, Córdoba, Seville, Granada, and Málaga. On

September 16 State Department and FBI officials interview Wright in Paris about his relationship to the Communist party when he goes to renew his passport. *Black Power: A Record of Reactions in a Land of Pathos,* about his African trip, published by Harper and Brothers September 22. Receives mixed reviews in America, but is widely praised in France. *Savage Holiday,* novel about psychopathic murderer, is published as a paperback original by Avon after having been rejected by Harper. Book attracts little attention in the United States but is well received as *Le Dieu de Mascarade* in France. Visits Geneva with Gunnar Myrdal for further research on Spain at the United Nations library. Lectures on Africa in Amsterdam in October, where he meets Margrit de Sablonière, his Dutch translator, and begins an important friendship with her. Returns to Spain on November 8. Hires a driver and travels through Irun and on to Madrid, where he stays before returning to Paris in mid-December.

1955

An old Chicago friend, the cartoonist Ollie "Bootsie" Harrington, arrives to live in France. Wright secures funding for his attendance at forthcoming conference of non-aligned nations in Bandung, Indonesia, from the Paris office of the Congress for Cultural Freedom, an international alliance of anti-Communist intellectuals. Returns to Spain February 20, and spends several weeks there, including Holy Week in Granada and Seville. Leaves Spain on April 10 for Indonesia. At Bandung, Wright shares room with missionary Winburn T. Thomas. Leaders attending conference include Nehru (with whom Wright speaks), Sukarno, Sihanouk, Nasser, and Zhou Enlai. Remains in Indonesia at home of Thomas until May 5, working on notes of his impressions, then returns to Europe via Ceylon and Kenya. Begins writing an account of the conference. Spends July to October with family at their new country home, a small farm in village of Ailly in eastern Normandy. Plans series of novels dealing with the conflicts between individuals and society (including one set in Aztec Mexico), but abandons the project on the advice of Reynolds and Aswell (now with McGraw-Hill). Returns to Paris when daughter Rachel falls ill with scarlet fever, then goes back to Ailly when her continued quarantine makes work at home difficult. *Bandoeng: 1.500.000.000 hommes,* French translation of book on non-aligned conference, published in December.

1956

Prepares manuscript of book on Spain in February and March, often living alone at Ailly, where he enjoys hours of gardening. Fearing deportation, remains silent on Algerian war of independence while in France (will offer guarded criticism of war when in other European countries). *The Color Curtain: A Report on the Bandung Conference,* with an introduction by Gunnar Myrdal, published March 19 by World Publishers in America and receives favorable reviews. Revises and cuts book on Spain. Adapts Louis Sapin's play *Papa Bon Dieu* as *Daddy Goodness* but is unable to have it produced. First Congress of Negro Artists and Writers, sponsored by *Présence Africaine* and which Wright had helped plan, meets in Paris in September, attended by delegates from Africa, the United States, and the Caribbean. Wright speaks on "Tradition and Industrialization: The Tragic Plight of the African Elites" and participates in several sessions. Suspects that *Présence Africaine* is being secretly taken over by the French government through anti-nationalist Africans and considers withdrawing from its activities. Lectures in Hamburg on "The Psychological Reactions of Oppressed Peoples" and tours the city with Ellen. Attends a meeting in London of the Congress for Cultural Freedom, organized by Arthur Koestler. Travels alone to Stockholm in late November for the Swedish publication of *The Outsider;* it sells 35,000 copies in four days (*Native Son* had sold 75,000 copies and *Black Boy* 65,000). Lectures in Sweden, Norway, and Denmark before returning to Paris in early December. Agrees to help found the American Society for African Culture, inspired by the French Société Africaine de Culture. Returning to native material, Wright begins work on novel set in Mississippi.

1957

Aunt Maggie dies January 20 in Jackson, Mississippi, where she had been taking care of Wright's mother (Wright has continued to help support them through the years). Mother moves in with a niece, then goes to Chicago at the end of June to live with Leon Alan. *Pagan Spain* published by Harper in February to good reviews but weak sales. Works at Ailly on new novel. Travels throughout Italy with Ellen during the spring. Visits West Germany in July to interview black American servicemen stationed there. *White Man, Listen!,* a collection of essays drawn from Wright's lectures, published October 15 by Doubleday (where Edward Aswell is now an editor). The book is especially well-received by the black press in the United States.

1958

Finishes *The Long Dream,* Mississippi novel, and begins "Island of Hallucinations," sequel set in France. Seeking to renew his passport, he is again compelled to report to the American embassy in February and sign a statement admitting his past membership in the Communist party. Becomes increasingly alienated from the black community in Paris, which is torn by suspicion and dissension; finds himself the object of resentment, including rumors that he is an agent of the FBI or the CIA. Depressed and isolated from other blacks, Wright suspects that he is being persecuted by agents of the U.S. government. Takes part in a session of the Congress for Cultural Freedom, and in seminars on American literature sponsored by the American Cultural Center in Paris. Supports Sartre and Simone de Beauvoir in their opposition to the new regime of General de Gaulle. Works on new novel at Ailly during summer. *The Long Dream* published by Doubleday in October to often hostile reviews and flat sales. When Leon Alan telegraphs that their mother is seriously ill, Wright is forced to borrow extra money from Reynolds to send to his brother. Edward Aswell, his long-time editor, dies November 5. Considers moving to England and enlists aid of Labour member of Parliament John Strachey, who obtains assurances from the Home Secretary that Wright's application for residence will be fairly considered. Wright distances himself from various organizations he had previously supported, including *Présence Africaine* and the Société Africaine de Culture.

1959

Mother dies January 14. Wright sends the manuscript of "Island of Hallucinations" to Reynolds in February. Later in the month, he spends a day with Martin Luther King, Jr., who is passing through Paris en route to India. Timothy Seldes (Aswell's successor at Doubleday) asks for major revisions in "Island of Hallucinations"; Wright puts book aside (it is never completed). Discouraged by financial worries, weak reviews, poor health, and frustrating state of his novel, Wright continues to curtail his public activities. Declines to attend the second Congress of Black Writers and Artists in Rome. Plans a study of French Africa. After Doubleday promises a $2,500 advance, Wright asks the American Society for African Culture for an additional $7,500, but is turned down; believes CIA infiltration of the organization is responsible for his rejection. Tired of what he considers to be growing American political and cultural influence in French life and in the wake of increased attacks by other expatriate black writers, Wright prepares to leave France and live in England. Sells farm at Ailly. His play *Daddy Goodness* is produced in Paris in the spring. Wright falls ill in June with attack of amoebic dysentery, probably picked up in Africa. Illness persists despite treatment at American Hospital. Vacations at the Moulin d'Andé near Saint-Pierre du Vauvray in Normandy. With daughter Julia now at the University of Cambridge, his wife Ellen and daughter Rachel establish themselves in London. Ellen works there as a literary agent and looks for a permanent home for the family. Wright begins writing haiku (eventually completes some 4,000 pieces). Harassed by British passport officials during visit to England in September. Sees George Padmore, who dies not long after Wright's visit. Wright returns to England for the funeral. Tries to obtain resident visa from the Home Office, but is denied one without explanation. Alone in Paris, he sells home on rue Monsieur le Prince and moves to a two-room apartment on rue Régis. Recovers from dysentery but continues to have intestinal problems. Among his close friends at this time are Michel and Hélène Bokanowski, Colette and Rémi Dreyfus, Simone de Beauvoir, Ollie Harrington, and the Reverend Clayton Williams. "Big Black Good Man" is included in *Best American Stories of 1958*.

1960

The Long Dream, adapted by Ketti Frings, opens on Broadway February 17 to poor reviews and closes within a week. Translation of *The Long Dream* well-received in France, but earnings are not enough to quell Wright's deepening anxiety about money. In April, driving his own Peugeot, Wright accompanies his gastroenterologist, Victor Schwartzmann, and Dr. Schwartzmann's father to medical conference in Leiden, Holland, where he visits Margrit de Sablonière. Selects and arranges 811 haiku for possible publication. Declines offers from Congress for Cultural Freedom to attend conferences on Tolstoy in Venice and New Delhi, believing that the organization is controlled by the American government (the Congress is later shown to have received substantial covert funding from the CIA). Records series of interviews concerning his work in June for French radio. Spends much of summer at Moulin d'Andé, where he begins new novel, "A Father's Law." Falls ill on return to Paris in September. Julia Wright decides to study at the Sorbonne and visits her father before returning to England to pack her belongings. In September, Dorothy Padmore comes to visit. Later, old Chicago friend Arna Bontemps makes his first visit to Paris. Wright delivers lecture on November 8 at the American Church on the situation of black artists and intellectuals. Accuses the American government of creating and manipulating dissension among them through spies and provocateurs. Continues to suffer from intestinal difficulties and dizzy spells. Finishes complete proofreading of collection of stories, *Eight Men* (published by World Publishers in 1961). Welcomes Langston Hughes to his home for a brief but enjoyable visit on the morning of November 26, then enters the Eugene Gibez Clinic for diagnostic examinations and convalescence. Dies there of a heart attack shortly before 11:00 P.M., November 28. Cremated, along with a copy of *Black Boy,* at the Père Lachaise cemetery December 3, where his ashes are interred.

Note on the Text

⚮

This volume presents the text of Richard Wright's autobiography Black Boy (*American Hunger*) from a complete set of page proofs dating from the spring of 1944. This is the last version of the text that Wright prepared without external intervention by the Book-of-the-Month Club. A great deal of material pertaining to the publication of this work, including typescripts, proofs, and correspondence between Wright and his publishers, is in the James Weldon Johnson Collection of the Beinecke Library at Yale University and in the Harper and Brothers archive in the Firestone Library at Princeton University.

Wright began intensive work on his autobiography, initially entitled "Black Confession," in 1943. On December 17, 1943, he delivered the manuscript, now titled American Hunger, to his friend and agent, Paul Reynolds. It was divided into two sections: "Southern Night," treating his life in the South before he moved to Chicago in 1927, and "The Horror and the Glory," continuing his story in Chicago into the 1930s. The work was accepted by Edward Aswell of Harper and Brothers in January 1944. By early May 1944 the book was in page proofs and scheduled for fall publication.

Aswell sent bound sets of page proofs to other authors for promotional statements in May. Around this time a copy was also sent to the Book-of-the-Month Club for consideration. Aswell had earlier gotten Wright's agreement to revise one scene in the book he thought might be considered obscene. By late June the club's judges had expressed interest, but they asked Aswell if Wright would agree to publish only the first section of the work. Wright sent Aswell the altered version of the scene (see note to pp. 188.16–24) and agreed to shorten the book if the club decided to adopt it. (The title page in a sheaf of page proofs of *American Hunger*, now held at Beinecke Library, bears written instructions, under the heading "If the Book Club Takes It," for the replacement of the objectionable passage and the elimination of the second section, with the proviso "Hold till Book of the Month decides.")

The book jacket had already been designed when Wright wrote to Aswell on August 10 to suggest changing the title to *Black Boy*: "Now, this is not very original, but I think it covers the book. It is honest. Straight. And many people say it to themselves when they see a Negro and wonder how he lives. Black Boy seems to me to be not only a title, but also a kind of heading of the whole general theme."

Late in August 1944 the work was formally accepted by the book club and re-scheduled for release the following spring under its new title. Wright supplied several pages of new concluding material, working with Dorothy Canfield Fisher of the Book-of-the-Month Club (see note to p. 257.20). Though Wright was pleased with the book's selection by the club and the income it generated, he wrote in his journal that pressure from Communists had led the book club to ask him to drop the second section, which dealt with his involvement with the Communist party in Chicago. Although "The Horror and the Glory" remained unpublished, selections from it appeared in magazines at the time: "I Tried to Be a Communist" in *Atlantic Monthly* (August–September 1944), "American Hunger" in *Mademoiselle* (September 1945), and "Early Days in Chicago" in *Cross Section* (1945). These articles were reprinted numerous times during the 1940s and 1950s. The entire text of the second section was first published by Harper and Row in 1977 from the surviving page proofs, under the title *American Hunger*, which Wright had originally applied to the work as a whole. The present volume for the first time brings together the complete text of Wright's autobiography, using the page proofs set before the intervention of the Book-of-the-Month Club.

This volume presents the proof and typescript text chosen for inclusion without change, except for the correction of typographical errors. Spelling, punctuation, and capitalization often are expressive features and they are not altered, even when inconsistent or irregular. The following is a list of the typographical errors corrected, cited by page and line number: 29.26, asker; 165.18, now."; 264.16, Dont'; 264.30, too; 274.5, mixed,; 274.7, thing; 311.21, talk; 314.30, value; 315.12, artist; 367.33, enemy, "I; 378.10, but not.

Notes

In the notes below, the reference numbers denote page and line of this volume (the line count includes chapter headings). No note is made for information available in standard desk-reference books such as *Webster's Collegiate* and *Webster's Biographical* dictionaries. Footnotes in the text are Wright's own. For more biographical background than is included in the Chronology, see: Michel Fabre, *The Unfinished Quest of Richard Wright,* translated from the French by Isabel Barzun, (New York: William Morrow & Company, Inc., 1973); Addison Gayle, *Richard Wright: Ordeal of a Native Son* (Garden City, New York: Anchor Books/Doubleday, 1980); Constance Webb, *Richard Wright: A Biography* (New York: G. P. Putnam's Sons, 1968). For references to works by Wright and to other studies, see: Charles T. Davis and Michel Fabre, *Richard Wright: a primary bibliography* (Boston: G. K. Hall & Co., 1982); and Keneth Kinnamon, *A Richard Wright Bibliography: Fifty Years of Criticism and Commentary, 1933–1982* (Westport, Connecticut: Greenwood Press, 1988).

2.1–2   *Part . . . —Job*] Omitted for the 1945 and all later editions set from that text.

39.3–4   *Bluebeard . . . Wives*] Traditional story; the classic version, *Blue Beard,* is by the French poet and author of fairy tales, Charles Perrault (1628–1703).

56.34   war . . . declared?"] The United States declared war on Germany April 6, 1917, and entered World War I, which had begun in 1914.

76.20   "The war is over,"] The armistice was signed November 11, 1918.

82.33   *Amazing . . . sounds*] Cf. *Amazing Grace,* line 1. Sometimes represented as a Negro spiritual, the hymn was composed by John Newton (1725–1807) and published in *Olney Hymns* (1779) by Newton and William Cowper. Newton, who from 1745 to 1754 had been a sailor on slave ships and the captain of a slaving vessel, underwent a religious conversion during a storm at sea in 1748. Later ordained, he devoted his life to the ministry and became an important influence on the life of perhaps the greatest English abolitionist, William Wilberforce (1759–1833).

102.1   Seventh-Day Adventist Church] The observance of the seventh day as the Sabbath derives from the commandment: "Six days shalt thou labor . . . but the seventh day is the sabbath of the Lord thy God." The sect originated as the largest branch of Millerism, an interchurch movement led by William Miller, who in 1831 began preaching that the Second Coming of Christ was imminent, and might occur in 1843 or 1844. A branch of the Millerites, or Adventists, that was later to adopt the name Seventh-Day Adventists, came to believe that the 1843–44 date related to the beginning of an "investigative judgment" in heaven, which would end with Christ's return and the final judgment at an indefinite time. The church was formally organized in 1863. Among the main tenets of this fundamentally evangelic Protestant creed are the divine and supreme authority of the Bible; the comprehensive authority of the Ten Commandments; and the divine example of Jesus Christ's life. The gift of prophecy is a significant part of church teaching. The literal, premillenial Second Coming of Christ is insisted on, starting with Jerusalem and extending to all nations; Israel will be specially favored and restored. The dead will rise at the resurrection, at which time the earthly acknowledgment of the righteous and the eternal punishment through final death of the wicked will come to pass. Members must accept the doctrine of the church, repent their sins, and accept baptism by immersion. The church is supported through not only tithing but also the expected additional material generosity of its members.

116.33   how Jacob . . . angel] Jacob hears an angel in a dream in Genesis 31:11–13, wrestles an angel in 32:24–31, and sees angels in 28:12 and 32:2.

126.5–9   *But the . . . as thou . . .*] Deuteronomy 5:13.

133.20–21   *Flynn's . . . Magazine*] Magazines first published by Frank Munsey (1854–1925): *Flynn's Weekly Detective Fiction* (1924–42), and

Argosy All-Story Weekly (1920–29), so-named after a merger of the fiction magazines *The Argosy* (1888) and *All-Story* (1889). (After another merger, it became *All-Story Combined with Munsey's* in 1929.)

141.7–9   elections . . . power] Under the first Reconstruction Act, passed on March 2, 1867, former Confederate states seeking to regain their congressional representation were required to adopt new constitutions enfranchising black males. Mississippi voters approved a new constitution meeting this requirement on November 30, 1869, and the state regained its representation in Congress on February 23, 1870. The Republicans won the state elections in 1869, and the legislature subsequently elected two black men, Hiram Revels (served 1870–71) and Blanche K. Bruce (served 1875–81), to the U.S. Senate. In 1875 white supremacists organized a campaign of violence and intimidation intended to win the state elections for the Democrats. After dozens of blacks were murdered in Yazoo City and Clinton in September, Republican governor Adelbert Ames asked President Ulysses S. Grant to deploy federal troops against the "White Liners." His appeal for intervention was unsuccessful, and the Democrats won an overwhelming victory in the November 1875 election. Their control of the state government effectively disenfranchised blacks in elections thereafter.

153.4   *This . . . know . . .*] From "This May Be the Last Time," a traditional spiritual.

153.13–14   *It ain't . . . prayer . . .*] From "Standing In the Need of Prayer," a gospel song.

153.32   "right hand of fellowship."] See Galatians 2:9.

166.32   *Southern Register*] The weekly, one of the first attempts to establish a black newspaper in Jackson, began in the autumn of 1923 and was edited and printed by Malcolm Rogers; Wright's story (no copies are known to be extant) is said to have appeared in the spring of 1924.

169.2   Get-Rich-Quick Wallingford series] Get-Rich-Quick Wallingford was the name of the character, and the title of the first book, in the series (1908–13) by George Randolph Chester in which Wallingford and his partner "Blackie" Daw, a pair of likable rascals, set about making a fortune. The first book was subtitled "A Cheerful Account of the Rise and Fall of an American Business Buccaneer."

188.16–24   "Richard . . . did it."] Revised in 1944 for the book club review to read:

"Nigger, you think you'll ever amount to anything?" he asked
in a slow, sadistic voice.
"I don't know, sir," I answered, turning my head away.
"What do niggers think about?" he asked.
"I don't know, sir," I said, my head still averted.
"If I was a nigger, I'd kill myself," he said.
I said nothing. I was angry.
"You don't know why?" he asked.
I still said nothing.
"But I don't reckon niggers mind being niggers," he said
suddenly and laughed.

244.3–5   *Commercial* . . . article] "Another Mencken Absurdity"
(May 28, 1927).

244.6   editor . . . *Mercury*] Mencken founded the literary magazine
American Mercury with George Nathan in 1924, and was its editor until
1933. In it he attacked, among other targets, Puritanism, conservatism,
religion, and what he called the American "booboisie." Contributors
included Theodore Dreiser, Eugene O'Neill, Sherwood Anderson, Carl
Sandburg, Edgar Lee Masters, and Carl Van Vechten.

248.4–8   *A Book* . . . *Prejudices.*] *A Book of Prefaces* (1917) comprises
four chapters: "Joseph Conrad," "Theodore Dreiser," "James Huneker,"
and "Puritanism as a Literary Force." Mencken published six collections of
essays called *Prejudices* (1919–27). Perhaps his best-known essay and his
liveliest attack on the white South, "The Sahara of the Bozart," appeared in
Prejudices: Second Series (1920).

257.20   I fled.] Added to the 1945 edition as a conclusion after the
second part was cut from the work:
The next day when I was already in full flight—aboard a northward
bound train—I could not have accounted, if it had been demanded of me,
for all the varied forces that were making me reject the culture that had
molded and shaped me. I was leaving without a qualm, without a single
backward glance. The face of the South that I had known was hostile and
forbidding, and yet out of all the conflicts and the curses, the blows and the
anger, the tension and the terror, I had somehow gotten the idea that life
could be different, could be lived in a fuller and richer manner. As had happened when I had fled the orphan home, I was now running more away
from something than toward something. But that did not matter to me.
My mood was: I've got to get away; I can't stay here.

But what was it that always made me feel that way? What was it that made me conscious of possibilities? From where in this southern darkness had I caught a sense of freedom? Why was it that I was able to act upon vaguely felt notions? What was it that made me feel things deeply enough for me to try to order my life by my feelings? The external world of whites and blacks, which was the only world that I had ever known, surely had not evoked in me any belief in myself. The people I had met had advised and demanded submission. What, then, was I after? How dare I consider my feelings superior to the gross environment that sought to claim me?

It had been only through books—at best, no more than vicarious cultural transfusions—that I had managed to keep myself alive in a negatively vital way. Whenever my environment had failed to support or nourish me, I had clutched at books; consequently, my belief in books had risen more out of a sense of desperation than from any abiding conviction of their ultimate value. In a peculiar sense, life had trapped me in a realm of emotional rejection; I had not embraced insurgency through open choice. Existing emotionally on the sheer, thin margin of southern culture, I had felt that nothing short of life itself hung upon each of my actions and decisions; and I had grown used to change, to movement, to making many adjustments.

In the main, my hope was merely a kind of self-defence, a conviction that if I did not leave I would perish, either because of possible violence of others against me, or because of my possible violence against them. The substance of my hope was formless and devoid of any real sense of direction, for in my southern living I had seen no looming landmark by which I could, in a positive sense, guide my daily actions. The shocks of southern living had rendered my personality tender and swollen, tense and volatile, and my flight was more a shunning of external and internal dangers than an attempt to embrace what I felt I wanted.

It had been my accidental reading of fiction and literary criticism that had evoked in me vague glimpses of life's possibilities. Of course, I had never seen or met the men who wrote the books I read, and the kind of world in which they lived was as alien to me as the moon. But what had enabled me to overcome my chronic distrust was that these books—written by men like Dreiser, Masters, Mencken, Anderson, and Lewis—seemed defensively critical of the straitened American environment. These writers seemed to feel that America could be shaped nearer to the hearts of those who lived in it. And it was out of these novels and stories and articles, out of the emotional impact of imaginative constructions of heroic or tragic deeds, that I felt touching my face a tinge of warmth from an unseen light; and in my leaving I was groping toward that invisible light, always trying to keep my face so set and turned that I would not lose the hope of its faint promise, using it as my justification for action.

The white South said that it knew "niggers," and I was what the white South called a "nigger." Well, the white South had never known me— never known what I thought, what I felt. The white South said that I had a "place" in life. Well, I had never felt my "place"; or, rather, my deepest instincts had always made me reject the "place" to which the white South had assigned me. It had never occurred to me that I was in any way an inferior being. And no word that I had ever heard fall from the lips of southern white men had ever made me really doubt the worth of my own humanity. True, I had lied. I had stolen. I had struggled to contain my seething anger. I had fought. And it was perhaps a mere accident that I had never killed . . . But in what other ways had the South allowed me to be natural, to be real, to be myself, except in rejection, rebellion, and aggression?

Not only had the southern whites not known me, but, more important still, as I had lived in the South I had not had the chance to learn who I was. The pressure of southern living kept me from being the kind of person that I might have been. I had been what my surroundings had demanded, what my family—conforming to the dictates of the whites above them—had exacted of me, and what the whites had said that I must be. Never being fully able to be myself, I had slowly learned that the South could recognize but a part of a man, could accept but a fragment of his personality, and all the rest—the best and deepest things of heart and mind—were tossed away in blind ignorance and hate.

I was leaving the South to fling myself into the unknown, to meet other situations that would perhaps elicit from me other responses. And if I could meet enough of a different life, then, perhaps, gradually and slowly I might learn who I was, what I might be. I was not leaving the South to forget the South, but so that some day I might understand it, might come to know what its rigors had done to me, to its children. I fled so that the numbness of my defensive living might thaw out and let me feel the pain— years later and far away—of what living in the South had meant.

Yet, deep down, I knew that I could never really leave the South, for my feelings had already been formed by the South, for there had been slowly instilled into my personality and consciousness, black though I was, the culture of the South. So, in leaving, I was taking a part of the South to transplant in alien soil, to see if it could grow differently, if it could drink of new and cool rains, bend in strange winds, respond to the warmth of other suns, and, perhaps, to bloom . . . And if that miracle ever happened, then I would know that there was yet hope in that southern swamp of despair and violence, that light could emerge even out of the blackest of the southern night. I would know that the South too could overcome its fear, its hate, its cowardice, its heritage of guilt and blood, its burden of anxiety and compulsive cruelty.

With ever watchful eyes and bearing scars, visible and invisible, I headed North, full of a hazy notion that life could be lived with dignity, that the personalities of others should not be violated, that men should be able to confront men without fear or shame, that if men were lucky in their living on earth they might win some redeeming meaning for their having struggled and suffered here beneath the stars.

278.6   While . . . stomach] "At night . . ." This and the following two notes show penciled revisions made by Wright on a copy of page proofs some time after the book club had decided to take only Part One.

278.11   my family.] "my people."

282.5   I spent . . . reading] "I read . . ."

296.8   Hoover . . . marchers] Between 15,000 and 20,000 unemployed World War I veterans gathered in Washington, D.C., in late May and early June 1932, camping on open ground by the Anacostia River and in vacant public buildings near the Capitol. The veterans sought to pressure Congress into passing an appropriation that would allow veterans of World War I to cash in at full value bonus certificates granted them in 1924; the certificates were scheduled to mature in 1945. A bill meeting their demands was passed by the House of Representatives on June 15, but was defeated in the Senate several days later. Several thousand men left Washington after Congress adjourned on July 16, but the remainder vowed to stay. President Herbert Hoover adamantly opposed the cash redemption scheme and accused the leadership of the "Bonus Army" of being Communists and radicals rather than patriotic ex-servicemen, as they claimed. On Hoover's orders, troops led by General Douglas MacArthur used tanks, bayonets, and tear gas to rout the remaining marchers from their camps and shelters on July 28, 1932.

298.26   "Big . . . Thompson] William Hale "Big Bill" Thompson (1869–1944) was mayor of Chicago from 1915 to 1923 and from 1927 to 1931. In 1931 he defeated Judge John H. Lyle in the Republican primary, but lost his bid for re-election to Democrat Anton J. Cermak.

304.32   Aschheim-Zondek tests] Selmor Aschheim (1878–1965) and Bernhardt Zondek (1891–1961) were German gynecologists and obstetricians who developed a test for pregnancy in which urine from women was injected into immature mice. Urine from pregnant women caused enlarged ovaries in the mice, as well as other noticeable effects. Rabbits were later used instead of mice.

304.33   Wassermann tests]   August-Paul von Wassermann (1866–1925) was a German bacteriologist noted for developing the Wassermann test for syphilis, which he announced in 1906.

315.11   *Anvil, . . .* Conroy,] *Anvil* magazine (1932–1935), a journal of fiction and poetry edited by Jack Conroy (1899–1980) and actively supported by the Communist party. Its motto was "We Prefer Crude Vigor to Polished Banality." In 1935, it merged with *Partisan Review* (begun as a John Reed Club magazine), but dissatisfaction with this arrangement led to the birth in 1939 of *New Anvil,* which lasted only six issues. In addition to Wright, the two *Anvil* magazines also published work by James T. Farrell, Langston Hughes, Nelson Algren, William Carlos Williams, and Meridel Le Sueur, among other notable writers. Conroy, a novelist with a particular interest in folklore, started out as a self-educated labor leader in his native Moberly, Missouri, before turning to a literary career.

315.12   John Reed Club] The John Reed Club was started in 1929 by the editorial board of *New Masses* in accordance with the principles of agitation, education, and propaganda enunciated the previous year by the Comintern (Communist International). It was named in honor of the poet and journalist John Reed (1887–1920), author of *Ten Days That Shook the World,* and the only American buried at the foot of the Kremlin wall with other heroes of the Russian Revolution. The club had as its major aim the broadening of the cultural appeal of radical socialism. By 1934, there were some thirty clubs in cities and towns across the United States. They attracted many of the leading progressive writers, especially among the young, including black Americans such as Wright and Langston Hughes.

316.26–27   *Left Front,*] A magazine of the John Reed Club, begun in 1933. It was one of several magazines of the 1930s specializing in proletarian literature.

317.1   *Masses*] *New Masses,* so-named after the radical socialist journal of art and literature *The Masses,* which was edited by Max Eastman from 1913 to 1918, and suppressed during World War I as seditious. *New Masses* commenced monthly publication in 1927 as a radical journal of art and literature. In 1934, after it became a weekly, *New Masses* emerged as perhaps the major journal of its kind in the United States throughout the 1930s. In

1948, following a marked decline in its influence, it was subsumed by the newly formed *Masses & Mainstream*.

317.6 *International Literature*] Published in various languages and strongly supported by the Soviet government, *International Literature* was perhaps the leading literary journal of the international Communist movement in the 1930s.

317.9–13 introduced . . . Czechoslovakia] Among those Wright met in Chicago were the artist Morris Topchevky, author Nelson Algren, and filmmaker Herbert Kline, who made the political documentary *Crisis: A Film of the Nazi Way* (1938), which ended with the German entry into the Sudetenland, annexed from Czechoslovakia after the signing of the Munich Pact.

334.27–335.1 Trotsky . . . activity] In April 1926 Leon Trotsky joined his former rivals Grigori Zinoviev and Lev Kamenev in forming a "United Opposition" to the leadership of Nikolai Bukharin and Joseph Stalin. Trotsky and his allies accused Bukharin and Stalin of failing to support revolutionary Communist movements outside the Soviet Union and demanded the curtailment of the party and government bureaucracy, an end to conciliatory policies toward prosperous landowning peasants, and the beginning of planned industrial development. Their views were rejected by a majority of the Communist Party Central Committee, and in October 1926 all three publicly abjured further opposition activity. They resumed their criticism of the leadership in May 1927 and in September defied the party Politburo by printing their political platform and attempting to circulate it among delegates to the forthcoming Fifteenth Party Congress. After the secret police seized their printing press, the opposition organized protest demonstrations in Moscow and Leningrad on November 7, 1927, the tenth anniversary of the Bolshevik Revolution. Trotsky and Zinoviev were expelled from the Communist party on November 14 for violating the ban against factions within the party, instituted by Lenin in 1921. In January 1928 Trotsky was exiled to Soviet Central Asia, and in January 1929 he was deported from the Soviet Union to Turkey. Zinoviev and Kamenev were shot in 1936 after confessing to counterrevolutionary conspiracy at a public show trial. Trotsky was assassinated in Mexico by a Soviet agent in 1940.

335.18 Stalin's . . . *Question*] *Marxism and the National and Colonial Question* (1934), a revised edition of *Marxism and the National Question*, first published in 1913.

343.36   People's Front] In the summer of 1934 the executive committee of the Communist International (Comintern) instructed Communist parties to begin forming alliances with non-Communist movements as part of the struggle against fascism. These instructions reversed a 1928 decision of the Comintern to abandon alliances with Western socialists and denounce social democratic parties as "social fascists." The new "people's front" strategy, also known as the "united front" or "popular front," became the official policy of the Comintern at its Seventh Congress, held in the summer of 1935, and remained in effect until the signing of the German-Soviet nonaggression pact on August 23, 1939.

350.9–10   Negro . . . Association] The Harlem branch of the Young Men's Christian Association, located on 135th Street near Lenox Avenue, was a focal point of cultural activity during and after the Harlem Renaissance of the 1920s, as well as the residence of many newcomers to Harlem during the same period.

353.18–19   article . . . Louis] In his first piece of journalism, "Joe Louis Uncovers Dynamite" (October 8, 1935), Wright described the reaction of Chicago blacks to the fight in New York, September 24, 1935, in which Louis defeated former world heavyweight champion Max Baer.

358.7   Communist International] The Third International, also known as the Communist International (Comintern), was founded by Lenin in 1919 to provide revolutionary Communist leadership to the worldwide socialist movement. It was dissolved in 1943.

364.2   Federal Negro Theater] A unit of the Federal Theatre Project (funded by Congress as a Depression measure, and headed nationally by Hallie Flanagan). The unit was designed to serve the perceived interests of blacks. Although most of the plays staged by the Theatre came from the traditional repertoire, the Chicago unit produced the premiere of Theodore Ward's *Big White Fog* in April 1937.

364.23–24   Works Progress Administration] A federal agency established by President Franklin D. Roosevelt in 1935 to combat unemployment as part of his New Deal policy. The WPA administered several cultural programs, including the Federal Art Project, the Federal Writers' Project, and the Federal Theatre Project, as well as a vast program of public road, bridge, and building construction. Its activities were curtailed by Congress in 1939 and the agency was abolished in 1943.

364.30–31   Charles DeSheim] DeSheim, an actor and director in reper-
tory and stock company productions, was later associated with the Old
Globe Theatre Shakespearean productions at the New York World's Fair
(1939–40), and in 1940 appeared in *Journey to Jerusalem* at the National
Theater in Washington, D.C. He died in 1941.

366.35   white . . . company] The Federal Experimental Theatre was
a unit of the Federal Theatre Project that emphasized avant-garde plays.
Although the FTP had as one of its central goals the encouragement of
uncensored adult theater, more plays by Shakespeare were produced than
works by any other author, with works by Eugene O'Neill and George
Bernard Shaw following closely in frequency. Because many controversial
political dramas were also produced, opposition to the FTP grew among
conservatives and resulted in its abolition by Congress in 1939.

381.33–382.7   *Arise, . . . earth!*] Verses 1–2 of "The International."
Written in 1871 by Eugène Pottier, a member of the Paris Commune, it
became the anthem of the international socialist movement, and was later
adopted by the Communists. Adolphe Degeyter composed the music.

382.28   *A better . . . birth . , .*] "The International," Verse 4.

About the author

About the book

Read on

Insights,
Interviews
& More . . .

Meet Richard Wright

Courtesy of the Granger Collection

BORN IN 1908 near Roxie, Mississippi, Richard Wright is the author of six novels, two collections of novellas and stories, and seven books of nonfiction, as well as numerous influential articles, critical essays, and poems. His first published book was a collection of novellas, *Uncle Tom's Children* (1938). *Native Son,* a protest novel published two years later, became the first novel by an African American to be featured as a Main Selection of the Book-of-the-Month Club. Together with *Black Boy* (1945), the book achieved vast critical acclaim, stirred fierce intellectual debate, and made Wright the first bestselling African American. The social zeal and technical skill of his entire oeuvre secured a place for Wright among the most important American writers of the twentieth century.

Richard Wright lived throughout the United States, including Memphis, Chicago, and New York City. He became a French citizen in 1947 and settled in Paris, where he died of a heart attack in 1960. For more detailed biographical information, please see the chronology following the text of *Black Boy.*

Chronicle of an American Classic

THIS VOLUME represents the text of Richard Wright's autobiography *Black Boy (American Hunger)* from a complete set of page proofs dating from the spring of 1944. This is the last version of the text that Wright prepared without external intervention by the Book-of-the-Month Club. A great deal of material pertaining to the publication of this work, including typescripts, proofs, and correspondence between Wright and his publishers, is in the James Weldon Johnson Collection of the Beinecke Library at Yale University and in the Harper and Brothers archive in the Firestone Library at Princeton University.

Wright began intensive work on his autobiography, initially called "Black Confession," in 1943. On December 17, 1943, he delivered the manuscript, now titled *American Hunger,* to his friend and agent, Paul Reynolds. It was divided into two sections: "Southern Night," treating his life in the South before he moved to Chicago in 1927, and "The Horror and the Glory," continuing his story in Chicago into the 1930s. The work was accepted by Edward Aswell of Harper and Brothers in January 1944. By early May 1944 the book was in page proofs and scheduled for fall publication.

Aswell sent bound sets of page proofs to other authors for promotional statements in May. Around this time a copy was also sent to the Book-of-the-Month Club for consideration. Aswell had earlier gotten

" This [volume] is the last version of the text that Wright prepared without external intervention by the Book-of-the-Month Club. "

Wright's agreement to revise one scene in the book he thought might be considered obscene. By late June the club's judges had expressed interest, but they asked Aswell if Wright would agree to publish only the first section of the work. Wright sent Aswell the altered version of the scene (see note to p. 188, lines 16–24) and agreed to shorten the book if the club decided to adopt it. (The title page in a sheaf of page proofs of *American Hunger,* now held at Beinecke Library, bears written instructions, under the heading "If the Book Club Takes It," for the replacement of the objectionable passage and the elimination of the second section, with the proviso "Hold till Book of the Month decides.")

The book jacket had already been designed when Wright wrote to Aswell on August 10 to suggest changing the title to *Black Boy*: "Now, this is not very original, but I think it covers the book. It is honest. Straight. And many people say it to themselves when they see a Negro and wonder how he lives. Black Boy seems to me to be not only a title, but also a kind of heading of the whole general theme."

Late in August 1944 the work was formally accepted by the book club and rescheduled for release the following spring under its new title. Wright supplied several pages of new concluding material, working with Dorothy Canfield Fisher of the Book-of-the-Month Club (see note to p. 257.20). Though Wright was pleased with the book's selection by the club and the income it generated, he wrote in his journal that pressure from communists had led the book club to ask him to drop the second section, which dealt with his involvement with the Communist Party in Chicago. Although "The Horror and the Glory" remained unpublished, selections ▶

> ❝ Though Wright was pleased with the book's selection by the club and the income it generated, he wrote in his journal that pressure from communists had led the book club to ask him to drop the second section. ❞

from it appeared in magazines at the time: "I Tried to Be a Communist" in *Atlantic Monthly* (August–September 1944), "American Hunger" in *Mademoiselle* (September 1945), and "Early Days in Chicago" in *Cross Section* (1945). These articles were reprinted numerous times during the 1940s and 1950s. The entire text of the second section was first published by Harper and Row in 1977 from the surviving page proofs, under the title *American Hunger,* which Wright had originally applied to the work as a whole. The present volume brings together the complete text of Wright's autobiography, using the page proofs set before the intervention of the Book-of-the-Month Club.

The first edition of *Black Boy* (1945) is a classic example of American autobiography, a subtly crafted narrative of a young man's coming-of-age in the United States. For slightly more than three decades, this version of Richard Wright's story of his journey from innocence to experience in the Jim Crow South stood as tragic witness to the collective, as well as the individualized, realities of movement from childhood to manhood in a particular time and place. One could question the reliability of Wright's memory, try to discriminate between fiction and fact in the densely woven texture of the autobiography, or inquire why Wright himself never capitulated to the dehumanizing norms of early-twentieth-century Southern culture. It was impossible to deny, however, that *Black Boy* was a work of stunning imagination and mythic power; here was a book that nicely blended the meaning, the challenge, and the significance of being Southern, black, and male in America.

Readers were confronted with a different challenge when *American Hunger,* the unused portion of Wright's original manuscript of his autobiography, was published in 1977. *Black Boy* had provided a certain pleasure of the text for readers, prior to the turbulent 1960s, who tended to be less than thorough in analyzing the institutionalized nature of racism in the United States. Migration to the North was accepted as an essential prelude to black people's enjoying the full blessings of liberty and citizenship; Wright's story of his life up to his leaving Memphis for Chicago reinforced the belief that the South was a socially unreconstructed region where blacks who asserted their basic human rights invited retribution or death. *American Hunger* suggested that what Wright had all along envisioned was certainly a fuller depiction of his American education. His "hazy notion that life could be lived with dignity, that the personalities of others should not be violated, that men should be able to confront other men without fear or shame" in the North was swiftly transformed by the urban environment into clear ideas about the pervasive constrictions placed on authentic human freedom in the North as well as in the South. That such barriers were different in kind and degree did matter. Nevertheless, what mattered more was Wright's recognition that the Promised Land in America was nowhere. The posthumously published segment of Wright's autobiography exposed the deepest ironies of equality in America.

In short, Wright's early experiences in ▶

❝ Wright's story of his life up to his leaving Memphis for Chicago reinforced the belief that the South was a socially unreconstructed region. ❞

the North were variations, within a bleak urban setting, of what had happened to him in the South. *Black Boy* documented in vivid and painful detail Wright's Southern education from the age of four to that day in 1927 when he boarded a northbound train "without a qualm, without a single backward glance." Readers who were not aware that other fragments of Wright's autobiography had been published prior to 1977 might assume that his reflections on childhood and youth ended with hope and promise. They could not know until the unexpurgated edition was published that Wright really ended his reflections on the South with a terse indictment: "This was the culture from which I sprang. This was the terror from which I fled."

The autobiographical inscription of the relations between a sensitive, intelligent, spiritually hungry native son and a racist social order (in the South) had ended textually (in 1945) with the prospect that perhaps human beings could attain "some redeeming meaning for their having struggled and suffered here beneath the stars." *Black Boy,* so much in the tradition of the slave narrative, belonged also, as Ralph Ellison discerned in one of the earliest reviews, to the tradition of blues. It was an elegant gesture of testifying "both [to] the agony of life and the possibility of conquering it through sheer toughness of spirit." Yet *American Hunger,* the continuation of Wright's autobiography, seemed to be a lamentation, an extended riff on his hazy notion that wholeness and decency and redemption lay up North. The analytic imagination that informed the Southern

> ❝ *Black Boy,* so much in the tradition of the slave narrative, belonged also, as Ralph Ellison discerned in one of the earliest reviews, to the tradition of blues. ❞

portion of Wright's life experience itself was transformed from a blues to a jazz mode in *American Hunger*. In that sense, readers—regardless of ethnic or racial identity—who might have felt free to cast aspersions on the South were compelled to inspect the dirty laundry of race, oppression, and class in the North.

The publication of Wright's autobiography in its entirety for the first time in October 1991 by the Library of America, despite an understandable reluctance to claim that the meaning of his story is radically changed, did make possible an greater access to Wright's intention in creating an autobiography and extended the possibilities of how one reads his text. That is to say, the unexpurgated text provides grounds for the claim that Wright originally wanted less to shape from his life a representative myth of growing up Southern than an American story which speaks to "the hunger for life that gnaws in us all, to keep alive in our hearts a sense of the inexpressibly human." Such a story, if it were to be an adequate critique of individuality and ethnicity, required the wholeness of Wright's Southern and Northern experiences. Reading the story whole (or maybe holistically), we have a stronger appreciation of the artistry in Wright's reflective movement from homegrown optimism to tested knowledge. The facts of publishing history that led to a truncated edition of Wright's autobiography being issued in 1945 may be of greater interest to literary scholars than to ordinary readers, but the restored text provides for a new opportunity to explore the authority of Wright's confirming the ▶

> 66 Reading the story whole (or maybe holistically), we have a stronger appreciation of the artistry in Wright's reflective movement from homegrown optimism to tested knowledge. 99

referentiality of autobiography, the complex contract to be maintained between autobiographer and reader. As readers, we become more aware of Wright's position and our positioning ourselves with reference to his text.

This volume presents the proof and typescript text chosen for inclusion without change, except for the correction of typographical errors. Spelling, punctuation, and capitalization often are expressive features and they are not altered, even when inconsistent or irregular.

The following is a list of the typographical errors corrected, cited by page and line number: 29.26, asker; 165.18, now."; 264.16, Dont'; 264.30, too; 274.5, mixed,; 274.7, thing; 311.21, talk; 314.30, value; 315.12, artist; 367.33, enemy, "I; 378.10, but not. ᴄ◟

Have You Read?
More from
Richard Wright

*From the introduction by Jerry W. Ward in the
1993 Harper Perennial edition:*

"In the books that followed *Black Boy,*
Wright yearned for authority and freedom
of an unusual kind. Like Cross Damon,
the hero of *The Outsider* (1953), Wright
longed to be existentially free, ultimately
responsible to the 'self' he endeavored to
create through the act of writing. If one
posits that this novel involves the intellectual
autobiography, the book gives us keys for
explaining the intrusive 'self' in Wright's
later works. Whether he was analyzing
the independence movement in Africa
(*Black Power,* 1954), reporting on the
Bandung Conference (*The Color Curtain,*
1956), or examining the intricacies of a
culture (*Pagan Spain,* 1957), Wright was
never the distanced observer. He was
essentially the brother in suffering, the
brother who had the strength to speak. The
voice in *White Man, Listen!* (1957) is not that
of victimized millions but rather that of the
man who feels outrages as he beholds the
world's injustice and disorder. In *The Long
Dream* (1958), the last book published before
his death, Wright sought to create in Rex
'Fishbelly' Tucker a childhood and youth
that fate had denied him. Wright's work was
strongly determined by autobiographical
impulses. *Black Boy* (*American Hunger*)
permits us to grasp afresh why Wright's life
as a wronged human being was so powerful
a stimulus for creative work." ▶

Have You Read? *(continued)*

UNCLE TOM'S CHILDREN

Set in the American Deep South, each of the powerful novellas collected here concerns an aspect of the lives of black people in the post-slavery era, exploring their resistance to white racism and oppression. Published in 1938, this was the first book from Wright.

This edition includes material that was left out of the original. Alfred Kazin said, "The Library of America has insured that most of Wright's major texts are now available as he wanted them to be read." In addition to the four novellas originally published—"Big Boy Leaves Home," "Down by the Riverside," "Long Black Song," and "Fire and Cloud"—this edition includes a nonfiction essay, "The Ethics of Living Jim Crow," and a short story, "Bright and Morning Star."

"I found these stories both heartening, as evidence of a vigorous new talent, and terrifying, as the expression of a racial hatred that has never ceased to grow and gets no chance to die."

—Malcolm Cowley, *New Republic*

NATIVE SON

Right from the start, Bigger Thomas had been headed for jail. It could have been for assault or petty larceny; by chance, it was for murder and rape. *Native Son* tells the story of this young black man caught in a downward spiral after he kills a young white woman in a brief moment of panic. Set in Chicago in the 1930s, Wright's powerful novel is an unsparing reflection on the poverty and feelings of hopelessness experienced by people in inner cities across the country and of what it means to be black in America.

"Certainly, *Native Son* declares Richard Wright's importance . . . as an American author as distinctive as any of those now writing." —*New York Times Book Review*

THE OUTSIDER

Wright presents a compelling story of a black man's attempt to escape his past and start anew in Harlem. Cross Damon is a man at odds with society and with himself, a man who hungers for peace but who brings terror and destruction wherever he goes.

As Maryemma Graham writes in her introduction to this edition, with its restored text established by the Library of America, "*The Outsider* is Richard Wright's second installment in a story of epic proportions, a complex master narrative designed to show American racism in raw and ugly terms. . . . The stories of Bigger Thomas . . . and Cross Damon bear an uncanny resemblance to many contemporary cases of street crime and violence. There is also a prophetic note in Wright's construction of the criminal mind as intelligent, introspective, and transformative."

"It is in the description of action, especially violent action, that Mr. Wright excels, not merely because he can make the reader see but because he compels him to participate. There is not a murder in the book that the reader, at the moment of reading about it, does not feel that he would have committed under the same circumstances."

—Granville Hicks, *New York Times*

Read on

EIGHT MEN: SHORT STORIES

Each of the eight stories in *Eight Men* focuses on a black man at violent odds with a white world, reflecting Wright's views about racism in our society and his fascination with what he called "the struggle of the individual in America." These poignant, gripping stories will captivate all those who love Wright's better known novels.

"There is not a touch of phoniness or fakery in the book. All eight men and all eight stories stand as beautifully, pitifully, terribly true. . . . All the way through this is fine, sound, good, honorable writing, rich with insight and understanding, even when occasionally twisted by sorrow."

—*New York Times Book Review*

Don't miss the next book by your favorite author. Sign up now for AuthorTracker by visiting www.AuthorTracker.com.